Dogma and Compulsion

DOGMA AND COMPULSION

PSYCHOANALYTIC STUDIES OF RELIGION AND MYTHS

by

Theodor Reik

GREENWOOD PRESS, PUBLISHERS
WESTPORT, CONNECTICUT

Library of Congress Cataloging in Publication Data

Reik, Theodor, 1888-1970.
    Dogma and compulsion.

    Includes bibliographical references.
    1. Psychology, Religious. 2. Dogma.
3. Bible--Psychology. 4. Sphinxes. I. Title.
BL53.R37 1973   201'.1   72-9369
ISBN 0-8371-6577-6

Translated by BERNARD MIALL

Copyright 1951, by International Universities Press, Inc.

Originally published in 1951 by International Universities Press,
Inc., New York

Reprinted with the permission of International Universities Press,
Inc., New York

Reprinted in 1973 by Greenwood Press
A division of Congressional Information Service, Inc.
88 Post Road West, Westport, Connecticut 06881

Library of Congress Catalog Card Number 72-9369

ISBN 0-8371-6577-6

Printed in the United States of America

10 9 8 7 6 5 4 3

CONTENTS

5

PREFACE

Freud never tired of emphasizing a point which seems to be somewhat alien to a great number of psychoanalysts, who are primarily—one is sometimes tempted to say, merely—therapists, and interested exclusively in neuroses and psychoses. What characterizes psychoanalysis as a science, says Freud (in his *Introductory Lectures on Psychoanalysis*), is less the material with which it "works than the method it applies. Without forcing its nature, one can apply it just as well to the history of civilization, to the science of the religions, and to mythology, as well as to the theory of neuroses. Its only aim and its only contribution is to discover the unconscious in the psychical life." Many psychoanalysts seem to think that the unconscious can only be found in the symptoms of neurosis and psychosis. In the discussions, held on Wednesday evenings at his home, Freud frequently pointed out that the time will come when the treatment of neurotic and psychotic patients will not be the main task of psychoanalysis. Those analysts—and they are quite large in number—who believe that our science is confined to the understanding and treatment of nervous diseases, do not realize that they are cutting off the bough on which they sit. One might be curious to know where they will turn their interests in the near future, when endocrinology and other medical disciplines will conquer the primacy and priority in the treatment of neuroses and psychoses.

Of the many contributions psychoanalysis has made in the field of the social sciences, those dealing with the history and the comparative study of religions seem to be most important and successful in their scientific results. Encouraged by Freud, who was a pioneer also in this area, particularly with his *Totem and Taboo*, I investigated the analogy between the phenomena of religion and those of obsessional neurosis. My book, *Ritual* (published in 1919), was followed by a series of studies which pursued the psychoanalytic research of the psychology of religion in new directions. These studies were originally published in German, some in book form, others in psychoanalytic journals. Their English translation appears now, for the first time, in the present volume.

THEODOR REIK

New York, December 1950

Part One

"It is lamentable that a man who has no knowledge of the inwardness of the human being should be able to endow with the fire of passion an idea which was narrow and one-sided in its very genesis. This may have disastrous results. . . . Such a movement is the psychoanalysis which had its beginnings in Vienna. When Freud casts his ideological net over the life of the psyche, what does he catch in it? . . . The answer is, of course, *only sexual things*. . . . Logic, above all, has much fault to find with the psychoanalytic method. Its terms are derived exclusively from the material world; what they should signify when applied to the psychic field is problematical. How false the whole method is we may judge from its attitude to *Catholic dogma*. . . . Dogma is eternal, and has never demanded practical confirmation. The peoples and the centuries have weighed it and have not found it wanting. . . . *Psychoanalysis can learn more from the Church than the Church from psychoanalysis*. . . ."

From an article on "Psychoanalyse und Katholizismus," by Prof. Dr. Linus Bopp, published in the *Katholische Weltanschauungswoche*, Vienna, May, 1929.

"His Eminence obeys, at least, as regards his intellect, the injunction regarding evangelical poverty."

Anatole France: *The Trees in the Forest.*

DOGMA AND OBSESSIONAL IDEA

PREFACE

There is no lack, in analytic literature, of works which deal with the major articles of belief, and point to their unconscious motives and instinctual basis. Freud's analytic explanation of the Christian doctrine of redemption is undoubtedly to be regarded as the most significant example of this kind.[1] In the valuable essays of Karl Abraham,[2] Ernest Jones,[3] Oscar Pfister,[4] A. J. Storfer[5] and other authors the ethnopsychological material and the psychic tendencies of religious conceptions are subjected to examination. To some extent my own contributions to the analytic examination of religion follow the same direction.[6]

The following study[7] adopts a different course. It does not place the chief emphasis on the analytic interpretation and explanation of religious ideas but focuses on the dogma itself as a problem of religious psychology. Thus it constitutes a first attempt to ascertain the position of dogma in the evolution of religion, to demonstrate its nature, and to describe the unconscious instinctual impulses and psychic mechanisms which govern the formation of dogmas.

The way in which this study came to be written must excuse the fact that it deals with the problem analytically only up to a certain point. This investigation was a by-product of my attempt to clarify the significance—as yet hardly realized—of *blasphemy*

[1] *Totem and Taboo,* New York 1918.

[2] "Amenhotep IV," *Imago,* 1912.

[3] "A Psychological Study of the Holy Ghost," in *Essays in Applied Psychoanalysis,* London 1923.

[4] "Die Entwicklung des Apostel Paulus," *Imago,* 1920.

[5] *Marias Jungfräuliche Mutterschaft,* Berlin 1914.

[6] *Probleme der Religionspsychologie,* Vienna and Leipzig 1919; *Your God and Mine* (in press).

[7] An expansion of a lecture delivered on January 16, 1924 before the Wiener Psychoanalytische Vereinigung.

in the growth and evolution of religion. The study of the religions requires, like the study of human history in general, a conscientious submersion in a confused admixture of insanity, crime, and pettiness. The value of this study cannot be denied. In one of the works of Anatole France an abbé, the director of an ecclesiastical seminary, speaks these memorable words: "Such is the force of theological discipline that it alone is capable of producing the great blasphemers. An unbeliever who has not passed through our hands has neither the strength nor the weapons to do harm. It is within our walls that all knowledge is acquired, even the knowledge of blasphemy."

Although I can only compare this inquiry—as far as its origin is concerned—with the by-products of a great industry, I will nonetheless express the hope that the experts may regard it—as they regard such by-products—as having a certain value and utility.

I. DOGMA

Analytic investigations of psychopathological phenomena have revealed an analogy between the obsessional activities of neurotic patients and the details of religious ritual. A closer examination revealed the existence of pervasive analogies, as well as profound differences, between obsessional actions and religious practices—a fact which justified Freud in regarding obsessional neurosis as an individual caricature of religion. Freud was then able to comprehend the origins of religion analytically, and to demonstrate the emotional roots of its operation. Following the method of my teacher, I have endeavored to pursue the parallels between religion and obsessional neurosis, and to demonstrate the connection of the two phenomena by means of individual examples. The science of religion, and theology, have followed these studies with increasing attention, which has often been accompanied by a considerable degree of anxiety. They are beginning, now that the usual period of latency has elapsed, to discuss with some eagerness the results of analysis in this field.

At definite points of this discussion of the analytic examination of religion we encounter an objection which seems even more menacing than the pious imprecations which call upon heaven to take note of the sacrilegious attempts of the investigators. The critics have expressed a foreboding that ritual does not possess the significance, in respect of religious life, which analysis has ascribed to it. Might not the critic justly point to the fact that religion is not dependent on the performance of specific ceremonies, or on the observance of certain rites; for example, that it is not attendance at Mass, nor prayer, confession, and communion, that determine whether a person is to be regarded as a Catholic? At the first glance it seems that one cannot deny that there is something to be said for this argument. Its relative validity is, however, related to the decline of interest in religion and the diminishing function of religion in the structure of modern

society. It is true, of course, that our educated contemporaries—
in so far as they find a religious belief at all compatible with their
scientific knowledge—connect, with the concept of religion, a certain emotional attitude which is almost independent of ritual
and ceremonial. It does not matter whether they have replaced
the notion of God by the notion of destiny, or whether they tend
toward a Spinozaistic identification of God and Nature, or other
abstractions. It does not greatly matter what illusion we choose
in order to make life tolerable. The broad masses of the population, in all parts of the earth, have held fast to the old notion of
religion. For them religion is by no means a private matter, since
they feel themselves to be members of a great community. Here
religion still takes the form of a powerful social institution which
finds its significant expression in the common observance of a
ritual. The ancients, as well as the primitive peoples of the
present day, obviously had this conception of religion: The observance of religious ceremonies is regarded as the most significant evidence of a person's religious persuasion.[1] The answer to
the question: "Tell me, what is your religion?" will be decided,
not by the facts of the emotional life, but by the observance or
nonobservance of the rites prescribed by a certain cult. Faust may
repeat the assurance that he reveres the holy sacraments, but
Margaret will always retort, "But without any passion; 'tis long
since you went to the Mass, or confession." Everyone knows how
far this attitude persists, in a more or less veiled form, at the

[1] "The Romans associated the word *religio*—however different its etymological interpretation may be in the later Roman authors—above all with
the notion of adhesion to certain norms of worship, which as such constituted
a part of the public organization. But this attitude of the individual to the
cult is a common characteristic of all the ancient religions. That faith and
worship are in correspondence appears so much a matter of course that one
cannot ignore the emphasis laid on a specific *regula fidei*. Only when philosophy began to examine and speculate upon the content of the belief underlying the cult did it also endeavor to formulate it in definite doctrines. With
that religious orthodoxy was made dependent not on ceremonial but on doctrine, and the doctrine was established by the profession of faith which the
believer expressed, not as before, merely by his actions, but in words, and
by testifying to his membership of the religious community" (Wundt, *Völkerpsychologie*, Vol. VI, 2nd ed., 1915, p. 545). Robertson Smith expresses himself at some length to the same effect (*The Religion of the Semites*, 2nd ed.,
London 1907). Cf. the discussion of the problem in my *Probleme der Religionspsychologie*, p. XVII.

present day. One can meet the objection, of course, with various historical and psychological arguments. Here we will confine ourselves to stressing the fact that we have chosen ritual as the starting point of our analytic investigation of religious experience only on heuristic grounds; because it has the advantage of lucidity and external conspicuousness, and because it offers greater resistance than other religious phenomena to the manifold factors, conditioned by cultural evolution, which make for change. While we have also stressed the importance of ritual as one of the most significant forms of expression of the latent, unconscious emotional tendencies in religion, we have never forgotten that profounder criteria determine the essential nature of religion.

The psychoanalysis of theology is still a young science which has had to contend with many difficulties, external and internal. In dealing with the great problems of an alien and jealously guarded science it can proceed only slowly and with caution. Its progress in the field of religious psychology will therefore be achieved only step by step. For all that, it has often ventured to claim its right to occupy a central position in the psychological comprehension of religious problems. The present essay constitutes such a step in the direction of the still difficult problems of religious psychology which call for an even more searching analysis. I am conscious of its incomplete and preliminary character, though I cannot say precisely where the inquiry will lead us.

We have decided to suppress our counterarguments, and for the time being to consider the objection that ritual is *not* to be regarded as decisive in respect of the psychic experiences of religion. Institutional religion must offer us tokens of a different kind which will decide whether a person is to be regarded as a follower of a specific religion. Does not language itself—as though fortuitously—give us a hint as to one of the most important criteria of religion? When we are speaking of the religious persuasion of peoples and individuals, we assert that they are Christian, or Islamic, or Buddhist *believers*. We also say that they *profess* this or that religion. We therefore regard *profession* as an expression of this *belief*. By this we consider that a man professes to believe the ideas or doctrines of the religion in question. We

say of an atheist that he does not believe in God—that is, in the
existence of God—and we regard him as being without religion,
owing to this lack of belief. We do not, of course, mean to assert
that faith alone is the essential feature of religion. There are
different kinds and degrees of belief, and many of the greatest
religious spirits were for a long while inveterate unbelievers. But
no one will deny that belief, and the profession of this belief, are
among the most significant of religious phenomena.

We shall therefore turn our attention to that deposit of faith
whose unconditional acknowledgment every one of the more
highly evolved religions, and every church, requires of its followers, in the name of Divine authority. It will readily be understood that such religious beliefs exist, in the germ, even in the
religions of primitive races, although they may not there assume
the same predominant importance. For example, the Jambin of
New Guinea believe in a spirit, Balum, and further that their
chieftains are equipped with demonic powers; Islam asserts that
Allah alone is God, and Mohammed His prophet; the Mazdaists
declare that "Ahura Mazda gives the kingdom to the prophets,"
and Christendom confesses to belief in God the Father and the
Divine Son. In principle, there is no difference between these
various beliefs.

Again, the mode of inculcation of the novices is everywhere
almost the same. In the Australian bush the men initiate the
novices in the belief in the totemistic ancestral spirit in essentially
the same manner as the priests, in church and school, initiate
European children in the concepts of the Christian faith. Nonetheless, it is, of course, obvious what important differences exist
between the articles of faith of these religions, and it will be
readily understood that these differences are attributable, in the
first place, to the different cultural levels of the believers. For our
specific purposes we shall stress only two of these differences: The
beliefs of the primitive races, and of the peoples of antiquity,
seem far more indefinite than those of Islam (for example) or
Catholicism, and the acceptance of these beliefs is not demanded
with the exclusive rigor which in our civilization makes the belief in specific propositions appear the central fact of every
highly organized religion. In the case of the great monotheistic

religions of the present time the fundamental religious concepts are by no means indefinite; they are expressed in rigid formulae, and their unconditional acceptance is required of all believers. This simple faith, which has no need to seek support in the study of the profounder meaning of the individual religious concepts (but must indeed exclude all criticism of them) is indispensable; it will, however, be regarded as sufficing.

The religious beliefs thus defined are expressed in separate and precisely formulated doctrines which, in the opinion of the supreme authorities, include the essential content, the quintessence of the religion in question, and are generally acknowledged by the community. Doctrines of this kind are called *dogmas*.[2]

Today, when we speak of religious dogmas, we generally mean the dogmatic doctrines of Christendom, but it is evident that this restriction is unjustified, for all the more highly evolved religions—Islam, Judaism, Confucianism, etc.—have doctrines which deserve this description.[3] If one wishes to study the psychological problems of dogma it will not matter, fundamentally,

[2] This word has undergone many changes of meaning. In classical literature it is used in the sense of a theological proposition or doctrine. In the New Testament it signifies an imperial prescription (Luke, 2, 1; Acts, 17, 7); or a conciliar decree (Acts, 16, 4). Modern usage has further enlarged the notion of the dogmatic, which at a later period was restricted to the religious conception of dogmatism, but has also given it the subsidiary meaning of a narrow and obstinately defended opinion.

The above definition of dogma is open to the same criticism as definitions in general. Harnack defined ecclesiastical dogmas as "the doctrines of faith, abstractly formulated in terms amenable to scientific and apologetic usage, which include the notion of God, of the world, and of redemption through Christ, and which represent the objective content of religion." (*Lehrbuch der Dogmengeschichte*, Vol. I, 4th ed., 1919, p. 3). According to Loof's (*Leitfaden zum Studium der Dogmengeschichte*, 5th ed., 1893, p. 7) they are "those articles of faith whose acceptance is expressly required of its members by an ecclesiastical community." Seeberg (*Lehrbuch der Dogmengeschichte*, Vol. 1, 1895, p. 1) stresses the point that dogmas are not just any theological propositions or formulae consciously advanced by the ecclesiastical community, but are only such propositions "as have become ecclesiastic principles: that is, such as are acknowledged, by public declaration, by the church as a whole, or by a branch of the church, as the expression of the ecclesiastical truth." I. Kaftan (*Dogmatik*, Freiburg 1897, p. 1) declares that dogmas are "the fundamental ecclesiastical truths which are regarded by the church as authoritative."

[3] Paul still described the Jewish law as dogma (Eph. 2, 5), and the Greek ʰers speak of the heathen dogmas in contradistinction to the Christian.

from what religion he takes his material for analysis, since in all religions dogma exhibits the same essential characters. Here we shall adduce the substance of the Christian dogmas as modified by various motives. It was Christianity that first gave the word, dogma, a religious meaning, and the development of Christendom really constitutes a culminating point in the formation of dogma. We could point to other reasons for giving our preference to material drawn from Christian sources: the historical and religious evolution of Christendom has been subjected to the most thorough research, and for the sphere of our western civilization its dogmas appear to be the most important.

How does a dogma come into existence? Here I am confronted with a difficulty. The Church asserts that it does not come into existence; it does not acknowledge the genesis and growth of a dogma. The "deposit of faith" (*depositum fidei*) which was given to the Church in the beginning, and comprises the sum of truth, cannot be something that came into being. Dogma existed always, and one can speak of its development only in a formal or abstract manner. This argument was, of course, inevitable, since the truth emanating from God had to be interpreted, elucidated and defended for the better understanding of the faithful, and as a defense against heretics and skeptics. The Christian Churches declare that the truths comprised in the "deposit of faith" are contained in the Holy Scriptures or in the Christian tradition, and can therefore be transmitted in dogmatic form. But it can be shown that the votaries of primitive Christendom knew nothing of such dogmas in the beginning.[4]

The Church formulated the dogmas in its synods and councils, those great and imposing assemblies of the higher clergy, which were rent by the most embittered disputes, though they were convened in the name and in honor of one who came to bring peace to mankind. The Holy Ghost, informing the bishops, spoke with the voice of the assembly, and made his opinion infallible. Nevertheless, the Pope, teaching *ex cathedra* the eternal

---

[4] The opposition to the dogma of the Trinity is often based on the fact that the doctrine is not taught in the New Testament. Even so ardent a defender of Christian dogma as Georg Lassen (*Grundfragen der Glaubenslehre*, Leipzig 1913, p. 128) is obliged to concede that dogma has given Christian truth a form which is not to be found in the New Testament.

truth contained in tradition, can at any time give it a form which will possess universal validity.[5] Whether a dogma was promulgated by a Council or declared by the Pope, it was always referred to the authority of God, and Divine revelation was accepted, *kat exochen,* as the foundation of knowledge.

If we wish to study the genesis and the essential psychological features of dogma we shall perhaps do best to begin with a specific and important example of representative significance. Let us take, from the mass of available material, the basic dogma of Christendom, the doctrine of the divinity of Christ, a dogma whose importance, we believe, no one can dispute.[6] This central doctrine of Christendom is an ecumenical symbol: that is, one of those universally valid professions of faith which are common to all the Christian Churches. The *Symbolum Nicaeum,* which was formulated by the First Synod of Nicaea (325)—though it assumed its final form only about the year 381—appears as the profession of faith of the Greek Catholic Church, as a eucharistic symbol of the Roman Church, as an article of faith of the Protestant Churches, and as a liturgical profession of faith (the "Nicene Creed") of the Anglican Church. It commends itself to us not only because of its pre-eminent importance in the body of Christian doctrine, but because it is chronologically the first precisely formulated dogma of the Church, and it is only from the date of its formulation that we can speak of a development of Christian dogma.[7]

5 The evolution of dogma in the western churches appeared to have ceased since the Seventh Ecumenical Council (787). Since then no further dogmas have been officially formulated in western Christendom. However, in 1870 the Roman Church promulgated a new dogma, on a par with the old. The older Protestantism replaced the ecclesiastical dogma by the biblical text as a whole, in so far as it has a definite doctrinal content. The confessional Scriptures served to determine the formulae which took the place of dogma. The evolution of modern Protestantism, which no longer regarded the Bible as the absolute authority, followed a direction which diverged from the dogmatic, while it could not entirely exclude the remnants of dogma.

6 "The dogma of the Three Persons of God is in Christian opinion at once the culmination of all theological knowledge and the exactest measure of all true theological culture." (Franz Friedhoff, *Katholische Dogmatik,* 2nd ed., 1871, p. 294.)

7 Harnack stresses the fact that one must look for the incident which determined the development of dogma "where for the first time an abstractly

In a footnote[8] we quote the definitive text of this Nicaeo-Constantinopolitan creed, which was for all time to establish the fundamental dogma of Christianity. Listening to the text of this clearly formulated dogma, which comprises the supreme doctrines of Christendom, one would never imagine to what conflicts with the obstinacy and incomprehension of Christian heretics it owes its precision of phrasing. For century after century, in the battles that raged about this dogma, which comprises the sublimest truths of Christianity—battles waged with the most fervid religious zeal—torrents of blood were shed by the faithful to whom Christ had declared: "Blessed are the peacemakers."

In the following pages we shall deal with the history of the genesis of the dogmatic formulae. For obvious reasons we shall deal more exhaustively with the last, decisive difficulties and conflicts which led to the constitution of the dogma. In so far as I endeavor to describe the processes which constitute the essential feature of the history of this most important of the Christian dogmas, I should wish, by a concrete example of representative importance, to describe the emotional premises and processes of

---

formulated article of faith respecting Christ, expressed through the medium of scholarship, is promoted to the central doctrine, and as such is universally promulgated by the Church. But this first came about when the doctrine that Christ was the pre-existing and personal Logos of God was triumphantly accepted as the fundamental dogma: that is, about the end of the third century and the beginning of the fourth" (*Lehrbuch der Dogmengeschichte*, p. 3).

8 "We believe in one God the Father Almighty, maker of heaven and earth, and of all things visible and invisible. And in one Lord Jesus Christ, the only begotten Son of God, begotten of His Father, before all worlds, Light of Light, very God of very God, begotten, not made, being of one substance with the Father, by whom all things were made; who for us men and for our salvation came down from heaven and was incarnate of the Holy Ghost by the Virgin Mary, And was made man, and was crucified also for us under Pontius Pilate. He suffered and was buried. And the third day he rose again, according to the Scriptures, and ascended into heaven, and sitteth on the right hand of the Father, and he shall come again with glory to judge both the quick and the dead: whose kingdom shall have no end. And in the Holy Ghost, the Lord and Giver of Life, who proceedeth from the Father, who with the Father and the Son together is worshipped and glorified, who spake by the Prophets. In one holy Catholic and Apostolic Church. We acknowledge one baptism for the remission of sins. We look for the resurrection of the dead and the life of the world to come. Amen." (Revised by the Council of Nicaea, A.D. 325; by Cyril, A.D. 362; by the Council of Constantinople, A.D. 381; by the Council of Chalcedon, A.D. 451.)

the dogmatization in general, while attempting to solve the problems: what a dogma means, in the psychological sense, and how dogmas ever come to be created. It would, of course, have been more convenient to select, as example, a less complicated dogma, whose genesis could be more easily traced. But such a concession to convenience might perhaps have led us, quite unjustifiably, to regard the psychological content of the dogma as simple, and might have deprived us of an insight into the most difficult problems of dogma in its highly organized form. The simplification which may prove to be necessary for the purposes of our investigation will manifest itself in other directions: in a restriction to the most important factor of the basic dogma; in refraining from a many-faceted treatment of the problem of the dogma; and in the manner of representation. In particular, we shall direct our attention to that part of the problem which has been of the greatest importance in the evolution of Christianity—the Christological question of the relation of God the Father and God the Son.[9] However, we shall endeavor to comprehend the genesis and

[9] For the study of the dogma of the Trinity and its development, in addition to the already mentioned histories of dogma by Harnack, Loof and Seeberg, the following works may be recommended: Heinrich Holtzmann, *Lehrbuch der neutestamentlichen Theologie*, 1897; Eduard Meyer, *Ursprung und Anfänge des Christentums*, 3 vols., 1921; F. C. Bauer, *Die christliche Lehre von der Dreieinigkeit und Menschwerdung Gottes*, 1845; Dorner, *Entwicklungsgeschichte der Lehre von der Person Christi*, 2nd ed., 1845–1855; A. Reville, *Histoire du dogme de la divinité de Jésus Christ*, 2nd ed., 1876; H. Schultz, *Die Lehre von der Gottheit Christi*, 1881; Gustav Krüger, *Das Dogma von der Dreieinigkeit und Gottmenschheit*, 1905. Also the article, "Christology," by M. Köhler and Loof in the *Realenzyklopädie f. prot. Theol. u. Kirche*, Vol. IV, 3rd ed., pp. 4 et seq. For the history and doctrine of Arianism: in addition to occasional references to the works of the Fathers of the fourth century (Athanasius, Hilarius, Hieronymus) and the ecclesiastical histories of Socrates, Sozomenus, and Theodoret, and the Vita Constantini of Eusebius, the following works were utilized: Hort, *On the Constantinopolitan Creed and Other Eastern Creeds of the Fourth Century*, 1874; H. M. Gwatkin, *Studies of Arianism*, 2nd ed., 1900 (popular abridgement, *The Arian Controversy*, 2nd ed., 1897). P. Snellmann, *Die Anfänge des arianischen Streites*, 1904; O. Seeck, "Untersuchungen zur Geschichte des nizänischen Konzils", *Zeitschrift für Kirchengeschichte*, Vol. XVII, 1–72, 319–363; Kölling, *Geschichte der arianischen Häresie*, 2 vols., 1874–1885; I. Gummerus, *Die homöousianische Partei bis zum Tode Konstantins*, 1900; Tillemont, *Mémoires pour servir à l'histoire ecclésiastique*, 1752; W. F. Walch, *Entwurf einer vollständigen Histoire der Ketzerei*, Vol. II, 1767; C. I. Hefele, *Conciliengeschichte*, 2nd ed., 1875; A. Hahn, *Bibliothek der Symbole und Glaubensregeln der*

development of this dogmatic problem only from the analytic standpoints. We are well aware that there are other aspects of the problem of dogma, which may be discussed in the light of religious and ecclesiastical history, the philosophy of religion, and systematic theology. But the restriction to the analytic explanation has seemed to us necessary. At the same time, we have not forgotten that it cannot and will not furnish us with a complete explanation. Accordingly, our exposition will renounce beforehand all those pretensions which must be advanced in the case of a historical description of dogma and ecclesiastical doctrine, or of a philosophical and systematically theological treatment of the subject, citing only those essential problems which will bring us nearer to our goal, the analytic investigation of the genesis of dogma, and its psychic significance.

Before we turn to the historical description of the most important beliefs of Christianity, a word of comment will perhaps be in order. The historical existence of a religious and social revolutionary, whose memory survives in the mythically enhanced figure of Jesus Christ, seems to me, despite the all too rationalistic criticisms of such authors as Drews[10] and Brandes,[11] probable if not absolutely proven. That the Romans, and with them the civilized world, knew absolutely nothing of this agitator is in some degree explicable. No one bothered his head about the theological disputes of a little sect of a small, despised people. Even if we assume the existence of a person closely resembling the figure of the traditional Jesus, we must not lose sight of the fact that the rabbi in question—whether we consider his teaching or the course of his life—would be by no means singular in the Jewry of the period. Even the story of the Passion loses its uniqueness when we learn that in the time of Trajan more than 700 Jews were crucified. Why should Jesus alone have died with

---

alten Kirche, 2nd ed., 1877; Rogulla, Die Anfänge des arianischen Streites, 1907; Bernouilli, Das Konzil von Nicäa, 1896; Duchene, Hist. Ancienne de l'église, Vol. II, 1907; F. Bethune Baker, Introduction to the Early History of Christian Doctrine, 1902; Revillont, Del'Arianisme des Peuples Germaniques, 1850; Gibbon, Decline and Fall of the Roman Empire, 1896, Vols. II, III et seq.

10 The Christ-Myth, 1912; The Denial of the Historicity of Jesus, 1916.
11 Die Jesusfrage, 1925.

a quotation from the Twenty-Second Psalm on his lips ("My God, my God, why hast thou forsaken me")? It has been justly remarked that in heaven an angel is no rarity.

In a scientific publication there is no occasion to examine the Christian myths from any but a psychological standpoint. A serious and critical demonstration that the Christian narratives are not consistent with the historical facts would be superfluous. The zeal with which these legends are still being exposed as incredible fictions is about as sensible as the criticism of *Gulliver's Travels* which—according to Swift—was offered by a well-meaning Irish bishop. The ingenuous cleric declared, with indignation,[12] that "the book was full of improbable lies and for his part he hardly believed a word of it."

[12] Leslie Stephen, *Swift,* London 1899, p. 171.

II. THE GENESIS OF DOGMA

We know how unreliable is traditional evidence; in how many respects it is distorted; how frequently falsehood is blended with truth; how often it has been revised before it comes down to us. No reasonable man believes it possible to reconstruct the history of the ideas of two thousand years as it really happened, and to recover its real meaning. In so far as we are able to find our bearings in the extremely turbid and uncertain illusion which the scholars like to call the evidence of historical tradition, the hypotheses for the unfolding of the dogmatic problem are as follows: Jesus announced the glad tidings of God throughout the world and to every individual soul. His faithful disciples, who forsook their master in the hour of his death, had regarded him, before the message of Easter came to them, as a man like other men. The heavenly firmament, to which it was believed he had ascended, now casts its reflection over his earthly life; and the story of the glorification of Christ is born. To Peter it seems, as he declares in his Pentecostal sermon (Acts, II, 36; cf. X, 42), that through his resurrection God has made this Jesus, whom the Jews had crucified, Lord and Christ. Not until later was the Divine embassy dated back to the baptism. Early Jewry saw in Jesus the bodily son of Joseph the carpenter, who through baptism, being filled with the Divine spirit, became the Messiah. The belief in the Resurrection, and the installing of Jesus on the right hand of the Father, became, in the course of time, an occasion for representing the beginning of his life in a corresponding spirit. Thus the simple faith of the Apostles in the acknowledgment of the God of Israel and of Jesus as the Messiah, a faith which was a bond between God and every individual soul, was established. The Messiah was the Way to the Father.

The deification of Jesus the carpenter proceeded gradually; about the year 113 A.D. Pliny heard from apostate Christians

that they had worshipped Christ as God,[1] and the heathen of
the apologetical era regarded the adoration of "Jesus, the crucified Sophist," as the mark of a Christian.[2] The religious adoration
of the Saviour is clearly recorded by Paul; not only does he himself pray to Christ (II, 128), but he regards the invocation of
Christ as a universal Christian practice. The Apocalypse testifies
to the invocation of Christ by those in the author's environment
(V, 13; XXII, 17, 20), and the Gospel according to St. John takes
the practice of praying to Jesus for granted. The Epistle to the
Hebrews and the Epistle of Barnabas often made no distinction
between Jesus and God. The second Epistle of Clement contains
the prescription: "Thou shalt deem of Jesus Christ as thou
deemest of God, as of the judge of the quick and the dead." In
Paul the image of the Messiah is that of a heavenly being. Jesus
is now no longer the Son of God who came to announce the
kingdom of the Father, but the manifest Godhead. The fiery little
carpetmaker from Cilicia, Saul, who has justly been described as
one of the founders of Christianity, and who had never seen
Christ with his bodily eyes, was full of his experience before
Damascus, an experience which remained with him to the end
of his days. We shall not discuss here and now the Christology of
the great evangelist. It is enough to stress the fact that by this
Christology the conception of the Messianic king of the line of
David is replaced by that of the Son of God, the herald of the
spiritual, heavenly universe.

Ignatius of Antioch, when he speaks of "Jesus Christ, our
God," of "the God who came in the flesh," already betrays conceptions akin to those of the Fourth Gospel. We do not know
who the author of this record was—the disciple of Christ, John,
to whom the Church ascribes its authorship, would have been
about 150 years of age when he began to write it!—but it was
certainly written in the second century, somewhere in Asia
Minor. But how far removed is it from the intellectual sphere,

[1] Lucian de morte Peregr. 13 opp. ed. Lehmann VIII. 271. Celsus in
Origenes c. Celsus 8, 12–14.

[2] XIV, pp. 3 et seq. Cf. Zahn for prayer to Jesus in the time of the
Apostles, in *Skizzen aus dem Leben der alten Kirche*, 1894, pp. 1 et seq.

from the modes of thought and the idiom of the disciples, who were uneducated Galilean fishermen! This Gospel is no longer the message of God, proclaimed by Jesus Christ. We read of the earthly transubstantiation of the Divine Word, which from eternity was with the Father, and now, becoming flesh, brought light upon the earth. The Christ of this Gospel is definitely another being than the Jesus of the Sermon on the Mount and the parables! We are told why the Divine Word, the Logos, was sent down upon earth by the Father. Let us recall the trumpet-like prologue of this Gospel: "In the beginning was the Word, and the Word was with God, and the Word was God . . . All things were made by him, and without him was not anything made that was made. In him was life; and the life was the light of men. And the light shineth in darkness, and the darkness comprehendeth it not." The Evangelist makes Jesus assert, over and over again, that he and the Father are one. Nevertheless, the Son is always subordinate to the Father. For Tatian the Logos was the first creation of God and the beginning of the Cosmos; for it was the Word of God, which said: Let there be light, and there was light. The heavens were created by the word of the Lord, and all its hosts by the breath of his mouth (Psalms, XXXIII, 6). A difficulty remains, but Tatian quickly disposes of it: the Logos proceeds from the Father by differentiation, not by separation, "for what is cut off is separated from the beginning, but that which comes into being through distinction has its part in the self-determination [of the Father] and therefore has not impoverished him from whom it is taken. For as from one torch many flames are kindled, but the light of the first torch is not diminished by the kindling, even so the Logos, inasmuch as it proceeds from the power of the Father, does not rob the Father of the Logos." Here we already note the intensified interest in a definition and elucidation of the relation of Father and Son.

In the first days of Christendom Christ was often naïvely allowed to take the place of the Father, without considering such matters as unity, differentiation, separation, deprivation and resistance. But by the second century the apologists clearly realized that such questions were extremely complicated. We shall understand the necessity of these fine and subtle distinc-

tions if we reflect that at this time the evolving religion had to
fight one of its most dangerous battles. The Gnostics had drawn
the extremest conclusion from the tendency to represent Christ
as the Godhead: they placed him not beside, but above God the
Father. God the Father of the Old Testament appeared to them
—and more especially to the disciples of Marcion and Valentinian
—as the actual enemy of true understanding. He was the Demiurge, the architect of the universe, who was overthrown by the
Saviour, Christ. With God the Father the Old Testament lost
its pre-eminence as the source of salvation.

The manner in which Marcion, for example, revises the
Gospel of Saint Luke is characteristic of the Gnostic Christology.
He simply deletes the story of Christ's childhood, combines the
beginning of the Third and the close of the Fourth Gospel, and
boldly represents Jesus as God: "In the fifteenth year of the
reign of the Emperor Tiberius God came down to Capernaum
and preached on the Sabbath." Christianity very nearly succumbed to Gnosticism: a religion of the Son, who had dispos-
sessed God the Father, and all but conquered the earth. It may
be said that the baptismal creed, which was derived from the
injunction given in the Gospel according to St. Matthew,[3] served
as a rampart against the disciples of Gnosticism. No one who accepted this formula, which first emerged between 150 and 175
A.D., professing his belief in God the Father, the Son, and the
Holy Ghost, could possibly accept the Gnostic doctrines.

During the first two centuries we see the evolving Church
waging a vigorous battle on two different fronts: against the
Gnostics, who degraded God the Father, seeking to suppress the
new religion, and against the various tendencies of Judaeo-
Christianity, which regarded Christ as merely a great prophet,
comparable to Isaiah and Jeremiah. And this was certainly the
view of the original Christian community. The Ebionites, for
example, were still faithful to the ceremonial law of Moses, and
declared that Jesus was the bodily son of Joseph.

We have followed the main lines along which Christology
evolved, and we seem to see how the Galilean rabbi was gradually

[3] XXVIII, 19: "Go ye therefore, and teach all nations, baptizing them in
the name of the Father, and of the Son, and of the Holy Ghost."

transformed into the Logos. Here we have a recurrence—of course, in a philosophical and allegorical form—of the old myth of God the Son, who ascends to the Father. The mythical figure of the great Saviour had become established.

It would be quite erroneous to conclude that the doctrine of the Logos was then the common property of Christendom. What had a community which consisted mainly of poor Jewish and pagan slaves, procurers, strumpets, and artisans, in common with speculations concerning the Logos? What were all these speculations beside the immediate assurance of salvation through Jesus Christ?

Even among the more cultured followers of the new religion there were serious misgivings in respect of the conception of the Logos entertained by such apologists as Tatian, Irenaeus, and others. Such a conception was in danger of leading to a relapse into the polytheism of the heathen. Was not Christ, if he was at once God and man, a second God, at the side of God the Father? We know that the Alogi, a communal group of Christians in Asia Minor, flatly rejected the Johannine Logos. They maliciously pointed to the fact that the Gospel according to St. Mark says nothing as to the heavenly origin of Jesus, and rejected the title of Logos as that of the Son of God. The Monarchians disputed the sole supremacy (monarchy) of God; they believed in a uni-personal God, and in the man Jesus, miraculously born of the power of the Divine Spirit, and inspired by the Divine Spirit, who, being after his death raised to divine rank, was adopted by God. Thus, in the early days of Christendom a pneumatic doctrine of Christ is opposed to an adoptionist doctrine. According to the one doctrine Christ was a divine being made flesh. According to the other he was a prophet raised to the status of a divine ruler. The conflict between these two doctrines continued for more than a century and ended with the defeat of monotheism and the victory of the doctrine of the Logos.

The men of the Monarchian party, who, like their opponents, were members of the evolving Church, were led, at first, by the cordwainer Theodotus, who was living in Rome about the year 190 A.D., and was described by the Fathers of the Church as "the father of the God-for-swearing apostasy." He was treated as

THE GENESIS OF DOGMA

a heretic and excommunicated by the Roman Bishop Victor—
the first instance of a professing Christian being punished as a
teacher of heresy. But the Monarchians went too far. They professed to represent the ancient, unalloyed doctrine of Christianity; and they invoked Jesus himself, who had described himself
as a man. The Old Testament prophecies had spoken, not of a
God, but of a prophet, like Moses, and therefore undoubtedly a
man. They went so far in their infatuation as to allude to the
Gospel according to St. Luke (I, 35), in which the angel does not
say that Christ is God, but only that he will be born of the
Virgin by the power of the Holy Ghost, and that "he shall be
called the Son of God." A group of Monarchians, called, after
their leader, Artemonists, even ventured to diverge from the
sacrosanct allegorical interpretation of the Scriptures. They accepted the canon, and also the Gospel of Saint John, but they
examined the Word of God in a manner which was forbidden—
that is, of course, critically—scrutinizing the versions which already contained discrepancies in order to obtain confirmation of
their views. They laid hands upon the Holy Scriptures under
the infamous pretext of correcting them, and applying their
reason to this damnable work of criticism. The Church could
point to numerous writings of the worthy Fathers—such as
Justin, Miltiades, Tatian—in all of which Christ is called God.
But the Monarchians persisted in their blindness. Eusebius
sadly reproached them for interesting themselves in geometry—
in studying Euclid, Aristotle and Theophrastus "as people who
are of this world, and speak the tongue of this world, and have
no knowledge of that which comes from above." The Monarchians
by no means denied that the man Jesus Christ, who was replete
in a mysterious manner with the spirit of God, and had revealed
God the Father to men, should be called His Son and worshipped
as such, but the Church sternly reproved them, complaining that
hereby they denied the divinity of our Lord, or reduced it to a
mere phrase. The Monarchians constituted a large and peculiar
community, which was to survive for many decades.

In the time of Zephyrinus, Bishop of Rome (199–218), this
forming of churches went so far that a cleric was appointed bishop
of the Monarchians. But visions that came to him gently re-

quired him to return to the orthodox faith; and when, despite such a kindly warning, he persisted in his heresy, the "holy angel" gave him such a thrashing one night that he penitently returned to the bosom of the Church which was the sole disposer of grace. We have little authentic knowledge of the doctrines of this heretic. God, in His foresight, destroyed the writings of this bishop who denied the Godhead of Christ, making use of the pious zeal of the true believers. Nevertheless, the representatives of the Adoptian doctrine were still treated gently.

Even by the middle of the third century the Christology of the Logos was not generally accepted in the East. Not until the bishop of the important see of Antioch, Paul of Samosata (about 260) once again proclaimed the doctrine of the human person of Christ did the Church resolve to have recourse to energetic measures. According to Paul, God was to be conceived simply as one person. It was true that in God a Logos could be distinguished, and this Logos could even be called His Son, but it was nevertheless a quality of God, an impersonal power. This Logos had operated in the prophets, and in Moses, and most powerfully in the Christ who was born of the Virgin. The relation of the Logos to Jesus was one of indwelling, of inspiration; wherefore the Logos was still to be distinguished from Jesus. It was greater than he. The Saviour, then, is a man, born in time. He is "of the world below," but the Logos in him operates "from above." Paul, indeed, says that Christ has confirmed himself through community with God, and by virtue of such confirmation is raised by God's grace, after death and resurrection, to the divine status, so that he can now be called "the God born of the Virgin." But Paul attacked the votaries of the natural divinity of Christ. He regarded this belief as evidence of ditheism which did not allow of the prefiguration of Christ. According to Bishop Paul, there was nothing meritorious in natural divinity.

Yet the most dangerous opponent of the Logos Christology toward the close of the fourth century was not the delusion of Adoptianism, but the doctrine that the Deity Himself was incarnate in Christ, so that Christ was regarded as God the Father made flesh. The great Fathers of the Church—Tertullian, Origenes, Novatian, Hippolytus, and many others—all opposed this view, which for a long while agitated the entire Church with desperate energy. If one seeks to comprise all the numerous groups which inclined to different forms of this doctrine, the description that suggests itself is *Modalism,* inasmuch as they all regarded Christ as another kind of embodiment (*modus*) of the one God. In Rome Modalism was for a generation the official doctrine of the Church. In fact, the growing Church had no easy time of it. If it avoided the Scylla of Monarchianism it incurred the danger of lapsing into the Charybdis of Modalism.

Among the modalistic doctrines there is one special form of which the pious Hippolytus, in his polemic against Noëtus, gives us a very clear description. The older Monarchians of whom we have spoken taught that Christ was himself the Father, and that the Father himself was born, suffered, and died. This opinion— that Christ was God the Father and that the Father-God had suffered—is known as *Patripassianism* (from Lat. *pater* = father, and *pati* = to suffer). Thus, the doctrine of Patripassianism, which for a long while was accepted by many bishops, and the broad mass of Christian worshippers, supported the doctrine of monotheism in the form which identified God the Father with Christ. It reproved its opponents as *ditheoi,* believers in two gods, insisting that they themselves were the first to have acknowledged the full divinity of Christ in every particular. The Patripassians naturally invoked the canon of the Holy Scriptures (and their opponents did the same). The logical difficulties which arose from these views they overcame by a sort of superlogical proof. The Roman bishop, Hippolytus, describing the doctrine of a leader of the party, Noëtus, and his followers in Asia Minor, reported as follows: "They say that one and the same God is Creator and Father of all things. Although He is invisible, of old time He appeared, in His bountifulness, to the righteous. That is to say, if He is not seen He is invisible; but if He allows Himself to be seen He is visible. He is incomprehensible if He does not wish to be comprehended; but comprehensible if He allows Himself to be comprehended. So, in the same manner, He is insuperable and superable, unbegotten and begotten, immortal and mortal." Accordingly no doubt is cast upon the manifoldness of the divine qualities.

The Modalists also experienced but little difficulty in respect of the earthly life of this Jesus identical with the Father. There are no contradictions in the broad conception of Noëtus: "In so far as the Father was not made He is rightly to be called Father. But in so far as He took time to undergo birth He is, as one born, His own son, not the son of another." This relatively simple genealogy constitutes the gist of God's biography; but it also confirms the monarchy of God.

Noëtus and his followers simply assert that what is called Father and Son is one and the same thing; one is not born of the other, but of himself. It is true that the two were at certain periods distinguished by name as Father and Son, but in fact there was one, who elected to be born of the Virgin, and who lived as a man among men. To those that saw Him He confessed Himself to be the Son, but from those who were able to comprehend Him He did not conceal the fact that He was the Father. He was put to death on the Cross, and gave up the ghost. He died and did not die. He awakened Himself on the third day. He was pierced by the spear, etc. In concise terms, with the consistent subtlety which the radical Monarchian standpoint seems to have conferred upon its adherents, Noëtus observes: "Now if I acknowledge Christ as God He is manifestly the Father, if in another manner He is God. Now, Christ suffered, who Himself is the Father; therefore the Father suffered, for He was the Father."

Another form of Modalism is connected with the name of the Libyan, Sabellius, who about the year 220 organized a community in Rome, where he had many followers. The unifying effect of the spirit of this community was apparent in its fundamental idea that Father, Son, and Holy Ghost were one and the same. This sublime identity implied that there were three successive manifestations of the one divine being. The effect of this illuminating idea, especially in the East, was extraordinarily persistent, inciting the Fathers of the Church to assail the heretical notion with their utmost zeal.

Among the most zealous defenders of the orthodox doctrines of this period was Tertullian, the son of a Roman centurion, born in Carthage. A man of wide culture, on his conversion to Christianity in 197 A.D. he turned away from all the ephemeral pleasures of this world, and the possessions which rust and moth corrupt, and persecuted art and science with the hatred which they deserved. He never wearied of explaining the mystery of the Trinity, constantly finding new phrases to confound the heretics. No one was more zealous than he in the fruitful task of describing the incomprehensible in the most meticulous formulae, and adducing the most circumstantial proof of the inexplicable. He waged a bitter war upon the ignorant and dull-witted people who regarded triality as destructive of unity, "whereas unity, which allows triality to proceed from it, is not dissolved by the latter, but confirms itself therein. Thus, they are always babbling to the effect that we preach of two or three Gods. But they themselves profess to be worshippers of the one God, as though unity, when restricted without reason, did not lead to heresy, and as though trinity, if rightly understood, did not comprise the truth." Nevertheless, even this eminent son of the *ecclesia militans* had to admit that the truth is not easily comprehended. He therefore preferred to resort to images in order to elucidate the difference between Father, Son, and Holy Ghost: the Son is to the Father as the ray of sunlight to the sun, the shoot to the root, the brook to the spring. With pulverizing arguments Tertullian attacked the blasphemy of Monarchianism: "Notwithstanding that I call a ray of sunlight by itself the sun, when I speak of the sun to which the ray belongs I am not therefore calling the sun a ray." With equally dazzling logic Tertullian speaks of the mystery of the theanthropy of Christ, and many other dogmas. Anyone who has made a profound study of the great Carthaginian will agree with the judgment of Vincent of Lerinum: he wins a victory with every proposition.[4]

The world owes the victory of the Logos Christology not only to Tertullian, Irenaeus and Hippolytus, but also to the great doc-

[4] Only ignorance or malice has ascribed to Tertullian the notorious *Credo quia absurdum est*. As a matter of fact, the sublime words of the bellicose Father were as follows: "Crucifixus est dei filius, non pudet, quia pudendum est. Et mortuus est dei filius; prorsus credibile est, quia ineptum est. Et sepultus resurrexit; certum est, quia impossibile est" (*De carne Chr.* 5). Our skeptical age is lacking in the comprehension and ready credulity which politely overlook such trifling contradictions. But the hope persists that the soul, which, as Tertullian was the first to remark, has a natural leaning toward Christianity ("*anima naturaliter christiana*") may recover its faith.

tors of the Church, Clement (about 210) and Origenes (about 250). Origenes, especially, who labored in Alexandria, was an important figure in the further development of Christology. In his exposition the relation between God the Father and the Son is so simply conceived that in later years the most antithetical ecclesiastical parties were able to invoke his authority. To the Logos are attributed almost all the qualities which must be attributed to God Himself, and nevertheless the Logos is independent. Origenes does not lapse into the crude doctrine of ditheism. The Logos is caused by the Father, whose creation—although begotten from eternity by the nature of God—is almost God's equal, and yet subordinate to Him. His begetting is a unique and indescribable act. There is nothing comparable to it, whether in actual facts or in thought; and this the more so, inasmuch as "there was never a time when He was not."

In the fifth century the pious Vincent of Lerinum called the theology of Origenes a temptation of God. As a matter of fact, it was difficult not to contradict Origenes; and it was even more difficult to contradict him. One of his pupils, Bishop Dionysius of Alexandria, did not escape the danger of misunderstanding his great teacher. In his very comprehensible aversion from Sabellianism, that reprehensible doctrine which regarded the Trinity as merely a manifestation of the Father, he went to such lengths that in his comparisons he did not escape the other extreme, the subordination of the Son. While he had sufficiently expounded the diversity of the two, he did not sufficiently emphasize their essential parity. In other words, he had rightly asserted that three are equal to three and not one, but he had shown too little comprehension of the fact that three can at the same time be one. The Son, he suggested in his perilous comparisons, is created by the Father, but is of a different essence; much as the vine belongs to the vinegrower, and the ship to the shipbuilder. Since the dignity of Christ appeared to be seriously imperiled by such undue subordination, pious men eagerly turned to the Bishop of Rome with their complaints. The Bishop, in the year 261, convened a synod in Rome, which condemned the expressions employed by the Alexandrian. After having received the Bishop's epistle, which demanded certain explanations, Dionysius of Alexandria was prepared to retreat from his position. In an essay of some length he explained that the Father was to the Son as the spring to the brook, as the root to the stem, as parents to their children.

The dispute between these two bishops may be regarded as a slight and insignificant prelude to the Arian mêlée. It was symptomatic of the contrast between the theologies of the East and West. The Romans, while accepting the doctrine of the holy Triad, maintained, without further speculation, the unity of Christ. In Alexandria the subordinationistic doctrine of Origenes was further developed, and the subordination of the Son to the Father exaggerated to the point of alienation.

Before enlarging upon the nature of Arianism, the conflict with which heresy first led to the establishment of the most important dogmas of Christianity, we must endeavor to grasp the general historical situation as regards the Church and its dogmas. Epiphanius informs us that the cause of the great conflicts which were beginning to occur within the Church was the fact that Satan entered into Arius and induced him to make shocking innovations. Without rejecting this simple and clear explanation, we must emphasize the fact that this was a time in which the doctrines of the Church were deplorably confused. The union of tradition, scripture, and speculation in the form of dogma was expected, but had not yet been achieved.

We have broadly indicated the central problems of Christology, and have endeavored to describe the doctrinal opinions of the period, their differences, and the attempts to bridge over these differences. We have seen how these differences were centered, as early as the second century, upon the question of the divine nature of the Saviour and his relation to God the Father. Two great movements were struggling for mastery: the one denied or diminished the divinity of Christ, degrading him to the status of man or demigod. The other accepted the full divinity of Christ, but saw Him as a manifestation of the Father, and lessened the possibility of a distinction. On the other hand, by the beginning of the third century there was no longer any dispute as to the validity of the text of the greater number of the books of the New Testament; and the Old Testament also was generally accepted, even by the Christian heretics. Further, the facts of the Gospel were unquestionable; Christ was generally identified with the Logos; and the beliefs in his pre-existence, his miracles, and his resurrection and ascension, were shared by every Christian.

We are confronted by an age which experienced the cruel persecutions of the Christians under Diocletian and Galerius, and, above all, the fury of Maximinius Daza. In Syria, Asia Minor, and Egypt persecution was still working havoc while Constantine was growing up. The first Christian ruler, the saviour of the Church, who remained unbaptized until just before his death, and manifested the sincerity of his Christian temper by the murder of his son, his nephew, his wife, and many of his friends, published, in the year 515, the famous Edict of Milan, thanks to which the new religion was enabled to exist unharmed beside the old.

We cannot here describe how the protection of the Church by Constantine, whose tolerance was very much facilitated by an insuperable indifference in matters of religion, led to the secularization of the Church.[5] Christendom was now for a long while to become the ally of the reigning emperor, but also his docile servant. Constantine and his successors took it as a matter of course that they should convene synods of bishops, and to a great extent determine the matters to be discussed, and persecute such heretics as seemed to them dangerous. The Arian dispute began when Constantine, having defeated Licinius, became the autocrat of the great Roman Empire. Arius, by birth a Libyan, became, in his later years, a presbyter in Alexandria. The earnest, ascetic presbyter, well skilled in dialectic, who according to Loof "flaunts his name through the centuries as that of the most

[5] The worthy Eusebius describes the banquet which the Emperor Constantine gave to the Bishops of Nicaea on the occasion of his jubilee. Here we see clearly enough how the persecuted religion had become a triumphant State religion: "The Praetorians and the heavily armed troops were on guard, with drawn swords, about the entry to the emperor's court. The men of God passed through their midst and entered the palace. There some reclined at the table with the emperor himself; others took their rest at either side on cushions. There one could well have believed that here was a picture of Christ's kingdom, and that this was not reality but a dream" (Const. Vit. III, 15).

accursed of heretics," was greatly respected by the ascetics and the pious virgins. The beginning of the dispute is recorded more or less in these terms by Socrates, the ecclesiastical historian (I, 5): One day Bishop Alexander was speaking in the presence of his presbyters and deacons of the mystery of the Trinity, whereupon he made certain pious reflections concerning Unity in Triality. It seemed to Arius that he could detect Sabellianism in the bishop's pronouncements, and he thereupon violently contradicted him. This little scene, which occurred about the year 318, was the occasion of the conflict which raged for centuries, constituting the gravest peril to which the Church was ever exposed, leading to countless massacres and cruel persecutions, and compelling the Church to establish the Christian dogmas, which again were to lead to the sacrifice of thousands of human lives by fire and the sword. Bishop Alexander seems to have found it necessary to intervene. His friendship with Arius, as well as the fact that he had no very definite opinions upon the matters in dispute, appear to have been of equal importance. A few minor assemblies were convened, in which Alexander calmly listened to Arius and his opponents, patiently biding his time. Presumably he hoped to settle the dispute quietly by means of theological discussions.

Of Alexander's contemporary, Pachomius, it is recorded[6] that once, when certain strange monks came to him, he noted a disgusting odor. He prayed that God would reveal to him whence this odor arose, and in a vision he received the explanation that the monks whom he was harboring were heretics—that is, followers of Origenes. It would seem that Bishop Alexander was not at this time endowed with the gift of such subtle spiritual discrimination, or he would not have waited so long before taking sides. In the end, in order to preserve his own dignity, he had to excommunicate, not Arius alone, but a number of deacons and presbyters. Arius fled from Alexandria, and sought to win over his old fellow students, who had plenty of *esprit de corps*, and held influential positions in the Church. The bishop of the imperial residence, Eusebius of Nicomedia, Eusebius of Caesarea, and a number of bishops and deacons went over to him. Presently

6 Grützmacher: *Pachomius und das älteste Klosterleben*, p. 75.

he was able to boast that two bishops of Egypt, seven presbyters, twelve deacons, and seven hundred virgins were on his side. He deployed a vigorous propaganda of his views, but Alexander also wrote numerous epistles, reporting what had been happening, and warning the bishops against the Arian heresy.

Before we go further we must consider these doctrines of Arius, of which Alexander complained in his *Epistola encyclica* to the Alexandrian and Mareotic clergy. The most important of the Arian doctrines are as follows: (1) God was not always the Father, but there was a time when He was not the Father. (2) The Logos has not existed from all time, but was created out of nothing. It had a beginning; there was a time when it was not. (3) In essence the Son is of a substance alien to the nature of the Father. If he were of the same natural modality as the Father there would be two Gods. The Logos is by nature variable, in contradistinction to the Father—that is, it could fall into sin. By means of biblical texts Arius demonstrates the ignorance, the anxiety, the resignation of Christ. (4) He is alien to the divine nature, distinct from it, and has not full knowledge of the Father, nor, indeed, has he complete knowledge of himself. (5) He was created for our sakes, in order that God might create us through him as instrument; he would not have existed but for ourselves. The Son existed before the world but is not eternal. Before he was begotten he was not, for he is not unbegotten, as is God.

If we look into these doctrines we recognize that they are influenced by the wish to represent the Father alone as unbegotten and unchanging, and to reject all emanations from the divine being. The point of the whole was turned against Sabellianism. But precisely because Arius made the Son a being substantially different from God, he destroyed the monotheism he was seeking to protect and reintroduced polytheism in the form of a demigod.

Bishop Alexander was appalled by the Arian heresy. He called Arius and his followers the enemies of God, and murderers of the Godhead of Jesus, and showered other amiable epithets upon them. He contradicted the propositions that the Son was not eternal, was created out of nothingness, was changeable, had undergone moral development, etc., on the ground of Holy

Scripture, which served him as well as it served Arius. As for Arius, he rashly derided the numerous contradictions in Alexander's arguments. If, as Alexander declared, the Son also was unbegotten, a curious relationship emerged: Father and Son were therefore brothers. Alexander's doctrine, that the Son was the complete replica of the Father, was developed *ad absurdum* by the Arians; for then the Son, like the Father, must beget offspring. And it was really difficult to imagine that the Son existed before he was begotten.

Arius, while he was still living in Alexandria, endeavored to win the masses. He wrote his *Thalia,* an exposition of his doctrine, partly in prose, partly in verse, and hymns in lively meters. Already the millers and dock laborers of Alexandria were singing "that the Father was not always a Father." Athanasius speaks with dismay of the proselytizing efforts of the Arians, who asked the marketwomen: "Had you a son before you gave birth to one?" The dispute had already involved all the coastal provinces of the East; not only did the bishops and the clergy quarrel most bitterly, but the people became extraordinarily excited. Everywhere the accursed problem gave rise to dissension in the family circle; the Jews and the heathens scoffed at the affair in the theaters, and the sacred treasures of Christian doctrine were made the subject of blasphemous jokes. Alexander spoke of a number of churches—as a matter of fact, he called them dens of robbers —in which the Arians, by day and night, hatched all manner of loathsome calumnies against Christ.

We can hardly imagine a state of affairs in which theological problems of such subtlety aroused the masses of the people to such a pitch of passionate excitement; but we have the most reliable evidence of the prevailing spirit of the period. Here I will cite only Gregory of Nyssa (died about 394), who wrote: "The whole city is full of suchlike nonsense—streets, markets, and open squares. If you ask hawkers, moneychangers or greengrocers the price of goods they begin to talk of the 'begotten' and 'unbegotten.' If you want to know what the bread costs the reply they give you is: 'The Father is greater than the Son and the Son is subject to him.' If you ask the bath attendant whether the bath is ready he explains to you that the Son emerged from nonentity.

What is one to call such a plague—craziness, madness, or what . . .?"

Now, when the godlike Constantine had become an autocrat, he threw himself into the conflict, which was threatening to spread. He wrote an exhaustive epistle to the bishop of Alexandria and his refractory presbyters, describing the controversy as an idle squabble over incomprehensible matters, since in respect of the main point the adversaries were in agreement.[7]

Six years had passed since the beginning of the conflict—in Egypt feelings ran so high that the emperor's statues were profaned[8]—and Constantine found himself compelled to convoke a general council in Nicaea. This first Ecumenical Council (325) —according to Athanasius "a true pillar and a sign of victory over all heresies"—passed resolutions which the Church regarded as eternally valid. None of the doctrinal declarations of Christendom approach the Nicaean resolutions in importance. As some 300 bishops were present, who constituted "the image of the choice of the Apostles" and "the repetitions of the first Pentecostal feast," Constantine opened the proceedings resplendent in gold and purple and jewels. The Arians had come to the Council full of hope; the Bishop of Nicaea himself was on their side, and they had good friends at court. However, as the first action of the Council the bishops proclaimed the doctrine that the Son was created out of nothing, and was of an essence different from the Father, to be a blasphemy. According to the vivid comparison of Ambrosius, the bishops used the sword which heresy had drawn from the sheath in order to smite off the head of the hated monster. The majority of the bishops were, of course, united in their condemnation of naked Arianism, but they had difficulty in expressing their opinions in words which were able to contend with the masterly sophistries of their opponents. The Arians, who were quick to realize the danger that threatened them, now re-

---

[7] Alexander should not have asked his questions and Arius should not have answered them. The adversaries ought to come to an agreement; the Emperor's great effort in the cause of peace ought not to be thwarted by this unnecessary conflict. The epistle concludes with the pathetic request: "Give me back my quiet days and carefree nights; let me not spend the rest of my life in grief."

[8] Vita Const. III, 4.

sorted to those evangelical virtues which the weaker side are
given to extolling; they recommended Christian moderation and
patience. They were even prepared to make great concessions,
inasmuch as they always secretly attributed to the bishops' formulae a meaning in consonance with their own ideas. But the
assembly was determined to defeat the Arians; it treated their
concessions with justifiable suspicion, and finally resolved to
define the relation of God the Father and the Son by the statement that the Son proceeded from the nature of the Father and
was of the same substance as the Father.[9] The majority of the
Arians submitted, at least officially, to the decrees. Arius himself,
and other priests who refused their signature, were banished.

   Homoousia, the consubstantiality of Father and Son, was
subsequently accepted, unanimously, by the Greek, Latin, Oriental and Protestant Churches as a fundamental proposition of
the Christian faith. Never again, says Harnack, never again in
ecclesiastical history was a victory so complete and so quickly
won as then in Nicaea. But it was a Pyrrhic victory. For the
Latins the notion that the Son is *ejusdem substantiae* with the
Father was a matter of course; however, the majority of the
Greek-speaking bishops, although they had acceded to the
resolutions and were not followers of Arianism, were opposed to
this doctrine of consubstantiality. They protested against the
term *homoousia,* since it does not occur in the Scriptures. It also
involved a danger of Sabellianism, and to dialectical thinkers it
seemed natural to regard an *ousia*—that is, an essence or nature
—which was common to both Father and Son, as a material,

   [9] We have every reason to assume that the Emperor Constantine attributed a special value to the word *homoousios* (of the same substance). Neither
the sermons of Arius nor the vehement counter-sermons of his adversary,
Athanasius, turned the scale. The Emperor, an excellent listener—especially if
the speaker said flattering things about him—intervened, with gentle determination, in these subtle attempts at dogmatic formulation. He did so, assuredly, with the best intentions, but the rough warrior was hardly a competent person to form a theologically unexceptionable decision in the dispute regarding a quality of the Second Person of the Trinity. Constantine,
who, although he was not yet a Christian, described himself as "conjoint
bishop," afterwards confessed his comprehension of the formula of homoousia, identity of substance, in a letter, in which he proclaimed that God and
the Saviour are one in such a degree that one can declare not only of the
first, but also of the second, that He is Father and Son.

primal form; as a third deity, so to speak. There was yet another serious objection to the word; fifty years earlier the Council of Antioch, in attacking Sabellianism, had rejected the expression *homoousios*.

That the Nicaean decision, instead of ending the conflict, had actually become one of its causes was due to the rigid conservatism which would not tolerate any unbiblical expression, as well as to the dread of Sabellianism in the Orient. The ominous word, *homoousia*, gave rise to a dogmatic dispute such as the Church had never seen. In the course of a few years eighteen different forms of religion were recorded, all of which proclaimed that theirs was the true Christianity.[10]

Of course, I cannot enter into the eighteen creeds, with all their minute differences, which attributed their origin to this unhappy dispute. The three main tendencies that united those who detested the *homoousia* and its most ardent champion, the great prince of the Church, Athanasius, were the following: the *extreme Arianism,* which subsequently flared up again, denied positively that the Son was equal to the Father. In its opinion there was an enormous difference between God the Father and the Son. The extremest consequence was that drawn by Aëtius, whom his adversaries, in their wrath, declared an atheist. This party had taken as its slogan the word *anomoios* (different in nature), which played a prominent part in its discussions. Another party, often called the *Semi-Arians* by writers on the history of dogma, were perhaps a little too demonstrative in their abhorrence of this radical group. They declared that the Son was different from all other creatures, and like the Father only. But

---

10 The pious Hilarius declared that in the ten provinces of Asia he found hardly a single priest who had preserved the knowledge of the true God. The Bishop of Poitiers, in the midst of this prolonged theological ferment, exclaimed in distress: "The *homoousia* has been rejected, condemned and refuted by successive synods. The partial or total similarity of the Father and the Son is a subject of debate in this unhappy age. Every year, nay, every month we are proclaiming fresh confessions of faith in order to describe invisible mysteries. We repent of what we have done, we defend those who repent, we anathematize those whom we defended. We condemn the opinions of others in ourselves or our own opinions in others, and inasmuch as we are tearing one another to pieces we are mutually the cause of our own overthrow."

they denied that the Son was of the same or even of a like substance with the Father, and expressed their aversion from the
homoousia in the most violent fashion. These *Homoians* were a
powerful group, to which many of the bishops adhered. The
third and perhaps the most important group, which had many
followers in Asia, had chosen the word *homoiousios* in order to
proclaim their opinion as regards the enigmatical similarity of
Father and Son. They acknowledged the Son to be of the same
substance as the Father, but not identical, as the Nicaean decree
had declared. The final conflicts, which raged in the Churches
for many decades between the Homoousians and the Homoiousians, were actually waged over what Gibbon has called "the important diphthong." Only laymen would assume that the Semi-
Arians of these groups, who proclaimed the essential similarity
of the Son to the Father, were related to the Nicaeans, who proclaimed their identity. The stupendous efforts of several successive emperors and the endeavors of numerous bishops were
directed in vain toward the reconciliation of these two groups.
For the sake of clarity I will roughly tabulate the more important
and fundamental views of these groups:

Homoousios = of identical nature (substance)
Homoiousios = of similar nature
Homoios   = of like nature
Anomoios   = of dissimilar nature

The provinces of Egypt and Asia were most susceptible to
the poison of the Arian heresy. The Western provinces, "less
sicklied o'er with the pale cast of thought," and less prone to
the excited discussion of the invisible, had acquired their knowledge of things divine through the cloudy medium of a translation.
When the Arian peril pressed upon their frontiers the Church
had equipped them with the *homoousion,* and so, since they
credulously trusted the Bishop of Rome, they remained obedient
to Rome.

At the Council of Rimini (360), which united the four hundred bishops of the Western provinces, Arianism appeared to
have but little prospect of success. But Valens and Ursacius, two
bishops of Illyria, who had spent their lives in court intrigues,

and had been trained in the religious conflict of the East, in all the subtleties of dialectic, caused the assembly the greatest perplexity. They were able, thanks to the simple ,honesty of the Latins, to induce the latter to subscribe to a confession of faith which in many of its phrases refuted the doctrine of consubstantiality. In consequence, as the pious Hieronymus declared,[11] the world was surprised to find that it was Arian. But in a little while the bishops of the Latin provinces discovered their mistakes. The decision was rescinded with appropriate contempt and abhorrence, and again the Homoousian standard was triumphantly raised in the West. Since Constantine and his successors imposed their will even upon the beliefs of their subjects, there was a conflict between the power of the King of Kings and that of the reigning emperor. Constantine, with the strong hand which had won so many battles, enforced the acceptance in Nicaea of the doctrine of identity of substance. Three years later, after he had banished Arius and his followers, and had burned the writings of the heretics, these again found favor in his eyes. Eusebius of Nicomedia, whom Constantine had ignominiously expelled from his bishopric on account of his leaning toward Arianism, now returned, and Arius himself was solemnly admitted to communion. After a visit to the imperial palace (336) Arius was suddenly taken ill in the street, expiring soon afterwards in a public latrine.[12] Constantine condemned the leaders of the Homoousian party, among them the great Athanasius, to banishment, and in the latest moments of his beneficent existence he received the sacrament of baptism from the Arian Bishop of Nicomedia.[13] His son Constantius favored the Arians, but en-

[11] *Advers. Lucifer,* Vol. I, p. 145.

[12] Even a hundred years later the faithful were shown the place where God's righteous anger smote the reprobate. The ecclesiastical historian, Socrates, assures us (I, 58) that the heretic, owing to the prayer of the pious Bishop of Constantinople, was summoned to the judgment seat of God. The fact that others suspected that a little dose of poison had increased the efficacy of this prayer by no means dispelled the belief that the Lord in his mercy had hearkened to this pious request.

[13] The mighty warrior was not sufficiently adept in theological debate. He never really understood what was in dispute, and he still believed, while protecting Arius and persecuting Athanasius, that the Nicaean Council was the special glory of his career. The simplicity of his childlike view of the

deavored to convince and convert their adversaries by arranging disputations. Ammianus, who had served in this emperor's army, complained that all the military highways were thronged with bishops who were hurrying on their way to assemblies which they called synods, and were ruining the public posting service by their incessant journeys; they went wandering all round the great empire in search of the true faith. The Emperor, after the end of the civil war, devoted himself, in Arles, Milan, Sirmium and Constantinople, to reflecting upon these important disagreements. The eunuchs, whom Athanasius described as the natural enemies of the Son, with the women, and many bishops, had filled his feeble mind with suspicion and abhorrence of the *homoousia*, but he was no less terrified of the Arianism of Aëtius. Incapable of coming to any decision, he alternately condemned and favored those professing the Nicene creed, spent his days and nights in searching for the adequate words, and numbering the syllables which the true creed should comprise, and his obsessional doubts followed him into his unquiet sleep. The sovereign's dreams were interpreted as heavenly visions, and he graciously accepted the title of Bishop of Bishops, which his clerical flatterers bestowed upon him. After many futile efforts, to which synods in Gaul, Italy, Illyria and Asia bore witness, he decided to convoke a general Council.[14] It seemed that the moderate form of Arianism was finally victorious.

We should gain nothing by following the further development of these dogmatic conflicts, which would call for an exhaustive description. Athanasius, the Bishop of Alexandria, whose

---

truth may be judged from the epistle which he sent, after the Council of Nicaea, to the community of Alexandria. There he says: "What has satisfied three hundred bishops is none other than the will of God."

14 The bishops of the East assembled in Seleucia; those of the West in Rimini. The Eastern Council broke up after four days of bitter disputation, without having arrived at a decision. The Western Council lasted for seven months, and the prefect of the praetorians guarding the *patres* had orders to keep the clergy together by force until the men of God had agreed as to the intimate nature of the relation of God the Father and the Son. Thanks to the sophistical ingenuities of Bishops Valens and Ursacius, to the effect of hunger and cold, and the melancholy of exile, the sovereign at last had the satisfaction of assembling the bishops in his palace, where they submitted a creed which propounded consubstantiality but not identity.

joy and pride and fame it was to have defended the Nicaean decrees, was five times driven from his see, and for twenty years ate the bitter bread of exile, without flagging in his holy zeal for the *homoousia*. Every province bore witness to his sufferings for this symbol. Through the reigns of Julian, Theodosius and Valentian, as in that of Arcadius, the embittered conflicts between the Homoousians and Homoiousians continued. Semi-Arianism was for decades the official religion of Christendom at court and in the empire, in the bishop's palace and in the hut of the simple believer. Torrents of blood were shed in these battles over the nature of the Saviour, and the Christians of all the various groups evinced a truly evangelical patience in their toleration of the fact that opponents who inserted or omitted the letter *i* were persecuted with utmost cruelty, martyred, and sent to render an account of themselves in a better world.[15] Not until two generations had elapsed after Arius was the conflict settled in favor of the Nicaean dogma.

Not until very much later did the Germans, who were almost all Arians, change over to the Christianity of the Homoousian brand. The first German translation of the Bible was that of the Arian bishop Wulfila. The Germanic tribes, who had but recently abjured their belief in Wotan, Thor and Loki, were hardly less fanatical in respect of consubstantiality and identity than the first professors of Christianity. When the Vandals, to whose primitive natures half-measures were abhorrent, fell upon the fertile provinces of Africa, their king, Hunerich, in his pious

15 Moreover, it must be remembered that the difference between *homoousia* and *homoiousia* was almost imperceptible, even to theological eyes. Under Macedonius, the Arian Bishop of Constantinople, an edict of Constantius directed against those Christians who would not accept the one *i* was executed with the beneficent severity which alone could save the heretic from eternal damnation. The defenders of the *homoiousion* tore babies at the breast from their mothers' arms in order to baptize them. The sacred host was thrust between the jaws of the recalcitrant, which were held open by mechanical devices, and the breasts of tender virgins were branded with red-hot irons. The chief assistants of Macedonius in his pious efforts were the bishops of Nicomedia and Cyzikus, who were greatly respected on account of their virtues and their compassionate nature. Ammonius was of opinion that the mutual hostility of the Christians by far exceeded the savagery of wild beasts (XXII, 5), but how should this heathen understand that only such sacred fury could lead men's souls toward eternal salvation?

Christian zeal, decreed that all those inhabitants of Tiglassas who in their blindness refused to accept the Arian creed were to have their tongues torn out and their right hands lopped off. Theodosius the Great, who was finally successful in suppressing Arianism, did his best—for the salvation of their souls—to convince 30,000 Christians, who believed only in the consubstantiality of Christ with God the Father, of the identity of the Father and the Son. They were massacred by the soldiery in an amphitheatre —an operation which was performed with agreeable facility.[16]

If this and other victories had not been achieved the Christendom of today would profess the impious belief that Christ was the only Son of God born of the Virgin, created out of nothing, and like God, but not his equal. Today the Christian knows, with the sacred certainty which only the true faith confesses, and which excludes all doubt, that Jesus is a being existing from all eternity, eternally equal to the Father, but proceeding from the nature of the Father, one of the perfectly distinguishable three persons which constitute an indissoluble unity.

16 In Odessa, where the Arians settled their theological differences in pitched battles, Julian, whom the Church called "the Apostate," without much deliberation confiscated the wealth of the Church and distributed it among the soldiers. With horrid irony he calls himself (Epist. LIII) the true friend of the Galileans, since their admirable doctrines had promised the kingdom of heaven to the poor. The Christians would follow the path of true virtue with all the greater zeal if with his help they were rid of the burden of worldly possessions.

III. DOGMA AND OBSESSIONAL IDEAS

It was necessary to treat the ecclesiastical hypotheses of the dogma of the Trinity in such an exhaustive manner, for I shall endeavor, by means of this representative example, to demonstrate the fact that the religious dogma corresponds, in the history of human evolution, to the obsessional idea of the neurotic; in other words, that it is the most significant expression of the obsessional thinking of the peoples. Further, it will be shown that the emotional processes which lead to the constitution and development of dogma obey the psychical mechanisms of obsessional thinking, and that in both cases the same motives are predominant. I shall also attempt to show that in the formation of dogma the same technique of defense is employed as in the obsessional processes in individuals. In the attempt to comprehend the problem of dogma formation psychologically I shall keep the development of the christological dogma in the foreground, because in this example almost all the typical mechanisms of reaction, distortion, and displacement can be clearly demonstrated. At a suitable stage I shall consider also the psychical genesis and development of other dogmas, in which we can study special processes. Here, in examining the nature of dogma, we shall not deal with the whole problem, as all that is necessary for the moment is to exhibit the essential conformity between dogma and obsessional idea, and the psychological foundations of both.

1. DOGMA AS THE COMPROMISE FORMATION OF REPRESSED AND REPRESSING TENDENCIES

The *ambivalence* which humanity developed in respect of the father complex was at an early stage displaced on to its relation to the Godhead, where it perhaps acquired its most significant form of expression in the early periods of cultural evolution.

The Christ myth, like the related myths of Mithras, Adonis, and Attis, records the revolt of the son and his punishment, tells us of the son's expressions of defiance, and his efforts to replace his father; but also of the father's impatience and the necessity of expiation. If we consider the genesis of Christianity we recognize that here, in obedience to the laws of compulsive repetition, the ancient revolt of the son has once again asserted itself under the combined influence of religious, economic and political motives. As yet it has hardly been demonstrated how in the synoptic Gospels the behavior of Jesus in respect of tradition is completely inconsistent, so that his attitude towards religious law, to the Thora and the synagogue, appears to be ambivalent. The same Jesus who declares that the Thora is sacrosanct, and who has come not to destroy the law but to fulfill it—who prophesies that not a jot or tittle of the law shall perish until heaven and earth shall pass away—the same Jesus proclaims that man is above such matters as dietary prohibitions and keeping the Sabbath holy. The same Jesus who preaches obedience to the scribes also reproves them severely. His pious regard for the faith men have inherited from their fathers is hardly less urgent than the zeal with which he seeks to supersede it. He who forbids his disciples to go forth to the heathen and the Samaritans, and harshly reproves the Canaanitish woman who pleads with him to heal her daughter ("I am sent to the lost sheep of the house of Israel"), has radically disintegrated the national self-consciousness of the Jewish people and assailed the exclusive status of the Jews. Now a conservative, pious adherent to the religion of the fathers, now a revolutionary for whom no tradition and no rabbinical doctrine is sacred—so he appears in the earliest records. "The Father and I are one" has a double meaning; but the loving identification is here more prominent than the hostile identification which seeks to take the place of the Father. Actually the Son proves victorious after death and atonement; he becomes God beside the Father, really in the place of the Father.

The religion of the Son constantly increases in importance. We have followed, in the history of Christianity, the transformations and formal expressions of ambivalence until the opposing instinctual tendencies unite, and the opposed conceptions achieve a compromise expression whose contradictory and seemingly absurd content bears witness to its genesis and its psychical composition. The genesis of the dogma is controlled by ambivalent tendencies. The expression of their struggle for mastery is doubt. *The dogma is a compulsive effort to overcome religious doubt.*

Dogma formation begins as a psychical reaction phenomenon. The young Church, before it had established itself, had to defend itself against a powerful enemy, to whose attacks it all but succumbed. The rebellious movements which supported the religion of the Son were exaggerated, in Gnosticism, to the point of degrading the Father-God. Jahveh becomes the demiurge who has created the world, but who is conquered by the strange God, the Soter (Saviour, Preserver) Christ.

It is here that we must perceive the genesis of Christian dogma. Dogma, as the history of religion tells us, arose from the fight against erroneous belief; against the heterodoxy which the Church itself was inclined to accept. The youthful Christendom had been almost submerged in the doctrine of the Gnostic Marcion; Catholicism, in Harnack's words, "was erected against Marcion."[1] If the revolution of the Son had established itself in early Christianity, now the psychical reaction phenomena declared themselves. Dogma is perhaps the most significant reactive phenomenon of this period: like the obsessional idea, it already bears traces of the first defensive battle. The forbidden movements which aspired to the complete elimination of the Father-God and his replacement by the Son-God were threatening to become completely victorious; and this was the goal of Gnosticism. All traditions were to be thrown overboard; everything that was not consistent with the gospel of the new God was to be eliminated; and the entire Old Testament was to be excluded. But now the young Church guarded itself against the attempt to proclaim the Son-God in the place of the Father by means of dogma, articles of faith, the canon, and the election of bishops. Whosoever professed, in the baptismal confession, belief in God the Father, Christ, and the Holy Ghost could not be a Gnostic.

The original obsessional idea was repulsed. Christ had not won a complete victory over the Father. Irenaeus and Tertullian,

[1] Harnack, *Marcion*, Leipzig 1921, p. IV.

in the battle against Gnosticism, made constant references to sacred revelation and to their reliance on the Old Testament. They sought to vanquish heresy by those passages which occur in both Testaments of the Holy Scripture, and which are intelligently reproduced and formulated.

The object of Gnosticism, the dethronement of the Father-God by Christ, was of an obsessional character, because it was pursued by instinctual forces. This compulsive tendency the Fathers of the third century now referred to the Old and New Testaments. The obsession was opposed by a counterobsession; the supremacy of Christ was contrasted with the worship of God the Father.

The path which leads from the baptismal formula by which the orthodox faith expressed itself in the battle against the Gnostics to the Nicaean decree which furnished the definitive formulation of Christology is the *via triumphalis* of dogma. We have seen how the motives—at first rejected—of the divinity of Christ and his equality with the Father—but really his superiority over the Father—was finding its way, in new, ever-changing forms, into the growing Church. In the same way obsessional ideas which were once successfully rejected return from repression in distorted forms—unknown to the consciousness, until they again find a place in it. We have followed the processes of distortion which can be demonstrated in Christology; we have seen how the contrast between God the Father and God the Son, which in latent form permeates the Christ mythus, was disengaged from its historical genesis, and how Christ gradually became a preexisting deity. The repressed tendencies are eventually victorious; Christ is not only present at the creation of the world, but he himself creates the world at God's command. It is here that Christology approaches most closely to its unconscious goal— the replacement of God the Father by Christ. Gradually and by circuitous routes the repressed impulses have found entry into the defensive structure, and even in distorted form they reveal their true nature: In the detail that Christ is conceived as preexisting we have the denial of the difference of age as the natural reason for the superiority of God. Christ himself creates the world; at this point the really infantile motive of sexual rivalry appears in a cosmological disguise. The conflict which has so deeply moved humanity since the dawn of culture is thus continued at a higher level, just as in the wars of Homer the battles of the immortal gods are fought above the heads of the Greeks and their adversaries.

Yet the complete assertion of the unconscious emotional impulses is opposed by powerful defensive forces: reverence, and love for the Father-God whose rights must remain inviolable. We see precisely the same thing in the genesis of an obsessional idea, in which revolutionary efforts endeavor to break through the opposition. The whole of the subsequent development of the Christ dogma was governed by these two powerful and contrary impulses: to award Christ the position beside or really above God the Father, and to preserve the unique position of God the Father. As in the symptomatology of obsessional neuroses now the one and now the other of two mutually conflicting impulses wins the upper hand; and as here two simultaneous trains of thought reflect the victory and defeat of one instinctual tendency after another, so in the dogmatic controversy, now the revolutionary and now the reactionary ideas appear in the foreground. Just as in obsessional neurosis, there is here a striving toward a compromise formation which shall achieve the unification and reconciliation of opposites. Here, as in the former case, it is short-lived, and its structure is eroded by undercurrents until it collapses. In the dogmatic conflict such a compromise was attempted through the comparisons beloved of the Early Fathers; such as Tatian's comparison of Christ to a flame by which a torch is kindled. Tatian anxiously denies the possibility that the light of the first torch can be diminished by the kindling of the second.

If it was possible to protect the position of God the Father against encroachment, there was a danger that the high estimation in which Christ was held might be diminished. If the divine rights of the Father were attributed in their fullness to the Son, there was a danger that the Father's rights would be prejudiced. The dogmatic process is precisely analogous to the mutual subjugation of opposing obsessional ideas. It cannot be denied that here, as in the obsessional ideas, the ambivalence is displaced upon the instinctual derivative: that is, each of the opposites is destined to be affected by the same ambivalential tension; for the ambivalence affecting God the Father was gradually transferred to his Son and rival. The revolutionary tendency was gradually directed against him who sought to set himself in the place of God the Father. Thus, not only does the appraisal of the one represent the contrary of the worship of the other, but the veneration of Christ is a continuation of the feeling relating to God the Father, just as hostility toward the Son continues the unconscious tendencies of rebellion against God the Father. The same process is apparent in obsessional thinking. What appears in the consciousness as an opposite appears to be effected alternately by impulses of affection and aggression, in such a way that one seems to recognize in the opposites the original unity of the objects which is subjected to the full tension of ambivalence.

Let us start with the dogmatic attitude as it first appears as a reactive phenomenon. Those movements whose unconscious, instinctual aim is the dethronement of God the Father and the enthronement of the divine Son are here repulsed by the counter-tendencies. This movement can be followed in varying forms from the Ebionites to the Monarchians. Despite all the energy, not to say fanaticism, which manifests itself in the passionate assertion of the superiority of God the Father, we can perceive, as in the development of obsessional thinking, how the defense gradually approaches more closely to the repressed tendencies. In obsessional neurosis, the longer the neurotic process continues, the more closely do the repressing tendencies approach those which are felt to be painful or inacceptable, until finally the tendencies which were at first repulsed are victorious. Whereas the Ebionites saw in Christ the human son of Joseph, the Arians, despite all their contentions *ad majorem gloriam Dei*, were of the opinion that Christ was divine, and took exception only to the notion that he was to be regarded as identical with the Father. The distance between the rejected and the rejecting tendencies had so far diminished in the course of three hundred years that it was almost indiscernible. Now, proceeding from the other extreme, which can be followed from the Gospel according to St. John to Sabellianism: If we go back to Patripassianism, for example, we come upon the opinion that Christ is identical with the Father, since Christ appears as the Father who suffered upon the Cross. We see the same tendency in Sabellianism, which conceived God the Father and Christ as phenomenal forms of the one divine substance.

We may now compare the conflict in which Christianity was engaged on two points with the obsessional thinking of a nervous patient who has to contend against blasphemous thoughts. He cannot pass in front of a chair, a table, a lantern, etc., because this means, for him, that he is higher and more indispensable than God. The action becomes a demonstrative proof of the thought of his superiority; the mental association is furnished by the idea *in front of*. But if he passes *behind* the chair, table, or what not, this means that he despises God, for he then behaves as one must not behave to God: that is, he himself is then equated with the chair or lantern, and leaves God *behind* him—does not give God the precedence. It is clear that in both cases his obsessional thoughts are conceived as a defense against his revolutionary tendencies. But the opposing tendencies correspond with the double identification in which the patient is alternatingly the wrongdoer and the affronted deity. It should be noted that the patient cannot pass either in front of the chair or behind it. In both cases a blasphemy is perpetrated, which he must avoid in his dread of a mysterious punishment. Yet it seems inevitable that he will offend God, since both the action and its avoidance are of a blasphemous nature. How can one avoid giving offence? The patient now employs a complicated ceremonial in order to ensure his safety. He goes round the object (chair, lantern, etc.) so often that he no longer has anything to fear. Of course, at this point he has doubts again, and the result is that the patient must go round the object a countless number of times. Here, however, a trait appears which is characteristic of obsessional symptoms; the defensive action enhances not only the measure of protection, but also the originally rejected tendency. In the period of which we are writing the Church found itself in a position similar to that of the neurotic patient; the christological problem was insoluble. If it avoided one way of offending God it could not escape the other. The path of the true faith had

grown so strait that no one could be sure that he was not following a false track.

The problem of the relation between God the Father and
God the Son now confronted the Church. It lay at the very center
of the emerging doctrine, but any assertion in respect of this
relation was dangerous. Men were uncertain as to the nature of
this relation, and accordingly, in order to overcome their doubts,
they sought to conceive and to describe it with greater and greater
precision. We have cited some examples from the great teachers
of the Church who endeavored to frame definitions. For the purpose of elucidation they make use of many images and comparisons: as those between father and son, the sun and a ray of
sunlight, a spring and a brook. But these very examples were
liable to conjure up the very danger of heresy which they were
intended to dispel; as is shown by the example of Dionysius,
and others also. The parallel to obsessional thinking becomes
even more striking when one and the same teacher, in his pious
eagerness to avoid one false path, strays into another. It was the
lot of Origenes, as of many another great teacher of the Church,
to be regarded as a heretic.

The process of dogma formation is governed by doubt, as is
that of obsessional thinking, in which a thought is pursued to an
extreme, only to give way to its very antithesis. This wavering
to and fro of trains of thought which are supported by mutually
conflicting tendencies leads in the end to the statement of a
dogma which seeks to dispose of the doubt in a radical manner.
The succession of mutually opposing ideas in the neurotic may
be compared with the historical development of dogmatic
contraries. If one of the effective tendencies in Sabellianism, for
example, which sought to merge the Trinity in unity, had gained
the ascendancy, the reaction of the opposition which it encountered was so vigorous that it ended up in the opposite and
forbidden quarter—in Arianism—just as in the obsessional thinking of the neurotic.

I will take one more example from the symptomatology of
obsessional neurosis in order further to elucidate the analogy
between the development of dogma and obsessional ideas. The

patient whom I have already mentioned used to retain his feces for a long while because with the act of evacuation he connected the idea of affronting God; that is, because he was compelled to bring God into mental association with this undivine function. Finally the whole mental process was converted into its contrary; if he had constipation and did not go to the toilet this was a blasphemy. He would now waver for hours between the two contradictory trains of thought; for a long while the doubt as to which of the two actions or ideas was sacrilegious was insuperable. After a prolonged mental conflict he did actually evacuate, but when he was about to wipe himself the obsessional notion occurred to him that the toilet paper might be the Gospel.[2] Then for an hour at a time he would wonder whether he would or would not clean himself. Was he to do it with the paper that represented so sacred a document, or should he remain in the hardly less horrible condition of filth?

If we collate the results of our historical survey of the processes which have led to the formation of Christian dogma, it becomes apparent that the repressed impulses of filial rebellion and revolution have played as large a part as veneration and love for the Father. The expression which these mutually conflicting emotional tendencies have achieved in dogma—for example, in the Nicaean decree—is a rational attempt to overcome this instinctual opposition by an intellectual formula. It is impossible to show here how in the formation of every dogma the same processes, which are striving to summarize opposing impulses in an emotional unity, are repeated in an intellectualized form. This representative example gives us a first glimpse of the psychogenesis of dogma. Dogma is a mental compromise formation of repressed and repressing ideas. In its historical development the part played by the repressed impulses, and by the repressing instances, may be perceived in alternate recurrence. Its structure is conditioned by the defensive battle against the repressed material, which re-emerges in distorted shape and in substitute

2 Anyone familiar with the uncertain, characteristic utterance of obsessional neurotics will know that this is only one of the mental forms in which the notion may be expressed that the toilet paper is a substitute for the Gospel; or, reducing it to its latent meaning, that the Gospel is fit only for such employment.

formations. The dogma is analogous to the obsessional idea, which also represents a compromise formation of repressed impulses and defensive instances, not only in its psychical genesis and structure, but resembles it also in the circumstance that the admixture of the two factors in its final expression is an unequal one. The obsessional idea, in its analytic reduction, may be recognized, despite all secondary elaborations, as a substitute manifestation of a repressed idea. Its character as a reactive phenomenon cannot disguise the fact that in it the unconscious instinctual impulse has achieved a partial satisfaction. It is the same in the dogma; there also, despite the efforts of the reactionary forces, the repulsed tendency remains to a great extent victorious. Despite all modifications and cautious formulations, we perceive in the Christ dogma the breaking through of the revolutionary impulses which enable the Son-God to triumph: "*Christus vincit, Christus regnat, Christus imperat,*" so men cried in the intoxication of victory when in Rome the images and altars of the old gods fell crashing to the ground.

2. DISPLACEMENT ON TO DETAILS

The analytic reduction of obsessional ideas, like that of religious phenomena, is made more difficult by the distortions to which the two phenomena are subjected in the course of their development. The mechanisms of generalization, displacement, and isolation serve to withhold the latent meaning of the obsessional idea, like the latent meaning of a dogmatic statement, from consciousness, to liberate it from its original association, and to transfer doubt to a seemingly insignificant detail. As an example of such procedure, of the process of displacement on to an insignificant detail, the following case may be adduced: A patient pondered for hours over the differences between a gentleman and a waiter. He considered the differences from every aspect, and was indefatigable in his meticulous distinctions. But his intellectual labors redissolved all the differences which he was trying to apprehend, and he found himself obliged to discover others. He at last concentrated on the portentous difference that the gentleman, when in evening dress, wore a white tie, while the waiter wore a black one. Only one who understands the history of the patient's childhood and youth, and the influence of his highly aristocratic environment, could detect the genesis of this obsessional idea. The fixation on the early homosexual objects of the boy, which were waiters or manservants, the arrogant attitude of his parents toward persons of lower social position, and his feelings of love and contempt for his parents, as well as their contraries, all played their part in the development of the obsessional idea. The boy's astonishment at the treatment of the admired waiter, the revolutionary impulses directed against his parents, as well as the inclination to share their views and to assume the defensive against his choice of object, are recognizable, in the comprehensive reflections upon the difference between an aristocratic man of the world and a waiter. The displacement of the obsession on to the trivial difference of the neckties conceals the origin of these reflections, so that we can hardly realize the violent emotions of rebellion, pain, and scorn —and also the respect for the parents, and the consequent obedience which have co-operated in the construction of the obsessional idea. One might consider that reflections concerning the difference in the neckties of the gentleman and the waiter are absurd and meaningless *facetiae*. Analysis shows that behind them are concealed the most serious conflicts, in which the most powerful interests of the boy are involved.

The Arian conflict, in its long development, offers more than one analogy to such an obsessional-neurotic displacement of the original idea upon a trifle. The great conflict regarding the supremacy of God the Father or of Jesus Christ was no longer recognizable as such in its later stages. It had become a verbal squabble over *homoousios, homoiousios* and *homoios*. Decades of disputation as to whether the Son was identical with the Father, or consubstantial, or of a like nature, bore evidence of the deep-seated opposition between two powerful instinctual tendencies. When the battle is fought over the difference between *homoousios* and *homoiousios* it really seems to be *"the difference of the important diphthong"* which divides the religious views of the Athanasians, the Arians, and the Semi-

Arians, and yet the decisive problems of Christianity are concealed in this detail. Mephistopheles, who advises the student to
rely only on words:[1]

> "An Worte lässt sich trefflich glauben,
>   Von einem Wort lässt sich kein Jota rauben,"

is perhaps thinking of this difference, in which there is literally
"displacement upon a detail." When in our colloquial idiom we
speak of a squabble over the dot of an *i*, of a futile dispute over
words, in order to signify meaningless trivialities, we do not
realize that we are conjuring up the shadow of the great conflict,
a battle of decisive significance for the Church, which for two
generations was fought to all appearance over the dot of an *i*.
But we should be wrong to laugh at this apparently trivial detail,
for it involves the entire difference between two religions.

A few cases may be adduced which show the process of displacement upon a detail combined with other features. The
Arian Eudokius proclaims in his sermon that God is *asebes,* but
Christ *eusebes.* Again, the difference of a vowel; the meaning
being that God worships no one, but that Christ worships God.
Yet such differences of a diphthong constitute the foundation of
whole creeds, and decide whether the individual is or is not
doomed to the most grievous earthly and heavenly punishments.

The persecution of Athanasius and so many venerable
bishops who suffered for the truth of their faith—or, to express
it in more skeptical terms, for the integrity of their error—
filled their followers with the profoundest grief, and the protests
against the acts of violence committed by the emperor were often
expressed in a singular manner. To speak of one of these methods,
which was devised and successfully employed in Antioch, and
which before long made its way through the whole Christian
world: The adherents of one party wished to give public proof
that they did not agree with the horrible blasphemies of the
Arians; those of another, that they did not partake of what
seemed to them the sacrilegious notions of the orthodox regard-

---

[1] Roughly paraphrased:
> "Words you can trust in, great or little:
> They can't be robbed of a jot or tittle."

ing the designations of God and Jesus. The doxologies or sacred hymns which faithfully glorify the Trinity are subject to neat little variations; for the essence of an orthodox, Arian, and Semi-Arian creed can be expressed with extraordinary lucidity through the difference of a disjunctive or copulative pronoun. A swarm of monks from the adjacent deserts and a choir of well-trained singers were established in the cathedral of Antioch, where they sang triumphantly: "Glory to the Father, to the Son, and to the Holy Ghost." This hymn constituted the gravest affront to the religious feelings of the Arian bishop, who at the Emperor's command had accepted the see of the venerable Eustachius.

Godefroy, who has studied the subject with meticulous care, tells us that in addition to this hymn, which had a sacrilegious sound in the ears of the bishop, and differed from the only truly orthodox hymns, there were three others which would certainly be regarded as heretical sooner or later. These ran as follows: "Glory to the Father through the Son and the Holy Ghost," "Glory to the Father and the Son in the Holy Ghost," and "Glory to the Father in the Son and in the Holy Ghost." The difference of the particle may seem unimportant to the layman, and the significance which was ascribed to it ridiculous or absurd. But it is clear from the analytic standpoint that it owes its importance to the processes of displacement, and that behind them those tendencies are operative which have given Christianity its present form. Only the layman, who lacks understanding of the genesis of religion, and the enlightened liberal theologian, who in his overzealous rationalism seeks to explain it in the most superficial manner, can think contemptuously of such minute differences. The Church has instinctively taken the difference of a diphthong seriously enough, because it reflected the difference between two religions, between two *Weltanschauungen* which were separated by a gulf. Of course, the faithful who sacrificed the lives of innumerable heretics on account of a divergent diphthong knew nothing of the importance which it had acquired through the unconscious process of displacement. They knew not what they did, and so will be forgiven in accordance with the word of the God in whose honor they slaughtered their fellow creatures.

3. DOUBT AND DERISION IN THE FORMATION
OF DOGMA

In the mechanism of displacement, as we have just shown it at work in the formation of dogma, something beyond the generalization of the persistent doubt, and its extension to all and sundry, has been at work. In addition to this and other unconscious aims, such as isolation, detachment from origins, and disguising an idea from the conscious mind, the large part played by *unconscious scorn* in the displacement processes is also perceptible.

The meaning of unconscious mockery does not appear conspicuously in the intellectually elaborated doubt, but the analytic reduction of the obsessional ideas which are so closely related to the dogmatic opinions points the way to their psychological comprehension. It will be shown that even in the formulation of dogma unconscious tendencies to derision can be demonstrated. Let us begin by examining the obsessional-neurotic doubts. In the psychical life of the obsessional neurotic the need to doubt finds its fulfillment in the uncertainty of his approach to every object and every action. The unconscious tendency to avoid any certainty is incessantly contending with the adverse efforts to achieve the greatest and most reliable certainty. The need of uncertainty and doubt is served also when the obsessional neurotic shows a preference for dealing with subjects whose nature ensures that we can know nothing of them with certainty: with paternity, with the expectation of life of one's friends and relatives, with the question of immortality. Here the analogies with religious phenomena hold good even in detail.[1] We have seen

1 Freud observes that the need of uncertainty goes so far that obsessional neurotics often show an aversion to clocks, which at least enable them to tell the time with certainty, and with unconscious dexterity are able to put out of order any sort of instrument that excludes doubt ("Notes Upon a Case of Obsessional Neurosis," *Collected Papers*, Vol. III, London 1925). The history of dogma suggests many interesting analogies to this behavior. For example, one of the Semi-Arian synods furnished its decrees, which purported to elucidate the relation between God the Father and the Son, with its date. Athanasius mercilessly ridiculed those who believed that the truths of the Faith, which were fixed from eternity, could be regarded as existing from a certain date.

how important to the Church were such questions as the following had become: How Christ was descended from the Father; whether he was created out of nothing, or whether he had always been with the Father, etc.

One may say, in respect of obsessional-neurotic doubts, which for outsiders often appear childish and absurd, and also in respect of the majority of the intellectual processes of the theologians, that doubt represents unconscious contempt and derision. The very formulation of the question is often in accordance with this feature. Its very possibility betrays the unconscious tendency. As a matter of fact, the heretics of the Church pounce upon these weak spots and transform the unconscious decision into open and aggressive mockery. When the Arians say that Christ must have begotten life, as his Father had done, if he is identical with his Father, they indicate, consciously, how nonsensical is the belief in identity. But the unconscious ridicule exists already in the assertion that God and Christ are identical and yet different persons.

The parallel is obvious between these obsessional doubts of the neurotics, who busy themselves with the question of immortality, and with all sorts of subtle ethical problems, and the formulation of religious questions, and the replies to them; since in either case the same themes are discussed, queried, and replied to. However, it may be objected that in theology the great problems that concern humanity are in question, whereas in obsessional neurosis the patient is troubled by problems of the utmost triviality. Yet the reference to the individual questions of the Arian controversy shows that this difference is not of a profound or decisive character. When it appears to be a *sine qua non* of eternal salvation to decide whether Christ is of like nature with God or identical with him, the analogy to the thought of the obsessional neurotic is already close.

Nevertheless, in the development of every fully evolved religion there are whole periods of concentration on the discussion of problems which in structure and content are precisely similar to those of the obsessional neurotic. For example, the climax of Scholasticism represents such a period for the Catholic religion. One of the keenest thinkers of this period, Peter the

Lombard (Petrus Lombardus, 1164), puts the following theological questions and endeavors to answer them: Whether a foreseeing or a foreordaining of God would have been possible if there had been no creatures? Where was God before the Creation? Can God know more than He does know? Could God do anything better, or in a better way, than He does now? Could God at all times have done what He has done? Further, Peter asked where the angels have been since their creation? Could the good angels sin, and could the bad angels live righteously? Have all angels bodies? Was the hierarchy of the angels determined from the beginning of the Creation? At what age was man created? Was Eve positively made out of a rib and not out of some other part of the body? Why did Adam sleep while this was being done, since the importance of what was happening should have necessitated his waking? Would man be able to live for ever if he had not eaten of the tree of knowledge? How would men have propagated themselves if they had not sinned?

Further, the great scholastic and his contemporaries were interested in the question: Why the Son, and not the Father or the Holy Ghost had become man? Could God have accepted the sacrifice made through Christ if the Saviour had been a woman? These questions elicited the liveliest exchange of opinions between the highest authorities. Great scholastics, like Duns Scotus, Petrus Lombardus, Thomas Aquinas, Occam, Bonaventura, and Albertus Magnus considered the question whether God's Son could change himself into an ox, an ass, a pumpkin, or even a devil? As late as the fourteenth century there were disputations among the clergy, and even at court, as to whether the light on Mount Tabor was a created or an uncreated light.

The questions relating to the Sacrament were especially subtle, in particular, questions relating to baptism. Is the essence of baptism in the Word or in the water? (In the Word, for otherwise fish would live in a state of baptism and an ass which drank the baptismal water would be a baptized Christian.) Did the water mixed with wine in the chalice turn into wine or into blood? Even Augustine stated a problem, asking whether every error was a sin; for example, as when one confuses twins or thinks that something sweet is bitter. One problem gives rise to hundreds: as, for example, in the discussion of the question whether God could make something that had happened not to have happened—say, the foundation of Rome (Petrus Damiani). Anselm anxiously pondered the question whether Christ's death benefited even his enemies who crucified him (*Cur deus homo.* II, 15).

Similar problems appear in the "Summis" of the scholastic theologians for some three hundred years, heating the brains and tempers of the best divines and engaging the interest of the clergy. The questions whether God the Father stood up or lay down, whether he could make a mountain without a valley, or a child without a father, or whether he could make a fallen woman a virgin again, absorbed the theological inquirers of the period. The hypercritical formulation of the problems, the ingenuity with which questions were answered, the renewed doubt which followed every attempt at solution, making this seem uncertain, or deriving fresh problems from it—all these are features familiar to us in the symptomatology of obsessional neurosis.[2] It is easy to see that such questions as these: whether God could at all times do everything that He has done, or whether He could make a mountain without a valley—questions which naturally could not be positively answered—must serve the underlying doubt in the omnipotence of God. The asking of the question whether man could have lived for ever if he had not eaten of the tree of knowledge suggested a doubt as to the prevision or the goodness of God. Only a theologically preju-

---

[2] Naturally enough, these features appear prominently in scholastic literature, but they also occur constantly in the theological literature of later times. In Leipzig, in 1705, a theme proposed for the dissertation to be presented by candidates for the doctorate was: "Whether the garments of the Jews in the desert outlasted all their hardships through a miracle or reproduced themselves." In 1795 there appeared an essay by Salomon Ranisch, "The Service of the Angel on the Marriage of the Pious." The consistorial assessor, Christoph Haymann, thought the subject important enough to justify a learned discussion with the author. From the innumerable writings of this kind we will single out for mention only the exhaustive inquiry of Johann Georg Walch, "Of the Faith of the Child in the Womb" (about 1750), which treated this theologically important subject with all becoming earnestness. Anyone familiar with the apologetic and casuistic literature of the contemporary churches will realize that there will always be such inquiries as long as Christian piety endures.

diced mind could fail to perceive that questions which attempt to elucidate the properties of baptism and other sacraments must at the same time give expression to the unconscious doubt in the efficacy of the sacraments. When the Scholastics seriously ask and discuss the question whether the Son of God could have redeemed the world in the shape of an ass it is obvious that in this discussion Christ is unconsciously brought into unbecoming proximity to a despised animal. The unconscious effect of the derision in the discussion of the sublime problem, "How many angels could dance on the point of a needle?" cannot be dismissed; nor can the underlying doubt of the existence of angels.

We shall see how the Church overcame such doubts. In individual cases it protested against the asking of such questions, as though it had some perception of the mockery concealed in them. Epiphanius described the ticklish inquiries as to certain details of the Virgin Mary's virginity as sacrilegious. But these questions were not avoided in theological disputations. Duns Scotus thought it probable that Mary was conceived without sin and was therefore ignorant of carnal desires.[3] When in 1462 a violent theological dispute broke out between Dominicans and Franciscans, as to whether even the blood shed by Christ on the cross had been associated with his Godhead,[4] or when Lombardus or Bonaventura applied themselves to the problem whether Mary, in concluding her marriage to Joseph, must not have accepted[5] a possible enforcement of conjugal rights, the Church—without realizing it—is making itself ridiculous.

As we have already indicated, subtle questionings and doubts of this kind, which are so closely related to those of the obsessional neurotic, must play a great part in any highly organized religion. One is reminded of the famous doubt of the Talmud, and of the many delicate problems which are there discussed. In spite of all religious differences, the questions of the Halachoth —for example, the speculations as to what may be worn on the

3 Sent. VII. Dist. 3. 0, 1.

4 Pius II decreed in the Bull of 1 August 1464 that the dispute was to be dropped and that neither side was to call the other heretical until a decision on the Apostolic throne was arrived at. This has not as yet happened.

5 Sent. IV. Dist. 30 B.

Sabbath, what must be regarded as a burden, and what as a decoration, whether one may wear a false tooth, whether in the case of an animal a bell is to be regarded as a burden or a decoration, etc.—all these remind one of the hair-splitting disputations of the Scholastics.

Islam exhibits the same features in its highly complicated Kālām, in which similar questions are discussed (whether man is completely master of his actions or is compelled to act by God's omnipotence; whether Allah could destroy himself, etc.). One notes the same atmosphere as in the dogma formation of the Church when the Mutalizites dispute the Islamic doctrine of the seven Attributes of God (the All-knowing, the Almighty, etc.), alleging that an eternal God and a number of simultaneous and eternal attributes are equivalent to a postulate of polytheism. One is reminded of the meticulous questionings regarding the possible sinfulness of Christ, when the great dogmatist Al-Ashari (died 941) declares that for the Prophet sin was indeed a possibility, but he was protected from its reality by divine Providence.

We may compare the prescriptions of the Talmud concerning the amount of water to be used for ceremonial purpose, or the discussion of the question how far one may travel on the Sabbath, with the prescriptions of the Church in respect of the consecration of priestly vestments (Gihr, *Das heilige Messopfer*, 4th ed., 1887, p. 255). "Ecclesiastical vestments lose their benediction through repair only if the new portion, replaced or inserted, which has not as yet been consecrated, is larger than the consecrated portion, but not if it is smaller," etc. Harnack (*Dogmengeschichte,* Vol. III, p. 710) unjustly calls such paragraphs "dreadful," and says that in such sacramentalia the Church has "legitimized Rabbinism and the theory and practice of the Pharisees and Talmudists in Christianity." This theory and practice are, as a matter of fact, not specific in nature, but correspond with a certain progressed stage of development of every highly organized religion.

The unconscious aversion and the latent ridicule in the asking of insidious questions, characteristic of obsessional neurosis, may be observed also in the religious speculations of all great religions. Even in the heart of Jewry the rabbis had to be on their guard against these tendencies. Thus, Rabbi Jehudah excluded a whole generation from his school, because, so he asserted, the pupils of Rabbi Meier were given to chicanery. "They come here not to study Thora, but they want to destroy me with Halachoth" (Kidduschim 52b, Nasir 99b). That the revolutionary tendencies which found a vent in the putting of subtle questions were really directed against the overstrict God is evident from many examples. I will therefore give only one example of the theological discussions of Jewry. In the third book of Moses (Lev. II, 55), we read: "And every thing whereupon any part of their carcass falleth shall be unclean; whether it be oven, or ranges for pots, they shall be broken down." The question was now asked in the Synhedrion, how it would be if one divided the oven into two parts and heaped sand between them. Would it then be unclean if it were touched by carrion? The Synhedrion replied in the affirmative; B. Elieser in the negative. The course which the debate had taken is described as follows: "On this day Rabbi Elieser adduced much evidence, but he did not gain his point. Then he said: 'Let this carob-tree decide!' Forthwith the tree removed itself a hundred ells, or many say four hundred, from its roots. But they answered: 'That proves nothing.' Hereupon Elieser called upon the river to judge between them. Immediately the river flowed backwards. When they did not accept even this proof, Elieser cried: 'Then let the walls of our school decide!' They bowed themselves and threatened to fall upon the assembly. Then the vice-president Rabbi Josua ben Chananja stood up and cried to the walls: 'When the wise men dispute together it is not for you to interfere!' Now the walls remained in a leaning posture. They did not fall, out of respect for Rabbi Josua, and they did not right themselves, out of respect for Rabbi Elieser. At last the latter said: 'So let the decision come from Heaven!' Then came a voice from Heaven: 'Elieser is right!' Again Josua stood up and cried: 'O God, thou hast told us: The Thora is not in Heaven! Further, thou hast commanded us: One shall judge in accordance with the majority.' Hereupon"—so the report concludes—"the wise men assembled together and laid the great interdict upon Rabbi Elieser" (Baba

Mesia 59 h). Here we see that God is defeated with his own weapons. However, the Talmud makes a characteristic comment upon the record. It relates that from time to time the prophet Elias appeared to a rabbi and reported on all manner of things which were happening in Heaven. On one such occasion the rabbi asked him how God had accepted Josua's correction. "He laughed," replied Elias, and said: "My children have defeated me." The commentator naturally did his best to dispose forthwith of a difficulty which presents itself at this point. It might be objected: "But it is said that since the destruction of the Temple God laughs no longer." But, says the conciliatory commentator: it was not a real laugh, it was only a smile. We see that the faithful will allow of no contradictions, and will restrict God's liberty on the rare occasions when He is tempted to laugh at this vale of tears which He has created, and in which there is so little cause for merriment.

4. DOGMA AND ANATHEMA, OBSESSIONAL IDEAS AND MECHANISMS OF DEFENSE

Psychoanalysis shows, in its regressive resolution of the obsessional idea, that this does not make its appearance in the patient's mind complete and fully formed, like Pallas Athene from the head of Zeus, but occurs at first as a vague notion, associated with somewhat elusive feelings. The obsessional idea then evolves, historically speaking, from the defense against the doubt which is directed against it. It gains in extension and stability, is isolated from the rest of the individual's mental life, is released from its historical limitations, and enters into new thought connections. As certain building materials appear to acquire a greater stability and power of resistance when exposed to wind and rain, so the obsessional idea gains renewed strength in fighting to defend itself against "reason." The persistent doubt which underlies it enforces the secondary elaboration, but conditions it, so that in evolving it forms new associations and anchors itself in the pseudo reasonable. Through this process it acquires a hold and a meaning in the psychical life of the individual, whereas before this it seemed entirely motiveless and meaningless.

Dogma, which we are comparing with the obsessional idea, reveals the same process in its development. Every effort, on the part of those who believe in dogma, to solve its unreasonableness, its many self-contradictions, and its incompatibilities with other beliefs, as with the realities of life, is doomed beforehand to fail, because to such people the dogma appears eternal and released from all temporal limitations. Nor is it possible to solve an obsessional idea by analysis, so long as one has not succeeded in bringing it into genetic and temporal relation with the patient's experiences. Only when this has been done, only when one can show the patient that his obsessional idea has not, so to speak, dropped ready-made out of the sky, do its agglutinative and enigmatic qualities disappear, while its latent meaning becomes apparent, and the mechanisms of its genesis and their derivation from strong psychical instinctual forces are explained.

Moreover, the dogma remains unaffected, despite all the rationalistic efforts of the antireligious critic, all attempts of the freethinkers to expose its absurdity, so long as its historical genesis in the psychical evolution of the peoples has not been understood. The history of dogma, the history of the Church, and comparative study of religions will here, to some extent, represent the analytic elucidation of personal prehistory in the individual. But the results which these scientific methods are able to achieve are capable only of providing external data and their connections as material for comparison. They cannot tell us anything about the psychical motive powers, the emotional mechanisms, nor their premises and their aims in the formation and development of dogma. Here the psychoanalysis of religion must intervene, and must find a way of employing the raw material furnished by the above-mentioned methods in the psychological elucidation of the problems in question.

The history of dogma tells us that in the early stages of religion there were no dogmas. The message of Jesus, for example, was entirely undogmatic; nor had he ever any intimation of a future church. Nothing was farther from his mind than the thought of dogmatic fixation. Nothing would have more greatly astonished him than the existence of Catholicism as an institution. Over and over again his utterances foretell the imminent end of the world, the Kingdom of God. He is possessed by the belief in the coming judgment, the end of things material. The time is close at hand when the power of Satan will be broken, when the perfected sovereignty of God will be established. The clock of the universe tells that the eleventh hour has come.[1] Jesus is living in the last days. He calls for repentance and conversion. How should he, who knew that the Last Judgment was close at hand, have established dogmas and canons of religious law?

The original Christian community, waiting for the imminent appearance, the *parousia* of the Kyrios, and still in the closest union with the Jewish mother religion, knew nothing of dogmas. Paul was to be the "founder" of Catholic ecclesiasticism. The Jewish zealot who had formerly so bitterly persecuted the Nazarenes was to conceive the first Bull of excommunication. He had resolved to surrender those who had defiled what was sacred "unto Satan, for the destruction of the flesh" (II Cor. V, 3 ff.). He was the first to fling his *"anathema sit"*—like the hierarchs of a later age—against any who should seek to preach another

[1] On sending forth his disciples, Jesus tells them: "Ye shall not have gone over the cities of Israel, till the Son of Man be come" (Matt. X, 23). The kingdom of God is at hand. He declares that "there be some of them that stand here, which shall not taste of death till they have seen the kingdom of God come with power" (Mark, IX, 1), and he exclaims: "Verily I say unto you that this generation shall not pass till all these things be done" (Mark, XIII, 30). Cf. J. Weiss (*Die Predigt Jesu vom Reiche Gottes*, 2nd ed., Göttingen 1900), who stresses the point that Jesus gave his life as a sacrifice for the early advent of the kingdom of God. Again, in Albert Schweitzer's great work (*Geschichte der Leben-Jesu-Forschung*, 2nd ed., Tübingen 1913) the eschatological theory of the imminent end of the world is given its true importance. The Catholic modernist George Tyrell (*Christianity at the Cross-road*, London 1910) accepted Schweitzer's "consequent eschatology" with enthusiasm, in order to justify, apologetically, the Catholic belief in the future world. But the official theology of the Church has protested very sharply against these views of Catholic Scholars, which reproduce a belief most unequivocally expressed in the New Testament. The authoritative decision of Pius X (in the *Syllabus Lamentabili* of 3 July 1907) declares: "Propositio damnata 52: Alienum fuit a mente Christi ecclesiam constituere veluti societatem super terram per longam saeculorum seriem duraturam: quin imo in mente Christi regnum coeli una cum fine mundi iamiam adventuram erat."

gospel than his: "But though we, or an angel from heaven, preach any other gospel unto you than that which we have preached unto you, let him be accursed" (Gal. 1, 8). Heiler has justly observed: "Paul coined the formula of excommunication with which the Councils and Popes of the Roman Church have branded heretics. There is no difference of kind, but only one of degree, between the Pauline anathema and the Roman."[2]

It cannot have been fortuitous that the same Paul who was so intolerant in respect of deviations from the faith was to lay the foundation of dogmatic doctrine in his Christology and soteriology. His myth of the Son of God furnished the basis of the subtle and richly ramified christological dogmatics of a later age. It was in Paul that the *Mysterium crucis* first took the shape of an intelligible doctrine, accessible to reason.

So we return to our assertion that dogma arises as a reactive phenomenon, reacting against heresy; that it is born of the defensive battle against doubt. Obsessional neurosis displays a two-fold character in its symptomatology; it devises prohibitions, precautionary measures, and penalties—that is, symptoms of a negative character; or, on the contrary, substitute satisfactions in distorted form. Freud has shown us that of these two groups of symptoms the negative and defensive is the older. With the continuance of the neurosis the substitute satisfactions move progressively into the foreground, so that they often very largely govern the clinical picture. Freud has drawn attention to a typical process, in alluding to the frequent triumph of the symptom formation. This occurs "when it succeeds in amalgamating the prohibition with the satisfaction, so that the originally protective command or prohibition acquires the significance of a satisfaction, to which end highly ingenious modes of incorporation are resorted to."[3]

Even in the development of dogma we perceive the rejection of heresy at the root of the dogmatic formula. This connection cannot entirely have escaped the theologians, nor yet the representatives of the science of religion. The dogmatists, when they

2 Heiler, *Der Katholizismus*, München 1925, p. 53.
3 *The Problem of Anxiety*, New York 1936.

allude to it, agree that while the dogma has of course existed from eternity it had to be formulated for the repulse of heresy and rejection of doubt, and also in order to deepen the understanding of the faithful. We have seen, in the case of the Christ dogma, how the Church, in its conflicts with the Gnostics, Monarchians, Sabellians, and finally the Arians, was compelled, more and more categorically, to formulate its beliefs with ever-increasing definiteness. Dogma finally became the bulwark which had to be erected against the persistent might of doubt. The whole history of dogma formation, and not of Christian dogma alone, but also of the dogmas of Islam, Judaism, Buddhism, etc., shows only too clearly the psychological laws of this process. Without Arius there would have been no Nicaean Creed; without Luther and Calvin, no Confession of Trent. Augustine himself testifies to this conditioning of birth of dogma when he exclaims: "Was Trinity ever fully described before the Arians howled against it?" (Ps. 54, n. 22). Over and over again we see the same process: just as obsessional neurosis seeks to banish doubt, so dogma seeks to banish heresy. One of the most eminent historians of Islam, Professor C. Snouk-Hurgronje, of Leyden, has clearly formulated the typical example of this process in the development of Mohammedanism.[4] "Not otherwise than in the Christian Church, in Islam also heresy became the midwife of dogmatics. The emergence of opinions which gave offence in the ruling circles compelled the latter to revise and classify their own views, and to defend them with weapons resembling those employed by their adversaries. Every heresy gave birth to one or more articles of faith."

Thus, in religious life, before the genesis of dogma, there were only beliefs of a more or less definite character, which had their roots deep in the unconscious, and whose conceptual content was comparatively simple. These beliefs, which had evolved from the animistic views of primeval antiquity, were now adapted to the cultural level of the believers, and are dated accordingly. They are not exposed to doubt on account of their

[4] In the *Lehrbuch der Religionsgeschichte,* Vol. I. Edited by Alfred Bertholet and Edward Lehmann, 1925, p. 723.

simple nature and their variable, indefinite forms.[5] Reason has nothing to do with them. Only when doubt arises do the premises of dogma formation emerge. All the enigmatic, fantastic and absurd features of religious ideas make their first appearance in the rigid formulation which doubt has compelled the Church to adopt.

Dogma consists in reality of two mutually connected parts, whose psychical validity is unequal: of the precise conceptual expression of the "true belief" and the expression of the rejection of divergent beliefs. In the course of religious evolution it so happens that this second factor recedes farther and farther into the background. The diminishing power of religion is very largely responsible for the decreasing violence with which divergent opinions are condemned. It is easy to be mild when one has become enfeebled. It can escape only the superficial survey of speculative theology that the condemnation of heretical views represents the essential and historically primary component of dogma. Although later on it may seem no more than a suffix, its importance, with regard to the genesis and the character of dogma, must appear undeniable to the analytic investigator. Here again appears the analogy with the obsessional idea, whose defensive side is the older, and which only afterwards thrusts the substitute satisfaction into the foreground. Here is a closely analogous example from the symptomatology of an obsessional neurosis: The patient whose blasphemous thoughts have already been mentioned kept on saying or shouting, from time to time, the words "God is a fox!" or more briefly, "Fox, fox!" Earlier still he had shouted: "The devil is an ass, but Fox" (= but God is a fox). The abbreviation is explained by the en-

[5] Here we will point only to primitive Christianity, in respect of which—as, for example, A. Dorner has emphasized ("Heilsglaube und Dogma" in *Beiträge zur Weiterentwicklung der christlichen Religion*, München 1905, p. 140) one cannot speak of a definitely worded doctrine: "The manner in which the content of Christianity finds expression here is not sharply conceived, but the belief is expressed in more indefinite, imaginative, rhetorical, poetical form. . . . One can no more speak of dogma than of a definitely worded doctrine." The same characteristics mark the beliefs of all religions in their initial stages.

deavor to ward off the obtrusive, blasphemous thoughts.[6] This formula shrank in the course of time to the abbreviated exclamation, apparently without subject or predicate: "Fox!" The omission of the blasphemous words and the abbreviation of the parrying formula were intended, the patient said, to make the defense against the objectionable thoughts more decisive. The patient himself explained that the peculiar force with which he uttered the word "Fox!" as well as the shortness of the word, was, towards the end, forced upon him, in a manner of speaking, because the blasphemies followed one another at ever shorter intervals, and threatened to attain even greater violence, so that he had to guard against them all the more rapidly and energetically.

In many respects these obsessional ideas may be compared with the dogmatic formulation of a positive religion. We see, for example, that in their development the forbidden or heretic thoughts, after a time, no longer find expression, but there is only a positive enunciation. However, no intelligent observer will deny that this development owes its psychical significance mainly to the repudiation of the suppressed, contradictory thought. Anyone who makes the acquaintance of dogma today only in its precise and positive form, as it occurs in any highly organized religion—for example, as a child learns dogmas in learning the catechism, or as the believer hears the priest proclaim them from the chancel—knows, as a general thing, little of its historical conditioning, in which the parrying of doubt plays so decisive a part. The dogma, as it is positively formulated, follows the *"anathema sit"* which since the Synod of Chalcedon has been the technical expression for the ecclesiastical interdict. It means that anyone who holds a view contradicting the opinion expressed

---

6 It is characteristic that the blasphemous railing was originally displaced upon the devil. The patient remembers that during his English lessons he often had to say "The devil is an ass and a fool." Finally his teacher had to reprove him for these "blasphemous" remarks: "That is not true, the devil is neither an ass nor a fool. On the contrary he is very clever." Since the temptation to reproduce this forbidden zoological idea on uttering the name of God became constantly stronger, the patient preferred to avoid the divine name. If, for example, he wished to recite the Belgian hymn, "Dieu, qui protège la Belgique," he said: "Le renard qui protège la Belgique," etc.

in the dogma shall be accursed and excluded from the community (*"si quis dixerit . . . anathema sit"*). The anathema represents the historically earlier and more significant part of the dogma, which afterwards surrendered its importance to the positive assertion of the dogma.[7] Just as it is quite impossible to guess the real wording of my patient's obsessional idea when one merely hears him shouting "Fox!", so it is equally impossible to recognize the true character of a dogmatic proposition unless one is aware of its history, and especially of its origination from the rejected heresy. The Church evinces a great deal of psychological understanding in repudiating, above all things, any research into the history of dogma or theology, unless this takes place under its own control, and subject to the restrictions inherent in the rules of the Christian faith. According to the Syllabus of 1907 any modern Bible criticism, or history of dogmatics, is really no longer justified in the theological domain. The reason is the same as that which represented Galileo's heliocentric theories as "dangerous errors and heresies" which appeared "pernicious to faith" (*in perniciem fidei*);[8] wherefore Galileo had to "abjure, execrate and abhor them" (*abjurare, maledicere, detestari*).

The incomprehensibility of dogma, and the frequently abstruse appearance of its façade, are often explained, on a closer historical survey, during the reconstruction of its historical genesis, and especially of the circumstances of its origin. Despite all the conservatism of the Church, scientific progress in this direction continues unchecked.[9]

7 An obvious analogy is presented by the formula of renunciation, the vow to repudiate the devil and all his works, which is made upon entering the community, and which finds its biblical basis in Mark, XXV, 41; John, XII, 31; Eph. VI, 11, 12; I John, II, 13; V, 19. This formula, preserved into the Middle Ages, was then dropped, and transferred to the sacrament of confession. In baptism also the separation of the faithful from the heathen, gnostics, and heretics, is historically the more important point.

8 Mirbt, *Quellen zur Geschichte des Papsttums und des römischen Katholizismus*, 1911, pp. 268 ff.

9 The eminent Catholic scholar, Friedrich von Hügel, who compares the attitude of the Church in respect of historical criticism with its attitude toward the progress in natural science of the seventeenth century, says: "It may well be that our difficulties do not appear more difficult to us now than their difficulties appeared to the astronomers and theologians of 1616 and 1633, and

Another peculiarity of obsessional neurosis is observed in the critical examination of dogma: it starts with the *words*. The importance of the choice of words, of the verbal formula, and the special emphasis laid on precise and definite expression, are features equally of the obsessional idea and of the dogma. They provide a solid counterpoise to the doubt which is inherent in the very wording of the dogma, and which is seeking to make a breach in the original ideas. These features offer a singular contrast to the vague, wavering, dreamlike indistinctness of the original obsessional idea, and it is obviously the aim of such formulation to banish all indefiniteness, and so ensure the psychical defeat of the doubt and its aggressive tendencies.

It is characteristic of obsessional neurosis that on every fresh formulation fresh doubts may present themselves, until finally one absurd and monstrous obsessional idea, which appears to be most pregnantly expressed, seems to dispel the doubts once and for all. The patient of whom I have spoken had to repeat to himself many times in the course of the day: "Three aristocrats in Heaven, two lackeys in Hell." To translate his obsessional jargon into our conscious idiom, he meant that on one hand there was the Trinity, and on the other were Satan and Beelzebub. In order to interpret this remark I had to recollect what he had said previously of his relation to the aristocracy and to menials. It was quite consistent with this that servants or other persons in subordinate positions should appear as devils, since they had been badly treated by his relatives, and according to the teaching of the Gospel one may show enmity only to the Devil. The mockery in the designation of aristocrats for the Trinity is plain enough. Of course, at the beginning of the analysis I found his obsessional-neurotic jargon difficult to understand. For example, he would say "Devil-girl" meaning "chambermaid;" "Church-devil" meant "sacristan" (a servant!). He once told me: "Satan and Beelzebub were with me today, and they asked me: 'If you please, would you like veal cutlets?' " It took me some time to

---

that some of these historical troubles of ours may last less than the two centuries required for the full tolerance of heliocentrism" (*Eternal Life*, 1913, p. 347).

understand the curious question of the "Sons of Darkness." It seemed that the head waiter and his assistant were consulting him as to the menu. When the patient was looking at Leonardo's "Last Supper" he felt obliged to call Christ "a drunken lackey." But then, in repudiation, he exclaimed, "Sober aristocrat!" When he said that he had driven past Hell and Heaven that day, this meant that he had passed the hotel, where there were so many servants, and the imperial castle. His statement that he had given Beelzebub a tip referred to the porter; his prayer, "Elegant lady, help me!" was of course addressed to the Virgin Mary.

Precision of formulation served to repress the blasphemous tendencies and to ensure definite belief in the idea expressed. It is characteristic of such obsessional-neurotic formulae, with their peculiar precision of expression, that in spite of all tendencies to definite and exact wording, they cannot escape a certain vagueness, and therefore, a persistent doubt. This is readily explained if we consider that in such formulae we are dealing with mixed products of repressed and repressing tendencies, and that the rejected doubts still unconsciously play a part in the formulation of the defensive thoughts, and develop their dynamic power. Moreover, it is often the very intention of checking all doubt as effectively as possible by its mere expression, and to exclude any misunderstanding, any intervention of the canceled interpretation, that in its exaggeration gives the obsessional idea some part of its absurd character; that is, it makes its wording appear nonsensical or bizarre.

I have said that the formulation of dogma shows the same seeming exactness and precision as we find in the obsessional idea, and in both cases this feature serves to eliminate doubt. The original beliefs of the Church, like the primary obsessional ideas, are vague and ambiguous, and it is only the attacks made upon them that compel the Church to express its religious opinions more clearly and exactly. Just as the constant gnawing of doubt often drives the primary obsessional idea to developments that end in absurdity, so dogma formation is forced to proceed to its utmost extremes, in order to deal with the critics in its own and in the enemy's camp. In the symptoms of obsessional neurosis the trains of thought which are adapted to the repulse of a specific forbidden thought have themselves become the object of doubt, so that by such a circuitous path the forbidden tendency returns.

Let us compare this characteristic mechanism with the analogous process in the history of dogma, and again let us take our material from the time of the Arian conflict, which has already afforded us so many valuable opportunities of comparison. It was of course inevitable that both sides, in defining their beliefs, should rely on the utterances of Holy Writ as the highest authority. What they wished to say regarding the relation of God the Father and God the Son had to be conceived in the terms of such utterances. But the Arians invoked the Scriptures just as the Orthodox did. When the bishops were seeking to define this basic relation in Nicaea, the Arians displayed an extraordinary dexterity, which Gwatkin has appropriately described as "evasiveness," when it was a matter of giving their own meaning to every definition of their opponents. When the bishops asserted that Christ was of God, the Arians could quietly agree, since all things were of God. If the Saviour, in conformity with the Scriptures, and in rejection of the accursed Arian heresy, was described as the very likeness of God, the Arians could slyly smile at one another and agree: "So also are we, for man was created in God's image." They could even accept the designation of Christ as the Son of God, since men also are the sons of God. Thereupon the bishops, in order to show where they differed from the Arians found themselves compelled to employ the word *homoousios*, the word that does not occur in the Scriptures, and which has brought such miseries upon the Christian world. There was no other way of countering the doubts of the Arians than to make oneself guilty of a kind of heresy. In this predicament of intellectual self-defense it must surely be permissible to employ a weapon which they felt to be unrighteous. And this process also, as we know, is repeated in obsessional neurosis, where the defense put up so long by the obsessional thoughts again evokes the forbidden thoughts, until the repressed ideas recur in the midst of the repressing ideas. The counterimpulse, which disturbs the defense put up by the obsessional ideas, and affects their wording, is manifest in every developed obsessional neurosis. Here is a little example which reveals the similarity to the theological conflicts between the Arians and the Homoousians. The patient of whom I have spoken was suffering under the obsessional conviction that his dearly beloved aunt would very shortly die, and he tried to ward off this fear by a prayer in whose wording he had to make constant alterations, because the repressed death thoughts (death wishes) kept on recurring and disturbing him. For some time the prayer ran: "Lord, I place all my hope in Thee, and I pray that my dear and beloved aunt may be granted a long life here below," etc. The origin of just this wording becomes obvious when he explains that he says Lord (*Seigneur*) and not God (*Dieu*), because God, invoked by this name, has nevertheless allowed many people to die. Even this explanation represents a rationalization, since it seeks to cover the repulsion of the obtruding blasphemy which attaches itself to the name of God. He employs the locution "a long life *here below*" so that there shall be no doubt that he is referring to this world, and not by any chance to life in the future world, etc. Thus, almost every word is determined by the power of the persisting countertendencies. Just think of the great dispute as to whether Mary should be described as having given birth to God, or as the Mother of God; and of the famous debate over the *Filioque*, which was to decide whether the Holy Ghost proceeds only from the Father, or from the Father and from the Son, etc.

The examples from the Halacha of Judaism and its dialectics are so numerous and so well known that we hardly need to adduce them. The typical form of the impact of doubt on the text of a doctrine may be seen in the Christian debate on the *ousia* (nature, being) of God, and in the Islamitish discussion of the seven attributes of Allah. If the Christians were afraid that the *ousia* of God might appear to be a divine Being existing beside God, so the representatives of the Kālām pointed out that the seven divine Attributes increased the danger of polytheism. The latent co-operation of heretics and doubters in the genesis and development of dogma is entirely analogous to the share of doubt in the production of the obsessional idea.

The anathema is of earlier origin than the dogma in whose company it appears. It serves not merely to repulse the erroneous belief; it is directed in particular against the believers' own doubts. This curse is directed also against the members of the community who are inclined to accept an opinion (i.e., a belief) not officially acknowledged. It represents an unconscious cursing of the self on account of doubt or an aberrant belief.

When ecclesiastical orthodoxy considers the heretics wicked men, seduced by the Devil, ever seeking for new things, who are doomed to the eternal pains of Hell, it sets itself up in opposition to these words of the Epistle to the Corinthians (I Cor. 11, 19), which express the depth of their need: *"oportet et haereses esse":* "For there must be also heresies among you that they which are approved may be made manifest among you."

5. CONTRADICTION IN DOGMA AND IN THE OBSESSIONAL IDEA

The Church owes to heresy more than the reaction against its erroneous or sacrilegious assertions. The saying of a religious critic, which we have already cited, that heresy is the midwife of dogma, has certainly some truth in it, but it might be added that heresy is often the mother of dogma. The historian of dogma would have little difficulty in showing that the heretical opinion of an earlier day has found its way into dogma and has thereupon been declared sacrosanct.[1] It is therefore correct to say that dogma is the elaborated, distorted expression of a heretical view; one might call it a blasphemy transformed into an article of faith. This is only an apparent contradiction of the notion of the determination of dogma as a defense against blasphemy. Let us go back to what has already been said, according to which the dogma represents a compromise formation of repressed and repressing tendencies. In this direction also the Church is a *complexio oppositorum.* The positive significance of heresy as one of the constituent factors of dogma is for the unprejudiced

[1] As regards Catholicism, Heiler has described the process correctly, although he did not understand the psychological necessity of the phenomenon. He stressed the fact that the consequence of the violent opposition and isolation of the heretic is "always a thorough revision and examination of the heresy's claim to be truth, which always ends with a partial and modified acceptance of the religious element maintained by the heresy, and therewith the restoration of the violated Catholicism, of the disturbed equilibrium" (*Der Katholizismus,* p. 639).

critic unmistakable in the history of all highly organized religions. It finds unequivocal expression in two directions: firstly, historicoreligious research reveals innumerable examples of the fact that what today the faithful regard as dogma may seem heresy the day after tomorrow, while secondly, and conversely, the day after tomorrow the heresy of today may come to possess dogmatic validity. But this is not all: the same opinion can, in a manner of speaking, be prescribed and prohibited at one and the same time. The Dissenters, reprobated by the reformers who established the creeds, advanced a number of ideas which the official Protestantism appropriated at a later stage. Arianism was for many decades regarded as the essential form of Christianity, and not only as a State religion, being acknowledged by the majority of the clergy and of the Christian communities. The Mutalizitic interpretation was officially proclaimed a State dogma by the Abassid caliphs.

We will take only one example from the history of Arianism in order to illustrate the contrary process: The Synod of Antioch had rejected the designation of *homoousios* (consubstantiality) for the relation between God the Father and God the Son. They wanted to avoid acceptance of the consequent doctrine that the common being could be the first and absolute being, from which the Father and Son derived as common sons. The Council of Nicaea had decreed the consubstantiality of God the Father and God the Son, although the word does not occur in the Bible. The worship of images, once an abomination before the Lord, seemed acceptable to the Lord in a later period, although the ancient prohibitions were still maintained. What had been deplorable heterodoxy became an official belief.

Doubt itself broke through into the fold, and soon it was no longer possible to distinguish outside from inside. If in the early days of a religion every opinion which was contrary to ecclesiastical common sense, or to the articles of faith, was regarded as a heresy, with the later development of dogmatics everyone was a heretic whose convictions diverged in the smallest point from the prevailing orthodox opinion, however orthodox he might seem in other respects. Not even Apollinaris, not even the great Origenes escaped condemnation. Whether anyone was regarded as orthodox or heretical had become a question of minority and majority; his status might be transformed overnight, and the roles might be suddenly reversed. Seeberg alludes to the terrible danger incurred by the Church[2] "when the path of truth becomes so narrow that only the experts—and these only in fear and trembling—can declare whither it actually leads."

So even the dogma, like the obsessional idea, becomes subject to all manner of uncertainties. Even in the domain of obsessional thinking the analyst will often perceive that the rejected idea suddenly becomes the subject of an obsessional impulse, an obsessional train of thought. The very impulse against which the obsessional idea was erected as protection becomes suddenly itself an obsession. When my patient had repeated his conjuration against blasphemy often enough he was compelled, against his conscious will, to utter the blasphemy itself as a form of prayer. When he had loudly asserted a hundred times "The whore is the wife of the Devil, but the Virgin is the Mother of God," he would unexpectedly find himself compelled to utter the reverse of this unambiguous statement. Not infrequently, when he had declared with sufficient frequency, "The Holy Ghost is elegant, but the Devil is very vulgar," he would transpose the persons.[3]

In the later development of the obsessional neurosis the idea to be repudiated usually overpowers the precautionary measures, and is victorious; there is an irruption of the prohibited satisfaction. But the other phenomena of dogma formation reappear in the distorted form of obsessional thinking, so that the obsessional neurotic finds himself oscillating between two sets of opinions. What is prohibited seems to him somehow what is commanded, and in what formerly seemed the only proper line of thought elements of the forbidden have introduced them-

[2] *Lehrbuch der Dogmengeschichte,* Vol. II, p. 9.

[3] The patient expressed his obsessional thoughts and the defense against them in various languages which he spoke as fluently as his mother tongue. This circumstance acquired some importance in the analysis, because the employment of this or that language made it possible to draw conclusions as to the historical conditioning of his ideas, which had almost the same validity as the analogous conclusions drawn by the geologist from the stratification of the subsoil. Cf. the sacramental languages employed in religion (Sumerian by the Babylonians, Latin by the Catholic Church, etc.).

selves. We have already alluded to the fact that in the obsessional symptomatology the same symptoms not infrequently combine prohibition and satisfaction; that is, in so far as they represent mental processes they combine heresy and dogma in one and the same expression. If we trace the evolution of all religions we see that it is often quite uncertain whether one and the same manner of viewing things is to be regarded as dogmatic or heretical. We remember in how many cases of obsessional neurosis "most of the symptoms have acquired, in addition to their original significance, also that of their direct opposites; a testimony to the power of ambivalence, which, though we do not know why, plays so large a part in obsessional neurosis."[4]

But what should immediately concern us here are the modes of connection which make it possible in the same symptom, in the same dogmatic formula, to weld together the prohibition and the prohibited satisfaction in one and the same expression. This process frequently produces a result which appears grotesque or absurd. It is the paradox of the dogma and the obsessional idea that the contradictory elements appear more nonsensical in their completed synthesis than do the individual elements in themselves.

The intellectual effect of this attempted reconciliation between repressed and repressing ideas is often an absurd synthesis which is bound to appear either comical or bizarre. For example, Christianity teaches us that Christ is very God, but also very man; the second Person of the Trinity, but also the son of the Virgin Mary; He has two natures, but consists of three substances (Logos, body and soul); the two natures are not mingled, but are nonetheless inseparable. Catholic dogma proclaims duality in unity as well as unity in duality. There is also a mutual exchange of divine and human qualities, in so far as the God has to be given human and the man divine attributes. We say that "God suffered" and that "this man is God." In Christ we have to distinguish two wills, and so forth. In this dogmatic doctrine we clearly perceive the endeavor to exclude various heretical views, as well as the attempt to accept them in some degree. The history of this dogma shows us how it emerged from the conflict with

[4] Freud, *The Problem of Anxiety*, New York, 1936.

Arianism, Apollinarism, Docetism, Monophysitism, etc., and yet the dogma has absorbed fragments of all these heresies. The notion to be repudiated was in the first place, for example, the idea that Christ was only a man and a prophet, so that his divinity had to be acknowledged and maintained. Then, as Docetism asserted that Christ has no genuinely human nature, but a mere semblance of a body, the reality of Christ's humanity had to be maintained. The analogy with obsessional phenomena holds good to this extent, that there also, if the patient follows a train of thought to the end, he always comes upon a forbidden idea against which he defends himself in order to repeat the same process in the contrary direction. Thus, in obsessional symptomatology we may speak not only of two-phased actions or symptoms, but also of two-phased trains of thought. But the characteristic trait of the fundamental dogmas and of the obsessional ideas is the fact that they endeavor, so to speak, to suppress the contradictions which have been created by ambivalence. They try to annul them, and to establish a unity which is superlogical and yet obeys all the laws of logic. Ernest Jones[5] mentions an obsessional-neurotic patient who was compelled, whenever his attention was called to an idea, to think the precise antithesis, and then to seek for the idea which would be exactly midway between the contraries, taking enormous pains to discover the most satisfactory intermediate idea. This manifests, in the domain of obsessional symptoms, the very process which the Church applies in the case of two contrary beliefs.

The absurdity of dogma is conditioned mainly by the underlying co-operation of the aggressive tendencies. It is this that determines the absurd disguise of the obsessional idea. In most cases repression has had the result that the content of the aggressive impulse is unconscious. It expresses itself only in the nonsensical or paradoxical wording of the obsessional idea, in so far as the patient is conscious of the wording. The absurdity then appears, as in a dream, as the substitute expression of scorn or ridicule. The aggressive, disparaging and scoffing tendencies appear to find expression in the formulation itself. It seems as

[5] Jones, *Therapy of the Neuroses*, 1921, p. 147.

though they are to blame if those who hear the obsessional idea expressed are moved to exclaim "What a crazy idea! What utter nonsense!"

Analysis shows us how much sense there is in all this confused absurdity. It shows, also, that what the obsessional idea is trying to express is ridicule of a conception which it contains in a state of latency. Let us refer once more to the crux of Christology, the *dualitas in unitate* and the *unitas in dualitate*. The dogma of the two natures of Christ, his true Godhead and his no less real humanity, may sound preposterous to the scientific thinker, especially when he considers the consequences of this hypostatic union. The Agnoetae and many modern theologians find it possible to describe Christ as the being who simultaneously knew, as God, what he did not know as man. Athanasius, the great advocate of true faith against the Arian heresy, even thought that Christ spat as a man but that his spittle was full of divinity.[6] The emphasis on the humanity of Christ, which has been as vigorously maintained by Catholicism as his Godhead, is, in its connection with his true divinity, an expression of aggressive instinctual impulses. It is as though the assertion of the dual nature or the dual will of Christ were trying to reduce the whole of Christology to absurdity. Derision and contempt are mingled indistinguishably in this pious belief, as though they really wanted to say: *Credo quia absurdum.*

This unconscious character of derision, of stubborn defiance, which not only sets its stamp on so many obsessional ideas, but also constitutes their real latent content, is common to the assertions of dogma. It is as though they wanted to say: If I am to believe in Christ at all, why should he not be God and man at the same time—why should he not possess two wills, three natures, etc.? Or, to put it more plainly: If it is true that there is a Jesus who was the Son of God, who came down upon earth in order to save us, and who, being crucified, rose again to Heaven,

---

6 Athanasius, ad Serap., IV, 14. Cf. Luther's vigorous opposition to this kind of Christology: "So the sophists have pictured Christ as he were man and God; they number his arms and legs and fantastically mix the two natures together, which is only a sophistical notion of the Lord Christ. For Christ is not called Christ because he has two natures. How does that concern me?" (*Werke*, Erlanger edition, XXXV, p. 207).

he may have been both God and man; he may have possessed all human functions, and yet he may not have possessed them—and so forth. It sounds like persiflage when Tertullian says, "Crucified was the Son of God; that is no disgrace, because it is a disgrace. And the Son of God died; that is credible, because it is preposterous. And having been buried he rose again; that is quite certain, because it is impossible." Here, in a curious "twist"—as though in mockery—nonsensicality is made the very basis of belief.

If I wished to present yet another pendant to this remarkable character of dogma, and to the predominance of the nonsensical or paradoxical in the symptoms of the obsessional neurotic, I might well refer back to the case of neurosis already cited. The patient who contended with his blasphemous doubts is of all obsessional neurotics I have observed the one whose symptoms furnish the closest analogies to the processes of dogma formation. As we have seen, he has devised a personal and typical obsessional-neurotic jargon which at first I had some difficulty in understanding. Thus, he would speak of the "sacred Prince Oldenburg service;" or he would say, pointing to the sky, "There reigns the great Prince Schwarzenberg!" or he would say, as though in sudden alarm: "Saint Count Kinsky!" If he wanted to quote the Bible he would do it, perhaps, as follows: "I am thy Duke of Hohenlohe, who takes vengeance on the sins of the fathers." He spoke of "Count Lobkowitz proofs" in the philosophy of religion, and he declared that he had "the body of the Princes of Thurn and Taxis in himself" if he wanted to speak of having taken communion.[7] It was evident that the names of aristocratic families were employed to indicate God; that by the Oldenburg service

---

[7] For reasons of discretion I have inserted other names, though these are characteristic of those which he actually employed. The symbol of the dove for the Holy Ghost struck him as inappropriate. He could not help thinking that it was perhaps blasphemous to represent the Holy Ghost as a bird, and finally came to the conviction that the Holy Ghost, in so far as it was a bird at all, must be a bird of aristocratic connections. There are, of course, *"des oiseaux de race,"* and *"des oiseaux vulgaires."* He therefore contrasted the Holy Ghost, who in bird form would certainly have carried the scepter and imperial globe, with a plebeian bird like the raven or the canary. Once, when he saw a sacristan collecting money in church, he thought: "The Holy Ghost with the cash," and found himself plunged into the depth of despair by this blasphemous allusion.

he meant the Mass, etc. But how did this distinguished intellectual come to set the aristocracy of his country in the place of
God? The explanation of this apparent insanity is found in the
history of his earlier life. As a youth he had noticed that his
rather snobbish parents esteemed people mainly on account of
their aristocratic descent, and set the greatest value on their
social relations with the nobility. These views of his parents were
in sharp contradiction to the ideas which he acquired from the
Gospel, and to the conspicuous piety always exhibited by persons whom he respected. It was apparently in extreme exaggeration of his parents' outlook that he set the Schwarzenberg princes,
or Count Kinsky, or the Dukes of Oldenberg in the place of God,
promoting them to divine rank; but in reality it was the expression of the bitterest mockery. It was as though he were trying to
say: If people find it possible to exalt human beings in this way
simply because they are aristocrats, why don't they straightway
put them in the place of God? But he was not conscious of this.
As far as he could remember he had shared his parents' opinions
of the aristocracy, and it was difficult to convince him that
people do not begin to be human only from the rank of baron
upwards. We begin to approach the christological problem when
we learn from this patient that it seems all wrong to him that
Mary should be "a dirty Jewess" and the Apostles simple people
like fishermen and carpet weavers. It had always distressed him
that Christ should have been the son of a common carpenter, and
he has pondered on a means of showing that he came after all of
aristocratic forbears. This is like an attempt to repeat the creation
of dogma under one's own control—to create, as it were, a religion
in miniature for one's private use. Who can fail to be reminded,
on considering these obsessional thoughts, of the dogma of the
dual nature of Christ, or the attempt to combine his humble
origin with descent from David's royal line?

The unconscious part of mockery in the absurdity of dogma
appears, upon analysis, wherever an elaborated dogma appears
in the history of religion: it is already determined in the dogmatic formulation. It does not matter whether we consider the
doctrine that Mary gave birth to Jesus *clauso utero,* or the doctrine that unbaptized children are condemned to the eternal pains

of hell;[8] or the dogma of the Trinity; of the "thorn-beset" doctrine of grace; of the transubstantiation in the Eucharist, which assumes the real presence of Christ in every particle of the host; of the Perichorese, the doctrine of the reciprocal penetration and indwelling of the three Persons of the Trinity. There is always a complete contradiction, which is "equally mysterious to wise men and to fools."

The ingenious nonsense of the dogma is the feature which relates it most conspicuously and significantly to the obsessional idea of neurosis. Here, in its mental trends, religion often enters the sphere of obsessional thinking. Here, if anywhere, the saying of Heraclitus is justified—that faith is "a sacred malady."

6. THE SECONDARY ELABORATION IN RATIONAL THEOLOGY

Religion is a system of thought which is comparable to the great illusory formations of neurosis and psychosis. Animism, whose hypotheses were taken over by religion, was such a system of thought; one which was common to primitive humanity. Our ancestors all believed in the existence and dominion of good and evil spirits in forest and plain. This belief was impregnable, and was therefore supported by excellent reasons. Today only our children believe in these beneficent and malevolent beings, and this only for as long as they read or listen to fairy tales. With us the belief in such animistic conceptions is succeeded by astonishment. We no longer share them, but we should like to know what they signify, how people came to hold them, what psychical

[8] In accordance with the strict theology which Augustine defended (Enchirid. 93), and which was confirmed by the decision of the Council of Florence, Hermann Schell, who ventured to doubt this dogmatic assumption (*Katholische Dogmatik,* Vol. III, Paderborn 1893, pp. 478 ff.), had to suffer for his humanity; his works were placed on the Index. The practical consequences of this belief are seen, for example, in the refusal of many Catholic priests to bury such unbaptized children in consecrated ground. If many a priest refuses to allow the (unbaptized) little ones to come unto him, the danger can be averted if, when a stillborn child is expected, "intra-uterine" baptism is administered by means of a special surgical instrument. (Exhaustive details are given by C. Capellmann, *Pastoralmedizin,* 18th ed., Paderborn 1920, p. 242.)

motives underlaid them, and to what purpose they were directed. A time will come when the religions of the world will be regarded from the same point of view. Neither the zeal of the believer nor the fanaticism of the freethinker will dominate our views of religion. In the place of belief we shall have research into belief. This development is already casting its shadow before it. I am not speaking now of the advance of research into comparative religion, and the psychology of religion, but of the penetration of the very fabric of religion by scientific points of view. The scientific elaboration may appear completely inadequate, purely dialectical, sophistical, and constrained by religious prejudice; it may be biased, seeking only to defend the standards of belief against doubt and to prove their reasonableness; yet its very necessity is an unequivocal symptom of future development.

The need of a comprehensive and rational consolidation of religious phenomena, the theological endeavor to secure a rational foundation for the standards of belief, already indicate, in the history of the religions, the beginning of the end. For criticism and doubt will at most transpose their activities; they will not abandon them; and the collapse of beliefs will result from the action of these strong psychical powers. Religion can maintain itself only if it makes concessions to reason, but these concessions will have to become larger and larger as the challenges of the adversaries become more urgent and peremptory. There is no means of checking what has rolled over the edge of a precipice.

A most imposing performance, and one which tries to protect the religious conceptions from destruction by the critical factors, inasmuch as it actually makes use of these latter, has been achieved by "rational theology." The formation of rational theology, which comprises both apologetics and dogmatics, is a process which becomes a psychological necessity in the evolution of all established religions. *"Ratio recta fidei fundamenta demonstrat."* This maxim of the Vatican Council comprises the programme of the rational theology, not only of Christianity, but of all highly organized religions.

Dogma itself, even in its formulation, is a hybrid entity, inasmuch as it seeks to reduce the ideas of believers to a precise and intelligible form, which will exclude all doubt and misgiving on the part of the faithful. It has the character of a compromise inasmuch as it seeks, in its formulation, to satisfy the requirements of reason as well as those of faith. As in an obsessional idea, the unconscious motivation in the rationalization process is replaced by a secondary motive.[1] If the dogma already bears traces of the secondary defensive conflict, the dogmatics of the belief is entirely dominated by this motive.

What is dogmatics? It is the doctrine of faith in the more restricted sense, in opposition to morality as a doctrine of ethics. It is distinguished from moral theology by the special point of view that it provides "not the supernatural standards of ethical behavior, but those of religious thought."[2] Dogmatics is the focal point of theology, which by the Catholic Church is designated "the science of belief" (scientia fidei). Dogmatics is the scientific elaboration and representation of the beliefs comprised in a religion. Its function is to extract doctrine from scripture and tradition, to link individual sayings in a reasonable manner, and to insure them against doubt and the contradictions of the inquiring intellect.

1 This compromise character of dogma, which it possesses in common with the obsessional idea, has not escaped the notice of religious historians. We need refer only to Harnack, who draws attention to the fact that the efforts of the Church to combine the traditional or legendary material of the community beliefs with philosophical concepts have engendered "the curious hybrid nature of the dogma . . . which is neither manifest image nor clear logical thought" (Dogmengeschichte, Vol. I, p. 424). Dorner calls attention to the fact that the dogma contains disparate elements (Heilsglaube und Dogma, p. 145): "Sometimes it comes into existence with the aid of science, and this demands free judgment, and yet this is refused by the Church, which makes it a compulsory belief. At other times it has emerged only at a later period, and yet it commonly claims that it is in agreement with the ancient traditions and the ecclesiastical canon which are held to contain the pristine sources of Christianity, and indeed there it expresses the true meaning of these authorities." The same author observes in another place (Grundriss der Dogmengeschichte, Berlin 1899, pp. 13 f., that dogma "has remained to some extent in imaginative form, partly because, on account of its semiscientific origin, it had no popular characteristics, and was therefore regarded as unintelligible to the people." It "wavers, owing to its semipopular and semicommunal character, between the direct form of a statement of belief and the scientific form, and represents a stage of the process of religious perception in which it is brought by the community to a state of provisional rest, which as a rule, however, is not of long duration."

2 Josef Pohle, "Christlich-katholische Dogmatik," in Systematische christliche Religion (Kultur der Gegenwart), Part I, Vol. IV, 1909, p. 52.

While in an earlier chapter I have defined religion as a system of thought, dogmatics may be regarded as the theoretical exposition of this system. We have come to understand the peculiarities of system construction in the psychical life of the psychoses and neuroses, and we know that in this there is an endeavor so to organize a mass of disparate, primarily incoherent and unintelligible material that it acquires unity, coherence, and meaning. This is precisely what dogmatics attempts to do in respect of the whole body of religious beliefs. Its efforts are directed toward representing the individual dogmas which derive from different historical strata, and which rest upon different assumptions, as homogeneous, mutually connected, and mutually consistent. This it does by means of a treatment which we have come to know in the psychology of dreams and neuroses as secondary elaboration. Here an intellectual function enforces unification, interconnection and intelligibility in the elements of the material under consideration, establishing a spurious connection when a genuine connection cannot be discovered.

The rearrangement of psychical material toward a new purpose is evident in dogma formation just as it is in obsessional thinking; it is, as our examples show, no less drastic in dogmatics than in the neuroses and psychoses. In both domains we note the same appearance of multiple motivation. Take, for example, a case of compulsive or obsessional washing. The patient will justify his numerous and extensive precautionary measures by referring to the theoretically unlimited possibilities of infection. His views regarding infection show a twofold motivation; one motivation derives from the presumptions of the system—in this case the possibilities of infection; the other, and really the effective motivation, refers unconsciously to the avoidance of physical contact: originally, of touching oneself, of masturbation.

The dogmatic system formation proceeds in just the same way; it rearranges the dogma, completes it, develops it in detail, and gives it a rational motivation, thereby disguising its genesis from the animistic myths whose real content was the expression of aggressive and sexual instinctual impulses. Dogmatics has a twofold foundation: Its lower regions are the rationalistic, reasonable representation and justification of its pronouncements; its deeper and really effective stratum is the struggle against blasphemous, depreciatory and rebellious impulses against those authorities on which it depends—God, Jesus, the Church, the Pope. Of course, this comparison is intelligible only to one who has penetrated into the inmost region, the *sanctissimum* of dogma formation, and has also acquired an analytic understanding of the psychology of obsessional thinking. But even the student of comparative theology will readily understand how in dogmatics a general modification and rearrangement of the body of the material, and of its individual elements, has taken place. The purpose of this secondary elaboration is, historically, in the first place, to break down the connections with the ancient, primitive conceptions of a superannuated stage or religious development, and to make every dogma appear the appropriate concept of a highly evolved religion.

The efficacy of the sacraments in the dogmatic interpretation reveals their derivation from the primitive notion of conjuration or magic only to the researches of religious criticism. The derivation of the Eucharist from the primitive totemistic feast is rationalistically disguised in dogmatic theory; the priest speaks the sacramental words of the Lord: *hic est enim corpus meum— hic est enim calix sanguinis mei,* and the bread is changed into the body of Christ and the wine into his blood.[3] The initiate will

[3] On this occasion, it may be noted, the power of the priest often threatens to exceed the Divine power. From Heiler *(Der Katholizismus,* p. 226) I quote a passage from a Jesuistic volume of meditations: "The power of Moses was great. A word from his mouth parted the waves of the Red Sea. Even the sun obeyed Joshua's word. Yet these were only individual cases in which these great men possessed a wonderful power over Nature. But the priest possesses this power over lifeless creation and *over the Creator Himself,* and this whenever he wills. A word from his mouth compels the Creator of the physical universe and the heavens to descend upon the earth, divests Him of His greatness, and conceals Him in the form of bread." The pastoral letter of the Cardinal Archbishop of Salzburg of the 2nd February 1905 proposes the following considerations: "Where in Heaven is there power like that of the Catholic priest? . . . Once Mary brought the divine Child into the world, but behold, the priest does this not once, but a hundred, a thousand times, whenever he celebrates the Mass. . . . To the priests He has transferred power over His sacred humanity, has given them, as it were, power over His body. The Catholic priest can not only demand His presence upon the altar, enclose Him in the tabernacle, bring Him forth again, and offer Him for the delectation of the faithful . . . Christ, the only begotten Son of God . . . is obedient to his will" (Mirbt, *Quellen zur Geschichte des Papsttums,* p. 401).

recognize, in the dogmatics of the sacrament, the primitive elements, one by one, in the individual dogmas, which in the Catholic religion have undergone an exalted and spiritualized interpretation, an anagogic transformation. But the analyst can still see behind them the latent, repressed instinctual impulses, to guard against which the dogma was created, and which have achieved a distorted expression in the dogma itself. He recognizes in the sacramental dogma the original concept of the taboo in the full efficacy of its ambivalence, in the Christ dogma the myth of the rebellious son, in the dogma of the Mother of God, the *semper virgo, Dei genetrix* and *corredemptrix,* the adoration of the great Goddess of Love, etc.

Our knowledge of doctrine formation enables us to dissect this great and decisive connection, to give the concrete dogmas an abstract form, and to grasp them intellectually. Faith, according to Freud, is the offspring of love, and in the beginning did not need to be argued.[4] Argumentation already indicates an enfeeblement of the power of faith. The justification of faith through its foundations is already a symptom of its decline.[5] An obsessional idea is awakened by obscure and unfamiliar instinctual impulses; it appears at first to be unmotivated and unsupported, and only later does it receive its justification and location in the psychical life, in so far as this can be effected by the patient's efforts at rationalization. In the same way religious beliefs derive from primeval views of an animistic character, and are first formulated and established on a higher level of development in concordance with reason.

An allusion to the connection between doubt and dogma which I have already stressed should enable the reader to realize that dogmatics has "gone to school," so to speak, with doubt and

---

[4] *Ges. Schriften,* Vol. VII, p. 463.

[5] Wobbermin was aware of the debilitating effect of the attempt to justify faith by scientific and theoretical arguments: "Thereby a necessary belief is somehow transformed into something to be regarded as a certainty: that is, it is deprived of the character of a belief, and the independence and characteristic nature of faith are imperiled. If the convictions of faith are somehow degraded to the level of rational logic they will be dragged down into the sphere of the hypothetical and relative, whereas faith seeks to uplift and exalt man above this latter" ("Apologetik," in *Die Religion in Geschichte und Gegenwart,* Vol. II, p. 559).

heresy. The defense of faith has acquired the weapons and the technique of the aggressor, and has learned to employ them in defense. Logic, the whole arsenal of argumentation, the drawing of conclusions, the establishment of connections—these things dogmatics has taken from doubters, heretics and adversaries, and has applied them to its own purposes.[6] This again is wholly analogous to the phenomena of obsessional thinking; the secondary elaboration is effected by the same means as those employed by the disintegrating factors of consciousness. The objections—e.g., to the washing obsession—which appeal to healthy common sense, are opposed to arguments from the same source. I was once a witness to a protracted argument between a famous bacteriologist, a professor in a foreign university, and an obsessional neurotic who was suffering from syphilophobia. The patient, who was wearing peculiar and specially constructed underclothing of his own design, in order to escape the treacherous spirochetes, had asked the scientist for a consultation, in order to obtain reliable information as to a certain possibility of infection. All scientific arguments were futile. The patient eagerly accepted them and so applied them that they encouraged his sense of insecurity, and at the conclusion of the interview the professor had to grant that in the cases under discussion a minimal possibility of infection could not indeed be excluded.

Dogmatics also employs the methods of doubt in order to assure the doctrines of faith. If doubt attacks the dogma from rationalistic standpoints dogmatics will rationally attack the doubt. If historical arguments are employed the evidence of tradition is adduced by the dogmatists. Finally, as a last resort, one can still appeal to the authority of God and the superrationality of dogma, which eludes rational explanation. Here the Janus face of dogmatics reveals itself; it emphasizes the differ-

[6] I may point, for example, to the dialectical elaboration, annotation and interpretation of the law in Judaism. The Gemara has a special phrase for this sort of exegesis: it is "declaring a dead reptile to be clean." According to Lev. II, 29 ff. he who touches a dead reptile is made unclean. But one may show by all manner of conclusions that this precept is invalid. There were Tanaits who could attain this result in 150 different ways. Rabbi Meïr had a pupil, Symmachus, who could prove in forty-eight ways that what the Thora calls clean is unclean, and the converse.

ence between *Dogmata pura* and *Dogmata mixta*. The former conceal their content after the fashion of the mysteries of faith, and are cognizable only through faith and revelation (i.e., the Trinity, the Incarnation, Grace); the latter are not mysteries, and are therefore cognizable by the reason, and thus are, or could be, the object of natural intuition (the unity of God, the Creation, the spiritual nature of the soul). We may conjecture that the *Dogmata pura* which contain the secret doctrines are the older and more important. Even by this distinction we shall be reminded of certain obsessional-neurotic phenomena. Obsessional thoughts, of course, are not divided into such sharply delimited groups, but one may often note that there are some which the patient tries to justify, and even ventures to discuss, while there are others which he carefully keeps to himself, and of whose virtue he has a profound inner conviction, mysterious yet peremptory.

Unquestionably the great dogmatists of all religions, who conclude that the inner content of the dogmas is of universal validity, and seek to demonstrate their relation to other examples of divine sapience, were originally the great doubters. Augustine, one of the greatest intellects of Christianity, once confessed:[7] "There is much in the Gospel which I believe only on the authority of the Church." It will be readily understood that they followed the technique of skepticism and heresy. The great teachers of the Talmud learned and practiced the sophistical and dialectical tricks of their adversaries. The great Al Asch'ari himself (874–935) had been a Mutalizite, and had introduced the science of the Kālām in the orthodox colleges of Islam. The great systematizer of Catholicism, Thomas Aquinas, the *Doctor angelicus* of the Church, reveals on every page of his mighty *Summa theologica* how much he had learned from doubt and unbelief. He himself makes a series of objections to the dogmas of the Church, bringing against them arguments and lines of reasoning which are finally refuted. Moreover, for every heresy he adduces a number of arguments in its favor, showing, for example, that *simplex fornicatio*, which is strictly condemned by

7 *"Ego vero evangelio non crederem nisi me catholicae (ecclesiae) commoveret auctoritas"* (Contra ep. Manichei, 5).

the Church, is not a deadly sin. In rational theology, in apologetics and dogmatics, heresy and dogma are in intimate contact. Here faith and doubt have their rendezvous, and since both are masked their countenances are hardly distinguishable. The primary ambivalence which conveyed the love of God and unconscious hostility toward God in the same expression appears in the endeavor of dogmatics to draw closer to God—as in the hymn "Nearer, my God, to Thee."

In all religions the secondary elaboration begins with the conception of God and the proofs of God's existence. The conception of God, as Freud has indicated, has grown out of those psychical conflicts which arose from the ambivalent impulses of the son in respect of the powerful father. The revolt of the son, the great primal act of patricide and the consequent psychical reactions of conscious guilt—the longing for the father and the defiance of the son—have uplifted the primeval father to the status of God. The proofs of God's existence are intellectualizing overcompensations in respect of an insurrection against God. The logic which deduces, from the contingency of all created beings, an absolute Being; from the causality of all things, a first, self-created Cause; from the voice of conscience, the existence of a universal moral law, is precisely like the logic of the obsessional neurotic. By just such pseudo logic the neurotic will seek to justify his belief in demons. Nothing more closely resembles the arguments of the obsessional neurotic in respect of the problem of the immortality of the soul than the justifications of various dogmas and apologetics. As the most certain proofs (*signa certissima*) of supernatural revelation such "external criteria" as miracle and prophecy are adduced. On studying the dogmatists the reader will often be struck by the comparison with the obsessional neurotics who speak of the "omnipotence of thought" because, having thought of a certain person, they immediately see him passing. In both cases we have a vicious circle. The belief is primary, and out of its hypotheses evidence is now fabricated in order to justify it. In the antimodernist oath the priest has to swear that the existence of God can be proved, that miracle and prophecy are the most certain proof of Divine revelation, that the Church was founded personally and immediately by the historical Jesus, etc.

In obsessional neurosis the compulsive speculation is extended more especially to subjects in whose nature it lies that we cannot know anything about them (immortality, duration of life, the life of the soul after death). The rationalization of the mysteries of faith is the basic character of the doctrine of dogmatics, "that curious hybrid formation of bold and religious fantasy and discriminating logic."[8] They determine most exactly the attributes of God; the difference between the genesis of the Son and that of the Holy Ghost is precisely defined (*generatio, spiratio*); the relations between these three Persons are described, the why and how of the Creation and the causality of God in respect of evil are expounded. The sins of the fallen angels, their punishment, and the precise constitution of the soul are established. The statements of dogmatics in respect of the modality, the hierarchy, and the distribution of the angels have that pleasing exactitude which is so deplorably lacking in scientific assertions. Science may pronounce only with hesitation upon death and life, the origin of the world, and the end of the world, but the catechism knows all about them. Here the indescribable is not only effected, it is also most precisely described.

It is particularly interesting to note the modes of connection into which the secondary elaboration enters in order to establish a relation between the latent and actual motives of an element. As in obsessional neurosis, so in theological thought this connection often depends upon the misunderstanding of the wording of a statement. In dogmatics the choice of words in the Old and New Testaments is adduced for the purposes of a pseudological justification of a statement. For example, the actual birth of Christ as the son of Mary is defended against the Gnostics by Tertullian by pointing to the fact that Christ, according to the Scriptures, was born not *per virginem* or *in virgine* but *ex virgine*.[9] Paul interprets the words of God in respect of the Creation: "Let us make men after our own image" as a proof of

8 Heiler, *Der Katholizismus*, p. 361.
9 *De carne Christi*, p. 20.

Christ's existence; for God says, "Let us." From the promise to the seed of Abraham (Gen. XXII, 18) he draws the following conclusion: "It does not say: 'to the seed' in the plural but in the singular; and *thy* seed—that is, 'Christ.' " From the wealth of material offered by the talmudic Halacha we will allude merely to the interpretation of the word "only" in the plan of Jisroel for the Jews; as an example of Islamic theology we have the statement that the appearance of Mohammed is prophesied in the New Testament, the word *Paraclete* being interpreted as *Periclytos.*

Another mode of connection is employed in dogmatics as frequently as in obsessional neurosis; namely, symbolical interpretation. Compare, for instance, the thoughts of my patient, who was struggling with blasphemous ideas, with the interpretations of the Scholastics. The patient once had the peculiarly nonsensical idea that a gold-embroidered armchair was writing in his album. The solution of this obsessional idea was furnished by its genesis: he must at some time when he was in the bathroom have struggled against the blasphemous thought that God was a toilet upon which one seated oneself.[10] In defense, he had at once to entertain the antithetical notion of a luxurious armchair from an aristocratic drawingroom. Later on in the day he thought, how many distinguished gentlemen had perpetuated their names in his album, and he indulged in all sorts of ambitious fantasies, how many of the great ones of the earth might not still write in it? It was not merely a continuation, but a grotesque satire of this train of thought, when he reflected that God Himself might sign His name in the album. The inclusion of this image of God, a gold-embroidered armchair, provides us with the solution: a golden armchair writes in his album.

10 Originally: did God also sit on the toilet? The association of blasphemous thoughts with coprophilic ideas is especially noteworthy. This patient immediately associated *water-closet* with the name Jesus Christ, because both designations consisted of two intimately connected words. An obsessional neurotic from a puritanical milieu was reminded, by the sight of the toilet, of the biblical phrase "the throne of Grace." As a candidate for confirmation a patient pondered over the question, whether the sacred host was expelled with the stools; the communion cup, in obsessional thinking, was likened to the bedroom chamber, etc.

We will take a relatively simple example of such a symbolical interpretation from the theological sphere: Paul, in those passages of the Old Testament in which the angel of the Lord is mentioned, saw Christ as the angel. The rock from which Moses drew water (Exod. XVII, 6) can, of course, only have been Christ, for they "did all drink the same spiritual drink, for they drank of that spiritual Rock that followed them, and that Rock was Christ" (I Cor. X, 4).

Dogmatics reminds us more especially of the curious mixed formations of obsessional neurosis which Freud has called deliria. Like these latter, they show that they cannot escape the influences and objections of conscious factors. In neurosis these mixed formations appear as products which establish themselves by rational means on morbid foundations. We may recall the speculations of Johannes Damascenus, as to which day of the week the angels were created; how they multiply themselves, since they have no bodies; whether they have a language; and whether they occupy space; and the calculations of Gregory of Nazianzus, as to how many angels there are. It was in this delirious fashion that Anselm answered the question, whether Christ's death benefited His enemies, who crucified Him (*Cur deus homo*, II, 13). Here too we may cite the satisfaction theory of Anselm of Canterbury. It is an excellent example of a delirious formation; it proceeds from the question whether Christ's death was voluntary. Christ acted on his own behalf, not as the representative of humanity. But the Father has to requite him for this. Yet nothing can be given to him, for he has everything. It would be a blasphemy to assume that all the actions of the Son were without effect. It is necessary that they should benefit another, and if the Son is willing the Father cannot resist him, for otherwise He would be unjust. So He attributes to men, as His kinsmen, the merit of Christ (II, 19). Here one thinks of the subtle considerations and justifications which the Talmud tractate Beza devotes to the problem, whether on the Sabbath it is lawful to pick up a splinter lying in the courtyard and use it as a toothpick.

One of the special tasks of system formation, and in particular of the secondary elaboration in obsessional neurosis, is the reduction and adjustment of the contradictions between the individual obsessional thoughts. As the patient endeavors to establish the freedom from contradiction and the continuity of his symptoms in his consciousness, so rational theology directs its endeavors to ensuring that the contradictions and inconsequences within the doctrines of religion shall be eliminated, bridged over, or veiled. The infallibility of the Church is dependent on this attitude. The attempts of the obsessional neurotic to form a closed system become intelligible. Åny considerable rift in the system causes the collapse of the whole fabric; or at least it will begin to crumble. The true believer can no more allow this than he can allow a stone of the house in which he is living to become loosened and give way. Like the casket in *The Merchant of Venice*, the Church seems to admonish the questioner: *"Who chooseth me must give and hazard all he hath."*

We are to understand that doubt in respect of an unimportant detail of the dogma is doubt of God himself. Scheeben[11] says very justly that the most essential thing is infallibility of doctrine, "so that if this doctrine were false even only for a day and on one point the Church would collapse, and all its erudite truths would lose their validity." The severest cases of obsessional neurosis exhibit the same iron consequence and the same tremendous resistance, and the same inflexibility, even in details, as orthodox Catholicism or talmudic Judaism. But the Church has made the most stupendous efforts to preserve the unity and the unassailability of its religious doctrines. A monstrous ingenuity was exercised, from the days of the Apologetics to the Dogmatists of our own time, and intellectual efforts and campaigns of a heroic nature were necessary in order to achieve this end. Renan exclaims in admiration that really, "fundamentally, few persons have the right to disbelieve in Christianity. If they knew how

11 M. J. Scheeben, *Handbuch der katholischen Dogmatik,* Vol. I, Freiburg 1873, p. 101. Ernest Renan has emphasized this imposing rigidity and inflexibility of Catholicism (*Souvenirs d'enfance et de jeunesse,* 1885). He understands how right was his teacher at Saint-Sulpice, that as a Catholic one must be consistent. "A single error proves that a Church is not infallible; a single inept passage proves that a book is not 'revealed'" (p. 292). And elsewhere (p. 301): "For the Church to admit that Daniel is an apocrypha of the time of the Maccabees would be to confess that it is mistaken in other respects, that it is no longer divinely inspired."

strong is the net prepared by the theologians, how difficult it is to tear one of the meshes, what scholarship has been expended upon it, and what practice is required before it can all be unraveled!"

Only the psychoanalyst, who for many years has taken pains to follow all the modes of thought, doubts, obsessional ideas, reasonings and mediations of the obsessional neurotic, can judge of the amount of intellectual energy and labor expended upon the construction, development, and systematization of obsessional ideas. And here again there is a kind of analogy between the attitude of the outer world toward the mental labors of dogmatics and toward those of obsessional neurosis. In most cases the family and friends of the neurotic have no notion of the extent, and still less of the intensity and scope of obsessional thinking. The lay believer has just as little notion of the intellectual achievements of dogmatics and apologetics.

Here the asocial character of obsessional thinking is akin to the nature of theological speculation, which is exclusive and accessible only to individual priests and religious scholars. But the congruity of the two phenomena goes even farther; for the believer is sometimes ignorant of the wording of the dogmas; he is not even aware of their exact content; he can say nothing as to their creation or their mutual interconnection. He may have vague, imaginative religious beliefs, but he certainly has no knowledge of the precise content of the views acknowledged by the Church. The religion of the priest and that of the simple believer are—strictly speaking—two different phenomena. For who would assert that the giver and the receiver of the sacrament have the same ideas as to its nature and effect? The subtleties of dogmatic Mariology have nothing to do with the popular conception of the sorrowful Mother of God, who graciously looks down upon the distress of Margaret. The Church is content with this state of affairs. Of Christians it requires only *fides implicita;* that they shall profess indiscriminately those beliefs which the Church prescribes. In all highly developed religions the knowledge of dogmatics is confined to a narrow circle. The simple sheep of the Christian community accepts without pondering upon it the belief of his pastor, just as the Amhorez of the ghetto accepts the ideas of the rabbi, and the unlettered Muslim the decisions of the Ulema. Even the obsessional neurotic is ignorant of the real wording of his obsessional ideas. He learns it for the first time through the painstaking analysis which undoes the work of an extended distortion.

It is indicative of the kind of secondary elaboration which we have described, and also, in particular, of the operation of unconscious psychical powers, that the methods which rational theology employs are the same in all religions, whether we consider the dogmatics and apologetics of Catholicism, or the Halachoth, or the Kālām. Everywhere we find the same triumphant syllogisms; the same dazzling pseudo logic, which works in the void; the same reference to ancient, mutilated and misunderstood texts; the same false associations and conclusions, which ignore all historical development; the same confusion of dates and circumstances; the same uncritical spirit as that prevailing in rational theology.[12]

The ontological proof of God's existence, as we read it in Anselm of Canterbury, appears in every rationalistic religion—from the fact that the conception of a perfect being exists it necessarily follows that we must conclude that he exists. The reference to sacred texts, the pseudohistorical tracing of a dogma into the remote past as though it had existed from eternity, these "mousetrap methods"[13] of theological logic and demonstration, the spurious consistency and conclusiveness, make their appearance in every theological system.

We find the same farfetched associations, the same omissions, the same unconvincing proofs, the same forceful attempts to exclude contradictory facts, in Catholic dogmatics, in the Talmud,

12 One has only to open any work of Catholic dogmatics—for example, Josef Pohle's *Lehrbuch der Dogmatik* in seven volumes—and read the traditional proofs, the justification by Scripture, the fundamental principles of interpretation and exposition, and compare with these the theological methods of proof and interpretation revealed by the Talmud, the entire syllogistic system as it slowly developed out of the rules of Hillel, as well as the corresponding portions of the Fikh books of Islam, in order to realize that these analogies are not fortuitous, but based upon profound psychical similarities.
13 Schopenhauer's term for the Euclidean method of demonstration in geometry.

in the Fikh literature of Islam, and in obsessional thinking.[14] The agreement between the kind and the operation of the secondary elaboration in theological discussion and in obsessional thinking will impress every sincere student of both phenomena.

In individual cases, in which religious problems occupy the foreground of the obsessional thoughts, they affect even the details, and thereby testify to the homogeneousness of the psychical life of humanity. The obsessional neurotic of whom I have spoken often employed the same arguments and counterarguments, in fighting against his blasphemies, the same doubts and the same alleged proofs, as those we find in the works of the Fathers of the Church and the Scholastics. But even in the cases of obsessional thinking which deviate from this any dogmatist who studied them objectively would detect similarities with the methods of his own science. It is this identity of the psychical motivation, and of the psychical mechanisms, the identity of the repressed instinctual impulses and the repressing factors, and not a revelation from Heaven, which gives the Church the courage to assert that it teaches *quod semper, quod ubique, quod ab omnibus creditum est.*[15]

14 Popper-Lynkeus points to the extremely interesting impulse of human nature "to support religious and metaphysical assertions by means of derisory arguments." To the thoroughly rationalistic thinker it seems that he has discovered a remarkable law, the law that in theology "in those cases where one wishes to operate with arguments founded on reason or with philosophical arguments, there is always a sort of concealed dishonesty (of course, usually unconscious), whose exposure is not always an easy matter, but which one senses even when one cannot detect it, and by whose cool audacity one is positively flabbergasted" (*Über Religionen*, 1924, p. 38). One sees how nearly Popper-Lynkeus has arrived at the analytic views of dogma, and yet how far he was removed from them, since he saw in it nothing but fraud and trickery. The associations which we have traced enable us to realize the unconscious necessity of this law, of which Popper-Lynkeus had no conception. I have alluded to what has been said in the above work in order to show how much deeper psychoanalysis leads us than a merely rational conception of the problem of dogma. Popper-Lynkeus's indignant repudiation of belief in dogma is perhaps explained by his description of the impression produced by the ontological proof of the existence of God: "After listening to such a philosophical-theological hoax one feels as though pinned to the ground, and positively paralyzed with astonishment at the nerve with which such juggling is accomplished."

15 Naturally, Islam makes the same assertion. The Catholic doctrine of

7. *FIDES ET RATIO:* THE TWO CONVICTIONS

The great Thomas Aquinas and all *doctores ecclesiae* have endeavored to bridge the contradictions between faith and reason. But these contradictions cannot be denied. Indeed, there are countless mutual disagreements and uncertainties in the Holy Scriptures on which theology relies. Sylvester de Sacey, who paid special attention to the quotations from the Old Testament which occur in the New, had much difficulty in justifying them. With a heavy heart, he had finally to agree on the principle that the two Testaments, each taken singly, are infallible; but that the New Testament is not infallible when it quotes the Old.

The magnificent attempt to harmonize *fides* and *ratio* which we find in the theology of Thomas Aquinas pointed the way for the Church. Faith becomes a recognition of God, a *cognitio* of the Divine. "The cathedral of the Christian theory of revelation has a portico in natural theology." According to ecclesiastical doctrine there is no contradiction between the truth of faith and the truth of reason, between *Lumen divinae revelationis* and *Lumen naturalis rationis,* since God is the source of all truth and knowledge.[1]

But there is "no religion within the boundaries of reason." Reason depends on the function of reality, but faith on authority. Ecclesiastical dogmas, as *"veritates a coelo delapsae,"*[2] and the views of reason cannot harmonize. From an early period insuperable obstacles made reconciliation impossible, especially as the Church sternly insisted on every point of its doctrine.

---

the infallibility of the *consensus* corresponds with the Islamic dogma of the *idschmā*. "My community will never agree in error," the Prophet is alleged to have said; thus constituting the recognized teachers of the community as a whole as an infallible Church. The Church is even on the point of "assimilating" psychoanalysis, by means of its infallible logic. It is true that it complains of the immoral "overvaluation" of sexuality, but it endeavors to re-create and transform that portion of the analytic doctrine which it is able to utilize until it believes it can recognize in it what the Church has always taught, and what is already written in the Gospels. A few clever priests have displayed a thorough understanding of psychoanalysis; but also the inflexible though concealed intention of employing it in the service of the Church.

[1] Thomas Aquinas, *Summa theologica,* I. 9. I. a I.
[2] Syllabus Lamentabili, prop. 22.

Today the Catholic is pledged to believe in the devil, and in exorcism, and to acknowledge the bodily admission of Mary into Heaven as the necessary *conclusio* of the Marianic dogmas. All interpretations are rejected. The fire of Hell is an actual fire. Anyone who assumes that the fire of Hell may be a metaphor for the spiritual torments of remorse is guilty of a *sententia temeraria* and incurs the danger of learning for himself the real nature of hell-fire.

When it comes to a conflict between science and faith, human reason has to give way to the supreme, Divine reason. The great truths of the sacrament or the Trinity are not contrary to reason: they are superreasonable, above ordinary human reason.

The contradictions between faith and science were at last dispelled by the doctrine of the twofold truth, which emerged in the Middle Ages. Siger of Brabant formulated this epistemological doctrine about 1270, which subsequently was accepted by many of the teachers of the Church. According to this doctrine a thing can at one and the same time be true for philosophy and untrue for theology. We see here that every possibility was provided for. If it proved impossible to bridge the difference between the contradictory statements by reality the second expedient was chosen. Faith must be permitted "to say yes when agnostic science says no."[3] Actually Abelard called his great work "Yes and No" (*Sic et Non*),[4] and for every thesis he wrote arguments *pro* and *contra*. In reading the works of such scholastics as these we find ourselves surrounded by the atmosphere of obsessional neurosis.

The doctrine of the twofold truth, which was first expressed by the Arab Averroes, may be regarded as a parallel, in religious psychology, to the peculiar trait which so often makes its appearance in the obsessional symptomatology: the existence of two convictions regarding one and the same thing. If, for example, an obsessional neurotic believes in the power and in-

[3] "Programme of the Italian Modernists," *Reformkatholische Schriften*, Vol. II, 1908, p. 147.

[4] Abelard's method was primarily directed to expounding the contradictions in tradition. The work has to all appearance a skeptical tendency, which undermines authority, but in the Prologue the author announces his intention of mutually reconciling the authorities ("*solvere controversias in scriptis sanctorum*").

fluence of demons, this does not by any means exclude the possibility of his being at the same time a freethinker. Lichtenberg once observed that one can be afraid of ghosts without believing in them. Obsessional neurotics often entertain two different and mutually opposed convictions, between which they oscillate. One is in accordance with their sane human intellect, or common sense, and the other in accordance with the morbid, obsessive nature of their mental operations. It is as though these two widely separated convictions lay upon different planes. In the "deliria" of the neurotic we recognize mixed formations containing both kinds of ideas, which may correspond to the rational endeavors of theology to explain the mysteries of faith. The ratios of admixture are different in every case and every situation. It may happen that an obsessional neurotic may smile contemptuously at some superstitious view of which he cannot divest himself, and which completely dominates him. This characteristic entertainment of the twofold conviction is in complete correspondence with the theological doctrine of the twofold truth. Even the arguments which are employed in defense of the twofold truth can be compared with certain considerations which the neurotic advances in order to suppress the resistance to the obsession. One of my patients made use of little amulets, such as ivory monkeys, images of Indian gods, etc., which he always had with him, in order to protect himself against the failure of his intentions, etc. When the analysis had progressed so far as to reveal to him the unconscious motivations of his phobias, and the protective measures which he had adopted, he no longer carried the amulets. But once, before taking an especially decisive step, he put in his pocket, before leaving the house, a little image of a god, which was supposed to avert all misfortune, telling himself: "Even if it's no use, it doesn't do any harm. But if anything were to happen to me I couldn't help thinking: this has happened because I hadn't the amulet on me." One may compare such reflections with the arguments which religious people employ in defense of their faith when all other resource fails them; as, for example, Pascal's reasoning, as recorded in his *Pensées:* "The reason cannot decide whether there is or is not a God. From this standpoint one can lay a wager as to whether there is or is not a

God. But one must wager that there is a God, and must live in this belief, because hereby one wins everything if God really exists; but loses nothing if God does not really exist; while by the wager that God does not exist one wins nothing if one is right, and loses everything if one is not right." As one sees, such reflections might very well be made by an obsessional neurotic. And they were indeed made by an obsessional neurotic!

The schism in the treatment of the dogmas, which are suprarational and yet amenable to rational consideration, corresponds completely with the schism in the obsessional ideas which exist deep in the unconscious, and resist all reasonable explanation, and which the patient still seeks to explain by rational motives.

It is difficult for us to enter into the psychical life of the obsessional neurotic, because we cannot easily judge the inconsistencies and contradictions contained in the contrast between a mentality adapted to reality and a morbid mentality, nor can we easily understand their coexistence. Only analysis has shown us how these peculiarities of obsessional neurosis are to be understood. In the majority of cases there is a splitting of the personality, in which an ego under the control of the repression is opposed to the rest of the ego. In these cases of obsessional neurosis the malady has not gained a hold upon the entire personality; large segments of it have remained intact, and treat the obsessional idea as something alien to the ego.[5] The historian of Japan, Michel Revon, tells us that some two hundred years ago the philosopher Arai Hakouseki summed up the result of his conversation with a Jesuit father who had come to convert the Japanese to Catholicism in these words: "In this man there are

---

5 The Benedictine Paschasius Radbertus, in his theory of the Eucharist (*De corpore et sanguine dei;* about 830 A.D.) was the first to express the belief that the sacramental body in the Eucharist is actually the same body which Mary bore and swaddled and laid in the cradle, etc. Harnack, in his abstract of Radbertus' manuscript, calls attention to the many problems which the great sacramental controversy, despite much ingenuity, has left unsolved: "Deep calls unto deep; inasmuch as in the time to come the men of greatest understanding give ear to this call, and notwithstanding remain reasonable in other respects, they prove that the most absurd speculations in the province of religion do not necessarily mean a sick mind" (*Dogmengeschichte,* Vol. III, p. 316).

really two men contained. When he speaks of the science of his country he is worthy of admiration, but as soon as he begins to speak of religion he talks at random and becomes childish. It is as though one listened first to a sage and then to a fool."

8. THE TABOO OF THE DOGMA

The estimation of the dogma as suprarational serves to protect it from disintegration; it forbids discussion by alluding to the inadequacy of the human understanding. Here is one of the traits which constitute the taboo of the dogma that appears in every religion. Its separateness from all other knowledge manifests this sacramental character: here again it is analogous to the obsessional idea, which does not exclude acute criticism and objective observation in the other departments of life. The imposition of the taboo shows how intense is the unconscious hostility toward the consecrated treasures of the faith. According to Dante, above the gates of the Christian Paradise stand the words: "Me also eternal love created." The history of the dogma, which leads to eternal blessedness, tells us that this inscription might more justly be: "Me also eternal hatred created."

It is a decisive feature of the taboo character of the dogma that it appeals to the *auctoritas dei,* from which it derives its origin. Any doubt of the dogma is therefore an affront to God; any criticism of the dogma is blasphemy. In all highly organized religions God is the *auctor scripturae,* the author of the Holy Script. The dogmas are therefore God's Word, and not only because they originate from God, but also because they have proceeded from God through the inspiration of the authors of the Scriptures. The Church proclaims the doctrine of *inspiratio verbalis.* Belief in the Scripture is more than an assent of the understanding; it is an agreement (*consensus*) on the part of the believer, who submits himself to the authority of God.[1] From the

1 Dogmatics emphasizes the point that God has the right expressly to require us to believe: "By God, then, who as our Creator and Lord is worthy of our absolute respect, and who can at the same time command belief, we are absolutely obliged, by reason of the respect which we owe Him, to take for granted the truth of His least words, when He commands our belief in a specific truth. Herein there is no necessity of positive proof or even the pre-

authorship of the dogmas it results that God is not only the content but also the basis of faith (*"Prima veritas auctoritas dei"*). The Vatican has declared that the truth of dogma is accepted *"propter auctoritatem dei revelantis, qui nec falli nec fallere potest."* The Vedas, the Thora and the Koran have to be accorded the same belief. The origin of the Vedas is described as an emanation of the god Prājapati, and as part of the creation of the world. Its meters and strophes are world powers, and the fate of the world hangs upon its literally correct transmission and exposition. While the Church declares that God dictated the dogmas to their holy authors as an ordinary author dictates to his secretary, the Jewish theologians inform us that there can be no contradictions and no omissions in the Thora, because it was dictated word for word to Moses. The authorities were unwilling to grant that even the last passages, in which the death of Moses is described, were as some think added by Joshua. Consistently, the rabbis consider that up to the last eight verses, in which his death is recorded, Moses repeated the words after God, and wrote them down; but these last verses he wrote in silence, with tears in his eyes. Islam asserts that the Koran is the eternal, uncreated word of God, and the extreme followers of Mohammed even declare that the individual written copies of the Koran will last throughout eternity. The Mutalizites, who considered that the Koran was part of the created world, and who had the impudence to doubt whether the suras in which Mohammed's uncle is cursed showed signs of divine origin, were treated as heretics. The dogma of the uncreated Koran was of course in many instances difficult to maintain in the face of the content of the book; nevertheless, all the contradictions arising out of its content must be tolerated if one would declare its eternal validity and unimpeachability. It is clear that the dogmas could exhibit no mutual contradictions if they were transmitted by God to Christ, by Jehovah to Moses, or by Allah to Mohammed. Accordingly no substantial alteration of a dogma was possible, and

---

sumption of the positive and absolute holiness of God, for the absolute presumption suffices that God could not possibly be personified untruth" (Scheeben, *Handbuch der katholischen Dogmatik*, Vol. I, Freiburg 1873, p. 278).

no progress, but only an explicit formulation. To be sure, there were dogmas which were not explicitly formulated, and which were subsequently proclaimed by a Council or by the Pope *ex cathedra*. Since Pio Nono, in 1854, declared that all believers in the doctrine of the Immaculate Conception of Mary must believe that those of another opinion were damned by their own judgment, there has been for the last hundred years a new condition of salvation, the belief in this dogma, which was not previously required. In this case there was merely a process of elucidation, which brought to light the dogma contained in tradition. The so-called included dogmas were thus transformed *in dogmata explicita*.

In the dispute regarding verbal inspiration it was asserted that God's authorship of Scripture extended even to the writing of the Hebrew vowels and consonantal points. The *traditio divina* had serious consequences: not only that Scripture itself was for all time valid, infallible and unalterable, but so also were the decisions of all those who like Scripture were filled with the Holy Ghost.[2] Sanctity and infallibility are contagious: Christ was the immediate ambassador of the eternal Father, and proclaimed that which the Father had deposited in him as "the treasury of the wisdom and knowledge of God." So the Apostles, sent forth by Christ, proclaimed what they had heard and received from Christ and his Spirit, which was entrusted to them as to "living books of the Holy Ghost." So the successors of the Apostles proclaimed what they had heard from them, and their successors proclaimed what their predecessors entrusted to their keeping. This truth transmitted by the Apostles and their suc-

---

[2] According to Heinrich Wetze and Welte (*Kirchenlexikon*, Vol. 2, Col. III, pp. 1879 f.) the reason for the concealment of such included dogmas can be equivocal: "It may be because the truth in question was indeed directly expressed, in Scripture, and in ecclesiastical tradition, or even in an instruction of the Church, but not with such lucidity that everyone, or at least every well-educated and discerning believer, could recognize it with ease and certainty. In this case the truth is directly revealed and propounded by the Church, but not with sufficient lucidity. There is here, as the theologians say, a *revelatio et propositio formalis et immediata, sed confusa et obscura*. Such a revelation has been called *quasi implicita*. For those truths are in the real sense *implicita* which are not directly and formally contained in the revelation and proposition of the Church, but only as it were in principle, from which they have followed by logical operation."

cessors is that *traditio apostolica* which demands unconditional belief.

The power of the Pope is based upon the continuing power of the religious taboo; and so is the inerrability of the successor of Peter as the supreme shepherd. Judaism, like the Church, declares that the whole doctrine, spoken and written, is one great revelation, comprising both earlier and later revelations. The Ten Commandments and the interpretations given many centuries later by the Sofrim were communicated to Moses on one and the same day (Meg. 196). The whole of the Mischna and the Gemara, all that in future ages a diligent scholar would recite to his teacher, were revealed to Moses, proclaimed upon Mount Sinai (S. Berg. 5a Meg. IV. 1). Thus God gave to Moses not only the oral but also the written Thora, which comprised everything, as the Bible contained all later dogmas. This oral tradition was transmitted from Moses to his successors, to the heads of the colleges of that period, and from generation to generation. The authorities so contrived, at least before the time of Hillel, that only such dogmatic decisions should be regarded as they had received from their teachers. These teachers, on principle, had acted in the same way, so that the opinion under consideration could be traced back to Moses. "They subjected the repository of the tradition to a regular examination. He had to confirm by an oath that he had heard the legal decision from his teacher."[3]

Here we have evidence of the uniformity of psychical processes: So long as Mohammed was alive, there was apparently but little difficulty in communicating directly with Heaven. On the transfiguration of the Prophet his speeches and his typical actions became the *Sunnah*, the standard of the community. Apart from Allah and his messenger, no authority was regarded as competent to establish a commandment. The life of the Prophet was rich in incident, but there were only a few persons living who remembered all its details. The questions asked were out of proportion to the existing material, for answers were required not merely to questions of religious worship, and dogma, and civil and criminal law. As a matter of principle, questions were put concerning the forms of salutation, table manners, what

[3] Cf. Jakob Fromer, *Der Talmud*, Berlin 1920, pp. 45, 77 ff.

should be said beside a sickbed, etc. Now a sort of *pia fraus* was perpetrated, precisely like that which we find in the Talmṵd:[4] "The customary form of obtaining information regarding a point in question was the following: A has told me that B told him that he had heard from C (and so on, according to the distance dividing the speaker from the age of Mohammed) that one day the Messenger said so and so, or acted thus or thus. The enumeration of the transmitters is known as *isnâd* (props); the text of the narration *matn* (text). The chain of witnesses and the text together constituted a *hadîth*, a tradition, and the totality of these narrations was also called *hadîth*." These collections of *hadîth* were now accorded canonical validity. The stupendous amount of material which these books contained, comprising every imaginable subject, and including the most heterogeneous components, was thus referred back to Mohammed. The continuation of the *Hadîth* collections, which was devoted to commentaries on the *hadîth*, was the Fikh literature.

We cannot expect to find exactly the same phenomenon in the domain of obsessional neurosis. After all, the dogma is a social creation, and not, in spite of all points of similarity, an obsessional idea. But there are similar phenomena which, *mutatis mutandis*, permit of further such comparisons. The taboo character of the dogma, which maintains its importance, has been produced by displacement. The protection which deity conferred was displaced upon all doctrines which related to the nature of God, all views concerning His worship, and all persons entrusted with ceremonial or ritual observances. Accordingly, all depreciatory and dubious and refractory thoughts were regarded as aggressive attacks upon these doctrines. The texts which express truths relating to God, Christ and the Church were protected no less than these sacred personalities themselves, and any contradiction of them was regarded as *crimen laesae majestatis*. There is no better safeguard than to allow such doctrines to emanate from God himself—to make him their author. They are thereby isolated and acquire a special position outside and apart from other declarations.

---

[4] See C. Snouk-Horgronje, in *Lehrbuch der Religionsgeschichte*, Vol. I, Tübingen 1925, p. 697.

This special treatment of the dogmas, which makes them taboo, reminds one of the oldest injunctions of obsessional neurosis—the taboo of touching. The avoidance of contact and touch plays a prominent part in obsessional neurosis, and becomes the central point of extensive and often complicated systems of prohibition. Freud has told us why it has such a great importance; touch is the most immediate aim of affectionate as well as of aggressive object cathexis. The mechanisms of displacement, and of regression, which lead to the replacing of thoughts by deeds, enables us to understand why associative connections, which might be called contacts of thoughts, are prohibited. The chain formations through which the dogma of Catholicism, Islam and Judaism demonstrates by intellectual transmission the continuity of its existence reminds the analyst vividly of those negatively accented delirium formations which in a neurotic suffering from a washing obsession represent the "impossibility," the taboo, of an object. Gloves, for example, are taboo because they were in the pocket of a winter overcoat which the patient was wearing when he passed through a street in which an acquaintance was living whose cousin died of tabes dorsalis after syphilis.

Every analyst is aware of the importance of the avoidance and prohibition of forbidden thoughts in obsessional neurosis. He knows that this difficulty of avoidance constitutes a special impediment to the resolution of obsessional ideas. Certain critical, aggressive and sexual thoughts are excluded, because they do not harmonize with the claims of the superego; and especially such thoughts as relate to persons near and dear to the patient. It is as though the inhibition had projected itself from action to mental activity. These thoughts ought not to be thought, and they are not consciously entertained. The associative link between them and other thoughts is broken. They are isolated, and their domain is like a reserved area.

The *noli-me-tangere* nature of dogma has peculiar consequences: It forbids one to take any further steps toward investigating that which might not be in agreement with the views of the Church. Strictly speaking it indeed forbids unbelievers, or those who differ in any point from the views of the Church, to concern themselves with theological questions. Even Tertullian (*De praescriptionibus haereticorum c. 20*) has declared that the Catholics denied heretics the right to make use of the Scriptures, making it impossible for them to formulate objections. Indeed, the Church declared that the direct employment of the Holy Scriptures "is not for all persons and under all circumstances salutary, so that the Catholic Church with exalted wisdom has decreed various precautions in this direction."[5] Here, then, as the Talmud puts it, "hedges about the law" are erected. Such intellectual avoidances are quite analogous to the precautions by which obsessional neurotics assure themselves against contact with forbidden impulses and thoughts. Tertullian says expressly that "familiarity with the Scripture has its roots in the ruminating spirit. The thirst for knowledge takes the place of belief; the thirst for fame takes the place of spiritual welfare. To know nothing contrary to the rules of faith is to know everything!" Later on the Church required of the layman only assent to the Creed, or *fides implicita,* and in other matters referred him to the discrimination of the Church. It knew that the researches of the individual would lead him into temptation and error, and sought, in its love, to protect him against this peril. In the Abbé de Ségur's book, *Brief and Confidential Answers to the Most Widespread Objections to the Catholic Religion,* we read: Question: How can the body of Christ actually be present in the consecrated Host? That is surely impossible. Answer: I have only one answer to give you, but that is surely sufficient. It is so, therefore it is possible. It is so, therefore you must believe it, even if you cannot understand how it can happen" (the words "It is so" are printed in especially large type).

The prohibition of thought which is thus implicitly imposed may be compared with the paralysis of thought which we often observe in serious cases of obsessional neurosis. The obsessional neurotic to whose symptoms I have often referred for comparison showed at one time such an intellectual inhibition. When blasphemies with all their corrosive power, were threatening to irrupt into his consciousness and win dominion over his

[5] Scheeben, *Handbuch der katholischen Dogmatik,* Vol. I, p. 124.

intellectual life, he forbade himself all reading, all conversation, all social activities, because everything he heard and saw suggested a blasphemy. He even wore dark glasses, so that he would not be obliged to see, and for several days he remained in a sort of mental lethargy, in which he vegetated, dull and mechanical, lest he should be compelled to blaspheme. I will only add, in order to indicate the practical thoroughness of such precautionary and conciliatory measures, that he was compelled, several times a day, to stand absolutely motionless in one spot, and to stare straight in front of him without seeing anything. He was positively the image of an Indian fakir; though he reminded me even more strongly of the pillar saints, the Stylites of the desert, which the Christian legends have described with such pious earnestness, and Anatole France with such covert irony in his *Thaïs.*

But the taboo of the dogma extends still farther; it relates to all who proclaim it. The Catholic priest is called "Right Reverend" with the very words employed for the Sanctissimum.[6] The entire clergy, up to the bishop and the Pope, is thus taboo. Boniface could say, "The faithful are obliged to follow the Bishops even on the road to Hell." Indeed, the faithful have often been overjoyed to follow their shepherds along this road, which is not paved only with good intentions.

It is characteristic that the Church can censure a heterodox doctrine, or one that in some respect is in disagreement with the dogmas, and that this censure possesses the same character of infallibility as its positive decisions. If we read the numerous stages of these judgments we shall realize how hard the Church has tried to maintain the taboo of the dogma and to protect it against all objections.[7] The graduations of censure, and also its

6 It is perhaps not generally known that a Catholic is actually forbidden to accuse or indict a priest in a secular court of law. "The fear of the taboo is so extreme among the Catholic people that no one dares to say anything detrimental to a priest without expressly exempting the sanctity of his office. The locution: 'Our pastor is a rogue—apart from his sacred function' may often be heard among the Bavarian countryfolk" (Heiler, *Der Katholizismus,* p. 180).

7 By the so-called *Notae theologicae vel ecclesiasticae* all the possible kinds of infringement of the Catholic creed are very definitely described. The judg-

justification, bring us back once more to the psychology of obsessional thinking. In this also the patients subject their own opinions to a censorship, and are careful as to which thoughts they admit to consciousness. When in analyzing an obsessional idea we think we have recognized the existence of an impulsion, an instinctual urge, or a thought as responsible for the obsessional idea, we often learn from the patient that such an impulse or thought did actually emerge on a certain occasion, but was repulsed as irrelevant, unsuitable, immoral, etc. From the nature of the psychical reaction we can then judge how profound or decisive the impulse or thought in question must have been.

We shall now more readily understand the phenomenon which recurs in every constituted religion—a phenomenon which shows that theology, as we saw in the Arian conflict, is literally unwilling that a single jot or tittle of its dogmas should be sacrificed. It is not only the fact that the dogma comes from God that determines this attitude. It is rather the taboo character of the doctrine that demands such absolute and literal reproduction. The Church declares that if it had erred in a single point, or in

---

ments pronounced by the teachers of the Church (*sententiae judicales*) are as infallible as the positive proclamations of the Faith. A proposition is called *propositio formaliter haeretica* if it contradicts a formally announced truth, and *materialiter haeretica* if this is not the case; whereas one which contradicts an assured theological doctrine which is not formally proclaimed is *erronea*. Of the other terms of censure a few may well be cited, because, as with the taboo, their designations appear to reflect the degrees of the greater or lesser danger which they represent in respect of the dogma to be protected: *Sententia haeresi proxima, sententia falsa, sententia temeraria, sententia scandalosa, sententia blasphemia, schismatica, seditiosa, sententia de haeresi suspecta* (which in itself may have an orthodox meaning, but according to the circumstances under which it is uttered, or on account of the personal or religious character of the author, etc., might be understood in a heretical sense). For example, the proposition that the sinner can attain justification through faith may under some circumstances be heretical, inasmuch as it might be suspected that this proposition is intended to express the doctrine of justification as preached by the Reformers (*sola fides*). A *sententia piarum aurum offensiva* is a proposition which offends pious ears ("One must not name to pious ears what pious hearts could not desire"). This is a proposition which might be given an orthodox meaning, yet in itself or by reason of external circumstances it might be regarded as a heresy. A *sententia captiosa* is a maxim which by reason of its artful phrasing attempts under the semblance of truth to conceal an unecclesiastical or heretical meaning.

so slight a matter, for example, as the nature of Cain's death, its entire edifice would collapse.

The obsessional neurotic thinks and acts in precisely the same manner. For example, if a nervous patient who is suffering from a germ-phobia, and who has been sacrificing many hours a day to his washing obsession, should chance to brush against someone in the street, or should notice a speck of dust on his clothing, all his precautions were evidently futile, all his pains were in vain, and he must again subject himself to an extensive course of purification. The breaching of the system at a single point, no matter how unessential, is treated, psychically, as though the whole system were imperiled. A single contradiction in a dogma, like the remotest contact with the prohibited in the obsessional symptomatology, is a mortal failing hard to bear, since in the one case it contradicts the secret prohibition, and in the other it is simply irreconcilable with the divine origin of the dogma.

By the restrictions of taboo which underlie the dogma we are reminded of the many restrictions and precautions which primitive peoples observe in respect of their chieftains and kings.[8] In respect of this analogy it will be understood that the tabooing of the "King of Kings" extends also, and in particular, to all thoughts referring to him, while the taboo of the savage is restricted to the acts of contact. In explaining this difference we shall not allege that the heavenly Ruler is so far removed that all palpable contact is impossible, for there was a time when the forests and meadows of this earth were peopled by Gods. We are thinking rather, in considering this extension of the taboo to the world of thought, of a development and displacement of the taboo in the sense of the progressive nature of the secular repression.[9] Thus, while in religion itself the Word progressively dis-

---

[8] Cf. Freud, *Totem and Taboo.*

[9] It is certainly in conformity with the character of unconscious processes that the old taboo prohibitions should remain in force even when fresh objects are interpolated. Naturally, the taboo of the priest persists. If we wish to gain some idea of the extension of the primitive taboo in Catholicism, we have only to recollect the contagious influence of relics, of the consecrated water (*aqua benedicta*), of the amulets bearing images of the heart of Jesus, Saint Benedict, Saint Aloysius, or Saint Anthony, of rosaries, of incense, and of

placed the Act, so the weight of the taboo was progressively displaced from action to the thoughts and feelings. In this we should perceive not only an enhanced conscientiousness, but also, assuredly, the reaction against the temptation to aggression displaced from motor activity to the realm of the intellectual faculties. Simultaneously with this extension and displacement of the taboo there is really an approach to the primitive phenomena of the taboo; for the restrictions of the taboo were imposed against aggressive, cruel and hostile thoughts and impulses.

If we study the taboo character of the Faith and its content it will be clear to us that here God appears as the wielder of the mysterious and dangerous power that acts like an electrical charge. In the taboo of the dogma we are dealing with the mental concern with this dreaded object, which is subjected to extreme restrictions. We shall understand that this charge of magic can be transferred, that faith must be protected against every trivial objection, and that the power of contact may find expression in a negative as well as a positive sense. We shall better understand, moreover, that the holiness of God and his decrees is communicated to his Son, his messengers, and his prophets, and is propagated to the first apostles and teachers, and so on, down to the present Pope, Khalif or Zadik. It makes no essential difference whether one says: these men to whom the magical power was communicated have much *Mana* or *Orenda*, or whether one declares that the Holy Ghost has enlightened them and conferred infallibility and inerrability upon their decisions.

In the sanctity of belief, moreover, we see yet another character of the taboo, which manifests itself in two mutually opposed forms of operation. Faith makes the believer blessed, but unbelief condemns him to eternal torment. A savage chieftain or a mighty king of the ancient world had only to touch a sick man,

the sound of bells. The Sanctissimum still retains the fullness of its sanctifying power. The connection between the Catholic religion in its developed form and the oldest and crudest forms of religion was never really interrupted. In the decree of the Holy Office of August 5, 1903 the ecclesiastical authorities gave it as their official decision that the swallowing of images of the saints dissolved in water is a permissible usage (Mirbt, *Quellen zur Geschichte des Papsttums*, p. 400).

and he was healed of his sickness in a moment. But if one of his subjects touched him or anything belonging to him the punishment inflicted for the violation of the taboo fell upon him and he died automatically of the consequences of his crime. We obtain a hint of the first kind of magical power from the theory of consecration, and also from the Church's doctrine of grace. A profitable task for a trained analyst and religious historian would be to refer the many and minutely different kinds and degrees of grace, which according to the Christian conception is a bestowal of supernatural aid from Christ's "Treasury of Merit," to these ancient tabooistic ideas.

But for the breach of the faith taboo there is punishment, and this, more especially, betrays the continued operation of the ancient conception of the taboo. The original, negative conception, which threatened the offender with the pains of hell, is gradually repressed by the positive conception, which assures believers of eternal blessedness. Although salvation may still constitute the central point of the believer's expectations, and although "going to Heaven" may be the final goal of all his wishes, these ideas are certainly not primary. They are not merely developed from the general belief in the continuation of our earthly existence in the other world, and in an eventual compensation for the renunciation of earthly joys. They represent rather a reaction against the calamitous expectations of believers subjected to temptation.

Belief has first of all to be confirmed by the salutary fear of death. The Church threatens the unbeliever with the most hideous punishments, with the hell where the servants of Satan torment the damned with red-hot pincers and frightful instruments of torture. Anyone who has heard a mission preacher of the Capuchin or Redemptorist orders preach a sermon containing a vivid and exhaustive description of the pains of hell will know why the Catholic demands absolution, the last unction, and the sacrament of the altar before he dies.[10]

[10] Even the belief of Christians in heaven and hell has decreased in our time. The other day a French writer cynically remarked that considering the climate, he preferred heaven, but with regard to company he would prefer hell.

It is no longer death that is dreaded, but the future world. Religion has intensified the fear of death. At the same time, by appealing to humanity's sense of sin and guilt it has touched on one of the most important sources of this fear. The notion of Resurrection and the Last Judgment at the end of time has still farther increased the individual's fear of death.[11] In fact, the feeling of doom in the beyond has sometimes replaced the fear of death. Hamlet wants to die but "there's the rub." For in that sleep of death what dreams may come is "the dread of something after death" that puzzles the will.

Here we perceive that the infringement of the taboo of the dogma brings with it consequences no less fearful than the infringement of a taboo among savages: he who does not believe incurs the punishments and pains of Hell. The character of belief, as an act of love, and of unbelief as the expression of unconscious hostility, explains this rigid consistency. The unbeliever's sense of guilt is the result of a reaction to those unconscious aggressive and revolutionary instinctual impulses against the Father Deity, and the neurotic's anguish of conscience, corresponding to this sense of guilt, is not unrelated to the "wailing and gnashing of teeth" of the believers who see themselves being swallowed by the jaws of Hell.

We shall understand presently why in the opinion of religion

11 It has also, of course, increased his hopes, unless he shares the skepticism of Heine:

> When we are dead, then you and I
> Long in the grave will have to lie.
> The Resurrection, I greatly fear,
> Will not so very soon be here!

For comparison, consider the eschatology of Islam. In this also belief is the condition of salvation. Beside the deathbed those present recite the 36th Surah of the Koran, and give the dying man the hastily whispered creed as viaticum. Even when he lies in the grave the creed will be recited to him. After he is buried the angels Munkar and Nakir will visit him and question him as to his beliefs and his works. If his replies are not satisfactory he will be chastised. At the end of time will come the Last Judgment, awaited by humanity with terrified anticipation. The final scene of world history is described in the eschatology of Islam with the same dramatic power as in the Christian eschatology. Gustav Mahler has expressed the sense of guilt associated with this conception in the last movement of his Second Symphony.

unbelief should be attended with such frightful consequences. Even the ancient religions—for example, the Egyptian—foresee a great judgment of the dead, but then only good or bad deeds will be judged. This, of course, is done according to the later religions also, but in the later stages of religious evolution the unbelief of heresy is *kat exochen* one of the most terrible sins. Here we will be content with the provisional statement that unbelief has taken the place of insubordination and aggression. This corresponds with our psychological expectations, with the spiritual bases of belief as described in these pages, and with the unconscious sense of guilt and anguish of conscience, if in the last resort not even faith alone is regarded as a sufficient protection against the repressed hostile impulses. Paul may proclaim the "law of love" as against the law of works (Rom. III, 27), and announce: "Without faith it is impossible to please Him" (Heb. XI, 6); yet the same Paul knows: "And though I have all faith, so that I could remove mountains, and have not love, I am nothing" (I Cor. XIII, 2).

Analytic examination of the nature of dogma reveals that it is inviolable and taboo, because every attack upon its content of belief includes an attack upon God and his representative. It is just the strict application of the taboo, prohibiting any criticism of dogma, any rapprochement of the *mysteria divina* and human understanding, that shows how intensive these unconscious hostile tendencies are. The taboo of dogma arises from the ambivalent emotional attitude of believers toward God and the beliefs associated with Him; His very existence is a reason for the unconscious lust of aggression on the part of His worshippers. It is not only the heretics, the apostates and atheists against whom the taboo of the dogma is established; but in particular the possibility of aggression on the part of believers has to be repressed and excluded. But is not that which is so carefully protected in urgent need of protection?

Dogma is supposed to point the right course to the erring and ignorant soul, as the lighthouse points the way to the ship tossing on the waves. But a profound saying tells us that "there is a darkness at the foot of the lighthouse."

9. THE COMPULSIVE FACTOR IN DOGMA

The taboo of the dogma may be derived from its origin in God and his chosen prophets. As the last representative of this inspired series appears the reigning Pope, who corresponds absolutely to the priest-king of primitive tribes. Through him speaks the spirit of God. *"Tu es Petrus et super hanc petram aedificabo ecclesiam meam et portae inferi non praevalebunt adversus eam."* These words, displayed in huge golden letters on the dome of St. Peter's Church in Rome, announce the solemn charter of foundation of the Roman Papacy. Christ, the Son of God, who of course never dreamed of the foundation of the Church, is supposed to have spoken these words in a solemn hour. The tabooing of the Pope expresses itself in those characteristic forms which we find in the injunctions of the priest-kings of the primitive peoples. Actually the Pope is "the prisoner of the Vatican."[1] But what power he possesses, this carefully guarded sovereign over millions of souls! And how much greater the power which he once possessed! His word is God's Word, perfect and infallible. The entire Catholic world bows itself humbly before the religious decisions of the occupant of the *sedes apostolica*.

The peculiar part played by faith in the nomistic religions is explained if we rightly estimate the factor of obedience in the act of faith. The Church declares faith to be an act of intellect no less than an act of will. Faith is an intellectual credence of that which God has revealed for the salvation of mankind. At bottom, however, it is in ecclesiastical doctrine an act of obedience, a deliberate submission to the *auctoritas dei*, which demands belief. Indeed, the Church itself speaks of *credere debere* (Tertullian, *de praescr. haer.* II), of the duty of belief, of obedient belief. In the *sacrificio dell'intelleto* which is made to faith no very great sacrifice is offered in the case of many pious folk. But in others the intellect's will to resist has to be broken

---

[1] Pius X once declared: "It is not enough that they have made me a prisoner; they are going to bar the doors too, and wall up the cellars, so that I cannot get out again" (Ignis Ardens, *Pius X und der Päpstliche Hof*. Transl. by Maria Textor, Leipzig 1908).

down. "The will overcomes all skeptical objections, it tramples underfoot all contrary personal opinions, and so compels the intellect to bow itself under the *lex fidei*."[2] Heiler records a categorical explanation given by one of the leading theologians in the Vatican to a German savant who complained of certain difficulties of belief: *"La chièsa non è un credo, la chièsa è una disciplina."*

In accordance with the obedience comprised in the act of faith, belief in Catholicism counts as a merit, and unbelief as a grave sin. The first "spontaneous" doubt is already a sin, which must be fought and suppressed. If it is inwardly approved it becomes a deadly sin.[3] In order to guard believers against the temptation of doubt they are forbidden, in the *Index librorum prohibitorum*, to read any dangerous literature. The "immediate occasion" is avoided, much as in the symptomatology of a *folie de toucher* a situation is avoided in which the dreaded contact with forbidden objects would be possible.

To the Curia freedom of conscience and freedom of expression are a *pestilentissimus error,* as Gregory XVI declared. The Church used to deliver Christian heretics to be broken on the wheel and burned at the stake. The beneficent flames of the pyre (*"O benedictas rogorum flammas!"*) with perfect impartiality saved Christian heretics and Jews and Mohammedans from living a life that was not worth living, since *"extra ecclesiam non est salus."* Anyone who has studied the history of religious persecution and the Inquisition knows that the pious zeal of the Church exceeded that of all other religions.[4] The pagan Romans sacrificed many Christians for political reasons, but they did not burn them *ad majorem Dei gloriam,* and the crudity of their philoso-

2 Heiler, *Der Katholizismus*, p. 242.

3 The coexistence of two convictions (which has already been mentioned) and also the continuous psychical effect of doubt, is demonstrated by the fact that in theology we can approach a dogma "not with the actual doubt" but with the so-called "methodical doubt" ("Christlich-Katholische Dogmatik" in *Systematische christliche Religion, Kultur der Gegenwart,* p. 53). The dogmatists would never admit that the "methodical doubt" might also be a real doubt, but they appraise it as a proof of the "dogmatic freedom of movement despite all constraint."

4 H. C. Lea, *History of the Inquisition of the Middle Ages,* 3 vols., 1888; and *History of the Spanish Inquisition,* 4 vols., 1906-7.

phy prevented them from correcting deviations from the orthodox faith by means of the rack and the autodafé.[5]

No pious believer, unless he is a theologian, has a precise
knowledge of the individual dogmas. But this is not necessary;
he has access to eternal salvation if he professes: "I entirely
believe all that the holy Catholic Church propounds for belief."

Luther's grim mockery of the *fides implicita,* of "blind faith"
(lit. "charcoal-burner's faith") did not prevent the Reformers
from punishing every serious doubt just as cruelly and rigidly.
Melanchthon claimed that authority should suppress the astro-
nomical doctrine of Copernicus as a revolutionary heresy, and
the physician Michael Servetus, who had cast doubt on the ecclesiastical doctrine of the Trinity, was burned alive in 1553 by
the Calvinistic Council of Geneva.

The *Fides implicita* is strictly required by the Church.[6]
Even the priest, whose faith is based on his knowledge of the
dogmas, and is therefore *fides explicita,* must profess, in the
antimodernist oath, that he believes every individual dogma (the
consecration of the seven Sacraments by Christ, his presence in
the Host, the immaculate conception of Mary, the infallibility of
the Pope) and that he expressly condemns all dissenting opinions.[7]

[5] "In no religious community on earth, apart from Islam, did the fanaticism of faith perpetrate so many bloody sacrifices as in the Roman Church.
While such a heathen religion as Buddhism has never in its long and ample
history erected inquisitory tribunals and pyres, the Church has practiced mass
persecutions of its Christian brothers" (Heiler, *Der Katholizismus,* p. 322).
Pius IX, only 80 years ago (1869), received one of the cruellest and most
bloodthirsty of the Spanish Inquisitors, Pedro Arbues, among the saints.
Nietzsche described Christianity as "an executioner's metaphysic" ("*Götzen-
dämmerung*").

[6] "*Ego firmiter amplector ac recipio omnis et singula, quae ab inerranti
ecclesiae magisterio definita, adserta et declarata sunt*" (Mirbt, *Quellen zur
Geschichte des Papsttums,* p. 426). In the *professio Tridentina* the formula
runs: "*Simulque contraria omnia atque haereses quascunque ab Ecclesia
damnatas et rejectas et anathematizatas ego pariter damno, rejicio et anathe-
matizo*" (Denziger, *Euchiridion,* No. 863).

[7] Pope Innocent III announced: "The *Fides implicita* is, as some say, so
valuable that if anyone, moved by his natural reason, is wrongly of the opinion that the Father is greater or earlier than the Son or that the three Persons are three spatially divided beings, or the like, he is not a heretic and
commits no sin, provided he does not obstinately defend this error, and believes it only because he believes that the Church believes it and thereby submits his opinion to the belief of the Church."

Not with the same strictness, but in the same sense, faith is required by all the established religions as a precondition of salvation.[8]

Augustine justified the custom of compelling those who had not yet obtained eternal salvation to enter the Church, since God had not spared his own Son and for our sakes had delivered him to the executioners. This principle of enforcement in the name of the Church—the formula *"compelle intrare"* corresponds with Islam's "holy war" (*jihad*), which originates in the belief that the Muslim theocracy is the only justified political community on earth.

The volitional factor in faith, the factor of submission which perceives in faith an act of obedience and which silences all objections, represents the factor of compulsion which finds its correlate in the psychical peculiarities of the obsessional idea. At the same time, we must not overlook the differences between the two phenomena. In the obsession of the neurotic we have an idea or an opinion of an individual which despite all objections is suppressed. In faith we have a great social phenomenon which requires obedience even despite the criticism of the human understanding. This difference is decisive in respect of the attitude toward the outer world. While the neurotic generally keeps his obsessional idea to himself, and, of course maintains it in spite of all his own objections, religion proclaims its doctrine, endeavors to become a general, comprehensive organization (*ecclesia catholica*), and in its periods of power does not hesitate to establish and confirm its supremacy over men's souls by violent means. Compulsion is for the neurotic as for the theologian an attempt to compensate for doubt. This attempt is made with the greater energy in proportion to the strength of the impulses against which faith has to defend itself. From the violence of the reaction we must deduce the intensity of the action. Obsessional neurosis is governed by a continual conflict with the re-

---

8 Even in Islam, for example, all depends upon faith (*imân*). There, as in Catholicism, faith is accounted a divine gift of grace. Of course, faith is withdrawn from human observation, so that even the believer himself cannot be confident of his own faith until he is dead. But he who makes his profession to Islam (*schahâdah*) and manifests submission (*islâm*) must be treated as a Muslim.

pressed material, which increasingly favors the repressing forces. In this conflict the obsessional phenomena are the defensive measures which most successfully prevent or delay the victory of the repressed impulses or thoughts. In the same way the obsessional element of a dogma is a means of making it impossible for doubt to irrupt into the fabric of religion.

The rigidity of a religious belief corresponds to the rigidity of the superego as it appears in obsessional neurosis. It is influenced by the regression and the admixture of impulses in the id, more importunately and unfeelingly than in hysteria. Through regression the aggressive tendencies of primeval times are reawakened, but a great proportion of the libidinous impulses themselves assume a cruel or hostile form. In religion also, through the influence of regression, the demands of love are frequently expressed in a violent and often cruel form. The Crusaders, who were inspired by religious zeal, massacred Turks and Jews with the cry: *"Dieu le veut!"* The love in whose name Christianity was founded had given place to hatred, to sheer hostility.[9]

There had been a time when the love of God embraced the community and made its members brothers in Christ, but with the passage of time blind submission to the Church was demanded and enforced with brutal severity. Christianity was a religious revolution, which was originally directed against the scribes and Pharisees, demanding freedom in place of the strict law of the Jewish religion. But the insulted and dethroned God revenged Himself; the *lex Christi,* no less dogmatic than the Thora, assumed supremacy. When the old imperatives were replaced by new, even more urgent, ones, the dogmas of Judaism were presently matched by a vast number of ecclesiastical dogmas. The path led from rebellion to subsequent obedience, just as we see it in the obsessional neurotic.

Faith may be demanded ever so categorically, representing the first and most important condition of salvation; a stern God

---

[9] The Headmaster of Eton in Shelley's time, Dr. Keate, who regarded thrashing as a necessary means of achieving perfection, ended a sermon on the Sixth Beatitude with the words: "Now, boys, be pure in heart! For if you are not, I'll flog you until you are!" (André Maurois, *Ariel: The Life of Shelley,* 1925, p. 1).

may demand first and foremost the elimination of the personal will and blind submission—just as the peremptory superego and the instinctual id of the individual obsessional neurotic compel him to admit the most absurd ideas—despite all that there is in the domain of religion also a hint that this obedience may not be the last and the spiritually decisive thing. Christianity knows that faith alone, unless hope and love (or charity) be added to it, "neither joins a man perfectly with Christ nor makes him a living member of his body" (Tridentinum, 6, c. 7).

In the place of the three faithful Parcae of the Greeks, Christianity has set three other sisters: Faith, Hope, Love. Analytically interpreted, these three principles appear as reactive phenomena: faith as a reaction against the impulses of doubt and rebellion; hope as a reaction against the foreboding of evil associated with the unconscious sense of guilt; and love as a reaction against repressed impulses of hostility.[10] According to Catholic doctrine, the order of this series is not reversible; the highest place is held by love. The history of Christianity, which I have placed in the foreground as representative of every religion, has demonstrated that religious evolution must lead to a reversal of the order. Love of the begotten Son of God, of the Kyrios and Saviour, stands sovereign and central in its early stage. The longing for salvation, the hope in the Kingdom of God, determines the character of Christian piety in its prime. Faith, or rather the profession of belief, becomes the criterion of the declining religion.

Religion has not conferred the same power of expression

---

[10] The Council of Trent cited first faith, then fear, whereby the sinner is profitably distressed; then mercifulness, in the hope that God will be gracious to him for Christ's sake; and finally the primordial love of God as the source of all righteousness. According to Catholic dogmatics it is accepted as a *fidei proximum* that the three godly virtues, Faith, Hope and Love, are infused into the justified soul simultaneously with the sanctifying grace (*virtutes morales infusae*). The above comparison of the three theological virtues with the Parcae is by no means arbitrary. Pohle (*Lehrbuch der Dogmatik*, Vol. II, 5th ed., 1912, p. 578) calls faith, hope and love the "exalted company of virtues." They appear as a sacred *trias* in I Cor. XIII, 13: "*Nunc autem manent fides, spes, caritas, tria haec; major autem horum est caritas.*" The three virtues appear personified in theological speculation as well as in the arts.

upon the three great sisters. Faith spoke aloud in the Creed and in dogma. Hope whispered and stammered in prayer. But the third . . . ah, the third stood beside them, and was mute.

10. THE LATENT CONTENT OF DOGMA

It cannot be denied that the obsessional element in religion becomes apparent at certain stages of the evolution of religion. It proceeds from its nature inevitably as cruelty and intolerance. There are, it is true, more kindly and tolerant religions. There are some which have encountered no appreciable opposition, or are no longer a match for the opposing forces. It is with religions as it is with governments; so long as they have no reason to fear for their sovereignty they are gentle and peaceable in their attitude to other states. They practice this virtue also when a conflict with more powerful nations is utterly hopeless. In our days there is so much humanitarian chatter about tolerance that in the interest of truth one ought to find the courage to say: Tolerance is in the first place a question of power. The beautiful souls who are never weary of announcing that man is good ought really to find cause for reflection in the fact that he inclines to tolerance only when he has unrestricted power or is completely powerless.

But we will not now discuss the obsession or compulsion in dogma, which is explained by its psychological premises; compulsion would at most yield a contribution to the psychology of the belief in the nonsensical content of dogma. What should concern us here is rather the problem: On what does belief in the reality of dogma depend? Or, in other words, the problem of the psychological nature of dogma itself. For many inquirers the question is answered as soon as it is asked: Dogma is simply priestly cozenage and mystification. For Popper-Lynkeus the nucleus of dogma may be defined as follows: "It is never anything more than indemonstrable conceits of superstitious fantasy, contrary to reason and science, which conceits are (suddenly) by ecstatics, or (gradually) by theologians administered to mortals in their feebleness, and subsequently, by all manner of means, surrounded with such a halo that in spite of their trivial or arbitrary character, or their absurdity, one no longer has the intellectual courage to reject them *a limine*" (*Über Religion*, p. 69). The humanitarian, the student of ethics and the rationalist in this philosopher, who all his life has sung the praises of the high achievement of the human intellect, has stated the problem too simply. Perhaps the shadow of Voltaire fell too darkly on the pages which Popper-Lynkeus wrote two hundred years after the great liberating works of the French Enlightenment. At all events, he comes nearer to the truth than the views of systematized philosophy, which boasts of its religious independence and its profound insight, but for which the dogmas are "to be apprehended as transformations of inherently transcendent intellectual ideas" (W. Wundt, *System der Philosophie*). A philosopher[1] of our own days speaks of the "transcendent superreality" of dogma. The object of belief is, of course, not actual as our house is actual; yet "it has in another sense an even higher reality than this; indeed the ordinary reality is to be regarded only as the temporally transitory modus of that . . ." Vague and unmeaning pronouncements of this kind do not become more comprehensible and sensible through being uttered, as it were, from the verge of the cosmos.

Theology says much the same thing, only in rather different words. Dogmatics will assuredly agree when the philosophers assert that the crucifixion of Christ is a profound allegory, and the sacrament the most significant of metaphysical symbols. Theology, of course, will at the same time declare that the Saviour, really present in the Host, was truly and actually executed by the Jews. But it wishes people would not speak of rope in the hangman's house, even in dogmatic parlance. From this point there is no path leading to the great mass of people who either believe in the dogma without knowledge of it, or who have not heard the Gospel and have not faith.

Here we shall consider faith as a kind of deliberate belief; an intellectual phenomenon which in certain directions is distinguishable from the purely emotional content of religion. The Church lays special stress on the volitional and intellectual elements in the act of faith. It is an intellectual, appreciative assent

---

[1] R. Müller-Freienfels, *Grundzüge einer Lebenspsychologie*, 1924, p. 297.

to the revealed truths taught by the Church. Every emotional apprehension—such as that expressed by Schleiermacher, for example, to whom the propositions of the Christian faith appeared as "verbal interpretations of the mental disposition of Christian piety"[2]—is flatly rejected by the Church. Faith is not to be regarded as the subjective aspect of piety, but as the belief in the objective content of dogma, the acceptance of its objective reality. What matters is not—primarily, at least—what religious feelings are aroused in the individual by thoughts of the Holy Trinity, but that he should believe in the existence of the Trinity and in its nature as represented in the dogma.

But what does this belief signify? How is it comprehensible that religion declares the real existence of the Trinity, and the effect of the Eucharist as that of the partaking of Christ's real flesh and blood, etc.? Are we dealing merely with priestly cozenage, the infatuation of the masses, and delusion, or are the dogmas actually to be regarded as "transformations of inherently necessary, transcendental intellectual ideas?" I think the alternative is inherently false. The question cannot be answered on this level. The problem will be more readily solved if we try to apprehend it from the psychological standpoint. We need not concern ourselves at this stage with the value or worthlessness of the dogma; what we wish to know is its psychological meaning. For even if it comes straight from heaven it is meant for human beings. It will become their psychical possession, it will meet with assent or rejection in the emotional life of humanity. The problem before us is therefore a psychological problem, and we are acting in a perfectly legitimate manner if as psychologists we deal with it according to our own methods.[3]

We must return to our narrower province, to psychology, if we wish to know what this belief is to signify. We find a related element in the psychology of the dream. It often happens that

[2] Schleiermacher, *Der christliche Glaube nach den Grundsätzen der evangelischen Religion*, Vol. I, 6th ed., p. 15.

[3] Here it may be mentioned that the older theologians distinguished between *Dogmata rhetorica* and *Dogmata practica*: revealed truths of the faith and revealed doctrines of morality. In the modern terminology the term dogma is restricted to truths of the faith in the narrower sense. The present volume conforms with this terminology, now accepted by theology also.

after waking from a dream belief in the reality of the dream images continues for an unusually long time, so that one can only with difficulty shake off the impressions of the dream. But we should be wrong to assume that we have here a delusive judgment, which is determined by the vividness of the dream, and that the peculiarly real character of the dream, which is productive of certain aftereffects, is entirely without significance. It would be equally a mistake to accept it literally as a confirmation of the dream content and to recognize it as characteristic of a prophetic dream which has lifted the veil before the future. These two opinions correspond more or less to the two attitudes toward dogma which we have already described as typical.

Freud has shown us that this feeling of reality after a dream is a psychical action in itself, a confirmation, depending on the dream content, that something really is as we have dreamed it. At the same time, there will often be distortions, due to displacement, which will prevent the conscious mind from realizing to what this character of reality should actually be ascribed. It is the same with delusions. If the patient firmly believes in his delusion this is not because his power of judgment is perverted, but because there is a iota of truth in his delusion; something is concealed in it which really merits belief. But this fragment of truth has been repressed long since. A distorted substitute for it has formed itself, and the sense of conviction, which is often extremely strong, now attaches itself to this substitute. The sense of conviction of the numerous possibilities of infection in a case of compulsive washing cannot be affected by argument. The patient sticks to his opinion, unshaken, because there is something in it that rests upon a fragment of experience: namely, the unconscious recollection of the temptation to masturbate.

The same thing occurs in the case of dogma. The convincing nature of the dogma, which is extremely potent, must depend on a repressed fragment of truth, which defies all objections, and which has found a distorted expression in the formulation of the dogma. At this stage the form of the dogma will trouble us as little as the form of a dream, or a schizophrenic hallucination, or an obsessional-neurotic group of symptoms. We must look for the element of truth which corresponds to the sense of conviction experienced by the theologian, and by the believer. In so doing we discard the hypothesis of priestly cozenage. The priests may be extremely clever men, equipped with extraordinary powers of suggestion, and great authority, but a dogma could not be imposed upon the masses by their sole influence if there were nothing that responded to it in the psychical life of the community. Something in the dogma must seem real to the believer and must seem to correspond with his psychological needs. To put it briefly: the dogma transforms a fragment of an outmoded religious idea which was converted into a standard belief and translated into the idiom of logical concepts. It is accordingly nothing new in the emotional life of the pious, but a fragment of repressed reality. Its formation, as regards its content, cannot be described as an innovation, but as a renovation.

Against this qualification, which does not attempt to provide a definition, but merely to offer a psychological explanation of the nature of dogma, a number of objections present themselves. I will only point to the fact that the multifarious, indefinite, fantastic and rambling form of an ancient myth is in sharp contrast to the terse, precise, and intellectual conception of the dogma. For the time being we will concern ourselves only with the content of dogma, reserving the question of its form for later examination. We do not, of course, assert that an ancient, repressed myth, with all its characteristic features, enters into the dogma unchanged and entire. On the contrary, we lay stress upon the fact that it has undergone an extensive remodeling and stratification; that is, a distortion. Unless I am greatly deceived, it is precisely this fact which has hitherto prevented religious writers from recognizing the latent content of dogma and its connection with the ancient myths. Let us revert to our representative example: What is the Christ dogma but the intellectual envelope of the revived myth of the revolutionary son who rises against his father and is therefore punished with death? What is the nucleus of the Mary dogma but the myth of the great and kindly Goddess of Love, which has undergone a great transformation?

Judaism had concentrated all its energies on the endeavor to suppress the great figures of the pristine myths; in Christianity they made a victorious reappearance. In the hosts of the saints and angels we see a revival of the Olympus of the immemorial pagan religions; in the devils, the degraded gods of the pre-historic ages. The conceptions relating to the Eucharist are the ecclesiastical transformations of the old totemistic views. The idea of holiness has grown out of the notions of taboo. Baptism repeats the puberty rites of the primitive tribes in a superficially altered form; exorcism originates in the ancient ritual of ex-pelling demons. The doctrine of the Creation can be traced back to the cosmological beliefs of the earliest ages, soteriology to long-forgotten legends of redeemers, and eschatology to the opinions of the Egyptians and Babylonians. Everywhere, through the strata overlying the primary cause, we see the glimmer of old, repressed opinions and beliefs, against which the Church had so long guarded itself, and which it was nevertheless compelled to accept and transform in the sense of anagogic interpretation. Thus Islam had to assimilate the ancient Arabic belief in demons, and the ancient Arabic rites. Buddhism, in its Mahayanic form, had to absorb the folk religion of India. Yet this is not the decisive point. The most recent writers on religion have often recognized and described, as an essential element in the life of the established religions, their impregnation with primitive con-ceptions. But they have not perceived, much less solved, the problem of their relations to the dogma process. And yet we have here one of the most essential elements of a new psychology of religion; and only from this standpoint can some of its most im-portant questions be answered. How does a new religion come into being? How are its beliefs and its dogmas evolved? Essen-tially, it is a process of regression to very ancient, repressed be-liefs, which have had to make way for more recent ideas, adapted to the level of contemporary civilization. These primitive con-ceptions, returning from repression, constitute the latent content of the new religion, and are now transformed in accordance with the intellectual requirements of the period, and its social and political necessities. The recurrence of repressed religious

notions in an organized religious community means the emergence of a new religion, which is really a revival of a derelict
religion.

Judaism had arrived at one of the starting points of its religious evolution—devout belief. The observance of the law
constituted its central point: Its dogma was petrified, and the
whole of life was entangled in a network of commandments and
prohibitions. The people was politically and socially subjugated
under the potent influences of an alien culture, yet it held on
tenaciously to its inherited ideas. This was the moment when
Christianity emerged; it brought about a reversion to old, repressed religious material, a distorted substitute for long submerged myths and derelict forms of worship. But how did its
dogmas arise? We have traced the paths which led up to their
formation.

The new religion has first of all to differentiate the primitive
conceptions returning from repression from those of the old
religion, to liberate itself from the matrix of the ancient faith,
and to clarify its doctrines. It has then to safeguard these new,
though really very ancient conceptions against doubt, which
attacks them from within and from without. It had then to
subject them to a secondary elaboration which conceals their
deeply buried primary motives, and to make them consistent,
uniform, and in harmony with the thought and knowledge of
the age. The contrast between the ideas originating from animistic beliefs, which have already been superseded, but have
again become dominant, and the critical requirements of the
intellect, does not merely dictate the superstructure of rational
theology, which seeks to enforce agreement between these two
opposing factors. This contrast also determines the increasingly
intense obsession which suppresses the objections of the conscious mind and of doubt, and silences all contradictions by in-
voking Divine authority.

The character of dogma gradually becomes clear to us. Its
more essential content is a fragment of a suppressed but re-
emergent primitive religion in the shape of a displaced and distorted substitute. Its form is determined by several factors,
among which the tendency to synthesis and agreement with

rational thought is especially noteworthy. One of the essential motives of its creation is the endeavor to repulse the doubts and contradictions of the primitive myths and cults, which are opposed by the criticisms of an advanced culture, so as to suppress these countertendencies altogether. At this stage we shall observe the existence of a curious religious cycle: The extensive and comprehensive development of dogma, suppressing all contradiction, is bound to lead to fresh revolutionary efforts whose aim is to revoke and shatter it. All this is entirely in agreement with the phenomena of obsessional neurosis, in which fresh doubts attach themselves to the developed obsessional idea, which is itself a doubt overcome. The character of reality peculiar to belief in the dogma may be thus explained: it relates to the unconscious contents of the dogma, to those ancient myths and cults, and those concealed instinctual impulses which have found in them their veiled expression. This belief is perhaps comparable to that of the onlooker at a performance of *Oedipus Rex*. He feels, unconsciously, that the same repressed desires are active in him as in the protagonist of the drama, and he liberates himself from their importunate power by identification with the hero. In the belief in the Christ dogma, for example, the rebellious and sexual impulses, the filial pride, the sense of guilt, and the craving for punishment will find their unconscious expression. In the belief in the Sacrament of communion, all those pristine cannibal tendencies which long ago became alien to our conscious thought are reawakened. In all such beliefs there is a re-emergence of the conceptions of taboo to which we have long been strangers. The unconscious awareness of these psychical contents produces, when it encounters their representation in the dogma, that sense of familiarity, that species of *anagnorisis,* which we rediscover as an element of belief. I think we may safely assume that as the individual unconsciously recognizes fragments of his own repressed instinctual tendencies in the dogma, so, in the belief in the dogma, long discarded convictions of a forgotten early age emerge; just as the community unconsciously rediscovers in the dogma a long silenced echo of events of its primeval history. In the myths and cults the unconscious memory of the prehistoric age of human evolution survives. There are the memories of the

patricide of which the primeval horde was guilty; of the institution of the fraternal clan, which re-emerges when the members of
the community avow their brotherhood in Christ; of the great
feast of the totemic meal which is revived in the Eucharist. Accordingly, the truth contained in the dogma cannot be denied.
It is based on a psychical reality which is unconsciously understood and is received and conceived by believers as a material
reality.

The psychoanalytic explanation of the dogma as I have here
attempted it—of its emergence, and its position in religious
evolution—is impossible without an understanding of the dynamic processes in obsessional neurosis. This attempt takes as
its model the results of research into the psychology of obsessional neurosis. The obsessional idea also reveals itself as a
fragment of repressed material which has re-emerged from the
individual's childhood, and now, in a distorted, displaced, unrecognizable form, has seized dominion over the emotional life
of the individual. The contrast between such a repressed and
outworn conception and the rational thought of the adult explains a good deal of the development of an obsessional idea—its
isolation from the rest of the patient's thoughts, its secondary
elaboration, etc. Here again the duality of conviction adheres to
the displaced substitute, as in the case of dogma. Here again the
obsessional idea acquires its conviction from the fact that one or
more elements in it have psychical reality, and are related to real
events in the life history of the patient. The obsession protects
the supervalent ideas, or the dogma, from criticism and doubt,
and isolates the ancient conception operative in the obsessional
idea, just as it declares the primitive religious nucleus of the
dogma to be sacrosanct. The nature of God, His qualities and
attributes, the Creation and the Trinity, the Fall of Man—the
most important of the early chapters of dogmatics—may all be
understood as collective correlates of those psychical elements
which play an essential part in the genesis of an obsessional
neurosis—the *pater familias*, the mystery of procreation, the
relation of the son to his parents, the expressions of infantile
sexuality with their important psychical reactions and repercussions.

Dogma is the imposing cathedral which lifts its dome above the beliefs and the cults of a highly organized religion, enclosing them and guarding them against the crude reality. The architects of the Middle Ages believed that such a sacred edifice was consecrated only if a living man was buried under it—a belief from the dawn of religion. Deep under the floor of the gigantic edifice, which encloses the holiest elements of a religion, an unknown fragment of reality is actually concealed. There lies buried the omnipotent chieftain of the primeval horde, who was once upon a time murdered by his united sons, and who afterwards became the Almighty God.[4] Though the pinnacles of the cathedral may soar toward the heavens, its foundations reach down into those depths in which the strongest and most primitive instinctual impulses, the sexual and hostile impulses of humanity, have found their concealed satisfaction.

11. MIRACLE IS THE FAVORITE CHILD OF FAITH

The facts of the supernatural order are of importance in respect of the knowledge of God, as premises of a rational proof of God's existence, and as *praeambula fidei* for the supernatural belief in God. "Not Nature alone (Creation) but also Supernature tells human reason of the existence of God, and far more persuasively than the visible world. The proofs of God's existence from the supernatural world—the fulfillment of prophecies, the miracles of both Testaments, Christ, and his work—are contained, by reason of their nature, in the province of history, so that they impress themselves most profoundly on the consciousness of the historical research worker, though even the layman cannot escape their compelling evidential power."[1]

The miracle of the preservation of Israel, the entire history of the Old Testament, are accepted by dogmatics as proofs of

---

[4] An anecdote of the Renaissance depicts a similar situation. A bold condottiere had once saved the city, and the citizens took counsel together: What imperishable reward could he be given for his unprecedented service? A wise councillor came out with the surprising proposal: "We will kill him and afterwards pray to him as the guardian saint of our city!" (Fritz Mauthner, *Der Atheismus und seine Geschichte im Abendlande*, Vol. I, 1920, p. 549).

[1] Pohle, *Lehrbuch der Dogmatik*, Vol. 1, p. 19.

God's existence; the appearance of Christ, as well as the miraculous fact that Christianity transformed the peoples that were walking in the ways of evil, enshrouded in the shadow of death. What, were the miracles of Christ and Mary not to be taken literally—could there be no violation of Nature's laws? Why was it credible that the lame should be made to walk, the blind to see, and the deaf to hear, but not that the earth should be stayed in its orbit, that an ass should speak, and that a tempest should be stilled by a word? But this would be to destroy the harmonious unity of the evangelical record, which spoke of these things in the same breath! It meant more than this; it would place an ineffaceable stain on the moral character of Jesus, would degrade him to the status of a despicable charlatan, a common cheat! Accordingly, the miracles are true. This is the typical logic of dogmatics. The *signa certissima* of the supernatural criteria of faith are miracle and prophecy. Only on the strength of this faith can one assert the real, actual, essential presence of Christ, with flesh and blood, body and soul, Godhead and humanity, in the Eucharist. If the consecrated host is broken into fragments, or if the cup is swallowed in sips, yet Christ's body is present as a whole in every crumb and every drop. Transubstantiation, that mysterious change of substance, with its essential characteristics: the fact that the mere forms of bread and wine can persist without the proper substance of bread and wine, with the spaceless, spiritual mode of existence of a human body; the simultaneous existence of Christ in heaven and in many places on earth—these are miracles.[2]

2 As we have already stated, speculative theology has nevertheless endeavored to explain the mystery. The theological fact of multilocation, which contradicts natural law (for every body is by its nature restricted to *one* place) is unshaken. For the Catholic dogmatist the *fact* of multilocation in the Eucharist is evidence of its *possibility*. Nevertheless, he will manage to prove that the real body of Christ is present in every particle of the host (continuous multilocation); that the same body is not in one host alone, but in the many hosts contained in the ciborium, and truly present also on all the altars on the face of the globe (discontinuous multilocation); and finally that the body of Christ does not leave Heaven while at the same time it is present on a thousand altars in the Sacrament (mixed multilocation). It is quite in accordance with the ponderings of obsessional neurosis that extensive speculations as to the nature of space should be derived from the doctrine of the Last Supper; for example, the question of the relation between the Eucha-

It is childishly easy to mock at the belief in miracles. It is more difficult to explain them. Many believers accept the miracle simply and do not think about it. And many freethinkers do not think about it because, on the whole, they are not much given to thinking. As a matter of fact, the attribution of the miracle to natural phenomena is not calculated to explain it.[3] It sounds more paradoxical than it really is if I say that it is more necessary to understand the belief in miracles than to understand the miracles themselves. It is no magical feat to demonstrate the weakness of an argument which sees a proof that the living God spoke with Moses on Sinai in the fact that Mount Sinai still exists.

Even to point to the fact that men's convictions very, very rarely contradict their desires is insufficient to explain the belief in miracles. The psychology of the obsessional symptoms gives us the first glimpse of an explanation. An examination of the phenomena of the "omnipotence of thought," of the overestimation of the psychical power of the human being, will perhaps help us to understand those reports in which Christ's supreme power over the laws of Nature is made apparent (as in the miracle of the loaves and fishes, the changing of water into wine) better than the superficial expositions of the rationalists. Recognition of the unconscious happening, of the blindfolding of the intellect by the power of psychical processes, of the unconscious conviction of our observations, of the little unconscious conjuring-tricks which help to condition the miraculous happenings, and the punctual occurrence of foreknown events in obsessional neurosis, seems definitely more necessary than the dogmatic, materialistic denial of all the real elements in miracles. Just as in dogma there is really something true—namely, a psychical reality—so in the belief in miracles we may find a fragment of psychical reality which, though distorted and displaced, is taken for and confused with the material reality.

---

ristic body and the transfigured body of Christ in Heaven. Since a fresh creation was excluded, the question was, how the body already in Heaven could be present in the Sacrament. And since the body appeared to be present as a whole in every separate particle of the consecrated bread simultaneously, it became necessary to speak of a "spaceless present."

3 "Convictions are more dangerous enemies of the truth than lies" (Nietzsche, *Human, All-Too-Human*).

The miracles of Mary, the Mother of God, are many. "Mary, help us!" the people cry, and the Divine Spouse performs miracle after miracle for the poor earthly children who flee for shelter to the shadow of her wide, blue mantle.[4] The writer, not long ago, had an opportunity of divining something of the psychology of the belief in miracle. Since he himself is in a state of unbelief (*in statu infidelitatis*) and would not be deemed worthy of the prevenient grace (*gratia praeveniens*) or the concomitant grace (*gratia cooperans s. adjuvans s. subsequens*) which are necessary for belief, he himself has never yet come upon a miracle. This may be why he has never as yet seen any proof of the many miracles which have been performed by Our Lady at Lourdes, or by the Queen of Heaven at Mariazell.

Here, as we are considering the analytic understanding of dogma, I shall attempt to make only a contribution to the psychology of the belief in miracle, so that such supernatural experiences as have not been vouchsafed to me would appear superfluous. I shall speak rather of a drama whose essential content is one of Mary's miracles—a miracle whose profound and even overwhelming effect upon many people has been witnessed by many thousands of spectators—I mean the *"Mirakel"* of Karl Vollmöller.[5] I shall not here attempt an analysis of this ancient legend, sensationally produced and remodeled to suit the taste of the larger public; it will be enough to sketch the action of the play in broad outline.[6] In a cloister of the White Sisters on the

----

[4] The famous *Memorare* of Bernard of Clairvaux begins with the words: "Bethink thee, O kindly Virgin, that it has never yet been known that one who has sought refuge in Thee, who has appealed to Thee for help, and has pleaded for Thy intercession, has been forsaken by Thee;" and the author of the "Glorie di Maria," Alfonso di Liguori, has even made the faintly blasphemous assertion: "It is difficult to attain salvation through Christ, but easy to attain it through Mary."

[5] It testifies to the immense effect of this play that since the first performance, which was given in 1911 at Olympia, in London, before 30,000 spectators, the miracle play has been witnessed in Stockholm, New York (a thousand performances), Los Angeles, Berlin, and Vienna, by millions of spectators. The large scale of the production, and the "playing to the gallery" by the crudest of methods, may have had something to do with its great success, but the essential factor was the latent content of the play.

[6] This beautiful legend, which Vollmöller reproduced in an unusually coarsened and vulgarized form, first appeared in Caesarius (Dial. 7, 59). There

Rhine there stood, in the Middle Ages, the miraculous image of Our Lady, which had already brought healing to many of the sick and oppressed. In this convent lived the young and lovely Sister Megildis, who on account of her piety was granted the responsible office of sacristan. The young nun fell in love with a handsome knight, who had entered the church in one of the many processions that came thither. She followed the knight into the world, where she tasted love and knew terror. In the frenzy of passion she passed from hand to hand, until one night she gave birth to a child. Broken and forsaken, she fled back to the cloister, and fell on her knees before the image of God's Mother. Her child, swathed in rags, she laid at the feet of the Madonna. There, before the statue, she found, intact, the robe, the veil and the cross which she had long ago faithlessly cast aside. The holy Mother had, in the meantime, assumed the outward semblance of the fugitive nun, had donned her robe, and during all the time of her absence, while the abbess and the sisters took her to be Megildis, she had filled the office of sacristan. Now, once again, the statue comes to life; bending over the child of the sinner, swathed in its rags, she bears it in her hands as of old she had borne the holy Child Jesus.

Was the powerful impression produced by this miracle play due merely to the transformation of the auditorium into a vast cathedral, with images of the saints larger than life, the carved tracery of the chancel screen, the crypt, the stained-glass windows, the organ, the chancel, the candles and incense, the whole of the pageantry which made the Catholic Church appear "the painted harlot" to the inexorable Oliver Cromwell? Assuredly, no; the beautiful old legend did far more than the setting to impress the onlooker, by its latent content which, thanks to the producer, made itself felt even through the tinsel realism of the scenery.

Since miracles, for some unknown reasons, are so seldom produced in our days, we will study the belief in miracles in this theatrical example. The nucleus of the medieval legend is the miracle by which the lifeless statue of the Queen of Heaven

---

have been modern treatments of the motive in Gottfried Keller's *Die Jungfrau und die Nonne*, in Maeterlinck's *Soeur Beatrice*, and in John Davidson's *Ballad of a Nun*.

is transformed into the errant nun, whose sinful life is hidden from her sisters, while her absence is not remarked. But from the analytic point of view this substitution signifies an unconscious identity; it means that the immaculate Mother of God and the sinful nun are one single woman. The assumption of name and function, the exchange of garments, the acceptance of the illegitimate child as the Infant Jesus, seem to the analyst evidence enough of the unconscious equating of the two figures. And here, believe me, is a miracle! Of course, this is intended only to mean that motherhood makes every woman, even the harlot, a *Mater dolorosa*. But the concealed identity of the two figures seems to point to yet another, profounder meaning. The analytic investigation of the genesis of this psychical divorce between the pure woman and the harlot in the love life of humanity shows that these opposites seem to have been, originally, really united in a single object; that they are connected with the libidinous interest of the boy, diverted toward the mother.[7] The fact that the sinner is changed back into the Madonna, which we find in the latent meaning of "the miracle," is not the miracle; for behind this change is Mary's virgin motherhood.[8]

The great impression produced on the spectator must be due to the fact that the miracle of the drama has brought him closer, regressively, to the repressed knowledge of the real nature of Mary. But the impression produced by this substitution could not possibly have been so extraordinary if it had not, on account of the represented relation between the contrasted figures, awakened in every spectator a group of unconscious ideas—if by it he had not been unconsciously reminded of that original identity. What in the consciousness of the man commonly appears as an irreconcilable contrast becomes, in the legend, unconsciously, an identity. Such a recurrence of repressed conceptions is possible only through the awakening of those ancient incestuous wish impulses. Through these we are reminded that the two apparently irreconcilable elements, the maternal and the libidinous, are operative in every woman.

[7] Freud: Über die allgemeinste Erniedrigung des Liebeslebens. *Ges. Schriften*, Vol. V.

[8] Cf. the study of sexual symbolism in A. J. Storfer, *Marias jungfräuliche Mutterschaft;* Berlin 1914, and my own book, *Your God and Mine* (in press).

We come nearer to a psychological understanding of the belief in miracle if we say: it appears only when a situation occurs which seems to remind us of something in whose reality we have long ceased to believe. This is by no means a trite remark. It tends even to emphasize a surprising condition of the belief in miracle. The first psychological premise of the belief in miracle is doubt. Without doubt there can be no miracle. To a little child, who is still so nearly an animist, it would not seem a miracle if a statue were suddenly to move. The adult, who has long ago got rid of his animistic convictions, would not regard such mobility as a miracle; he would assume that natural causes were the reason of such movement. Only he whose animistic beliefs are not entirely discarded, who, in addition to his free-thinking views, has still unconsciously retained a remnant of his old opinions, can participate in the grace of the belief in miracle, if his reality testing is impeded or has broken down. If the crowds who massed before the grotto of Lourdes, in search of healing, had been fully convinced of the enormous influence of psychical processes on organic maladies, their faith in the miraculous would have been shaken; that is, they would still regard the cures as miraculous, but not as miracles. Yet the knowledge of miracles must have been in their minds; it had attached itself to the figure of the Mother of God, who for all of us represents, in the unconscious, the mother, our own mother, who consoled us in our childhood. The faith in the power of love, which we once received from our mother, was displaced upon the *advocata*. The essence of the miracle is thus the reawakening of a repressed desire, which has become unconscious, by the displacement substitute of a definite situation. In the belief in miracles we have clearly to distinguish three elements: a given situation; the return of an unconscious wish from repression; and the projection of this wish upon the outer world, through the transference of the omnipotence of our own thought to higher powers. The important point here is not the trivial fact that the nucleus of the miracle is a natural event, but the more significant fact that a psychical instance in the belief in miracle is struggling against the recognition of the natural character of a situation, being unwilling to accept it as natural.

The avoidance of the test of reality and the attribution of an event to higher powers—those two essential factors of the belief in miracles—are not mutually independent. It is clear that in this belief animistic conceptions, and notions of magic, are resuscitated, but these ideas may no longer be associated with our own person. The belief in miracles first arises when the magical ideology has already been to some extent discarded, and the powers of magic have been transferred to the gods. To the savage, whom the tribal wizard heals by his touch, his healing is no miracle but a matter of course, for which the *mana* of the wizard is responsible. The impression of the miraculous is dependent on the psychical process by which a situation is deprived of its natural character, determined by the laws of Nature, and transformed by the belief in the "omnipotence of thought," into a supernatural situation. The interpretation of a given external event in the sense of these tendencies to wish fulfillment is one of the essential factors of the belief in miracles. It must already be regarded as a sign of a partial resignation of the belief in the power of one's own wishes if the operation of higher powers is manifested in the miracle.[9] Accordingly, the belief in miracles must be regarded as a relapse into the childhood belief in the omnipotence of our parents, with the difference that we have put God and the saints in their place. We might sum up by saying: The impression of a miracle is produced when an external event seems to reawaken in us the recognition of our belief in the omnipotent power of our parents (in the displacement; of God or divine persons).[10]

[9] The difference between the belief in miracles and the impression produced by the uncanny, which has been analytically elucidated by Freud ("The Uncanny," *Collected Papers*, IV), must be carefully investigated.

[10] A delightful episode in Wilhelm Busch's "Der heilige Antonius von Padua" hints that the miracle may often consist of the transference to the higher powers of knowledge which should have remained secret. Certain worldly persons have complained to Bishop Rusticus that Antony is working miracles in Padua. The Bishop sends for the saint.

> "Such stories of your art I hear:
> Now, what shall I believe of that?"
> Straightway Antonio doffed his hat:
> A radiant beam of sunlight made
> A peg for him, and there it stayed!"

The co-operation of human wishes in the production of a miracle is most evident in cases of the healing of the sick through the intercession of saintly persons. Here the significance of the psychical translation of an external event in the sense of wish fulfillment is especially evident. To the Mother of God at Kevelaer the sick bring, as sacrificial offerings, waxen models of limbs "and many a waxen foot and hand."

> "Who offered a waxen hand there,
> His hand was healed of its wound;
> Who offered a waxen foot there,
> His foot became strong and sound."

It is not recorded that there were waxen models of the human brain among the sacrificial offerings.

Even in the belief in miracles we have found a real element, a psychical reality; the belief in the omnipotence of human thoughts and desires, which was eventually transferred to divine persons.

It often seems that in a miracle, as the Gospels and the legends record, opposites are sundered which were once combined in unity; just as in obsessional neurosis a united whole, which has

---

The Bishop is still undecided; after all, this might be the work of the Devil.

> ". . . Played in the dust or sucked his thumb
> A foundling child, both deaf and dumb.
> Nor sire nor mother did he own:
> His parentage was all unknown.
> Quoth Antony: Say who, my dear,
> Your father and your mother were!
> O wonder! He who till this hour
> Could never speak, now had the power.
> "Why, Bishop Rusticus is—"
>   "Stuff!"
> The Bishop cried: "But sure enough
> Thou art a saint, Antonio!"
> And from that hour, as all men know,
> Antonio wore, is wearing now,
> A shining halo round his brow!"

One sees that in this version by the great humorist the displacement of the psychical accent from a psychical to a material reality appears to be the miracle.

become the object of the ambivalence of the emotional impulses, is presented as two opposites. Often a second miracle reveals the concealed reactive character of the first. The analytic comprehension of the second miracle then offers an explanation of the latent meaning of the first. As in the two-phased symptoms of the compulsion neurosis, the reaction against a forbidden instinctual impulse is the first to appear, after which it obtains satisfaction through a displacement substitute. Perhaps I can best conclude this excursion into the psychology of the belief in miracles by citing a fine example of this species of multiform miracle. A pious legend relates that when Anthony wished to bury the corpse of Paul he was greatly distressed, because he had no spade. Thereupon there hastened out of the desert a monstrous lion with waving mane, which began to scrape at the earth most zealously with his claws. Having completed his task, he bowed his head before Anthony and licked the saint's hands and feet. Thereupon the saint broke forth into praises of Christ, because even the dumb animals recognized that there is a God, and he rewarded the lion by blessing him. This had the curious effect that the lion thereupon encountered a sheep, which he immediately tore to pieces and devoured.

12. THE RETURN OF THE REPRESSED

The unconscious content of dogma, to which allusion has been made, will have told us that in the formation of dogma the same concealed instinctual forces are operative as in the renovated and distorted myths and cults. Indeed, one may say that in dogma, and especially in dogmatic explanations or discussions, these forces are often much more clearly revealed than in the primitive products of the unconscious mind. Thus, very often in a late stage of development of an obsessional neurosis, the repressed content suddenly breaks through and appears in the midst of the repressing forces. The constant repudiation has by way of reaction made the attack more unequivocal and violent. The patient of whom I have so often spoken had, during an analytic session, a blasphemous thought, connected with the notion that his recumbent position was disrespectful to God, of whom

he was then speaking. The resolve to stand up must have con-
flicted with his comfort, for suddenly, to his distress, the thought
presented itself: "It isn't worth while to stand up for such a
fellow!" Another time, in order to repel ideas which were an
affront to God, he endeavored to represent to himself the exalted
attributes of God. But since he was constantly perturbed by opposing tendencies he resolved to think no more about God's attributes. So thinking, he represented to himself a zero, 0, as visual
confirmation of this resolution. But he naturally had to reject this
notion, since it might be directed blasphemously against God,
meaning that God was nothing. In order to cancel this notion he
thought of two zeros, 00, but this reminded him of the sign of a
public washroom.[1] Just as here an "unheard-of" blasphemy sud-

[1] I hope elsewhere to describe this case of blasphemous obsessional ideas
more fully. It is worth noting that the same problems appear in dogmatics;
and of course, the same difficulties. It has been suggested that for fear of
anthropomorphism one dare not assert anything concerning God; and the
response to this suggestion is that the attributes which we ascribe to God
(goodness, wisdom, truth, righteousness, etc.) are naturally crude debasements
of the conception of God if they are understood in the sense of identity, but
are necessary and true if they are interpreted in the sense of analogy. Dogmatics points to three ways in which one can proceed from the completeness
of the created creature to the estimation of the Divine. The way of causality
(*via causalitatis* or *affirmationis*) affirms the creative perfections of God as
their cause, since what is in the effect must also be in the cause. But reason
immediately perceives that created things are burdened with incompleteness
(for example, becoming and passing away). Hence by this second way (*via
negationis*) God appears as the pure opposite of the creature. Accordingly he
is absolved of all essential creaturely imperfections. But on this way of the
dismissal of all finite and limited things one arrives at pure negation. "It is
not enough to say what God is not, but whosoever would inquire into the
nature of Being must also say what He is. For he who only asserts what He is
not is acting like one who to the question: How many is twice five? replied:
Not one, not two, etc.; but did not say, Ten" (Gregory of Nazianzen, *Orat.
Theol.* 2a). Now one proceeds by the third way, that of increase (*via superlationis*), on which one attributes to God the creaturely perfections purified and
intensified until they are glorified in God. (Cf. the congruent definitions of
this threefold path of knowledge in the dogmatics of Bartmann, Simar,
Pohle, etc.) One can also say of God, *via affirmationis*, that He is wise; *via
negationis*, that He is not wise; and *via superlationis*, that He is supremely
wise. The similarity of this logical "process of purification and elucidation"
(Pohle, *Lehrbuch der Dogmatik*, Vol. I, p. 39) to the following, contradictory
trains of thought, which are determined by ambivalence, is as clear as the
irruption of blasphemous ideas at certain points (*via negationis:* God is not
wise, not good, etc.).

denly emerged from the intensified rejection, so in dogmatics and dogmatic conflict a sacrilegious thought may irrupt at unexpected points.

Here we may consider the "gynecological fantasies" (Harnack, III, 308) of Radbertus, Hieronymus, and other Fathers of the Church, who had concerned themselves with such questions as: Of what did the *"essentia virginatis materialis"* of Mary consist? How did natural birth occur *clauso utero?* How did Joseph behave with regard to the exercise of connubial rights? We have noted how much attention was given in christological dogma, from the time of Origenes down to the Arian conflicts, to the mystery of the begetting of Christ.

The irruption of the original meaning of the Eucharist has often been only too plainly evident in dogmatic disputes—more plainly than in the overelaborated analogous cults of the days of paganism. The suppressed, primitive characteristics emerge in these speculations upon the essence and the accidents of the sacrament, upon the space occupied by the body of Christ, and the discussion of the question whether the breaking of the bread referred to the real body or to the *species sacramentalis*,[2] and whether Christ had eaten himself, etc. When Gregory of Nyssa describes the Communion Supper,[3] at which Christ bids us "eat our fill of his flesh," while "our tongues are reddened with the most awful blood," and when this saint exclaims: "He has given us His body pierced with nails, that we may hold Him in our hands and eat, in proof of His love, for that which we greatly love we are often wont to bite," the recurrence of repressed cannibalistic symbols becomes obvious.

In the exactness of the dogmatic formula, of the symbol, and of the creed, we find manifestations of sublimated anal erotism, as well as of conscientiousness, which corresponds to obsessional-neurotic components. In the rigid, obstinate adherence to these prescriptions the anal stubbornness, and in the harmless custom of burning alive and beheading those who think differently the primitive cruelty will find their satisfaction.

[2] Thomas Aquinas, *Summa P.*, III, Q. 75 (itself the repudiation of a blasphemous idea: *"Corpus Christi non frangitur"*).
[3] Hom. 24, 1 cp. and Cor. IV.

But the sadistic instinctual components have already appeared as such in the world of theological thought. The epistomephilic instinct—the "instinct to know"—governs them, just as in many obsessional neuroses it dominates the clinical picture as an intellectualized power drive. Brooding, rumination, then appear as main symptoms, showing that the mental process in its fervent longing to embrace the whole faith has become sexualized. So, finally, in the last stage of the dogmatic process, the aggressive components of the instinct to know take possession of God and of sacred objects by means of intellectual processes, taking by violence the insoluble mysteries of belief. To some extent this drive will *unthink* them and intellectually grind them to atoms, pulverize them.

In the symptom complex of obsessional neurosis it often happens that prohibition is intimately allied with satisfaction, and the original act of rejection becomes also the agent of satisfaction. Thus, the intellectual labor which dogmatics has performed to the glory of God may also be a great labor of destruction over which the devils rejoice in triumph. The hymn of praise which solemnly arises to heaven sounds a *requiem aeternam Deo*.

13. THE PLACE OF DOGMA IN RELIGION

The solution of the problem of the rise and development of dogma points the way to another problem: What is the position of dogma in the evolution of the religions? We have seen that the early Christianity and the beginnings of Islam knew nothing of dogma. Conceptions were wavering; the doctrines of the young religions were indefinite; the practical, emotional, and imaginative motives, like the theoretical elements, were still blended together. The most disparate views of the most important problems of Christology still existed side by side; contradictions were still able to tolerate one another. For a long while to come a free development of doctrine was permitted. It was some time before there were serious debates over individual problems. Again and again, we are bound to conclude, the decisions concerning certain debatable questions were based on definite historical and psychological hypotheses, for every Church eliminated the mental process which had led to the formation of the dogma, broke off its connection with the situation from which it emerged, and declared it to be eternal. Its origin is perceived in divine revelation. This procedure is important, because—like the dissociation of an obsessional idea from its situation of origin—it impedes the search for the most essential cause.[1]

The word, dogma, in its very change of meaning, gives an indication of the alterations which the significance of religious ideas have undergone inside the religion; and it seems to me that from the expression *dokei moi* a broader path leads to the significance of the notion of dogma, as we understand it today; that is, as a rigidly held, intolerant norm of belief. In the religious field the conception of belief has undergone a similar change: belief means, in distinction from knowledge, an uncertain opinion, not consistent with evidence. The belief of theology is the most fundamental and unshakable certainty to which knowledge must defer.

It has been rightly suggested[2] that one can speak of primitive

[1] Dorner stresses the importance of this motive to Christian dogma. "Since this decision can be recorded only in brief formulae, the result is that at a later period, far removed from the disputations which gave rise to the decision, and no longer aware of the circumstances in which this formulation of the doctrine was produced, this formula is as it were uplifted into timelessness, and is thus made a more or less mechanical, authoritative law" (Dorner, *Heilsglaube und Dogma*, p. 144).

[2] By Marianne Beth, in an essay "Zur Psychologie des Glaubens" (in *Religionspsychologie*, Veröffentlichungen des Wiener Religionspsychologischen Forschungs-Instituts, Vol. II, 1927, p. 123). The author rightly points to the fact that in the world of the primitive peoples there are enough beliefs to qualify as contents of faith, and asks: "Why do they not become matters of faith—why do they remain in the elastic and harmonious framework of a religious mood? However much one may resist the conclusion, it seems that there is nothing left us, in view of the findings of religious history, but to resign ourselves to accepting the apparently paradoxical answer that one speaks of religious ideas and perceptions so long as one does not speak of the contents of faith, so long as everyone believes them as a matter of course. However, closer consideration shows that this is no paradox. Primitive thought, and above all, naive thought, has not yet divorced religion from *Weltanschauung*. There is no literary fixation of either. A great elasticity, even of morals and usages, allows every new religious experience to utilize and adapt the existing religious picture, or even to erase parts of it. There is no instance which can apply a normative standard to new experience. There is not even a standard, indeed there is not the lucidity of thought, the conscious realization of one's own religion, which could even note discrepancies." I cannot help expressing

religion, but not of primitive belief; that one can no more speak of Maori belief than of Greek or Roman belief. As a matter of fact, with the emphasis on belief, and with dogma, something new entered into the world of religion, which had previously existed only in rudiments. This estimate shows that cult and tradition, prayer and myth, are no longer enough. It reveals a momentous displacement, which indicates the decline of the function of religion. Dogma is one end product of religion wherever it appears, however long it may resist criticism and contradiction. I have already indicated that it has made important concessions by clothing the mysteries of faith in the form of rational statement. It shows by this that it makes allowance for doubt inside religion, and permits of speculation in the place of a sense of "absolute dependence." According to Nietzsche: What has long been thought becomes questionable. What has first to be rationally proved will not be believed without contradiction. The transference of the psychical accent from vague but massive emotion to the impulse to comprehend indicates, in religion, the incipient decline of the certainty of faith, for faith needs no reasons, no arguments.[3] Every proof of an article of faith betrays its weakness. We know why this must be so, and can comprehend it through our knowledge of the psychology of the neuroses, because in the case of the obsessional idea argument shows that the obsessional conception is defending itself against normally sane reason. The obsessional idea is at the summit of its strength and has great power over individuals so long as it expresses itself in vague notions, which emerge mysteriously, associated with peculiar feelings of aversion, anxiety, or satisfaction, which to the individual seem strange and unfamiliar. Thus, Pascal measured the strength of belief by the weakness of its justification. He saw the "erroneous" elements in certain dogmas,

---

my regret that the writer seems unacquainted with the methods of psychoanalysis. Her admirable work, of which only the first part is so far available, would have gained in essential depth by such knowledge.

3 Marianne Beth writes in the same spirit: "But the farther the certainty of faith declines, the more firmly does dogmatics believe that it must stress its importance for the religious life, until finally *credere*—to believe as true— is of sole value and pleasing to God, at least in the popular consciousness" (p. 120).

the "repulsive" and the "absurd" elements, "which were dragged in by the hairs;" he saw the elements that contradicted experience, yet he accepted everything. In religion the maxim is true of the believer: If he has begun to doubt he has ceased to doubt. Luther made passionate war upon the "fool," the "harlot," the "devil's bride:" Reason. He knew that "a thing is to be believed outright and altogether, wholly and absolutely, or not at all."[4] As in the persistence of the obsessional idea the secondary defensive struggle already constitutes an indication of an incipient subjugation, so the dogma becomes a demolition product of religious faith. "Who dare name it, who confess it?" This is the primary, elementary expression of faith as against the precision and the zealous profession of rational theology.[5] The admission of elements of thought adapted to reality, the consideration of real motives, is already a part of a primitive recovery process, a kind of revision or correction of the obsessional idea. The correspondent processes in dogma formation already show a leaning toward the kingdom of this world.

It is evident that dogma, in the end, according to the laws of the psychical life, must lead to the decline of religion. It bears within it all the seeds of extremism, and stern rulers do not reign long. The history of all religions shows that they begin with vague and wavering beliefs, and then move onwards toward their dissolution, when they have sacrificed to reason and reality too much of their mystical content. Finally religious emotion is succeeded by historical interest, by religious research. The evolution of humanity is extraordinarily slow, and yet one may venture to prophesy this end for all religions. In this gradual process, this conflict between the beliefs emerging from the depths of the unconscious, and the conscious findings of religious research, dogma plays an important part, and its culmination marks the

---

[4] Luther, *Kurzes Bekenntnis vom heiligen Abendmahl*, Erlanger ed., XXXII, 1545, p. 415.

[5] The ambiguity of dogmatics is shown by a story relating to Simon de Tournay, of whom it was told that once, when at college he had distinguished himself by giving an ingenious proof of the truth of the Catholic religion, he cried out: "My Jesu, how greatly have I contributed to the confirmation of Thy teaching! If I were to appear as Thy opponent I should be able to find still stronger reasons for refuting it!" (Mauthner, *Der Atheismus und seine Geschichte im Abendlande*, Vol. I, p. 266).

destined hour of the change.[6] The tenacity of dogma in the life of the peoples is, of course, as great as that of a major obsessional idea in the life of the individual. Its dissolution proceeds very gradually and without much ado; it may take centuries to reach completion. When the *Sanctus Spiritus* has fled religious inertia still persists, but this has nothing in common with a living religion.

The attempted regeneration of religion begins with movements of reformation, which occur when religious oppression has become too great and when dogma and ritual threaten to stifle all free impulses. It is a paradoxical feature of the effect of all these efforts at reformation that they reveal the narrowness of the norms of faith and diminish the burden of the laws of religion. They lead either to a violent reaction or to unbelief. Officially, it is true, Protestantism made an end of dogma, but it continued to exist surreptitiously. The liquidation of frontiers involved the dangers of weakness and inconsequence, of numerous concessions and contradictions. As we have said, there is no religion within the frontiers of reason.

Liberal Protestantism means the end of Christianity:—it is really an atheism covered with a thin layer of belief in God.[7] "With God everything is possible, even that He should exist," said Ernest Renan. We must not deny that Protestantism has done a great service by increasing intellectual independence throughout the world. We only insist that every reform movement of this kind, whether it be Liberal Protestantism, or Reformist Judaism or Brahmanism, must necessarily end in atheism or in a still more rigorous established religion. Logically, if one wishes to be religious, one can only be orthodox, or one is no longer religious. The situation in which Liberal Protestantism

[6] Harnack (*Lehrbuch der Dogmatik,* Vol. I, p. 20) says of the dogma of Christianity: "Between religious faith, by which theory and practice protect themselves, and the historical and critical record of the Christian religion and its history, we can no longer interpolate a third element without coming into conflict either with faith or with the historical findings; the only practical task left is to defend the faith. But in history, as religion has experienced it, a third element has been interjected—dogma . . ."

[7] "Protestantism is the only religion—of the Western world, at least—in which one can become an atheist without realizing it and without resorting to any violent measures" (I. M. Guyau, *L'irreligion de l'avenir,* 1910, p. 156).

finds itself is like that of the Emperor Trajanus, as recorded by the preacher Johannes: Saint George wept at the thought that this righteous but heathen ruler was damned to all eternity. Thereupon God released the soul of Trajanus from eternal torment. It remained, of course, in Hell, but from that time it suffered no harm.

The Catholic Church has justly described dogma as *vinculum unitatis*. In Protestantism the intellect dances in the chains which it dragged out of prison after it.[8] In the course of obsessional neurosis also there are periods of relief and alleviations of the obsession, but they lead either to a violent reaction, to a reactive exacerbation of the obsession in the displacement substitute, or they end in the gradual relaxation and finally in the complete disappearance of the obsession.

14. A FEW DISTINCTIONS

There are still a few questions to be answered. The first, since we have tried to point to so many similarities and analogies between dogma and obsessional neurosis, concerns the essential differences between these two phenomena. They are to be attributed more particularly to the fact that dogma is a collective, psychical product, whereas the obsessional idea is an emotional phenomenon in the life of the individual. While obsessional ideas show that neurosis arises from the defensive battle against instinctual sexual impulses, religious research shows that dogma

[8] An Anglican missionary who was sent to Siberia related that when he arrived in Irkutsk a conflagration had reduced three-fourths of the city to ashes. In the devastated portion only one chapel had remained unconsumed; the Russian clergy took this fact for a miraculous portent. The missionary, however, explained it by the circumstance that the chapel alone was built of brick while the rest of the city consisted of wooden buildings. The same clergyman, who in this case denied the intervention of Providence, thought it consistent with his views to refer to Providence in another instance. He reflected that if one of his horses had not run away he would have arrived in Irkutsk earlier, and then his luggage would certainly have been lost in the fire. He thanked God for inspiring his horse to break its traces (Henry Lupsdell, *Through Siberia*, London 1882; cited from Guyau's *L'irreligion de l'avenir*). We see that the belief in Providence is absurd if a Greek-Orthodox chapel is in question, but natural and evident when the property of an Anglican missionary is at stake.

has built itself up as an institutional defense against aggressive and revolutionary tendencies which in this case have assumed the character of the epistemophilic instinct—the "drive to know." The difference between social and individual psychical products may perhaps explain the incomparably greater diversity and difference of obsessional ideas as against the recurrent and rather stereotyped dogmas of the religions.[1] This difference, of course, loses its distinctive character when we reflect that analysis may refer the diversity of obsessional ideas to a series of definite and basic forms of thought. On the other hand, in the various religions dogma exhibits a difference of kind and development corresponding to the religious and national character. The central position of the father in the obsessional ideas corresponds to the principal dogmatic problem of religion—that of the Godhead. One might also observe that the private character of the obsessional idea, which is usually carefully concealed by the patient, is in complete contrast to the communal character of religious conceptions. But this difference also becomes less extreme when we consider that neurotic patients often express and discuss their obsessional ideas when these, through a secondary elaboration, have become more intelligible to others, and when the patient can be sure that his ideas will not be too severely condemned or derided. On the other hand, it must be emphasized that the communal character of religious ideas first becomes conspicuous when the members of a religion are confident that they will no longer be persecuted, and when the church has evolved from a martyrdom to an *ecclesia militans*. The initial secrecy in respect of the symbols and the discipline of the Christian religion, with analogous procedures in the other religions, bear witness to this essential feature of religious evolution.

I think the difference between religious conceptions, dogmas, and the contents of rational theology (apologetics and dogmatics) is worth psychological consideration. Perhaps the foregoing inquiry will have shown how greatly such a differentiation is impeded by the variable character of these religious conceptions

[1] This difference may be compared with that alleged by Freud in his paper on "Obsessive Acts and Religious Practices," *Collected Papers*, Vol. IV, London 1925.

and the constantly varying progress of the history of religions.[2] We may best hope to represent the decisive psychological differences correctly if we continue to draw the analogies between religious ideas and dogmas and the phenomena of obsessional thinking. It would not be unduly rash to assert that *religious beliefs correspond to obsessional conceptions, dogmas to obsessional ideas, and the considerations, proofs and conclusions furnished by rational theology to the deliria of humanity in its religious evolution.*

15. RELIGIOUS LAW AND THE MORAL LAW

The association between the religious law and the moral law seems indissoluble to the religions. The strict observance of

[2] By this we mean that beliefs are those religious contents in whose reality a community believes although this belief has not assumed a rigid and perfectly definite and formulated shape, and has not been promulgated by spiritual authority as a religious norm. Dogma is the totality of the "infallible" ecclesiastical decisions as to doctrine; dogmas are the individual doctrines of this nature. The contents of dogmatics, as of dogmatic discussions, are dogmas and opinions in matters of faith, but also the refutation of heresies, unbelief, and erroneous beliefs. It is clear that the essential psychical content of the three phenomena is the same, however they may differ in form and intention. Thus, a belief, in more or less distorted form, may become a dogma or the object of dogmatic disputation. The greater complexity of the dogma, its sanction by divine and ecclesiastical authority, its precise conceptual formulation, and its greater resistance and tenacity, as well as its rejection of heretical opinion, distinguish the dogma from the religious belief.

I think it would be as well to differentiate between the designations, obsessional notion, obsessional idea, and deliria, even though analytic practice shows that such differentiation of the fleeting phenomena of obsessional thinking may often have only theoretical significance. Freud himself has reserved the description of *deliria* for those forms of obsessional phenomena which establish themselves by rational means on the foundation of morbid thought ("Notes Upon a Case of Obsessional Neurosis," *Collected Papers*, III). He also speaks of the great difficulty of delimiting the individual obsessional structures, since the patients, "with their peculiar tendency to vagueness, mass together the most disparate psychical formations as obsessional ideas." Nevertheless, it seems to me proper to regard those obsessional formations as obsessional notions which are rather indefinite and not clearly formulated, and have as yet undergone no secondary elaboration—or very little—and often assume only a temporary form. Obsessional ideas seem to me such notions as have acquired an exact conception in the patient's thoughts and already bear definite traces of secondary elaboration, and are capable of establishing an enduring existence in the psyche. The frontiers between obsessional notions and obsessional ideas are as unstable as the frontiers between doctrine and dogma.

religious law forms the precondition of the observance of the law of ethical life. The validity of the Decalogue depends upon recognition of the One God; that of the "five foundation pillars of Islam" upon the belief that Allah alone is God and Mohammed His prophet; and the deportment of the Buddhistic *pañčasila* upon faith in the Enlightened One. Only if the dogmas of the Church are divinely revealed truths are the ethical commandments a divine moral code. Only he can obey the fourth commandment, says the Church, who has learned to obey the first. If the dogmatic teachings are false there is no longer any reason for burdening oneself with the many restrictions and prohibitions imposed by religion. The religions feared, with a certain justification, that the decay of faith must lead to the irruption of the elementary instinctual impulses. Swift relates that a man who heard that a text which had hitherto been regarded as a proof of the existence of the Trinity was differently worded in one ancient manuscript, jumped to the surprising yet logical conclusion: "Why, if it be as you say I may safely drink on and defy the parson!"[1]

The norm of faith thus protects the moral norm, the commandments imposed by the ancestors, which had to be set up against the elementary instinctual impulses of violence, of aggression, and of sexual drives. We shall understand this if we recall that the norm emanates from divine authority, and that faith depends above all on the recognition of that authority. While in the primitive community the essence of religion consisted of the observance of the rules of taboo and the commandments of totemism, in the highly organized religious communities the principal accent was displaced upon faith. We have

---

[1] Freud refers to the novel *When It Was Dark,* in which the enormous moral effect of the disintegration of a dogmatic faith is described. The novelist relates—writing in the present tense—how a conspiracy of enemies of the personal Christ and the Christian faith succeeds in discovering a tomb in Jerusalem bearing an inscription in which Joseph of Arimathea confesses that for reasons of piety he had secretly removed the body of Christ from his grave on the third day after his sepulture, and had buried it here. Thereby the resurrection of Christ and his divine nature are disproved. The consequence of this archaeological discovery is the collapse of European civilization and an extraordinary increase of all crimes of violence, which cease only when the forgers' conspiracy is exposed.

traced this process of psychical displacement to the transference of
the original impulses of cruelty and aggression from material
action to mental activity. Since with progressively increasing
repression thought increasingly replaces action, prohibitions
have to be imposed upon thinking also. If doubt becomes too
powerful there is a danger that the restrictions of taboo may
actually be infringed. So the normative element is displaced
from the commandment or prohibition to perform or not to
perform such or such an action on to the commandment to
believe. The rule of faith becomes the rampart of the laws of
morality. Thus, in the symbolism of the Athanasian Creed the
attainment of blessedness is four times over made to depend on
the precisely formulated faith.[2] The suppressed sadism, returning
from repression, which expresses itself in the sublimated form
of doubt, has made it necessary to transfer both commandment
and prohibition to the intellectual sphere. There it reappears as
the compulsion to believe.[3]

But then comes doubt, disturbingly interposing itself between the commandment and its execution, between the prohibition and its observance. The Pharisees and Rabbis of Judaism,
the Ulemas of Islam, the moral theologians of the Catholic
Church, have fabricated an extraordinarily constituted moral
theology which is supposed to keep all disturbing thoughts at a
distance, and which decides what is good and what evil (*Eritis
sicut deus, scientes bonum et malum*). Thus, it was decided by
Catholic casuistics whether the prescribed abstinence from drink
before Communion would be broken by merely a few drops of
water for brushing the teeth; and whether the formula of absolution could still be efficacious at a distance of twenty paces.

[2] In this process, according to Harnack (*Lehrbuch der Dogmengeschichte*,
Vol. II, p. 313) we have "the transformation of the doctrine of the Trinity,
as an intellectual belief to be privately assimilated, to an ecclesiastical order
on whose observance salvation depended."

[3] It must be noted that religious compulsion creates peculiar mixtures of
sadistic instinctual satisfaction and reaction formation, which find expression
in anxiety for the salvation of others. People must not be allowed to attain
salvation in their own way, because there is only one way of attaining salvation. When the tortured Mohammedans, Jews, and heretics screamed with
agony at the stake the banners of the Holy Inquisition waved consolingly
above their heads, bearing the device: *Misericordia et justitia.*

Casuistics ascertained precisely how many grams of meat could be eaten on Friday, how many pages of a forbidden book one could read, and how many days one could keep such a book in the house without committing a grievous sin (strict moralists reply: three pages, one day; milder casuists, six pages, three days).

But in casuistics a possibility was at last discovered of evading ecclesiastical law. Thus, the reading of a forbidden book is permitted if one reads it not in print, but in manuscript, or if one has it read aloud by a servant. The doctrine of mental restriction makes it possible for a wife who is accused by her husband of unfaithfulness flatly to deny the offence if in the meantime she has confessed it and received absolution. If a Catholic is asked whether he belongs to the Reformed Church he may reply in the affirmative, because the Catholic Church was "reformed" by the Council of Trent, and many chapters of the Council's decrees bear the heading *de reformatione*.[4] And further,

---

[4] This, and the following, statement is taken from Heiler's *Der Katholizismus*, pp. 296 ff. It would be easy to point to the analogies between obsessional-neurotic behavior and the attitude encouraged in the Church through the principle of *probabilism*. This principle serves as orientation in those cases in which a doubt exists as to whether an action is permitted or not permitted, enjoined or not enjoined. In such cases one should perform the action with a quiet conscience in accordance with the principle of probabilism, if there is a probability that it is permitted, and even if there is a greater probability that it is not permitted. ("*Si opinio est probabilis licet eam sequi, licet opposita sit probabilior*"—Bartholomäus de Medina, 1577.) The analyst will understand, psychologically, how things had to end in the construction of probabilism. As against the extreme increase of conscientiousness in obedience to the laws of faith and morality some way out of the conflicts of conscience had to be found. But this alleviation led with psychological inevitability, like a relaxation of the obsessional-neurotic system, to the irruption of instinct on an ever-increasing scale. Cardinal Aquina writes (cf. Döllinger-Reusch, *Geschichte der Moralstreitigkeiten in der römischen Kirche seit dem 16. Jahrhundert*, Vol. I, 1899, pp. 121 f.): "In our time there is hardly any divine or human, hardly any natural or positive law, which many do not evade on all sorts of pretexts, under the empty pretense of probabilism. The extreme form of probabilism, *laxism*, had at length to be condemned by Innocent XI on account of its disastrous effects (Denzinger, *Euchir.*, No. 1020). *Moderate probabilism* continued to exist, either in the form of *equiprobabilism* (one may follow a certain opinion if its probability is only equal to that of the contrary opinion), or *probabiliorism* (one must obey the law unless the opposite interpretation, making for freedom, is more probable), or *moderate tutiorism* (the opinion favoring liberty must be the most probable of all possible opinions). *Absolute tutiorism*, which requires that in the case of doubt

moral theology, which takes the religious dogma as its basis, must allow an action otherwise prohibited to be performed in the name of religion, and must even agree that it appears to be highly praiseworthy. So, in obsessional neurosis, the forbidden action or the rejected thought, for the sake of whose rejection the symptoms were built up, becomes often the central point of the obsession. The synthesis of forbidden and commanded actions or ideas in a compressed form of expression is as frequent and as conspicuous in religion as in obsessional neurosis.[5] The Catholic legend relates that Mary was delayed by a deep river on her pilgrimage from Egypt to the Saviour's tomb. Since she had no silver coin for the fare she offered her pure body in payment, and by this sublime example showed that all the lust of the senses is as nothing compared with the longing for eternal salvation.

CONCLUDING REMARKS

We have come to the end of our inquiry. Our survey has followed the genesis and development of religious dogma. It must also glance at its future. With the decay of religion among the civilized peoples dogma must collapse, and with it rational theology, apologetics, and dogmatics must disappear. This, of course, does not mean the end of dogma itself. In the place of religious dogma another dogma will appear—perhaps socialistic,

---

one should always follow the law, was condemned by Alexander VIII in the Sinnichius (Denzinger, No. 1160). According to the Decree of Promotion of Pius LX (Mirbt, p. 370), the equiprobabilism, represented by Alfons di Lugori, is the most recommendable. The analogies between probabilism and those gaps in an obsessional-neurotic system which allow for the satisfaction of instincts and the ego interests of the patient become evident on analysis.

[5] The religions assert that the moral law and religious law are equally derived from Heaven. The accuser at the Last Judgment, before which God might be cited by His creation, could justly exclaim as Mephisto does:

"He would live a somewhat better life
Had'st Thou not given him the gleam of Heaven's light."

And he might add:

"He calls it reason — and it helps him, see,
Far beastlier than any brute to be."

perhaps scientific. Its external forms and psychical effects will not differ essentially from those of religious dogma.

Harnack once observed: "Nonsense and authority are in a sense the mark of the higher truth" (*Lehrbuch der Dogmengeschichte,* Vol. III, p. 507). We may be sure that in this direction there will be no great changes. The capacity to doubt, and in particular the ability to endure doubt for a long time, is one of the rarest things on this planet. As a matter of fact, man is a mammal who cannot well endure uncertainty. He cherishes a profound longing for firm convictions. The craving for immediate and impregnable security and certainty show how little man has evolved during the millenia.

So it may be that the perhaps imaginary progress of humanity will be expressed, at most, by the substitution of one dogma for another. Humanity is not capable of enduring life without illusion. The content of the illusion is not of crucial importance. *Plus que ça change, plus c'est la même chose.* Holy Scripture tells us that on the sixth day "God saw everything that He had made, and behold, it was very good" (I Gen. i, 31). Dogmatics, which knows precisely and has described the transcendent and absolute attributes of God, has therefore neglected to credit God with the attribute of supreme modesty.

Part Two

THE FINAL PHASES OF RELIGIOUS AND OBSESSIONAL-NEUROTIC BELIEF

My aim is to indicate the phases through which religious belief passes, and to follow the comparison between religion and obsessional neurosis down to the final development of both phenomena. This I have done here not by methodical investigation, but by the description of three examples which are representative in character. I shall not attempt a complete exposition but rather the elucidation of essential features. This chapter, therefore, must be regarded as provisional, since the analytic discussion of the problem is continued only to a certain point, and then broken off. The problem is stated, and the nature of its possible solution indicated, but the solution itself cannot be given here. It will have to be sought on a much broader basis.

One of the motives that have determined me to publish anything so incomplete is the realization that theology has not yet even so much as perceived the problem under consideration. The means of the discipline which investigates the genesis and the phenomenal forms of the religious life have hitherto been insufficient for the development and exposition of such questions. This has first become possible through psychoanalysis, which provided the means of investigating the essential psychic processes that determine religious experience, and of carrying this investigation to depths which had hitherto been inaccessible to research.

The three examples described show how the psychic motives and mechanisms which are characteristic of religion operate in the decadent and transitional forms of this social product. The first example is taken from the province of religious worship; the other two seem to belong to a totally alien atmosphere, having nothing in common with the psychic hypotheses and aims of religion. Nevertheless, analytic examination is able to reveal in them the repercussions of the same psychic forces that give religious experience its special content and its specific form. It is perhaps needless to state that the comparison of religious phenomena and obsessional-neurotic symptoms can, and will attempt to, explain only a fraction of the psychic connections between the two categories.

1. *PIA ET IMPIA FRAUS*

According to the prescriptions of the Israelitish religious ceremonial, a pious Jew must not extinguish a light on Friday evening. A Jew whom I had occasion to observe hit on an ingenious expedient which enabled him to have all the light he needed on Friday evening, and also darkness when he retired for the night—without, in his opinion, disobeying the religious prohibition. He wanted the lights to be dowsed at a certain hour, but his religious conscientiousness would not allow him to turn off the gas or turn down the lamps himself. He rejected the method adopted by so many Jews, who simply ask someone who is not a Jew to extinguish the lights. He had no intention of tempting anyone, even though a follower of another religion, to commit a "sin." His house was lit by gas. He hit on the following highly ingenious expedient; he connected an alarm clock with the gas tap in such a way that at a given hour the mainspring of the alarm turned the tap. On Friday afternoon he set the alarm for the time when he wanted the lights to be extinguished. When the hour arrived the alarm sounded and the spring turned off the gas; there was no need for the pious Jew to lift a finger. This ingenious person could not be persuaded that this whole device was, so to speak, a way of outwitting God. No clear-thinking person will deny that it was an evasion of the religious commandment which he achieved by taking advantage of the precise form of the prohibition.

This way of observing a commandment may be compared with the obsessional symptoms in which sane thinking is blended with obsessional thinking in an apparently homogeneous structure. Reality obtains access to the realm of obsessional phenomena and imperiously demands consideration. In this way mixed formations are often produced, in which the obsession is partially observed, but is also disregarded. In a certain phase of the evolution of these disorders the compulsion is obeyed and disobeyed in the same action. This is done in such a way that actually the greatest triumph of the repressed impulse is achieved by the most exact and conscientious observance of the obsessional commandment. Here is an example: An obsessional-neurotic girl is obliged to convince herself, hundreds of times a day, that the water tap in her bathroom is turned off. Analysis traced the origin of this symptom to a sexual incident in which the girl's fiancé was involved. She had then been afraid that the man would have an ejaculation and make her pregnant. Her compulsive action is therefore of a precautionary character; at the same time it gives her an opportunity of touching and playing with the tap. In a later phase of her disorder the observance of the precautionary measure became more and more an occasion to turn on the tap, while she nevertheless wished to convince herself that it was turned off. This turning on of the tap occurred precisely when she wished to take the compulsive measure of precaution.

The compromise character of the compulsive symptom undergoes modification in a certain direction during the final phases of the neurosis. The original defense against prohibited impulses becomes weaker, and the part played by concealed instinctual satisfaction becomes more obvious. We know from the analytic investigation of the obsessional symptomatology that the decisive irruption of these originally repressed instinctual impulses marks the end of many obsessional neuroses in their original form.

The greatest increase of obsessional-neurotic and of religious conscientiousness which characterizes the end phases of both developments leads inevitably to the irruption of the forbidden impulses. The underlying countertendency has asserted itself precisely when the pious believer was taking especial pains to observe the commandments of religion. Anatole France once spoke, in conversation,[1] of the great impression made upon him by the confidence and familiar trust which the believers in

[1] Recorded by Jean Jacques Brousson, *Itinéraire de Paris à Buenos-Ayres,* Paris 1927.

Rome displayed toward their God. For example—one day a respectable Roman matron came up to the high altar with her child in her arms. The child attempted to grasp the white Host with his innocent little hands, taking it for a sweetmeat or a butterfly. The priest gently put the blasphemous little hand aside; but at last, in order to guard the bread of the angels against the unhallowed contact, he whispered a warning to the child: "Kaka, my little one, kaka!"

2. AN OBSESSIONAL NEUROTIC
PLAYS AT PATIENCE

A lady who had contracted an obsessional neurosis boasted of being a complete freethinker in respect of religion. She did not observe the prescriptions of religion; she derided the credulity of other people, and often made fun of their religious beliefs.

She was fond of playing patience. In this card game, which is usually played by one person, the cards are laid beside or upon one another in a certain sequence. If all the cards are used up by laying them in accordance with the rules of the game the player has won. This is the most matter-of-fact and certainly the least usual way of playing patience.

This lady played patience in accordance with a certain hypothesis, as is more generally done. She told herself, before she laid out the cards: "If 'it' comes out, this or that, for which I hope, will happen; if it doesn't come out, my wish will not be fulfilled."

It is evident that this more general form of patience is simply a modern substitute for the oracle. The question which was put to Fate is here answered, favorably or otherwise, by the cards. The Pythia of the Greeks is represented by the fortune-teller from whom the women of the people seek to learn their future. Patience is one of the modern forms of the oracle; it does not differ essentially from the hepatoscopy of the Babylonians. The manuals of patience are analogous to the "Handbooks of the Soothsayer's Art" which have come down to us from the time of Asurbanipal.[1] In the days of the Hammurabi dynasty (about

[1] Cf. Artur Ungnad, *Die Deutung der Zukunft bei den Babyloniern und Assyriern. Der alte Orient*, Vol. X, No. 3, Leipzig 1909.

2230 to 1930 B.C.) hepatoscopy (the scrutiny of the liver) had already been elaborated into a complete and complicated system which, from the psychological standpoint, is analogous to the rules of patience. The difference between the result and the interpretation of a hepatoscopy and the corresponding procedures in patience is almost negligible. We can learn a great deal of the procedure of the ancient hepatoscopy from the records of priests; for example, from the record which a priest made of the inspection of the entrails of an animal sacrificed before the statue of King Hammurabi, who was worshipped as a god, on the 21st day of Adar in the tenth year of the reign of Hammurabi's great-uncle Ammizaduga (about 1975 B.C.). The parallel between the statement, "If the base is long so will the days of the sovereign be long," and the interpretation, "If the Ace falls on the King of Hearts I shall have a very long life," is astonishing.

One may compare the unfavorable issue of a game of patience, and its interpretation, with the Babylonian method of fortune-telling by inspecting the contents of a beaker, as described in two handbooks (whose date is possibly 2250 B.C.): "If the oil (poured into the beaker) spreads out and fills the beaker the sick man will die." We know now, as the result of analytic research, that this same order of thought, which has the significance of an unconscious oracle, plays an important part in the clinical picture of obsessional neurosis. Freud has shown us from what psychic motives it arises, and to what goal it is directed.

However, we cannot at this stage enter into an exhaustive description of the manifold forms in which the ancient oracle survives in our midst and in ourselves. We will turn our attention rather to certain psychic processes in the mind of the lady who is playing patience. She tells us that she is doing this only for amusement, as a pastime; but the tone of her voice, as well as her subsequent honest confession, shows that she does not regard the game as merely a game. Thus, we are reminded, by the conscientious observance of the order of precedence in laying the cards in patience, of religious ceremonial. What would it matter, for example, if she were to hesitate as to whether the knave of hearts or the knave of diamonds should be laid uppermost? She explains that for her the knave of hearts means her "friend," the knave of diamonds her husband. Has she not betrayed to us, by her hesitation, something more and something of profounder significance than her doubt as to the hierarchial order of the cards? Did her hesitation refer merely to this conventional system of valuation? Is the game played in earnest, or is it not rather the case that the player's earnest desire is concealed in the game?

By the analysis of her further statements we shall discover that she takes the play-oracle more seriqusly than she is willing to admit. At all events, we get this impression from her prolonged consideration of the questions to be asked, of her constantly recurring doubt, and her endeavors to subdue it. One of the questions is: "Will Franz [her husband] get a job within the next six weeks?" A doubt presents itself: "Within the next six weeks" is too indefinite. "Within" might mean at once or at the end of the term. And the term was too short. The question ought to be: "Will he get a job next year? *The* next year? As measured by the calendar? But does that mean within the present year? Am I thinking of the Gregorian calendar? There's a Jewish calendar too. And what about the Russian calendar?" We see that doubt is now intruding itself into the question of the calendar; it will now lead the patient into meditations upon the calendar, and will hinder her in her intention of questioning the oracle. Now such questions as these suggest themselves: "Do the Russians still—since the Revolution—adhere to their old calendar?" And the calendar leads her back to the ancient Romans. "The ides of March—on the ides of March Julius Caesar was murdered." The proposed question is not asked; fresh doubts are constantly intruding before she can realize her intention. If we follow the course of the associations we recognize that doubt represents unconscious hostile impulses, whose content becomes plainer in one of the end associations (the murder of Caesar). One recognizes, too, the unconscious motive that hinders her in the execution of her intention. It is her belief in the omnipotence of her own thought, displaced on the cards.

In opposition to the recurring doubt the text of the inquiry is often meticulously worded, authenticated, emphasized, repeated, criticized and corrected. For example, one must not ask:

Shall I find a house within three months? One should ask: Shall I find a suitable house (not just any house) for myself (not for others) in Berlin (not elsewhere) within two months from today (not at any odd time)? Later on, of course, the card-oracle will be questioned as to the probable outcome of the analysis: "Will my treatment be completed within the year 1929?" As she begins to lay the cards the first doubt presents itself, so that she repeats the question: "Who is being treated? Dr. R. or myself? Am I perhaps treating Dr. R.? I must ask: Will my cure be finished within the year 1929? But what does 'finished' mean? I must say: successfully finished. But what does 'successfully' mean? Is the restoration of mental balance, for example, a successful result? Don't I perhaps hope for some other result?" The new text is repeated, but a fresh addendum proves to be necessary: "Will the analysis be finished because he [Dr. R.] says it has been completed? He can say it has been completed without being satisfied with the results obtained. I must say: will he say it has been completed and that he is satisfied with the result?" But while the card is still in her hand, about to be laid on the table, a fresh doubt emerges, and has to be answered. We know how the unconscious, hostile component of the ambivalent tendencies constantly finds some new way of expressing itself. The doubt that is representative of this hostile impulse is naturally directed against the undefined force which has to give the answer.

We find the same phenomenon as an expression of the decline of religious faith in antiquity. From a wealth of examples we will take a question which was asked of the Sun-God Schamasch—according to the experts—some time in the seventh century B.C. The petitioner puts his question in the form of a prayer, couched in the following circumstantial terms: "Schamasch, great Lord, in response to what I ask of you give me your faithful answer! Between this day, which is the third day of this month, the month of Ijar, and the eleventh day of the month of Ab of this year—that is, within the hundred days and the hundred nights of the time appointed for the soothsaying—will either Kashtariti and his warriors, or the warriors of the Cimmerians, or the warriors of the Medes, or the warriors of the Manaeans, or any other enemy whatsoever, accomplish their plans? Will they by assault or deed of violence, or by force of arms and battle, or by breaching or destroying the walls, by siegeworks of all kinds and starvation, or through the special decree of a god or goddess, or by friendly speech and friendly argument, or by any kind of stratagem of war, such as leads to the taking of a city, take the city of Kischassu? Will they enter into the city? Will their hands conquer this city of Kischassu? Thou knowest, great God! Is the taking of this city of Kischassu by the hands of some enemy between this day and the end of the term which I have stated ordered and decreed at the behest and the command, of thy great Godhead, O Schamasch, great Lord? Will the eyes see this and the ears hear?"

After a prayer in which the god is asked graciously to pardon any possible oversight of a ritual character, the petition is repeated more briefly: "I ask thee, Schamasch, great Lord, whether between this day, that is, the third day of this month, the month of Ijar, and the eleventh day of the month of Ab of this year, Kashtariti with his warriors or the warriors of the Cimmerians or the warriors of the Manaeans or the warriors of the Medes or any other enemy will take this city of Kischassu and enter into this city of Kischassu, whether their hands will conquer this city of Kischassu, and whether it will be allotted to their hands?"

After the sheep, set aside for this sacred transaction, had been slaughtered, a priest who had been specially trained for such purposes subjected the animal's liver to a thorough examination, making notes of his observations. These notes were added to the request, and the whole was handed to the college of sooth-saying priests for further elaboration.

We find, in the peculiar exactitude of the wording of the request, the same uncertainty and the same endeavor to overcome it; the nature of the request must be indubitable, and pains are taken to avoid any possible misunderstanding. The precisest formulation of every detail should exclude the malice of destiny. My patient justly pointed to the example of agreements in civil law, which she cited in comparison. A carefully worded agreement avoids the necessity of legal proceedings. The analyst will know where to look for the secret motives of this striving for exactitude. The oracle is to reassure the petitioner in respect of the unknown evils which he anticipates—evils which are constantly threatening him. Its purpose is to warn him of threatening dangers and help him to avoid them. Examination of the psychic life of the obsessional neurotic shows that there are good psychological reasons for this exaggerated caution; its function is to banish the anxiety which constantly re-emerges as reaction against the patient's unconscious hostile and cruel wishes and impulses. The powers of destiny, which are interrogated, are represented, in unconscious dread of retribution, as peculiarly malicious and treacherous. In the representation of this treachery the unconscious "bad conscience" of the patient is reflected. We must assume that the oracles whose decisions were recorded by the writers of antiquity gave cause for the same excessive distrust. The enigmatical utterances of the Gods have led many mortals astray, and the gods who gave oracles seem to have been hardly more capable of foretelling the outcome of an undertaking with any certainty than their worshippers, who turned to them for aid and counsel. Or were the gods merely envious and jealous? Did they speak so ambiguously with intention, in order the more surely to lure their questioners to perdition? We know little of their nature, but it seems as though doubts were at work in the believers as they pressed forward to question the oracle, as though the powers of conscience strove within them against the fulfillment of many of their plans. The emissaries of Croesus, who asked of the Delphic oracle whether he should take the field against the Persians, received the reply from Apollo: "If Croesus takes the field against the Persians he will destroy a great empire!" Was there not already, before the campaign, an unconscious countertendency at work in the ruler? Did not his false interpretation of the oracle mean that he willed and desired his own defeat in an unconscious intention of suicide?

Doubt adheres not only to the wording of the question. It finds expression also in the inhibition against asking certain questions. Thus, certain "ultimate" questions must not be asked by my patient. She is afraid, of course, that destiny might return an unwelcome answer, which might then appear irrevocable. In the background, again, her belief in the power of her own secret thoughts emerges. Especially important desires should not be expressly betrayed to Fate. Often, of course, she is able to disguise her questions so skillfully that they could not be regarded as the direct expression of these desires. But then it is not surprising that the information of the patience-oracle should be so ambiguous that it can be interpreted in a positive or a negative sense, while its symbolism is obscure.[2] The doubt which has expressed itself in the interrogation will be perceptible also in the reply. Thus the patient dares not ask questions which involve her most important interests, or whose answer would decisively affect the welfare of those dear to her. Accordingly, before playing patience she has carefully to sift her questions, rejecting many as "too important," and replacing them by substitute questions of less importance. In doing this she has always to consider the degree of their importance. Sometimes she has to interrupt her interrogation, on account of sudden misgivings. In her case certain precautionary measures have to be taken before undertaking a compulsive transaction—a protective ceremonial, quite analogous to the ceremonial which the Babylonians performed before consulting the oracle, or the Roman augurs before observing the flight of birds.

Naturally, then, the patient can ask questions in respect of her wishes only when these are not "of the greatest importance." Questions of rather less importance, if asked at all, must not be spoken aloud. The consequence of the constant observation of all sorts of precautions and considerations, the constantly recurring doubts, and their rejection or justification, is that a game of patience takes many hours to play—if indeed it is ever completed. Very often the unconscious countertendency makes itself felt by the fact that the question is forgotten, the interrogation is broken off as too important or unimportant, or the text of the question, through constant correction, has become confused. In respect of all these phenomena comparative history of religion can point to numerous analogies.

In the analysis of these obsessional doubts it becomes evident that it is dread of the anticipated evil that inhibits the player in completing her consultation of the patience-oracle. This

2 The ambiguity of the Delphic oracle was notorious. The mysterious and symbolical character of Apollo's answers was generally admitted.

fear is by no means alleviated when the game "comes out"—that is, where Fate appears to give a favorable response. A fresh doubt then awakens—a doubt as to whether the favorable constellations were not incorrectly interpreted, or whether Fate will not realize its evil and secret intentions just when one thinks one is safe. The religions and superstitions of all peoples reveal the same dread in respect of the subtle sophistics which seems a monopoly of the higher powers. A legend relates[3] that Pope Sylvester II (999–1003) made a pact with Satan when he was a student in Cordova. With the aid of the Devil he learned geometry, algebra, botany, and other ungodly sciences. Among other tricks he owed the art of becoming Pope to his devilish teacher. According to the treaty which Sylvester concluded with the Prince of Hell, the latter would gain possession of his soul if the Pope should end his glorious career in Jerusalem. It is not certain whether Sylvester still had hopes of salvation, or whether he did not like the prospect of residing in Hell. At all events, he took good care not to make the pilgrimage to Jerusalem. But one day, as he was reading Mass in one of the chapels of Rome, the Devil came to fetch him. Since the Pope protested against this presumption, his partner in the treaty pointed out that the chapel in which they were then standing bore the name of Jerusalem. The conditions of the treaty were fulfilled, and now the sinful soul must go to Hell. According to Dante[4] the Devil, with a mocking smile, whispered into the ear of the outwitted Pope: *"Tu non pensavi ch'io loico fosso"* (You did not consider that I am a logician).

3. THE INSURANCE POLICY

In the foregoing examples a definite, personal attitude to religion was represented. In this attitude the analytically trained student of the psychology of religion can detect unequivocal signs that the person in question is unconsciously seeking to break away from his religious belief. In the above-described hybrid forms we can still find the belief in the omnipotence of

[3] Cited by Heine in his *Elementargeister.*
[4] *Inferno,* 27, V, 125.

thought, the anticipation of disaster, and the protective and defensive reactions which dominate the religious and obsessional-neurotic attitude of the individual.

In contradistinction to these phenomena, which are related to the individual, we will now turn our attention to a social institution, to *insurance*. By insurance one understands the conclusion of a contract according to which one party promises the other to indemnify him for the loss or injury which he may possibly suffer from a contingent event or accident of the nature defined in the insurance policy. (This labored but inadequate definition is taken from a dictionary.) The one party to the contract is usually an individual; the other, a state, a province, an insurance company, a trade union, etc. A distinction is drawn between the insurance of property against damage or destruction (e.g., insurance against fire, hail, failure of harvest, breakage of windows, etc.) and personal insurance (against accident, sickness, old age, etc.). As a rule an application form comprising certain questions is filled out. On the acceptance of this form the applicant receives an insurance policy. He pays, once for all, or at periodical intervals, a fixed amount, known as the premium. By the payment of premiums, which are determined by mathematical and statistical calculations, he acquires the right to claim a definite payment or indemnity if he should suffer loss or injury. If the sum total of the paid-up premiums does not suffice to cover the liabilities, the undertaking in question—that is, the insurance company—has to make up the deficit. The premium demanded from the insured person is always a gross premium—that is, it includes certain additions to the amount determined by calculation—the net premium. The purpose of these additions is to cover the costs of administration and to render possible the building up of reserves (reserve capital, expense fund, etc.).

The history of insurance companies has not yet been adequately investigated, but it seems to be established that even in antiquity social institutions resembling our insurance companies were known. The *Collegia tenuiorum* of the Roman Empire corresponded approximately to the modern burial club, while the Greek *Koinonia* performed very much the same function as the modern marine insurance companies. Marine insurance underwent progressive development during the Middle Ages. The seventeenth and eighteenth centuries saw the beginnings of fire, industrial, and life insurance in England, France, and Germany. Our own period has seen a tremendous development and expansion of insurance and there has been an increasing recognition of the social value of the various forms of insurance. Of this evidence may be found in the extension of insurance to all the great industries, and its international character; also in the tendency toward the nationalization of insurance; and in the comprehensive legislation relating to insurance, and the emergence of a specific science of insurance.

The insurance of life and property, whose social advantages need no elucidation, is, of course, a sensible arrangement, whose rational basis is obvious. In my opinion, this social institution represents a modern substitute for various religious institutions which were based upon definite religious ideas and beliefs.

Such an assertion may at first sound fantastic. This impression, however, is due to the peculiar share of the rational element in insurance. In order to elucidate the essential meaning of my assertion I propose, to begin with, to exclude the category of money, which, as a modern motive, originally alien to the phenomenal world of religion, is represented in the insurance policy. The quintessence of insurance then appears as a precautionary measure of human beings who wish to insure themselves against the consequences of the occurrence of accident or other calamity, and who hope to achieve this purpose by the voluntary observance of certain regulations. Here we already find ourselves on familiar ground. To begin with, we can only vaguely distinguish the underlying connections which unite the modern institution of insurance with the ancient phenomena of the offering or sacrifice, and the vow. We cannot for the moment enter into the historical and psychological differences between the religious institutions of sacrifice, vow, and prayer. Even a criticism of the theological investigation of these ideas must be postponed to another occasion.

Here we shall only note that scientific theology has demonstrated the fact that there are various forms of offering—the offering of homage, the offering of gratitude, the offering of expiation, etc. The notion of offering generally indicates that the believer surrenders to the divinity a portion of his possessions; a portion that for him represents a definite value. As a religion evolves the nature of the offerings changes. Originally they are regarded as purely material. The gods are well pleased by offerings of the flesh and blood of man and beast. After a time no more human offerings are made; only animals are sacrificed; and later still the offerings are inanimate. In the end instinctual renunciation is the only sacrifice esteemed by the god. In Psalm 50 we are told that Jahveh values obedience above all material offerings.

The regulations concerning the nature and the time of the offering, and the form in which it is to be rendered, are very precise in the highly organized religions; in making a sacrifice or oblation the rules must be exactly observed. In the period of the later Roman empire the offering assumed more and more definitely the character of a commercial transaction: *Do ut des.* The cultic decalogue already comprised definite rules in respect of offerings, which were subsequently discussed in the minutest detail.

Psychoanalysis is now in a position to explain all these different oblations as variations of a single form of offering. Offerings of homage, gratitude, expiation, etc., are developments and modifications of the defensive sacrifice, whose purpose is to avert a threatening disaster, or a dreaded punishment, and to appease the wrath of the gods. This sacrificial tendency is frequently unconsciously expressed even in the psychic life of modern humanity, which has discarded its belief in sacrificial services and offerings. Freud, in his *Psychopathology of Everyday Life,* has shown that many human actions which are otherwise incomprehensible have the unconscious significance of the sacrifice. The symptomatology of the obsessional neuroses reveals the same phenomena, and also their emotional premises.

The oblation of the ancient religions was a common action of the tribe and the people. There were, indeed, individual offerings, but these represented a late and derivative form of the religious activity of the community. The offering required, so to speak, the sanction of the tribe. The promise of a future sacrifice is a familiar vow. It consists as a rule of an introductory clause and a conclusion. The introductory clause states the condition on whose fulfillment the believer will provide the promised sacrifice. The formula is generally as follows: If Jahveh is with me and realizes my hopes, then I will sacrifice this and that to Him (Gen., XXVIII, 20 ff.).

The vow is related to the offering and is derived from it; it consists of a solemn promise to do something if a certain condition is fulfilled. Its relation to the sacrifice becomes clearer if we reflect that the content of the vow, in the majority of cases, and certainly in the beginning, was the promise to bring an offering. Many vows have the character of offerings. In many others there is a complete or preliminary payment made to the divinity, who is thus subjected to a sort of compulsion to grant the prayer. A careful study of religious evolution shows us that more and more complicated conditions are attached to the vow, and that it soon acquires the character of a business agreement. It assumes, so to speak, a commercial form, and often enough, if we study the documents of the later phases of the ancient religions, we have the impression that the petitioner is bargaining with the god.

The comparison of these religious phenomena with the institution of insurance does not now seem quite so paradoxical. In each case the predominant motion is to guard against a dreaded evil, or to mitigate its consequences. Whereas prehistoric man, when he went hunting, brought an offering to appease the god, and to protect himself against a danger threatening his life, the man of our own time takes out an insurance policy. The payment of premiums—regarded from the bathypsychological standpoint—corresponds to the offering or sacrifice, and one is quite justified in comparing the votive tablets of the ancient Babylonians (for example), on which the believer promises a sacrifice to Istar if a danger is averted, with an insurance policy. The modern practice even reverts to the more primitive form of sacrifice, in which the petitioner voluntarily surrenders part of his property to the deity. Theological science tells us that the sublimated forms of the sacrifice are of secondary occurrence. In the case of insurance a quota of material wealth is offered up in order to guard the insurer against the worst consequences of a contingent misfortune. The times of sacrifice correspond to the dates for the payment of premiums, and the conditions of insurance to the precise and businesslike formulation of the amount of the sacrificial offering, and the manner in which it is to be made. Now the other partner to the agreement is not God, but the state or a company. In the social obligation to insure which is more and more strongly emphasized by great industrial concerns and companies (insurance against accident, illness and old age) one may perhaps detect a trace of the original tribal character of the sacrifice. It can hardly be denied that here we have a perpetuation of religious institutions adapted to the realities of life, institutions whose heritable characters have impinged themselves on many of the features of the modern institution. This *perpetuation* is of course at the same time a *substitution,* which bears evidence of the decline of the social function of religion. He who leaves all things to God needs no insurance.

This is not the time to discuss the risks which the individual runs if he leaves the protection of his interests to the gods, or to an insurance company. We know that the promises of the gods are not always kept. (For that matter, insurance companies have been known to become bankrupt.) Despite such divine and earthly failures, man will continue to devise measures of protection against the disasters that threaten him. The Jew Shylock reminds himself that Antonio has one galley bound for Tripoli, and another for India; a third is sailing to Mexico and a fourth to England. "But ships are but boards, sailors but men; there be land-rats and water-rats, water-thieves and land-thieves, I mean pirates, and then there is the peril of waters, winds and rocks."

For man's anxiety in respect of all the perils and uncertainties to which his ship is exposed there are sound psychological reasons. Yet in the end the sense of adventure is victorious. One must put to sea: *Navigare necesse est.*

THE PRAYER SHAWL AND THE PHYLACTERIES OF THE JEWS

A Psychoanalytic Contribution to Hebrew Archaeology

"But Freud, in my opinion, lays too little stress on the fact that he . . . is referring merely to the European *Christian* culture, the promises of whose religion no longer appears worthy of credence. . . . Neither the law nor the moral prescriptions in the Old Testament are in contradiction to the laws of thought. . . . The Old Testament knows nothing of mythology or symbolism. . . . This tribe must have had a natural predisposition to the conception of things that rebelled from the outset against the polytheism of its environment. . . . We have endeavored to show that religion is by no means an illusion. By the application of psychoanalysis to religion it rather seems to us that Freud has dragged down the noblest and most wonderful conception of the human spirit into the atmosphere of everyday happenings."

Dr. Heinrich Haase, in *Religion oder Illusion?* A discussion of the latest work of Prof. Sigmund Freud, *The Future of an Illusion.*

"O God, where do I find Thee?
And where do I find Thee not?"

Jehuda Halevi

1. "THEY MAKE BROAD THEIR PHYLACTERIES AND ENLARGE THE BORDERS OF THEIR GARMENTS"

In one of his sermons Jesus reproves the scribes and Pharisees for the hypocrisy and superficiality of their outward piety. "Whatsoever they bid you observe, that observe and do; but do not ye after their works; for they say, and do not;" for "all their works they do for to be seen of men: they make broad their phylacteries, and enlarge the borders of their garments" (Matt. XXIII, 5). We are in no doubt as to the Saviour's meaning in uttering this reproach. The exhibition of piety, the demonstrative character of religious exercises, are indicated by a representa-

181

tive example. The Pharisees—so the Lord declares—make the bands or thongs of their prayer satchels, the *tephillin*, broad and conspicuous; they enlarge the borders or fringes which the Jews wear upon their garments in obedience to the commandment, in order to demonstrate their loyal observance of the law. The wearing of these prayer satchels and fringes was a religious custom which in the Saviour's time was conscientiously observed by every Jew. The Saviour did not attack this ritual as such, but only its exaggerations and aberrations. He himself wore such hems or borders, in compliance with the law, and the Gospel according to St. Matthew tells us that those who believed in him held that there was healing in the touch of these hems or fringes (in the Hebrew, *zizzith*). The people of Genesareth asked that the sick should be allowed to touch the zizzith of his garment. Those who touched it were made whole (Matt. IX, 20). "A woman who was diseased with an issue of blood twelve years came behind him and touched the hem of his garment . . . Jesus turned him about, and when he saw her, he said: Daughter, be of good comfort; thy faith hath made thee whole. And the woman was made whole from that hour."

The problem of such a singular therapy naturally excites our curiosity. We should also like to know more of the peculiar objects which were of such great religious significance. It is not difficult to satisfy our curiosity. We have only to observe a pious Jew as he repeats his morning prayer; we shall then have an excellent opportunity of obtaining a clear notion of this religious practice. We see how the pious Jew throws a cloth, which is like a shawl, and is called the *tallith*, over his head and shoulders. We note the four tassels at the corners of this article of clothing, and we see that thongs on which little satchels are fastened are wound in a special manner about the left arm and bound upon the forehead. Although these ceremonial objects may have altered a little in shape, they are in essentials what they were in the days when the Lord was wandering on the hills of Galilee. They have the same function today as they had twenty centuries ago, when Jesus brought mankind the joyful news of imminent salvation.

To us these objects appear no less peculiar than the praying

gloves, prayer mills, and prayer pennants of the peoples of the
Far East. Let us first of all consider the combination of the
satchels and thongs. Actually we have here two fairly similar objects, one of which is bound on the left arm, and the other on the
forehead. The head tephillah—in Hebrew, *schel rosch*—consists
of a leather box which is made from the hide of a ritually clean
animal,[1] and is fastened by means of leather thongs. This little
black leather box contains four compartments; in each is placed a
copy of certain passages of the Bible, written on a specially prepared vellum. On one of the outer sides of this box we see the
Hebrew letter *schin,* with three teeth; on the opposite side is
the same letter with four teeth. This four-celled box is sewn to
its leather support with twelve stitches of the sinew of a ritually
clean animal.[2] These stitches, according to tradition, represent
the twelve tribes of Israel. The thongs which fasten this head
tephillah are bound round the head in such a manner that the
box rests on the edge of the scalp, between the eyes. At the
back of the neck the looped thongs form the Hebrew letter
daleth. This, with the letter *schin* (on the outside of the box)
and the letter *jod* which is formed by the thongs of the hand
tephillah, spells the name of God, *Schaddai* ("Almighty"). The
sacred character of the tephillah boxes is apparent from the special prescriptions as to their manufacture: the strips of parchment within them must be of a special kind; the Assyrian script
on the strips must be written with extraordinary calligraphic and
masoretic exactitude. Before the scribe begins his work he must
solemnly proclaim: "I am writing this for the holiness of the
Tephillin." If he omits even one letter the whole inscription is
worthless. The verse of the Scripture which he has to write must
not be written from memory, but must be copied from the roll
of the Law. Every letter must be particularly clear; none must be
out of line with the rest; none must overlap or rise higher than
another letter. A definite space must be left between the letters,
and between the individual words, lines and verses.[3] The scribe
must write the name of God—and only Jews may write these

---

[1] Men. 42 b; Yad III, 15.
[2] Schab. 28 b.
[3] Yad II; Orach Chajim 32, 23 and 32.

tephillah verses—with special reverence and a sense of its exalted significance. The injunction to the effect that the writer's attention must not be diverted during his labor is so imperative that even were he greeted by a king he would be forbidden to respond to the greeting.[4] The text which is recorded with such special precautions on the parchment consists of four passages of the Bible. They are the following:

1. Exod. XIII, 1–10: "And the Lord spake unto Moses, saying: Sanctify unto me all the first-born, whatsoever openeth the womb among the children of Israel, both of man and of beast; it is mine. And Moses said unto the people: Remember this day, in which ye came out from Egypt, out of the house of bondage, for by the strength of hand the Lord brought you out from this place; there shall no leavened bread be eaten. This day came ye out, in the month Abib. And it shall be, when the Lord shall bring thee into the land of the Canaanites, and the Hittites, and the Amorites, and the Hivites, and the Jebusites, which he sware unto thy fathers to give thee, a land flowing with milk and honey, that thou shalt keep this service in their mouth. Seven days thou shalt eat unleavened bread, and in the seventh day shall be a feast to the Lord. Unleavened bread shall be eaten seven days; and there shall no leavened bread be seen with thee, neither shall there leaven be seen with thee in all thy quarters. And thou shalt show thy son in that day, saying, This is done because of that which the Lord did unto me when I came forth out of Egypt. And it shall be for a sign unto thee upon thine hand, and for a memorial between thine eyes, that the Lord's law may be in thy mouth; for with a strong hand hath the Lord brought thee out of Egypt. Thou shalt therefore keep this ordinance in his season from year to year."

2. Exod. XIII, 11–16: "And it shall be, when the Lord shall bring thee into the land of the Canaanites, as he sware unto thee and thy fathers, and shall give it thee, that thou shalt set apart unto the Lord all that openeth the matrix, and every firstling that cometh of a beast which thou hast; the males shall be the Lord's. And every firstling of an ass thou shalt redeem with a lamb; and if thou will not redeem it, then thou shalt break his neck; and all the first-born of man among thy children shalt thou redeem.

[4] Yad II, 15; Orach Chajim 32, 19.

And it shall be when thy son asketh thee in time to come, saying: What is this? that thou shalt say unto him: By the strength of hand the Lord brought us out from Egypt, from the house of bondage. And it came to pass, when Pharaoh would hardly let us go, that the Lord slew all the first-born in the land of Egypt, both the first-born of man and the first-born of beast; therefore I sacrifice to the Lord all that openeth the matrix, being males; but all the first-born of my children I redeem. And it shall be for a token upon thine hand, and for frontlets between thine eyes; for by strength of hand the Lord brought us out of Egypt."

3. Deut. VI, 4–9: "Hear, O Israel; The Lord our God is one Lord: And thou shalt love the Lord thy God with all thine heart and with all thy soul and with all thy might. And these words, which I command thee this day, shall be in thine heart: And thou shalt teach them diligently unto thy children, and shalt talk of them when thou sittest in thine house, and when thou walkest by the way, and when thou liest down, and when thou risest up. And thou shalt bind them for a sign upon thy hand, and they shall be as frontlets between thine eyes. And thou shalt write them upon the posts of thy house, and on thy gates."

4. Deut. XI, 13–21: "And it shall come to pass, if ye shall hearken diligently unto my commandments which I command to you this day, to love the Lord your God, and to serve him with all your heart and all your soul, that I will give you the rain of your land in his due season, the first rain, and the latter rain, that thou mayest gather in thy corn and thy wine and thine oil. And I will send grass in thy fields for thy cattle, that thou mayest eat, and be full. Take heed to yourselves, that your heart be not deceived, and ye turn aside, and serve other gods, and worship them; and then the Lord's wrath be kindled against you, and he shut up the heaven, that there be no rain, and that the land yield not her fruit; and lest ye perish quickly from off the good land which the Lord giveth you. Therefore ye shall lay up these my words in your heart and in your soul, and bind them for a sign upon your hand, that they may be as frontlets between your eyes. And ye shall teach them your children, speaking of them when thou sittest in thine house, and when thou walkest by the way, and when thou liest down, and when thou risest up. And thou

shalt write them upon the door posts of thine house, and upon thy gates. That your days may be multiplied, and the days of your children, in the land which the Lord sware unto your fathers to give them, as the days of heaven upon the earth."

It should be mentioned that there were prolonged discussions among the talmudic commentators, entering into all manner of details, as to the arrangement of these four passages of the Bible; that is, their arrangement on the parchment strips of the tephillin. Thus, the highly respected Rabbi Tam decided in favor of one arrangement, while the no less respected Rabbi Raschi recommended a different order.[5] This slight uncertainty, which is not without symptomatic significance, although it refers only to the order of the last two passages of Scripture, finds expression in the fact that in many tephillin rolls the order prescribed by Tam is followed, and in others that favored by Raschi. We note, moreover, that many pious Jews, incapable of deciding whether they should follow Rabbi Tam or Rabbi Raschi, have hit upon this method of ensuring that they have fulfilled their religious duty: They wear two head tephillin, one of which is arranged in accordance with Raschi's prescription, while the other observes the order favored by Tam.

These four passages of Scripture, which in the head tephillah are inscribed upon four rolls of parchment, are compressed into one roll in the hand tephillah, which is only about half the size of the head tephillah. The little box of the hand tephillah is fastened with a long leather thong, which is wound upon the left arm. The hand tephillah is adjusted first, in such a way that the box lies on the inner side of the left arm, under the joint. This position, in which the tephillah is carried near the heart, is in fulfillment of the rabbinical interpretation of the admonition contained in Deut. XI, 18, that "ye shall lay up these words in your heart . . . and bind them for a sign upon your hand." When the little box is fastened upon the bare arm the thong, which is passed through a loop, is first of all wound three times about the arm. At the same time the prayer is recited: "Praised be thou,

5 Rabbi Tam proposed the sequence: Exod. XIII, 1–10; Exod. XIII, 11–16; Deut. XI, 13–21; Deut. VI, 4–9. But Raschi proposed: Exod. XIII, 1–10; Exod. XIII, 11–16; Deut. VI, 4–9; Deut. XI, 13–21.

Lord our God, king of the world, who hast hallowed us by thy commandments and hast bidden us to wear the tephillin." The thong is then wound three times about the arm in such a way that its convolutions form the four-branched Hebrew letter *schin*. The head tephillah is then placed in the middle of the forehead, and a blessing is invoked.[6] The thong of the hand tephillah is then wound three times about the middle finger, so that it once again forms a letter *schin,* while a short length of the thong is left hanging down. While the thong is being wound around the hand the words are recited: "And I will betroth thee unto me in righteousness, and in judgement, and in loving kindness and in mercies; I will even betroth thee unto me in faithfulness; and thou shalt know the Lord."[7] After divine service the thong is unwound from the middle finger; then the head tephillah is removed, and finally the hand phylactery. The tephillin are then kissed and laid aside in a special bag or satchel.

Originally the tephillin were worn all day[8] (but not during the night); now they are put on during the morning worship only, except on the Sabbath and on holidays.[9] It is the religious obligation of every Jew to put on the tephillin daily after he has reached the age of thirteen years and a day.

We now have a fair notion of the objects for whose exaggerated dimensions the Saviour so sternly reproved the scribes and Pharisees. The other object which was mentioned by the Lord, and which he himself wore, as the Gospel records, is still in daily ritual employment among the Israelites. We see the fringes concerning whose dimensions the Saviour of the world was so indignant, on the prayer shawl which every male adult Jew has to wear during his prescribed devotions. This prayer

6 If anyone has spoken between the fixing of the hand tephillah and that of the head tephillah he must repeat the two invocations on applying the head tephillah (Men. 36 a; Yad l.c. IV, 4, 5).

7 Hos. II, 4, 19. One may compare with this a passage in Goethe's letter to Frau von Stein: "The Jews have thongs which they wind about their arms when they pray; so will I bind thy lovely riband about my arm when I make my prayer to thee, hoping to share in thy goodness, wisdom, moderation and patience."

8 Men. 36 b.

9 Ber. 14 b.

shawl is known as the *tallith*. It is a large, white, quadrangular cloth of sheep's or lamb's wool; or it may be of silk. The silken shawls will be prized as more valuable, but pious worshippers will prefer the woolen shawl, especially if its wool is that of the lambs of the Holy Land. The tallith is drawn over the head so that it covers the forehead and the back of the head, while its four corners hang loosely upon the shoulders. The four tassels which we see on these corners, and to which Jesus referred in his sermon, are known as *zizzith*. They are expressly required in Num. XV, 37–40,[10] and in Deut. XXII, 11 and 12.[11] These tassels —in Luther's translation called *Läpplein* (lappets)—consist of four white and four blue threads of the same material as the tallith. The rabbinical prescriptions relating to the zizzith are marked by a characteristic minuteness and precision which deal exhaustively with every detail; in fact, they fill many pages. Of the eight threads which form each tassel one is longer than the rest; it is known as the servant, *schammisch*. After the zizzith is fastened to the shawl this *schammisch* enters into action. It is bound first seven times and then eight times round the other threads, a double knot being tied between these windings. The thread is then wound eleven times round the others, and again a double knot is tied; and finally it is wound thirteen times round the rest, and again a knot is tied. This sequence of threads and knots has been compared with the knot-writing of ancient civilizations—for example, the *quipus* of the Peruvians. As a matter of fact, the medieval Jewish mystics attributed many secret meanings to the numbers of the windings and of the knots. One of these interpretations conceives the whole as a symbol of the Torah: the numerical value of the letters of the

---

10 "And the Lord spake unto Moses, saying, Speak unto the children of Israel, and bid them that they make them fringes in the borders of their garments, throughout their generations, and that they put upon the fringe of the borders a riband of blue, and it shall be to you for a fringe, that ye may look upon it and remember all the commandments of the Lord and do them; and that ye seek not after your own heart and your own eyes, after which ye used to go a whoring; that ye may remember, and do all my commandments, and be holy unto your God."

11 "Thou shalt not wear a garment of diverse sorts, as of woollen and linen together. Thou shalt make thee fringes upon the four quarters of thy vesture wherewith thou coverest thyself."

word *zizzith* is 600; if we add the eight threads and the five knots we get 613, which according to rabbinical calculations is the precise number of the positive (248) and negative (365) prescriptions of the Law. According to another version the numerical value of the knots and windings gives us the words *jahwe echod*—Jahveh alone (is God). There are many other speculations of this kind; the one thing they have in common is the connection between the zizzith and belief in God and the Law. The wearing of the zizzith was often regarded as equal in importance to the observance of all the laws.

These zizzith, however, are found not only on the special prayer shawl, the tallith, but also on another ritual article of clothing, which may be described as a sort of miniature tallith. Actually this article is known as *tallith kothen,* "the little tallith," in opposition to the *tallith godel,* "the large tallith." Another and frequently used name for the prayer shawl is *arba kamphot.*

While the tallith is worn only during prayer, this particular article is worn all day by pious Jews. It is simply a square of cloth that covers the breast and back and is worn under the outer garments. This shawl is slightly different in shape from the longer tallith, but like the latter it has the zizzith affixed to its four corners. This twofold use of tallith can hardly be explained by the historical development of Jewish dress. In ancient times the Hebrews wore a large piece of cloth not unlike the Arab burnouse;[12] it wrapped the whole body, and was probably used also as a nightdress. The usual tassels or "fringes" on the corners of the garment are prescribed by the Priestly Codex. These zizziths on the outer garment, which was so much larger than the later tallith, must have been (as we learn from Jesus' sermon) much larger and much more conspicuous than the tassels which we may see today on the ritual garment. The woman who was suffering from an issue of blood laid hold upon the Saviour's zizziths in the midst of the people.

As time elapsed the Jews approximated to the clothing worn by foreign peoples. The tassels on the outer garment were recognized as Jewish peculiarities. As the hatred of the Jewish

12 It may also be compared with the Greek *hymation,* a word which the New Testament actually employs in its translation.

people increased it became advisable to conceal them. This explains the use of the tasseled tallith which was worn only during the morning prayer, and the origin of the special article of clothing which was worn under the outer garments. Or so the scholars tell us. No doubt their explanation is correct, yet it surely does not reveal all the essential motives of the development.

As the tallith is put on the prayer is spoken: "Praised be thou, Lord our God, king of the world, who hast hallowed us by thy commandments and hast bidden us to wear garments with the zizzith thereon." As the tephillin are kissed, so the zizzith are kissed when the tallith is put on or removed. This the pious do in order to fulfill the commandment: "Ye shall look upon them."

There was an embittered discussion between the talmudic schools of the Rabbi Hillel and the Rabbi Schamnai as to whether the tallith had to be worn by night as well as by day. It was decided that this was not necessary, since the darkness made it impossible to obey the injunction to look upon the zizzith and in so doing call to mind the commandments of God. The pious Jew is forbidden to sell such a garment, provided with tassels, to anyone who is not a Jew, unless the zizzith are first removed.

2. THE RELIGIOUS SIGNIFICANCE OF THE PHYLACTERIES

The natural method of learning anything as to the significance of these mysterious religious objects is to apply to the Jewish authorities. One would expect that the Talmud, the vast, comprehensive lawbook of the Israelitish religion, would give us exhaustive information. As a matter of fact, the religious literature of Jewry contains a bewildering wealth of statements relating to the tephillin and zizzith. We are told how long a man should fast if he should drop the *tephillin,* and how they are to be cleansed. There are exhaustive discussions as to the proper manner of writing the tephillin; we learn how large the little box should be, and how long the thongs, etc. The tephillin were revered almost as much as the Holy Scriptures.[1] We learn that they, like the Scriptures, might be saved from a conflagration on the Sabbath.[2] In Berak. III, 5, this question is discussed: What is to be done with the tephillin when the pious Jew goes to the privy? (It will be remembered that in the time of the Talmud the tephillin had to be worn all day.) It is recommended that they should be laid down at a distance of four ells from the privy; but it is also debated whether they should be held in the hand during evacuation. The possibility of holding the tephillin in the clothes is rejected, as they might be in danger of falling. It is decided, for example, that it is allowable to take the tephillin into a permanent privy where there is no siphon, but not into occasional toilets where there are siphons.

The following story, which is recorded in the Talmud, testifies to the great respect with which the tephillin are regarded: It so happened that a youth laid aside his tephillin in an alcove near the street while he went to a toilet. A harlot came by, picked them up, and went into the school house, saying: "See what that fellow has given me in payment." When the youth heard this he climbed to the summit of the roof and threw himself down and died. In the same treatise the problem is debated, between the Rabbis Josefs, Nehunja and Jehuda, whether one should place the tephillin under one's pillow. It is stated emphatically that they must not be placed under one's feet, since that would be to treat them in a contemptuous manner. Should they be laid between the bolster and the pillow, and would this be allowable if his wife were to lie with the pious Jew, etc.?

The question as to what animal's hide should be employed in preparing the tephillin is answered by referring the matter to Exod. XIII, where it is said: "It shall be for a sign . . . that the Lord's law may be in thy mouth." This means: what you are allowed to take into your mouth; that is, only a ritually clean animal. That the tephillin must be square was revealed to Moses upon Sinai, and also that they must be wrapped round with the

---

1 Jadajim III, 3.
2 Schabbath XVI, 1. See also Emil Schürer, *Geschichte des jüdischen Volkes im Zeitalter Jesu Christi*, 2 vols., 4th ed., Leipzig 1907, pp. 569 f.

hair of a beast and sewn with its sinews. Even the color of the thongs—which must be black—was revealed to Moses upon Sinai (Sabbath II, 3). God himself taught Moses on Sinai how to prepare and bind the tephillin (Berach. I, fol. 7). It is expressly stated that God himself wears tephillin. This is proved by the passage in Isa. XVII, 8, which says: "The Lord hath sworn by his right hand, and by the arm of his strength." His right hand, according to Deut. XXXIII, 2, means the law; but his right arm means the tephillin, for it is said (Psalm XXIX): "The Lord will give strength unto his people." But how—it may be objected —can it be proved that the tephillin are a strength unto Israel? The answer will be found if we refer to Deut. XXXIII, 10, where we read: "And all the people of the earth shall see that thou art called by the name of the Lord; and they shall be afraid of thee." Rabbi Eliezer the Great explains that what the peoples will be afraid of will be the tephillin of the head. The statement that God Himself wears tephillin is apparently insufficient; the sagacious Rabbi Hijas b. Abin (Berach. I, 2) even went so far as to determine what is written in the Lord's tephillin, reciting the precise text contained in each compartment.

From the judgments of the decisors of the Middle Ages we see what importance they attributed to the wearing of the tephillin. Ula, for example (Berach. II, 11), says that if anyone reads the *Sch'ma,* the most important prayer of Jewry, without having put on his tephillin, it is as though he had given false witness against himself. Rabbi Hija b. Abba, on the other hand, compares such behavior to that of a man who has brought a burned offering without meat or a sacrifice without a libation. Rabbi Hija says also: "He who purifies himself and washes his hands and puts on the tephillin and reads the *Sch'ma* and prays, he is accounted by the Scripture as one who has erected an altar and offered up a sacrifice thereon, for it is said: 'I will wash my hands in innocency, so will I compass thine altar' " (Psalm XXVI, 6). The observance of the injunction as to wearing the tephillin is thus held equal to an offering upon the altar. Rabbi Schescheth decreed that he who does not wear the tephillin violates eight commandments (since the injunction occurs eight times in the Torah; Berach. 44, 1). Rab numbers those who wear no tephillin among the apostates (S. Rarch Hasch. 17 a). In the paraphrases of the Targum to Canticle 8 it is stated emphatically: "So saith the community of Israel: I am chosen from among all the heathen peoples, because I bind the tephillin on the left hand and about the head, and fasten the mezuzah on the right side of my door, that the evil spirits may have no power to harm me."

It is a fact that in the Talmud the tephillin, the zizzith and the mezuzah (the capsules containing biblical verses, fastened to the doorposts), often figure as apotropaic agents, and are usually named together. Maimonides (Yad IV, 25, 26) testifies to the sanctifying and protective action of the tephillin; so long as a man has the tephillin on his arm and head he will be humble and God-fearing, and will not turn his thoughts to sin and idleness. Tephillin, zizzith and mezuzah, in the Jewish belief, are a protection against sin (Menach. 43 and elsewhere). This belief was so general that various rabbis surrendered themselves to the most wanton delights, believing themselves to be insured against the danger of sinning, because they were equipped with the tephillin. When Abaji (in the third century) was one day seated before Raba, and remarked that the latter was behaving in a dissolute manner, he referred him to Psalm II, where it is written "Rejoice with trembling," but Raba retorted: "I have put on tephillin" (Berach. 30 b).

We shall not be surprised to note that the religious opinion of modern Jewry repudiates the belief in the magical character of the tephillin, ascribing to them only an exalted symbolical significance. Thus, according to L. Zunz,[3] though they remind us of things "heavenly" they also warn us against things forbidden: "For if hand and eye are dedicated to God we think with silent reproach of whatsoever of impure captures our eye and pollutes our hand." The connection may seem very vague to us, but it is stated with great emphasis: "The sign on thy left hand can hold back thy right hand from striking thy brother. The holy memorial that encircles the head fetters the foot when it hastens toward sin." Here, apparently, is no question of a simple defensive mechanism, since from the left hand it reaches

---

[3] "Thefillin, eine Betrachtung," *Gesammelte Schriften*, Vol. II, Berlin 1876, pp. 172 ff.

the right, and from the forehead its influence reaches the intention to transgress. The matter becomes even more complicated and enigmatical, inasmuch as the satchel and thong are supposed to awaken the religious sense of fraternity. We are told: "So often as the symbol is visible on our outward person, so often does the old love bestir itself within, drawing into its hallowed circle all who share our convictions."

Let us now turn to the second object of which the pious Jew must be heedful when he prays, the tassels or "fringes" which adorn the tallith. The name *zizzith* is related to a root which means "to show forth," so that the word may correctly be translated as "show-threads" (German: *Schaufäden*). Moreover, the scriptural injunction bids the faithful to look upon these threads. The significance and the religious importance of the prescription regarding the zizzith are indicated, not only by the careful exactitude with which it is followed, but also by the repeated expressions in the Talmud, which show what value was attached to the observance of this injunction. The Gemara says:[4] "This commandment is as important as all the commandments in the Torah." "Whoso obeys the commandment regarding the fringes, for him it will be as though he had obeyed all the commandments."[5] In a noteworthy talmudic interpretation it is said in the passage relating to the fringes, "and ye behold Him" (God); but not, "and ye behold them" (the fringes). This means that he who obeys the injunction relating to the fringes may be said to have received the Lord.[6] Similarly, it is said:[7] "Whosoever is diligent in the observance of this injunction, he beholds God," for it is said "and ye behold Him" (Num. 15, 38). In connection with these statements individual records are cited which show what importance the zizzith possessed in the eyes of the pious. The son of a famous rabbi was asked, what commandment his father had enjoined upon him above all others. He replied: "The law concerning the zizzith. Once, when my father was descending from a ladder he stepped upon one of the threads

---

4 Menachoth, 43 b.
5 Sifre ‡ 115 to Schellach lacha, 35.
6 Sifre ‡ 115.
7 Schabb. 118 b.

and tore it, whereupon he refused to move from the spot until the thread was repaired."

Rabbi Resch Lakizeh paints a vivid picture of the rewards which await the pious in the next world. He declares that no fewer than 2800 servants will wait upon every Jew who has observed the injunction relating to the zizzith.[8] For confirmation of this statement he refers to the prophet Zachariah, VIII, 23: "In those days it shall come to pass that ten men shall take hold out of all languages of the nations, even shall take hold of the skirt of him that is a Jew, saying: We will go with you; for we have heard that God is with you." The pious man now calculates in the following manner the precise number of servants who in future would wait upon every Jew: He proceeds from the fact that there are 70 principal languages; he multiplies the number of the lappets of the coat (4) by 10, and so obtains the figure of 2800. It is also related in the Talmud that the zizzith once saved a pious man inasmuch as when he was minded to sin they intervened, as it were, as living witnesses, smiting him in the face "as a reproach."[9]

In the example of a rabbi intimidated by the movement of the zizzith, as in other instances, the "fringes" figure as a kind of magical instrument. In the course of time this original character became less marked, until they came to be regarded as a symbolical admonition to obey the commandments of God. As an instance of such an anagogic conception of the zizzith I will cite a few sentences from Langfelder's *Die Symbolik des Judentums*.[10] This author emphasizes the fact that the "fringes" of the Jews "remind them at all hours of the day of the existence of a supreme Judge of the world and Creator: The twisted threads, which have one blue thread in the center, represent a complete symbol of the whole of our human life on earth. On firmly entwined and also innumerable threads the fate of humanity depends on the will of the Eternal . . . The fringes at the four corners of the garment bear witness that the power of God pre-

[8] Shab. 32 b.
[9] Men. 44 a.
[10] Klausenburg 1876, p. 97.

vails and rules in all four corners of the universe." The fringes in themselves are of course mere threads of white and blue wool. But for the enlightened, for those who have been instructed as to their meaning and their importance, "they comprise a momentous symbol, which represents the relation of mankind to God." Thus, the blue thread reminds us "that we are all bound to the heavens, to God, with indissoluble bonds. Because heart and eye inconstantly lust after all earthly joys, and because man is wholly enmeshed and imprisoned by eye and heart, these fringes are so ordered and arranged as to provide and oppose an effective counterpoise to the enticements of the senses." We may listen indeed to this comprehensive message, but we may yet be unable to believe that the god of a Bedouin tribe can have ordained for his believers so sublime a symbol, which would give rise to such trains of thought. The woolen threads are to remind one of human destiny, which is bound up with the will of God; the four corners of the garment typify the four quarters of the universe; the blue thread the infinity of heaven—here is an *embarras de richesse* in symbolical meanings which is surely too momentous even for primitive shepherds who have abundant time for meditation. It is difficult also to imagine why fringes should point to the existence of a supreme Judge of the universe, and what precisely may be the effective counterpoise that is "provided and opposed to the enticements of the senses."

It amazes us to reflect what exalted ethical and religious ideas these threads at the corners of the garment of a nomadic people are supposed to represent. Langfelder, whom I have quoted as the spokesman of modern religious opinion, comes to the following conclusion: "If monotheism has such vitality and viability in Judaism that the 'fringes' can bring the whole order of monotheistic ideas plainly and lucidly to the mind of the beholder, then the rest of the commandments, which convey and represent the same meaning and significance . . . will not be unobserved and disregarded."

If we agree with this conclusion the chances that the rest of God's commandments will be obeyed in the future are somewhat scanty, and the pious man may look toward the days to come with some misgiving, for then the whole order of monotheistic ideas as represented in the "fringes" would no longer be so clear and intelligible as one might wish.

The explanations which the religious and legal traditions of Judaism have to offer us may often sound full of meaning, but they are seldom clear.

3. THE THEORIES OF OLD TESTAMENT SCHOLARSHIP AND COMPARATIVE RELIGIOUS CRITICISM

Let us now turn to the representatives of Old Testament scholarship. Though in the literature of Judaism there may be obscure suggestions of the hidden meaning of the prayer thongs and fringes, the sober scholarship of the Hebrew archaeologists, which in the last few decades especially has made such great progress through the labors of so many scholars, is certainly better adapted to give us decisive explanations. Here we encounter the cool, transparent atmosphere of rationalism. Here the intellect is supreme, weighing and scrutinizing evidence, and forming its clear judgments. Therefore we may hope for a prompt and reliable solution of the riddle.

As a matter of fact, the critics have long been considering the nature of these mysterious objects. If I now give a brief selection of their theories, this will help to show the direction followed by inquiry, and the nature of the results obtained. If we wish to determine the original significance of the tephillin, our first step should be to discover the etymological meaning of the name of these enigmatical objects. In the Old Testament the designation *totaphot* occurs, a term whose meaning is doubtful. The Talmud calls them tephillin, which may mean head bands or prayer thongs; the Gospels employ the term phylacteries. The Hebrew archaeologists were assisted by their knowledge of biblical exegesis, which explains the meaning and the relevance of those passages of the Bible in which there is mention of the tephillin. It was also useful to obtain such data from the experts in comparative religion as would point to the observance of similar customs among other peoples and in the religious practices of other communities. Talmudic archaeology, and an exact knowledge of the Jewish liturgy, were called in to assist the work of research.

The still readable essay on the totaphot which Gottlieb Klein[1] published in 1881 derives this word from a Hebraic verb meaning to strike or beat. From this the author derives the meaning "lightly touched symbols." According to him, the tephillin were originally a kind of emblem branded upon the forehead. From the context in which the commandment relating to the totaphot first appears, Klein thinks it probable that a bodily mutilation was first indicated by the enigmatical term. The relevant injunctions appear in various passages of the Bible in connection with the feast of the Passover and the feast of the first-born. In Exod. XIII, 1–2, God requires that "all the first-born" shall be "sanctified unto me." Thus, the Passover offering of the first-born, which was made once a year, was no longer sufficient; all the first-born must bear the sign of dedication to God. This must be the meaning of Exod. XIII, 6: "And it shall be for the sign (*ôth*) unto thee upon thine hand, and for the memorial (*totaphot*) between thine eyes." It is significant that the commandment relating to the totaphot is intimately connected with the dedication of the first-born at the Feast of Passover. Originally, children were sacrificed at this festival; a later age endeavored to obliterate all vestiges of this heathenish method of revering God. The totaphot is, as it were, the last surviving vestige of this sacrifice. The author, or the authors of the other passages in which the totaphot is mentioned (Deut. VI, 8 and XI, 8), were no longer aware of this connection. They no longer understood the original significance of the totaphot as a physical mutilation, conceiving that the injunction was one relating to amulets. According to Klein, we have to distinguish between the original meaning of the totaphot (physical mutilation) and a later meaning (amulets containing verses from the Bible, which originated on Persian soil and under Persian influences). Even the Greek name, phylactery, points to the fact that the totaphot was of the nature of an amulet.

One's first impression of this theory is definitely favorable;

---

[1] "Die Totaphot nach Bibel und Tradition," *Jahrbuch für protestantische Theologie*, Vol. VII, 1881, pp. 666 f.

more especially because of the context in which the commandment relating to the totaphot first appears. Another point in its
favor is that it invokes the genetic standpoint, and is not content
with a superficial interpretation of the meaning of the totaphot.
It seems probable that there was once a connection, which was
no longer recognized at a later period, between the Passover
festival and the totaphot. But it is precisely here that our objections to Klein's ingenious theory have their origin; he claims
that the totaphot is derived from the dedication of the first-born;
but later on the law obliged every Jew to dedicate himself to
God by special signs upon the hand and between the eyes. But
why was every Jew to sanctify the human first-born? And what
was the nature of the connection between that offering and this
sign? Why was it to appear on the hand and between the eyes?
The derivation of the word totaphot from a verb that means to
strike or to beat is more than doubtful; and the interpretation
of the word as "burned-in symbol" is arbitrary. The totaphot
never appears, in the Bible or the Talmud, as a mutilation; yet
there is evidence enough that such religious mutilations did
occur. The path leading from these supposed self-mutilations to
the institution of the satchels and thongs, which were to be
worn constantly, is by no means clear, and is difficult of explanation. The assumption that the misunderstanding of later generations was responsible for this substitution is not a satisfactory
explanation. It seems to us highly probable that the totaphots
originally had quite a different significance, which is unknown to
us, and that it was only at a later period that they came to be
regarded as amulets.

The continuity of psychic events seems to require that this
evolution should be such that an inner, psychological connection
would exist between the primary, uncomprehended meaning and
the subsequent amulet-like character of the totaphot. Also, the
shape and structure of the tephillin can hardly, without coercion,
be referred back to a bodily mutilation. The details of the construction of the satchels and thongs, the particulars of their manufacture, the conspicuous and complicated method of applying
them, and the extraordinary opinions held concerning the tephillin can be explained neither by assuming them to signify bodily

mutilations nor by regarding them as amulets. The impression which we received on examining Klein's hypothesis is perhaps that of an observer who notes how a wanderer first follows the right path, only quickly to lose it, and ends by going far astray. We feel that a fragment of the desired explanation is contained in the introduction to the theory, but what we were trying to grasp soon escapes us, and leaves us empty-handed.

The explanations furnished by Bernhard Stade[2] constitutes a long step further in the false direction followed by Klein. It is not offered expressly as an attempt to explain the meaning of the tephillin, but it seeks to elucidate the nature of the sign which Jahveh, in the biblical narrative, gave Cain for his protection. Stade tries to establish a connection between this sign of Cain and the wearing of the tephillin. He believes that the sign of Cain was a primitive tattooing. He refers to Lev. XIX, 27 f., where the Jews are forbidden to "round the corners of the head or mar the corners of the beard;" nor shall they make any cuttings in their flesh for the dead, nor print any marks upon their bodies. In the Apocalypse the worshippers of the Beast bear the name or the number of the Beast on the hand or the forehead.[3] The 144,000 who stand beside the Lamb on the hill of Zion bear the names of the Lamb and his Father written upon their foreheads;[4] they are sealed the servants of God with the name of God upon their foreheads.[5] One of the relics of such an ancient sign of Jahveh, almost effaced by the hand of an editor, will be found in the passage of Exod. XIII, 9, in which the "law of the totaphot" appears. It is evident that the object mentioned is a cultic memorial emblem; that is, a sign which reminds the wearer of his membership of a cult. The passages in Deut. XI, 8 and VI, 8, express the obligation to bear the commandments of God in memory ("in their heart"), in the plastic form; they are to be bound upon the hand and worn as totaphot between the eyes. The choice of the expression "bind" indicates that here the plastic image is em-

---

2 "Das Kainszeichen," *Zeitschr. für alttestamentliche Wissenschaft*, Vol. XIV, 1894.
3 Revelation, XIII, 16 f.; XIV, 9; XVI, 2; XIX, 20; XX, 4.
4 XIV, 1.
5 VII, 2 ff.; IX, 4.

ployed in a secondary sense, since what is bound on is detachable. This choice of words represents the attempt at a later, material interpretation. By this the step was already taken which in Judaism led to the invention of the talmudic tephillin, the Judaeo-Hellenic phylacteries. The ancient custom of tattooing, which was afterwards felt to be heathenish, was now eradicated by the innovation:[6] "The sign scratched or burned into the body, since it had become repugnant in a religious sense, will have been replaced by a substitute which was no longer repugnant." The law intervened, taking the place of the old heathen magic, as it has often done in the Christian church also. The old cultic importance of the Jewish tephillin is revealed only by the fact that "these articles of clothing, inherently difficult of explanation," were worn during religious worship. The "mark of Cain" is identical with, or related to, the Israelitish totaphot.

One must admit that this aspect of Stade's theory represents an advance upon the earlier views, since it emphasizes the character of the totaphot as a cultic emblem. What there is to be said against it was said in our discussion of Klein's opinion. We feel that it is advanced by an inquirer who has not made a sufficient endeavor to find a basis for his views. It does not explain how a system of satchels and thongs could develop from the practice of tattooing, and it throws no light on the special importance in Judaism or on the peculiar ritual of the tephillin.

Baentsch likewise believes[7] that the totaphot are to be regarded as amulets. The practice of wearing amulets on the forehead is only a modification of an older practice—that of cutting or scratching a Jahveh sign on the forehead. The old sign was intended to remind the wearer of his cultic obligations. The passage in Exod. XIII, 16, signifies that the offering of the first-born was to be such a token of remembrance and admonition. It reminds Israel that Jahveh once smote the first-born of the Egyptians. Like Stade, Baentsch comes to the conclusion that the literal understanding or misunderstanding of this passage, or of other parallel passages, led later on to the invention of the tephil-

[6] Stade, "Das Kainszeichen," p. 312.
[7] *Handkommentar zum Alten Testament,* ed. by Nowak, Exodus—Leviticus Numeri, 1903, p. 113.

lin or phylacteries. The development was therefore as follows: An ancient tattooed cultic emblem—an amulet—the invention of the tephillin. Holzinger also thinks of a tattooed Jahveh sign.[8] Wellhausen considers that the totaphot were amulets fastened upon headbands.[9] According to Robertson Smith the phylacteries[10] are survivals of ancient superstition, and their employment during prayer may indicate the nature of this superstition. They are appliances for the purpose of increasing the efficacy of prayer.

The belief that the totaphot are amulets is supported also by Grünbaum,[11] Blau[12] (who refers to the scarabs of the Egyptian priests), and Bousset[13] ("If the New Testament calls them amulets the original significance of this custom is correctly indicated . . . The prayer capsules will have suppressed the original practice of bearing tattooed emblems of Jahveh on forehead and arm"). Similar opinions are held by Schürer[14] (the Greek designation shows that the chief importance of the tephillin consisted in the fact that they "kept evil spirits at a distance during prayer"), Wünsche,[15] Kittel,[16] Nowak[17] and many other scholars.

It became more and more obvious that the progressive representatives of religious research believed that they had solved the problem by resorting to the designation of phylacteries and regarding the tephillin as amulets. Here again the scholars have, on the whole, obeyed the wise advice to rely on words. Only rarely does there emerge a timid doubt as to whether this can be the real meaning of the tephillin. Such doubts were unwelcome,

---

[8] *Kurzer Handkommentar zum Alten Testament,* Tübingen 1900 (Exodus discussed by Holzinger).

[9] *Reste arabischen Heidentums,* p. 165.

[10] "Divination and Magic in Deut. XVIII, 10 and 11," *The Journal of Philology,* Vol. XIII, 1885, p. 286.

[11] Max Grünbaum, *Ges. Aufsätze zur Sprach- und Sagenkunde,* Berlin 1901, pp. 208 f.

[12] Ludwig Blau, *Das altjüdische Zauberwesen,* Strassburg 1898, pp. 87 f.

[13] Wilhelm Bousset, *Die Religion des Judentums im späthellenischen Zeitalter,* 3rd ed., 1926, p. 179.

[14] Emil Schürer, *Geschichte des jüdischen Volkes im Zeitalter Jesu Christi,* Vol. II, 4th ed., Leipzig 1907, p. 568.

[15] *Realenzyklopädie für protestantische Theologie,* Vol. V, p. 693.

[16] *Geschichte des Volkes Israel,* Vol. II, 4th ed., Gotha 1922, p. 76.

[17] *Hebräische Archäologie.*

and were quickly dispelled by the calm certainty of traditional learning. Thus, Friedländer's opinion that some other sort of sign must be in question was thrust aside as irrelevant. Friedländer's argument proceeded from a curious passage in the Mischna:[18] "Whosoever bears the tephillin on the forehead or on the palms of the hands, he is following the custom of the Minaeans" (heretics). Friedländer sees the explanation of this enigmatical decision in the fact that the Minaeans used to wear certain cultic emblems which the rabbis endeavored to replace by the tephillin. For example, they were substituted for the *signum serpentinum* of the pre-Christian Gnostics. The rabbis sought to obliterate every trace of such heretical symbols. In support of his opinion that the tephillin were not a genuine Jewish creation, but were employed to suppress the Gnostic *signum serpentinum*, Friedländer referred to the many indications of uncertainty in the talmudic discussion of the tephillin; for example, the debate as to whether they should be worn on the right hand or the left, and the hesitation to regard them as directly commanded by the Torah, etc. According to Friedländer's views the course of development would have been more or less as follows: Gnostic signs introduced themselves into the broad masses of the Jewish people. Then, since they could no longer be suppressed, "they were sanctioned, having been first given a Mosaic garment."[19] It was easily shown that this hypothesis of Friedländer's was untenable; the religious practice of wearing tephillin dates back to a time far earlier than that of the Jewish Gnostics. Still, despite the justifiable rejection of Friedländer's theory, one could not refuse to recognize the spark of truth contained among so many errors.

The question over which the scholars are still debating is whether the biblical passages in which the injunction regarding the totaphot appears are to be accepted literally or metaphysically. Emil G. Hirsch,[20] for example, begins by stating that these four passages in the Bible seem to prove that the custom of wearing amulet-like objects on the hand and the forehead was very

[18] M. Friedländer, *Der Antichrist in den vorchristlichen Quellen*, Göttingen 1901, pp. 161 f.

[19] Friedländer, *l.c.*, p. 157.

[20] Article on "Phylacteries," *The Jewish Encyclopedia*, Vol. X, p. 26.

widespread. The later rabbinical exegesis has taken the simile contained in these passages literally, and has proceeded in accordance with the literal meaning. Edward Mack[21] inclines to the opinion that in these biblical verses there is an allusion to visibly worn jewels or amulets, such as were worn by the neighboring heathen tribes, and that this allusion is a poetical comparison. A careful reading of the passages in question yields proof of their purely metaphorical significance. Thus, the ceremonial of the tephillin represents a degradation of an idealistic figure of speech occurring in the Old Testament. "Only the formalism of later periods could interpret this metaphor in the crude and materialistic practice of wearing phylacteries."

A. R. S. Kennedy, too, after an exhaustive examination[22] of the passages in question, comes to the conclusion "that the language of these verses is purely symbolical."

Kennedy, with reference to "the sign upon thine hand," points to the general practice of tattooing among primitive peoples. The forehead also is a favorite place for such tattooed symbols among half-savage tribes. We find that Kennedy returns to Stade's theory, and confirms it, inasmuch as he cites other passages of the Bible which he regards as evidence of such practices: the young man who bore a sign upon his forehead which showed that he was a prophet; the cross mentioned by Ezekiel, and the "sign of destruction" on the forehead of the wicked.

The scholars have debated the meaning of the word "totaphot" which is used in these passages (Exod. XIII, 16; Deut. VI, 8; XI, 8) for the token which Jahveh requires to be worn on the arm and the forehead. Knobel derives the word from a root which means "to strike" and then "to make an incision." Thus, totaphot would signify a tattoo mark or a branded mark. Klein, Siegfried, Stade, Nowak, and many other scholars support this opinion. On the other hand, König and other scholars have agreed that the word comes from a root which is related to the Arabic *tâfa* (to encircle), and has been produced from this by reduplication. From this, as Gesenius, Dillmann, Driver, and others maintain, is

[21] "Phylacteries" in *The Internat. Standard Bible Encyclopedia*, Vol. IV, ⧧2392.

[22] "Phylacteries," in *A Dictionary of the Bible*, Vol. III, by James Hastings, pp. 871 f.

derived the meaning "that which goes round the forehead"—a head band. Steuernagel also proposes the meaning "an encircling band."

If the derivation from the Arabic *tâfa = circumire* is correct, then the interpretation of the word as head band is not consistent with the explicit description, "between thine eyes." Kennedy, moreover, stresses the point that such an interpretation is not compatible with the group of ideas from which the metaphor is taken. Yielding to the force of this argument, recent research has again rejected the derivation from *tâfa*. In the absence of any other reasonable interpretation Kennedy refers the word to a root which means to drop or to drip. It then belongs to the order of designations for the apotropaic jewels which were worn in Israel. The author of Deuteronomy did not hesitate to employ so crude a metaphor in order to express the notion that the commandments of Jahveh should always be as close to the thoughts of the people and as highly treasured as were the most precious jewels among their superstitious contemporaries.[23] As a curiosity, it may be noted that König has derived the word totaphot from another Arabic root, which points to the meaning "field of vision." In correspondence with this interpretation, König translates Deut. XI, 8 as follows: "All the more shall ye lay up these words in your heart and your soul and bind them as a sign of remembrance on your hand and let them be as a field of vision between your eyes." This version is not lacking in elegance, but it may arouse a slight doubt as to whether the scholar has completely grasped the spirit of this passage.

The other problem—as to the date when the wearing of the tephillin was introduced—is closely connected with the question which has just been discussed. If we are dealing, as the majority of the scholars believe, with a novel institution, which was based on the misunderstanding of a biblical text, it should be possible, through research into the existing sources, to determine, approximately, the date of this new religious practice. The Talmud, of course, assures us that the wearing of the tephillin was in accordance with instructions given to Moses by God on Sinai. Wünsche attributes the introduction of the totaphot to the pre-

[23] Kennedy, in *A Dictionary of the Bible,* p. 871.

Christian era.[24] Klein[25] believes that it originated on Persian soil. Buhl[26] suggests a hypothetical date on the grounds that "the later use of the totaphot or tephillin, evoked by a more comprehensive grasp of the passages in question, cannot be proved in the Old Testament scriptures." This is true, but what is adduced as proof has itself to be proved; the question which is here represented as settled by an incidental attribute is the question whether such a later and more comprehensive grasp of the relevant passages was a reality. Kennedy[27] asks himself in what period of Jewish history were those four passages first interpreted literally? If we compare similar turns of speech employed in aphorisms with these, we arrive at the year 300 B.C. as approximately the *terminus a quo*. The *terminus ad quem* appears to be given by the famous letter of the pseudo-Aristeas, in which it is stated that Eleazar taught that Moses commanded us, in addition to affixing tokens of remembrance on our clothing, and verses to doorpost and gatepost, also to fasten signs upon the hand. Here, then, is an unmistakable reference to the hand tephillah. In this way Kennedy arrives at a period extending from 250 to 150 B.C.[28] On general and psychological grounds, moreover, it seems probable that this period saw the introduction of phylacteries, since it was marked by the rise of the ritualistic fanaticism which attributed the greatest importance to literal obedience to the Torah. During this period the Pharisees acquired great influence over the people, and enforced their rigorous opinions in matters of ritual. It is probable that the religious practice of wearing the tephillin was among the observances enjoined upon the people.[29] Josephus regarded the

[24] "Tephillin," Herzog's *Realenzyklopädie für protestantische Theologie*, Vol. XIV, 1907, p. 512.

[25] *Die Totaphot*, etc., p. 678.

[26] "Gebet im Alten Testament," Herzog's *Realenzyklopädie*, Vol. VI, p. 393.

[27] In *A Dictionary of the Bible*, p. 872.

[28] *Die Apokryphen und Pseudoepigraphen des Alten Testamentes*, Vol. II, ed. by E. Kautzsch, p. 19. Aristeas' letter of 159 B.C. (according to Wendland's translation) states: "And he expressly commanded that the commemoration signs should be applied likewise on the hands." Cf. also Hody, "Aristae Historia," in *De Bibliorum textibus*," p. XVIII.

[29] A critical examination soon exposes the weakness of this argument. Kennedy's choice of a date is based upon aphoristic expressions and their period. He assumes without question that he is dealing with a metaphorical

wearing of the tephillin as an ancient practice; and his con-temporaries[30] were of the same opinion.

If we have no definite information as to when the custom of wearing the tephillin originated in Jewry, the pronouncements of the Mishna give us abundant information relating to the period after the birth of Christ. We have already mentioned most of these disputations, prescriptions, and questions. The great mass of the people, during the Middle Ages, seem often to have wavered in their obedience to this particular law. At all events, in the eighth century, and more particularly in the tenth, the tephillin were less highly regarded; indeed, in many regions the religious practice had almost entirely lapsed.[31] It seems as though the faithful reverted to it with increased zeal after the many attacks from the advocates of reforms.

The religious ceremonial of wearing the zizzith has been discussed by the scholars no less exhaustively than the wearing of the tephillin. But in this case the agreement has been general that the practice is of great antiquity. As we see on the monuments of Persepolis, similar tassels or "fringes" were worn on the corners of the garments of the ancient Persians. Thureau-Daugin has shown that in the time of the first Babylonian dynasty the impres-sion "of the fringed border of a man's mantle" served as a seal or signature.[32] The representations of Syrian and other Asiatic peoples on ancient Egyptian monuments furnish evidence that this kind of ornament was habitually worn by the tribes neighbor-ing upon Israel.[33] Kennedy points out that the position of the "fringes" on the four corners of the garment is connected with certain superstitious notions which have left their traces in

---

mode of expression, and so arrives at a definite date. But it is extremely doubtful whether these verses of the Bible are of a metaphorical character. What he alleges in favor of the Pharisees, as a psychological probability, is somewhat superficial, and one has the impression that his judgment is un-consciously influenced by the recollection of Christ's protest. That the tephil-lin were worn at this time does not prove that they were not worn long be-fore this period.

[30] Ant. IV, VIII.

[31] Rodkinsohn, *Ursprung und Entwicklung des Phylakterienritus bei den Juden*, 1883. See review in the *Revue des Etudes Juives*, Vol. VI, p. 288.

[32] *Rituels Accad.*, 57n. 95.

[33] Wilkinson, *Anc. Egyptians*, ed. by Birch. Plate II b.

Hebraic legislation. He mentions, as an example, the bells on the official robe of the high priest,[34] which McNeil[35] has explained in a similar sense. Kennedy comes to the conclusion that the tassels were originally amulets. Baentsch also thinks that the wearing of such tassels may "somehow" be referred to an ancient custom, and the people of a later age, who no longer understood the meaning of the practice, evolved the explanation which appears in the Israelitish law. At all events, the tassels or fringes, like the tephillin, had originally the signification of phylacteries or amulets.[36] König thinks it obvious that the notion of Israel's special relationship to the Deity was to be symbolized by the attachment of tassels to the blankets of Israel. This scholar, however, whose originality we have already acknowledged, is remarkably backward in explaining how the addition of tassels to blankets is supposed to symbolize "the special relationship of Israel to the Deity." However, other scholars who have interested themselves in this detail of Hebraic archaeology have observed that originally the zizzith had doubtless the character of amulets. In this connection we should give special attention to Robertson Smith's reminder that among the ancient Semites the hide of certain animals was sacred, and that its use had originally a religious significance. Smith suggests that the fringes prescribed by the Jewish law are more or less distantly related to the *raht* or *hauf*, an Arabian girdle, or short fur tunic, such as was worn by maidens during menstruation and by the faithful before the Kaaba. With these one may compare the thongs of the *Luperci* in ancient Rome, which were cut from the hide of sacrificial animals. This theory, which Robertson Smith advances incidentally in a footnote, seems to me to come nearer to an understanding of the mysterious tassels than the other attempts at explanation on the part of the Old Testament and Near Eastern experts. Here we find a fresh point of view which the other scholars did not and do not now take into consideration: for the first time attention is given to the material from which these mysterious fringes were pre-

---

[34] Exod. XXVIII, 33; XXIX, 25.

[35] Namely, as a survival which, like the fantastic animals in our churches, served to intimidate the demons and evil spirits. *The Book of Exodus*, 1908, p. 185.

[36] *Lectures on the Religions of the Semites*, 1899, p. 334.

pared. The sacredness of the hide of certain animals acquires a special significance under this hypothesis. We may anticipate that the prosecution of Smith's theory will lead to definite conclusions as to the meaning of this custom. Such research seems all the more necessary if we wish to learn why such an important role was ascribed to tassels or fringes in particular, what their original meaning and function can have been, how they acquired the character of amulets, and how the complicated talmudic prescriptions are to be explained. Smith, in this hypothesis, has achieved more than all the efforts of the archaeologists and biblical critics. It is definitely important, for it is highly suggestive; but the explanations which it has afforded so far are too general to solve the enigma of the zizzith.

4. EXEGESIS AND THE CRITICISM OF SOURCES

We must once more return to the four biblical passages in which the prescriptions as to wearing the tephillin are contained. Exod. XIII, 9 forms part of a chapter which contains the commandments relating to the feast of the Mazzoth and the offering of the first-born. Here, suddenly—apparently without transition—appears the commandment: "And it shall be for a sign (ôth) unto thee upon thine hand and for a memorial (zikkaron) between thine eyes that the Lord's law may be in thy mouth; for with a strong hand hath the Lord brought thee out of Egypt."[1] The passage is very obscure. Dillmann and Kautsch assume that the text is imperfect. The question naturally arises as to what such a sign would be. The text says "it." Immediately before this is the commandment to eat unleavened bread for seven days. Baentsch[2] straightway assumes that the enigmatical "it" relates to this custom. Holzinger,[3] on the other hand, considers that the sentence is overloaded; the subject is not clearly indicated. Baentsch would interpret the verse thus: "Israel is to keep the Torah of Israel in its mouth; that is, diligently meditate upon it and make it the subject of instructive and improving speech." But this can-

---

[1] In the Latin version of the Bible: "*Et erit quasi signum in manu tua et quasi monumentum ante oculos tuos et ut lex Domini semper sit in ore tuo.*"
[2] Baentsch, *Exodus-Leviticus-Numeri* in Nowak's *Handkommentar*, p. 111.
[3] Holzinger, *Exodus*, Tübingen 1900, p. 41.

not possibly be the original meaning of the passage, for according to the context the Torah does not yet exist. It will be given to Israel only very much later. Can the "it" relate to the offering of the first-born, which is mentioned in the following passage? But what could be meant by the statement that "it" shall be "for a sign unto thee upon thine hand" and "a memorial between thine eyes"? The injunction is repeated in Exod. XIII, 16. There (XIII, 14) we read: "And it shall be when thy son asketh thee in time to come, saying, What is this? that thou shalt say unto him, By strength of hand the Lord brought us out from Egypt, from the house of bondage. And it came to pass, when Pharaoh would hardly let us go, that the Lord slew all the first-born in the land of Egypt, both the first-born of man and the first-born of beast; therefore I sacrificed to the Lord all that openeth the matrix, being males; but all the first-born of my children I redeem." Now, almost unaltered, follows the commandment: "And it shall be for a token upon thine hand, and for frontlets between thine eyes," etc. Baentsch observes at this point: "This custom also is to serve as a memorial," though it is difficult to see what connection there can be between the sacrifice of the first-born and the sign upon the hand and between the eyes. Kennedy[4] is of much the same opinion as Baentsch: The feast of the Mazzoth, like the sacrifice of the first-born, is to serve as a perpetual memorial of the liberation of the Hebrews from the Egyptian captivity and of the Lord's requirement of them.

The context of the third passage, Deut. VI, 6 ff., is as follows: "Hear, O Israel: The Lord our God is one Lord. And thou shalt love the Lord thy God with all thine heart and with all thy soul and with all thy might." According to Bertholet[5] this paranetic introductory speech is characterized by "its own urgent warmth of tone." "The speaker addresses himself *ad hominem* and expressly emphasizes the intimate relation of the human being to God." The continuation of this appeal, which has resulted in its being recited, morning and evening, by every adult Jew as a confession (*sch'ma*), is as follows: "And these words which I com-

---

[4] *A Dictionary of the Bible*, Vol. III, p. 871.

[5] Alfred Bertholet, "Deuteronomium," in *Kurzer Handkommentar zum Alten Testament*, Freiburg 1899, p. 23.

mand thee this day shall be in thine heart; and thou shalt teach
them diligently unto thy children, and shalt talk of them when
thou sittest in thine house, and when thou walkest by the way,
and when thou liest down, and when thou risest up. And thou
shalt bind them for a sign upon thine hand and have them as
totaphot between thine eyes," etc. Steuernagel[6] observes that the
relative clause, "which I command thee this day," seems to
postulate their relation to the Law. He proposes to omit the
clause, since "a reference to the law in this form before its com-
munication would not be really intelligible." In Steuernagel's
opinion we have in this relative clause one of the favorite conventional additions of the transcriber, who was always thinking
only of the Law. In Deut. XI, 18–20 the commandment appears
again in almost the same words. The biblical scholars consider
that in this passage there is a quotation from Deut. VI, 6–9; we
have apparently a late version, since the text of the first passage
is not completely reproduced.

These two passages in Deuteronomy are in Kennedy's[7]
opinion "the cardinal passages" on which the ancient Jewish
usage of the phylacteries is based. "We have to ask ourselves, do
these passages command and sanction the religious usage or do
they not command it? To answer this is by no means so easy as
may appear at first sight, for it is not only a matter of exegesis,
but it involves the consideration of problems of biblical criticism
and etymological research." Kennedy, returning to the hypothesis
already mentioned, suggests that the author or rather the authors
of these passages have here employed a metaphor, and interprets
the word *totaphot* as "drops" or "jewels."

Other Old Testament scholars have carefully examined the
text of these four passages to which the institution of the tephillin
is attributed. They have striven, with extraordinary care, to
identify the various sources of these verses, and to place them in
the known religious and historical context of Israel's development. If we summarize the views of the scholars regarding these
important passages, we find a consensus of opinions that they are
to be accepted metaphorically. It may well be—so many of them

---

[6] *Ibid.*, 2nd ed., 1923.
[7] *L.c.*, p. 871.

consider—that the editors of the Bible have made use of a comparison which is based upon the practice of an ancient national custom, a tattooing or a Jahveh sign; but no doubt we are dealing with a figure of speech.

Be this as it may, it seems to us that we may usefully note a few characteristics which these four passages appear to have in common. The law, or whatever the "it" may signify, is to be for Israel as an *ôt*—a sign, *signum*—on the hand, and as *zikkaron* or *totaphot* between the eyes. We know neither "what" this sign is to be, nor its nature, since according to the experts we have to regard the invention of the tephillin as a later institution, based upon a misunderstanding of the text. But it is undeniable that here the reference is to a sign or "memorial." Further, we note that in all four passages there is the recommendation to teach "them" to the children, to "talk of them." One other common feature may be mentioned; that is, the circumstances under which the commandment is uttered: it is somehow connected with the feast of Passover. The first-born, the sacrifice of the firstlings, have something to do with this mysterious memorial sign. In three passages this sign is designated by the word *totaphot*. The meaning of this word is obscure; the Greek translation is *asaleuton*, something immovable; the Vulgate says *appensum quid*, something attached. In any case the word is used in the same sense as *ôth* and *zikkaron*, and subsequently it acquired the meaning of sign or commemorative sign. For the moment, we incline to the opinion that the root of the word originally meant to go about, to circumscribe.

We now find ourselves in a curious situation. On the one hand, religious tradition tells us that the tephillin are memorial signs; that God commanded the Jews to use them, speaking to Moses on Sinai; and that they are of the greatest religious importance. We do not know, indeed, of what they are supposed to remind the bearer. We do not believe that Moses received a revelation from God; and we do not understand why such importance should be ascribed to a combination of satchels and thongs. Old Testament scholarship asserts, in opposition to religious tradition, that we are dealing with a late invention, which has no connection with the original Israelitish religion. A biblical text which should have been understood in a metaphorical sense was understood literally and misunderstood, many centuries later. From this misunderstanding the institution of the tephillin originated. They were amulets, intended to keep evil spirits at a distance.

The ancient, traditional view seems to be wholly absurd; at all events, as regards its connection with the religious use of the tephillin it is unintelligible. A literal understanding of the biblical passages appears at first sight to make sheer nonsense. The explanations of the biblical archaeologists cannot eliminate all contradictions; there remain, so to speak, errors of weaving in the carpet which they offer us, but it seems reasonable and consistent with our way of thinking. Thus, the choice before us is not a difficult one, if we accept the rational solution. It must be confessed, however, that there is a trifling obstacle in the way of our wholehearted acceptance; just one of those curious contradictions which the rational approach is unable to solve.

5. A NEW APPROACH

In situations of this kind psychoanalysis seems to me particularly appropriate. We know the judgments which the strict theologians have passed on the achievements of analysis, in so far as they relate to religion and religious problems. In particular, they reproach the psychoanalysts with introducing hypotheses which cannot be proved, or do not appear to have been proved; that they apply, without any justification, results obtained in the alien sphere of the psychology of the neuroses to the investigation of religious problems. We psychoanalysts cannot regard these reproaches as a reason for discontinuing our work in the theological field. We even feel that in this field we are pioneers, and that we can wait until the theologians recognize what a rich and fruitful region we have conquered for them to investigate.

Here, by exception, and only in this special case, a concession may be made, in order to satisfy the requirements of the theological discipline. In the following attempt to divine the original meaning of the tephillin and zizzith, not a single analytic hypothesis arising from the psychology of the neuroses has been applied. None of the results obtained by such analytic treatment have been adduced. Here psychoanalysis is applied only as a heuristic method. As such it should prove whether it is possible to solve a special problem of theological science without hypotheses—one of those numerous problems which this science is unable to solve by its own methods. On the basis of small and hitherto unregarded individual features psychoanalysis yields results in connection with this problem which even the representatives of the alien science will be obliged to accept—surprising and unfamiliar though they may at the first glance appear. We are not, however, especially interested in this result; but we should wish to see the method applied in its purest form to the work of research, and this precisely where the methods hitherto applied by theological science could result only in flagrant failure.

An old book which came into my hands by chance may serve as the starting point of our analytic investigation. It is entitled: *Die Alten Jüdischen Heiligtümer / Gottes-Dienste und Gewohnheiten / für Augen gestellet / in einer ausführlichen Beschreibung des gantzen Levitischen Priestertums / und fünf unterschiedenen Büchern etc.*, Hamburg 1701.[1] Its author was Johannes Lund, represented on the title page as a faithful servant of the Word of God at Tundern in the Duchy of Schleswig. This old book gives a faithful description of the religious institutions of the Israelites in antiquity and in the author's own time, in clear and vigorous German. One section is devoted to the tephillin. The "faithful servant of God's word" exactly describes these peculiar religious objects as they lay before him. Of the strips of parchment inscribed with biblical verses which are contained in the tephillin he says: "These are wound about with the hair of cows or calves / which are pulled out of their tails / and previously well washed and purified. These hairs, however, are not knotted at the end / but only twisted round with the fingers / so as to allow one hair / to stand out / so that it is seen from without . . ."[2]

---

[1] "The Ancient Jewish Sanctuaries / Divine Service and Customs / Made Plain / in an Exhaustive Description of the Entire Levite Priesthood / And Five Separate Books, etc."

[2] Lund, p. 800.

Now, we already know that these parchments are tied with the hair of a ritually clean animal. It may well be that the end of a hair protruded from the capsule. As a matter of fact, in the tephillin of orthodox Jews we still find that the hair with which the parchment is tied protrudes a little way from the capsule. But after all, how does this bit of hair concern us? It may or may not protrude a little from the head tephillah; surely this detail is meaningless? Nonetheless, let us read on and see what the faithful Johannes Lund has to tell us concerning this usage. He is not content to examine and exactly describe the religious objects before him; he has made exhaustive inquiries as to their details of the authorities of his day. Thus, he tells us of an interview which he had, in respect of this very usage, with a rabbi of Amsterdam. First of all, he informs us that he observed this peculiar hair in the case of this rabbi's tephillah: "A red hair was hanging out of it / almost as long / as one and a half joints of the finger. I inquired as to the reason of this. He said / it would be in remembrance of the red cow / and that they prayed to God / that / as the red cow had taken their sins upon her / and cleansed them of their impurities / God would also cleanse them of their sins / Novarin Schediasn, book 5, chap. 28 writes / he too had questioned a Jew as to this / and received the answer / that they were reminded thereby of the golden calf / which they had worshipped in the wilderness."[3] Now, here is a detail which is quite unimportant even for those who are interested in the evolution of religious beliefs. We are certainly not impressed by the statement that the Jews connect this little bit of hair protruding from the head tephillah with the red cow or the golden calf. How should such a detail, such a trifle as an inch of hair, set us on the track of the original significance of the tephillin?

The analytic method insists that it is just such unregarded details which are of the greatest heuristic value. Another of its methodical principles is to take the hints furnished by tradition seriously in a psychological sense, however foolish or meaningless they may seem. We follow the methodical hint which it gives us: What can it signify that this tip of a hair should remind pious Jews of the red cow or of the calf that their ancestors once wor-

[3] *Ibid.*, p. 802.

shipped in the wilderness? What heuristic value can attach to such a mystical or seemingly absurd statement? If the head tephillah is to be applied to the forehead near the edge of the scalp, and if the hair of a cow or a calf protrudes from it, and further, if the Jews assert that this hair is to remind them of the red cow, or of this calf on Sinai—is there not a suggestion that the head tephillah itself is an article of clothing or a disguise which represents the wearer, symbolically, as a bull, or—in more general parlance—as an ox? The material of which the head tephillah is made is in no way inconsistent with such an assumption; for the law itself requires that it should be made of the hide of an ox. Even its form supports the theory; for we have here a relic, a suggestion, of the horns of the beast, which jut forward from its head. The hypothesis at which we should arrive by following this line of thought, fantastic though it may seem at first sight, would be as follows: The head tephillah is a relic, a survival, of a disguise which the Israelites adopted on certain occasions. From this point of view it would not be difficult to offer an explanation of the meaning of the hand tephillah and the thongs, or of the tallith and the zizzith. We should conclude that these articles of clothing also represent some such primitive fashion of disguise. The hand tephillah might represent the hoof of the ox; the leathern thongs, as *pars pro toto,* would represent its hide. And even the tallith, made from the wool of a ritually clean animal, might be the substitute for the fleece of a ram, originally roughly cured and worn by the Hebraic tribes. The zizzith would then be allusions to the animal's four legs, and the knotting of the many threads would represent the joints. We should thus have uncovered the traces of an ancient tribal custom, from which the original meaning of the tephillin and the zizzith is derived.

In the arms of the city of Danzig are the words: *"Nec timide nec temere."* Let them serve as the motto of our inquiry. The analytic method has led us, through the psychological consideration of this detail, to a seemingly fantastic assumption as to the meaning of the phylacteries. If we wish in all seriousness to maintain our allegation it is incumbent upon us to establish its probability. First we must deal with all the objections which our hypothesis is bound to provoke, disregarding all the contradic-

tions which it seems to contain, and ask ourselves: What could
be the meaning of such an animal disguise? What could be the
motive of such a device?

6. THE LIVING RAIMENT OF GOD

Comparative ethnology tells us that the majority of primitive
and semiprimitive tribes employ such disguises for purposes of
magic. The belief that by putting on the hide of an animal one
becomes that animal is general among primitive peoples. Frazer
describes how the savage wraps himself in the skin of a totemic
animal, or fastens upon his person certain parts of the animal's
pelt, in order to make sure of the totem's protection. Certain
Indian tribes wrap themselves in the skins of wolves; a hole is
made in the skin, through which the head of the man protrudes,
while the head of the wolf hangs on the warrior's breast.[1] Lewis
and Clarke[2] report that on certain occasions the Teton Indians
wear a raven on the head, the body being divided, one half coming down on either side of the human head. Most of the Indian
tribesmen appear on solemn occasions, as at feasts or dances, in
such animal disguises, and as a rule every tribesman wears at
least a recognizable portion of a totemic animal on his person.
For example, the Condor Indians in Peru wear on their heads the
feathers of this bird, from which they trace their descent. The
warriors of the Buffalo Indians arrange two locks of their hair in
such a way as to imitate the horns of the buffalo. Many Australian
tribes cut thongs from the hide of certain animals and fasten them
all over their bodies, in order to resemble the animals.

The peoples of antiquity held the same views concerning
the special significance of an animal's hide or pelt. W. R. Smith[3]
tells us that among the Semitic tribes in ancient times the hide
of the sacrificial animal possessed a character of special sanctity.
It was employed in the ancient religions to clothe either the
image of the god, or his worshippers. The significance of this

[1] J. G. Frazer, *Totemism and Exogamy*, Vol. I, 1910, pp. 26 ff.
[2] Lewis Clarke, *Journey to the Source of the Missouri River*, Vol. I, p.
123. Cited from Frazer.
[3] William Robertson Smith, *Lectures on the Religions of the Semites*, 3rd
ed., London 1927, pp. 436 ff.

custom was obvious in a phase of religious evolution in which the god, his worshippers, and the sacrificial victim were all members of the same tribe. Smith argues that the worshipper of the god who clothes himself in the skin of a sacrificed animal thereby invests himself with the sanctity of the animal, so that for half-savage peoples clothes are a permanent factor of the social religion, a token of membership of the religion. Herodotus tells us that the *aegis,* the goatskin, was a sacred garment among the Libyans. Smith compares the tassels or fringes on the garment which are prescribed by the Jewish law with the thongs of the sacred goatskin. He likewise observes that at a later period the hide of the sacrificed animal always played an important part in connection with religious usages and especially in the ceremonial of atonement. The Assyrian worshipper of Dagon, who offers the mystical fish offering to the fish-god, wraps himself in the skin of a fish. When a sacrifice was offered to the sheep-goddess of Cyprus the worshipper wrapped himself in a sheepskin. In Hierapolis the pilgrim placed the head and feet of the sacrifice on his own head, while he knelt on the skin. In certain late Syrian cults a boy received religious lustration through a sacrifice, his feet being shod with shoes made from the skin of the sacrificial animal. Even in the later forms of religion the old usages persist, at all events in the religious employment of animal masks. In almost every crude religion there are related features; they will be found also in the Dionysian mysteries and other Greek rites.

We think we can now guess what motives led the ancient Israelites to disguise themselves with animal skins or parts of an animal. They were the same motives as those that actuated the Semitic peoples of antiquity, and which actuate the primitive peoples of the present day, and which bestow on these animal disguises their special religious and social significance. We may then assume that originally the Hebraic tribes clad themselves in the skins of their totemic animal, whether this may have been the bull or the ram.[4] They identified themselves with the sacred animals so completely that they regarded it as their tribal ancestor and protector. This was their way—and the way of all

[4] A discussion of the problem as to which was the original totemic animal of the Israelites will be found in my book *Das Ritual,* 2nd ed., 1928.

ancient peoples—of showing that they were proud of the blood relationship with the animal, and of partaking of its qualities. We must naturally imagine that originally it was almost the entire hide in which the ancient Hebrews wrapped themselves. With the decline of primitive totemism, and under the influence of various other motives, many changes occurred in this religious custom. They cannot have been only social reasons which forbade them to wear the old tribal tokens proudly and openly; the totemic religion itself gradually lost its importance. As among other half-savage tribes, at a later period only individual parts of the animal's skin were employed to indicate an identification with the totemic animal, and to place the wearer under its protection. What was once of the greatest importance now seems reduced to the extreme in its dimensions; what was formerly of the greatest significance is now merely indicated and transferred to the merest detail. In the place of natural members of the animal—perhaps the horns of the bull—artificial substitute devices, allusions to the originals, must have made their appearance. Their connection with the ancient token consists only in the identity of their material and their similarity of shape. Their special sanctity, and their employment in ritual and cultic exercise, were indicated by the fact that they had to continue the ancient function.

From the position which we have now reached it should not be difficult to define the difference between our views and those of our predecessors. These Old Testament scholars were mostly of the opinion that the totaphot were originally either bodily mutilations or amulets. This cannot be the case, though the tephillin might subsequently have acquired the character of amulets, just as every portion of a totemic animal can assume the function of protection, and often does so. There is no evidence to connect the totaphot with bodily mutilations. Nevertheless, this hypothesis leads us toward the actual origin of the tephillin. The tattooings or bodily markings are attempts at assimilation to or identification with the totem of the primitive tribe. Those investigators who assume that the totaphot were originally Jahveh signs or national emblems were on the right track. They cannot tell us, however, what was the nature of the sign, what function it had, and why it took this particular form. One might say that most of the representatives of Old Testament archaeology had individual fragments of the great complex in their hands, but that the factual and psychological connection between these elements was wholly lacking. We have to thank psychoanalysis for a hypothesis which can supply the "missing link": The tephillin are a substitute for those portions of the totemic pelt which the ancient Israelites wore in order to identify themselves with their totemic god.

From this it becomes evident how erroneous is the opinion held by the majority of archaeologists; i.e., that the institution of the tephillin was an invention of the late rabbinical Judaism, having originated about a century before the birth of Christ. Of this there can be no question; our views concerning the original significance and function of the totaphot refers the origin of the tephillin to the prehistoric age of the Israelitish tribe, when totemism was still a living memory. When, later on, the worship of Jahveh suppressed the old totemistic ideas these latter were not eliminated; a process of interpenetration and amalgamation of the two orders of religious ideas occurred. For a long while the new religion of Jahveh, fighting for its existence, made use of the old totemistic forms, and indeed never entirely superseded them. Subterraneously, and in new psychological connections, which were not perceived consciously, the ancient totemic cult forced its way through the laws of the new faith, and the inherited notions spread rapidly over the now enforced ideology, to which the conservatism and stubborn tenacity of the Hebraic tribes refused for a long while to adapt themselves.

While at a later period the tephillin may have assumed the indifferent character of religious amulets, everything goes to indicate that they were once the substitutes for the sacred animal pelt, the living garment of the god. While their function, within the framework of an "enlightened" Judaism and a tepid rationalism, may have been merely accessory and purely symbolical, analytic investigation is able to show that the unbroken psychical association of the pious with the emotional and intellectual life of their ancestors comes closer to the mystery than the rigid *akribia* and seeming objectivity of a science which approaches the unconscious without preconceived opinions. Psychoanalysis is able to give us profounder conclusions concerning the apparently unimportant detail of the tephillin than theology, which can do no more here than recognize some sort of indifferent cultic signs, or the relics of incised emblems. Our inquiry seems to result in the admonition: *Introite, et hic dii sunt.*

7. OBJECTIONS, CORRECTIONS AND ADDENDA

It is true that many problems remain to be solved; but now it is time to deal with the objections which we have for so long disregarded. The most important of these is based on the fact that our theory contains inherent contradictions which must endanger its validity. For example, we have assumed that the tallith is a relic of a representation of the sacred ram's fleece. The zizzith would then represent the four legs of the animal. The arrangement of threads and knots which we have observed represents, by allusion, the muscles and joints of the sacred animal. Here, of course, it may be objected that these threads, in their arrangement, can hardly be compared with the feet of an animal, but the brevity of the tallith belongs to a later stage of development. Originally it was a long garment. Lund[1] tells us that the tallith "were so long that not a hand's breadth of the undergarment could be seen beneath them. The fringes had to hang to the ground in such a manner that the above-mentioned Rabbi Jacob Abraham and also Christian Gottlieb assured me that in Poland many rabbis wore their Arba Canpos or the Jewish dress with fringes so long that the latter reached the ground and often trailed after them." The abbreviation of these combinations of threads, which were at first worn long, had thus resulted in making their original signification unrecognizable. A similar reduction of certain features of religious usages under the influence of cultural changes has often resulted in obscuring the primary significance of a cult or of many of its rites. Often enough another, secondary meaning is given precedence over the old meaning which has already become unintelligible.

When the original significance of a rite or custom has been

[1] *L.c.*, p. 798.

discovered by research a psychological analysis should succeed in showing that numerous connections exist between the secondary and the primary meaning. The change of meaning may be said to follow a prescribed path. Thus the tephillah, which was originally a portion of the divinity himself, became an amulet; which means that he who wears such a fragment of the god upon his person, or carries it with him, is under the special protection of the god. Such a significance is naturally a derived one; originally the wearer of the tephillin became the god himself, and gods have no need of amulets. Even in the later, artificially established, associations the original meaning still glimmers through the apparently uninterrupted context, as the first text of a palimpsest may often be deciphered between the letters of the later script. Do we not recognize it when religious tradition declares that the thongs of the head tephillah form, in their convolutions, the letters of God's name? Here the original meaning of the tephillin glimmers through the latest interpretation; the prehistoric totemistic god of an age which certainly knew nothing of letters reappears in this indirect manner in the curiously formed letters. Can we not recognize the original character of the zizzith in the mystical allusions to their numerical value? Do they not now say that "the Lord is one," and now give the numbers of the religious commandments? But the essential law of the primitive religion is really this identification of the believer with his god, whose garment he wears. The Lord himself wore tephillin—for confirmation, think of the original significance of the horns which adorn the sacred animal. The Talmud explains the biblical prophecy according to which the peoples of the earth were to be afraid before Israel by stating that the nations were to be afraid before the head tephillah. Can we not here detect an allusion to the original meaning of the national totem, worn on the head? The other talmudic interpretation, which explains the passage "ye behold him" (not: "ye behold them"—namely, the fringes) as meaning that God receives him who wears the fringes, is akin to the former. What it really says is: He who beholds the zizzith sees God, and this is true in the sense of *pars pro toto,* for the zizzith are the substitute for a fragment of the divinity; they represent themselves. In the Talmud the wearing of the zizzith is equivalent to obey-

ing all the commandments of the ceremonial religion. Psychologically this is correct: The identification with the ancient totemic god was the first and most important commandment of the
primitive religion.

Another objection to our hypothesis could be derived from
the hypothesis itself. If the tephillin, prepared from the hide of
the ox, point to identification with the ancient bull totem of the
Israelitish tribes, how can we explain the sacral character of the
tallith (and for that matter the zizzith) which consist of sheep's
wool? It is not difficult to dispose of this objection, if we refer
to the evolution of totemism—that is, to historical motives. The
exchange of totems, the replacement of one kind of animal totem
by another, may be observed in the course of the history of many
ancient peoples. In such cases the old totem often persists for a
long while unaltered, or acquires a different value when the new
totem has victoriously established itself. Thus, for the initiated
there is nothing surprising in the coexistence of tallith and
tephillin.

Religious usage ultimately points in the direction which we
have already been following; namely, the injunction to kiss the
tephillin reminds us that the ancient Semites used to cover their
religious symbols and idols with kisses. But their sacred stones,
trees, etc., were not regarded by the Semites as images of the gods,
but originally as the gods themselves. The Israelite who kissed
the zizzith performed, in a barely recognizable form, the same
religious act as is performed by the Arab who kisses the Kaaba, or
the pious Catholic who kisses the Pope's foot. The objection that
here a lifeless object is in question is of course irrelevant; in the
Catholic church the faithful pay their last homage to a deceased
Pope in the same manner. The feet of the holy man protrude
through the grille of the Chapel of the Sacrament so that for three
days the pious are still able to kiss them.[2] The recollection of
this original sign of religious veneration has long survived, in an
extraordinarily different form.[3] This is a fitting moment to recall

[2] Cf. Hermann J. Wurm, *Die Papstwahl*, Köln 1902, p. 94.

[3] No one familiar with the subject will harbor any doubt as to the connection between these two religious objects, though to the best of my knowledge no one has hitherto elucidated the connection. The scapular consists of
two scraps of woollen cloth which are so connected by two strings that one of

that the miracles recorded in the Gospels are effected by contact with the fringes of Christ's garment; miracles of the same nature as the miraculous results produced by the clothing of holy individuals, and the therapeutic effects of tabooed objects.

Perhaps this is also the moment to suggest that the tallith is to be regarded as the prototype of the consecrated article of

---

the pieces of cloth lies on the chest, and the other between the shoulders. "The material of the scapular must be wool, not cotton, linen, or silk, and a woven woollen fabric is required, not knitted or otherwise prepared. . . . As regards the shape, the scapular must consist of two square pieces of woollen cloth. When the sacred Congregation was asked whether round or oval or polygonal scapulars can be effectively consecrated, the answer was: *Nihil esse innovandum*" (Beringer, *Die Ablässe, ihr Wesen und Gebrauch*, 10th ed., Paderborn 1893, pp. 557 ff.).

Not only the form and function, but also the particular features of the scapular recall the corresponding features of the tallith: the scapular must always be worn, day and night. If one were to go a whole day without wearing the scapular one would not be able to obtain indulgences for that day. Also, it must be worn in a certain manner, so that one of the woollen strips hangs over the breast, etc. The further development of the ritual of the scapular became more and more complicated as the number of scapulars increased. Thus, the red scapular of the Passion was introduced by Pius IX, in 1847, and provided with special indulgences, on account of an apparition which the Saviour vouchsafed to a Sister of Mercy. The blue scapular of the Immaculate Conception was revealed in the seventeenth century to the Venerable Ursula Berincasa, in Naples, while the Heart of Jesus scapular is attributed to Maria Alacoque. Beringer (p. 374) asserts that devotion to the Lord Jesus scapular has greatly increased, "since in the war of 1870 its miraculous effects were noted in the case of many soldiers." Devotion to the brown Carmelite scapular, the most widespread of all, is due to a famous apparition of the Mother of God, which was vouchsafed on Sunday the 16th July 1251 at Cambridge to the holy Simon Stock, the general of the Carmelites. The Holy Virgin addressed the Saint, showing him a scapular, and saying: "Whosoever dies with this upon him will not suffer the eternal fire." The Virgin, however, vouchsafed yet a further privilege to those who devoutly wear the scapular of the Carmelites. This assurance was communicated to Pope John XXII, to whom the Virgin appeared, promising him to liberate the wearers of this scapular from Purgatory as quickly as possible, and explicitly on the Saturday after their decease. The Pope announced this grace, the so-called Privilegium Sabbatinum, in the Bull of 5 March 1330. Benedict XIV undertook to defend this privilege against its presumptuous critics. Many Popes, among them Clement VII, Paul III, Pius V and Gregory XIII, have declared themselves as enthusiastic supporters of this privilege. By the decree of the Congregation of 27 April 1887 it was decided that with regard to the special reverence and devotion pertaining to this most ancient scapular, it shall not be worn with other scapulars, but shall be consecrated and worn separately.

clothing which assures the Catholic of the forgiveness of sins; I mean the scapular. We know that the wearing of the scapular is accompanied by numerous indulgences, just as the wearing of the tallith was regarded as conferring religious merit.

We have now surveyed the hitherto unrecognized connection between the totemic disguises of the primitive peoples and the ancients and the religious use of the tephillin and the tallith among the Israelites, as well as the analogous use of the scapulars by the Catholics. In this connection a wealth of theologically interesting material presents itself, but here we must be content with the above-mentioned instances.

It may be noted, however, that in the light of our hypothesis Klein's old view of the subject, which stressed the connection between the law of the Tephillin and other injunctions, is rehabilitated. It obviously cannot be a matter of indifference that the ritual should be mentioned in connection with the extremely ancient feast of Passover, and that it should be enjoined that the father should answer his son's question by informing him that the tephillin are tokens or memorials. The archaic nature of this feast is attested by many witnesses. The law that the *passah* must not be eaten raw points to an earlier custom of devouring the bloody and still quivering flesh of the animal. Equally primitive are the spattering of the doorposts with blood, the old-fashioned nomadic garments, and the warning to leave some of the meat of the sacrifice until the dawn of the following day. There is no doubt that the animal slain and devoured was originally the sacrificed god, of whose flesh the clansmen ate in common, thereby renewing the community.[4] It now seems to us very reasonable that the law of the tephillin, which were evolved from the skin of the animal, should be connected with the festival of the great totemic banquet. The "it" which is to be shown to the sons as a sign or memorial is simply the divine hide, not the law, which belongs to a later period. To be sure, in this injunction we are dealing with a metaphorical mode of speech, but behind it is concealed the old, original meaning, which was entirely objective; namely,

[4] Cf. Georg Beer, *Pascha*, Tübingen 1911, pp. 18 ff.; and N. M. Nicolsky, "Pascha im Kulte des jerusalemischen Tempels," *Zeitschr. für alttest. Wiss.*, Vol. III, 1927.

the identification with the old totemistic cattle-god.[5] This crude material interpretation which Stade and so many other scholars have confirmed leads us back in reality to the oldest religious stratum; i.e., to the horns of the totem of the ancient pagan religion. Perhaps we shall also obtain an explanation of the enigmatic significance of totaphot, which, I believe, can really be derived from the root *tâfa*—to surround. Since to the scholars the meaning of "a band that goes round the head, a headband" seemed improbable, and with reason, this etymological possibility was disregarded; as I think, too soon. Is no other explanation possible? The allusion to the encircling of the sacrificial beast about to be slain, an old Semitic practice, may suffice to make this explanation seem probable. Thus, this expression would indicate the connection of the tephillin with the national cultic feast of the Passover.[6]

We must not conclude this section without a few words to show how near the pious Jew who puts on the tallith and tephillin at his morning prayer is to the child who sticks a feather in his hair and plays at "Indians." What in the one case is done with the fervor of a religious exercise and in the other makes us laugh at a childish game, had once all the gravity and seriousness of a vanished culture, which today seems to us alien and mysterious.

Returning to our point of departure, we think we can see why the Saviour reproved the pious with especial bitterness because "they make broad their phylacteries and enlarge the borders of their garments." They imagine themselves to be especially pious because they so conspicuously display the emblems of the living God. Here our reading of the matter coincides once more with the traditional interpretation of this passage of the Bible; nevertheless, we do not believe that the way which we have followed was an unprofitable bypath.

[5] The Passah sacrifice consisted now of sheep and goats (Exod. XII, 1) and now of sheep and oxen (Deut. XVI, 2). One may assume that originally the bull was the Passah or paschal animal.

[6] The circling round the sacrificial animal is followed later by the circling round the altar. This constitutes the most important part of divine worship among the ancient Arabians (cf. Wellhausen, *Skizzen*, III[2], p. 109; *Heiler, Gebet*[2], pp. 101, 103). For the Old Testament cf. I Kings XVIII, 26; Psalm 42, 5; 118, 27 ff.

8. CONCLUSION

We have, of course, every reason to think modestly of the upshot of our endeavors, for their essential result has been already forestalled by other psychoanalysts. As long ago as 1920 Karl Abraham had already explained the prayer shawl of the Jews as a substitute for the totemistically revered fleece of the ram,[1] and recently Frieda Fromm-Reichmann, basing her assertions on Abraham's investigations, and on mine, has pointed out that the tephillin are the means of identification with the animal totem by wearing its hide and horns.[2] In this essay we have not been so concerned to claim priority for our thesis as to furnish, as far as possible, a scientific justification and proof of the assertions which are contained in these incidental and aphoristic observations.

Here we return to the special characterization and appreciation of the method applied in this inquiry, for the theological result which we have obtained we owe to the psychoanalytic mode of approach. Whatever its value may prove to be, it could not have been obtained by the other methods at the disposal of the theologian. Our method consists in the psychological appreciation of otherwise unnoted and often barely perceptible

[1] "Der Versöhnungstag," *Imago*, Vol. VI, 1920.

[2] "Das jüdische Speiseritual," *Imago*, Vol. XIII, parts 2–4. This appreciation of my predecessors, whose analytic conclusions agree in essentials with those developed in these pages, does not mean that I share their opinions in every detail. For instance, the explanation of the origin of the head tephillah in Fromm-Reichmann's treatise appears to me extremely improbable. The authoress holds that we are dealing with the result of "a simple displacement mechanism," "when the second cube, that is, the second horn is removed from the forehead to the upper arm." In my opinion this displacement mechanism is neither so simple nor so obvious as she supposes. Presumably we have an artificial substitute for the hoof of the animal, which was originally represented quite realistically on the hand, but which subsequently, under the combined influences of various motives, among which the tendency toward disguise was especially prominent, was moved higher up the arm. For the rest, we have now seen by what obscure byways the orthodox tradition of the Judaic law returns to indicate the original significance of a cultic detail. When many pious Jews, in order to overcome the uncertainty arising from the discussion between Rabbi Raschi and Rabbi Tamm decide to wear two head tephillin, we may readily recognize, in this distorted form, the ancient sign of the paired horns, the return of the repressed.

details. Such a detail, hitherto absolutely unregarded, was the point of departure which led us to the comprehension of the significance of the tephillin; i.e., the tip of a hair that protruded from the head tephillah, which assuredly had not hitherto attracted the attention of any investigator. Here was a trace whose attentive psychoanalytic investigation led to a barely disputable theological conclusion.

The analytic valuation of this hitherto unregarded detail seems in this case—and only in this special case—to justify the assertion which one so often hears repeated as a criticism of psychoanalytic investigations; here the result obtained was really and truly dragged in by the hair!

PSYCHOANALYTIC STUDIES OF BIBLE EXEGESIS

1. THE WRESTLING OF JACOB[1]

Gabriel:

> Yet once again, my Jacob, sink again
> Back on thy stone and rest thou yet awhile!
> Think, when today thou wrestlest with the stranger
> It is with God the Lord thou dost contend!
> Thou in thy seed shall ever trembling cherish
> Remembrance of this night—thus His decree!
> Behold, His morning reddens on thine eyelids!
> Go forth—behold—and hearken Jisro-El!
>
> Richard Beer-Hofmann—*Jadkobs Traum*

In the difficult art of describing psychoanalytic insights there are worse methods than that which shows how the psychoanalyst seemingly comes upon a problem by chance, and then step by step, overcoming external obstacles and his own objections, seeks to approach its solution. We shall follow this method in this essay.

If we turn from current literature to the Bible, we become aware as never before of the rejuvenating effect of the elementary eloquence of the Old Testament. We read, for example, the story of Jacob; his birth, his crafty overreaching of his brother, his wooing of Rachel, his period of service under Laban, and his flight; and now we come to the passage which describes, enigmatically enough, Jacob's wrestling with God. We are faced with a problem.

Like a block of stone rolled hither by Cyclopean hands this narrative of ten verses stands out from the gentler pastoral landscape of Jacob's history. It is the night before Jacob is to meet his dreaded brother Esau.[2] "And he rose up that night, and took his two wives, and his two women servants, and his eleven sons,

1 Read before the Psychoanalytical Society of Vienna.
2 Gen. XXXII, 23–33.

and passed over the ford of the Jabbok. And he took them, and sent them over the brook, and sent over that he had. And Jacob was left alone; and there wrestled a man with him until the breaking of the day. And when he saw that he prevailed not against him he smote him upon the socket of the hip joint.[3] But Jacob put his own thigh out of joint as he wrestled with him. And he said: Let me go, for the day breaketh. And he said, I will not let thee go except thou bless me. And he said unto him: What is thy name? And he said, Jacob. And he said: Thy name shall be called no more Jacob, but Israel, for as a prince thou hast power with God and with men and hast prevailed. And Jacob asked him, and said, Tell me, I pray thee, thy name. And he said: Wherefore is it that thou dost ask after my name? And he blessed him there. And Jacob called the name of the place Penuel: for I have seen God face to face and my life is preserved. And as he passed over Penuel the sun rose upon him, and he halted upon his thigh. Therefore the children of Israel eat not of the sinew which shrank which is upon the hip joint;[4] because he smote Jacob upon the socket of the hip joint."

The attempts to elucidate this obscure passage, in commentaries, in articles published in various periodicals, in exegetical essays, and also in histories of the Israelitish religion and of the peoples of the Orient, constitute a whole literature, and the psychoanalyst, overcome by a momentary diffidence, may well ask whether he, with his defective knowledge of the subject, can contribute anything new and decisive toward elucidating an episode which has baffled so many versatile scholars. However, when his confidence in his science has revived a little, he will seek, first of all, to determine the actual nature of the difficulties. He will inquire what questions were asked by biblical research, and at the same time it will become apparent to him that in addition to these questions there are new enigmas, which complicate rather than simplify the old problems.

The difficulties begin with the classification of authorities. I am presupposing that the Bible, as we have it, represents a relatively late revision. We know how these legends came into

---

3 A.V., "touched the hollow of his thigh."
4 A.V., "the hollow of the thigh."

existence, and how they were modified by a tradition many centuries old; and finally, that the collective text is not the work of one hand or of one period, but that we have to distinguish between the compilations of the Jahvists, the Elohists, the Priestly Codex, and the final editors. An attribution of sources which is based mainly on the use of the different names of the Deity cannot be strictly relied upon here, since the word Elohim is used in a descriptive sense, while the name Jahveh is carefully avoided. Here I shall not attempt any textual criticism of the passages under consideration, but will only refer to the fact that Holzinger, Luther, E. Meyer, Proksch and Gunkel attribute individual verses to different editors.[5] This will be enough to show how difficult such an investigation must be, but also how essential it is for the proper comprehension of the text.

Even in the first three verses two authors may be clearly distinguished. In the one version it is said that Jacob "passed over the ford Jabbok;" in the other he remains alone on the hither side of the brook. And there he is attacked by an unknown person: "*isch*," says the Jahvist, a man, someone. Who this person is we learn subsequently. It is God. But which God? Can it be Jahveh? No, say the commentators; for Jahveh is the god who loves Jacob and helps him. This divine figure, if we accept Gunkel's interpretation,[6] is an important contribution to our knowledge of the pre-Israelitish religion which was suppressed by the religion of Jahveh. This is a being hostile to mankind, who falls upon the unsuspecting wanderer and seeks to kill him. J. S. Frazer, who has dealt with this passage exhaustively in the *Anthropological Essays*,[7] thinks that it must have been the *numen* of the river, which was angry with Jacob because he had passed over the ford. He attempts to support this opinion—that Jacob's adversary was the river-god of the Jabbok—by alluding to the customs of primitive peoples on crossing rivers. From the wealth of examples adduced by Frazer a few may be selected as representative: When the Persians under Xerxes came to the Strymon in Thrace

[5] Cf. *Genesis, übersetzt und erklärt von Hermann Gunkel*, 3rd ed., Göttingen 1910, p. 360.

[6] *Ibid.*, p. 364.

[7] Oxford 1907, p. 136.

the magi sacrificed white horses and performed other ceremonies before they crossed the river. We are told that the Kaffirs, on crossing a river, spit upon stones which they throw into the water, in order to appease the ancestral spirits in the stream. Similarly, the Bushmen on such occasions would sacrifice portions of the game they had killed; or, if they had no game, they would throw a javelin into the stream. Of course, this theory leaves many things unexplained: the blow upon the hip joint, the blessing, etc. There is an instructive parallel in Exod. IV, 24–26, where Jahveh falls upon Moses in order to slay him, and is appeased by the circumcision of his son. At all events—and here the commentators are agreed—the whole description of the episode —the mysterious picture, glowing with a Rembrandtesque chiaroscuro, of an unknown god falling upon a man in the darkness, intending to slay him—shows that the legend is very ancient. Thus, in the oldest myths, Hercules wrestles with Antaeus; while both Hercules and Samson wrestle with lions. Some commentators, of course, being scandalized by the notion that Jacob should fight with God, have sought to give their own interpretation of the nature of the contest. Many have sought in vain to transform the material fact here recorded into a purely spiritual procedure. Following the example of Herder in his work on the spirit of Hebraic poetry, many believe that the passage describes Jacob's striving for God's mercy, a wrestling in prayer, in dread awareness of the sin committed against Esau; the purgation of his offence. A poet may seek to interpret the content of the myth in the sense of his visions (Beer-Hofmann), and a highly cultured age may find a wealth of abstract ideas, thoughts and emotions in the narrative—but any such sublimated exegesis of the primary content of the hoary legend is out of the question. By the first assumption—that the passage describes an obscure vision—the matter is not in any way elucidated—at all events, from the psychoanalytic standpoint. We should first have to try to learn the inherent meaning of the dream or vision. The second hypothesis—of the wrestling in prayer—is untenable, for even in the most desperate striving for God's mercy it is not usual to dislocate the hip joint. There is nothing for it but to accept the passage as it stands, with all its numerous contradictions and obscure profundities. Perhaps the very fact of the contest conveys a hint as to its hidden meaning; God and a human being fight one another, with almost equal strength. Indeed, in the end the man defeats the god. Jacob, therefore, as Gunkel insists,[8] is conceived as a kind of giant, a human being approaching divine status.

But now we come to what is perhaps the most unintelligible verse: "And when he saw that he prevailed not against him he smote him upon the hip joint" (or "touched the hollow of his thigh"). If one reads this rapidly it seems to make sense. But actually the passage is especially obscure, and its exegesis is extremely difficult—owing to the absence of explicit statements, and the change of subject during the sentence—a characteristic Hebrew peculiarity. Which of the two adversaries smote the other upon the hip joint? Here the obscurity seems impenetrable. Of course, the next sentence tells us that God has struck Jacob, but then we cannot understand how Jacob—as is expressly stated—should be the victor. Eminent biblical scholars, such as Max Müller, E. Meyer, Luther and Gunkel[9] explain, giving serious reasons for their opinion, that this is the later version of the episode; that the god defeated the man seems the only acceptable version for a later age. But the context becomes far more intelligible if we assume that in the first place Jacob defeats the god; we shall then understand why the god, so sorely hurt, and incapable of further wrestling, beseeches Jacob to let him go. One objection to the later version arises from the fact that in the whole course of the narrative there is no further mention of Jacob's injury, or of his limping. In Hosea, moreover, we find it expressly stated, in respect of Jacob's wrestling, that "he had power over the angel, and prevailed; he wept, and made supplication unto him" (XII, 4). Let us note what Gunkel says of this obscurity:[10] "When Jacob sees that he is not equal to the other in bodily strength, he resorts—and this is perfectly in keeping with his general character—to a wrestler's trick (much as Odysseus did, II, XXIII, 725 ff.), and smote his adversary on the hip joint

8 *L.c.*, p. 361.
9 Cf. details in Gunkel, p. 361.
10 Here we may regard him as spokesman for his colleagues.

—that is, the socket (hollow) of the thigh joint." It may be asked, of course, whether the inclusion of this incident, "perfectly in keeping" with Jacob's general character, may not indicate—like that character itself—a secondary revision of the legend.

In all probability the original hero was a violent character, ruled by powerful instincts; not a cunning and treacherous adversary. In obedience to certain tendencies the narrative was revised in accordance with the taste of a later period. But even if we grant the plausibility of this view, the fact remains that the text asserts that Jacob suffered a dislocation of the hip joint. We have to decide, one way or the other: either God injured Jacob, or Jacob injured God. There is no other possibility. The following verse, strangely enough, is in contradiction to both assumptions, since it asserts that in the course of the struggle Jacob himself put his thigh out of joint. Riddle follows upon riddle. In an unorganic and loosely knit narrative there are contradictions in close juxtaposition. Not a single ray of light penetrates the darkness.

God says: "Let me go, for the day breaketh." A passage in the Amphitrio of Plautus offers an admirable parallel: *"Cur me tenes? Tempus est exire ex urbe priusquam lucescat, volo"* (I, 3, 34 f.). Here, too, we are reminded of the ghost of Hamlet's father, which must begone before the dawn. The god fears the dawn, which for him constitutes an undefined peril; it is as though the sun must not be allowed to shine upon him. To us, of course, the reason for this divine terror is unknown.

And now comes the saying which to us has always seemed so strange: "I will not let thee go except thou bless me." We have been wont to associate with this saying ideas that have a certain nobility of content: we think, perhaps, of the research worker, striving to achieve the solution of a problem; or of the artist, struggling, as his work takes shape, with the dark powers of matter. As a matter of fact, the passage has no such secondary significance. The exclamation, "I will not let thee go," is originally meant in the purely physical sense. To bless means to speak a word that will be operative in the future. The blessing, to the ancients, was not merely a pious wish, a matter of words, of breath and resonance, but something effectual, something actually operative. It does not merely announce the future—it creates it. Gunkel, in another passage,[11] points to the fact that legends in which a blessing is bestowed always give this a place of great prominence. The blessing is the main thing, "because it indicates what still exists as the enduring impression of this story; what else occurs does no more than state the purpose, cause, and occasion of this speech." Does this perhaps suggest how we should understand the legend? But the blessing is preceded by a sort of dialogue. God asks Jacob: "What is thy name?" and learns his name. What are we to make of this? The meaning of the question can only be that God does not know who Jacob is. Can Frazer be right in assuming that this deity is a river-god who indiscriminately attacks all those who seek to cross the stream? Something deters us from accepting this hypothesis as adequate: it leaves so much unexplained, and it degrades the legend to the lower status of a local incident. But since for the moment we see no way of overcoming this difficulty, we find that here too all is wrapt in obscurity, an obscurity that awaits elucidation. The god now utters the blessing, inasmuch as he changes the name of Jacob into Isro-El [he who fights with God], justifying the change of name by the assertion: "For thou hast power with God and with men and hast prevailed." Does the blessing, which seemed so important in anticipation, amount to no more than a change of name? To us modern readers there seems to be a curious discrepancy between the wonderful words: "I will not let thee go except thou bless me" and this very prosaic change of name. Yet we recall the fact that such changes of name constitute a very widespread custom among primitive peoples today, as they did among the peoples of antiquity, and these changes are of special significance. "The changes of name," says Heitmüller, in his book *Im Namen Jesu*,[12] "are not merely symbolical in character —they have a real value. The name is for its bearer a source of power and skill." For the psychoanalyst in particular this significance of the name is most enlightening; and he, of course, has already realized the importance of names from his analysis of dreams and of psychoneurotic symptoms, and also from his ob-

11 Gunkel, *Genesis*, p. 80.
12 Cited from Gunkel, p. 268.

236 PSYCHOANALYTIC STUDIES OF BIBLE EXEGESIS

servation of children. Further, we note that in the ancient East the name was changed on the birth of the first son, and from that time onwards the husband was known as the Father of So-and-so, as though his old existence had been canceled by the new paternal dignity, while a new life had begun for him.

We do not deny that these explanations are still far from adequate, and that they make no essential contribution to the elucidation of the whole procedure. The question as to how Jacob acquired his name cannot possibly be answered by a purely etymological explanation. We begin to realize that this change of name must have a special significance, and that it must have a prominent part to play in the legend. Yet while we are trying to grasp the latent meaning of the passage a new problem emerges: Why does God refer to Jacob's previous conflicts with gods and men? We know of no tradition to that effect. There is no allusion to anything of the kind; so there can only be a very strained comparison of Jacob's outwitting of Laban and Esau to a wrestling match—a comparison quite inconsistent with the ancient point of view in respect of such matters. And how strange that God, who had just asked the unknown Jacob for his name, should suddenly know the details of his adversary's life! What an enigmatic and inconsequent God! It is curious, too, that God, when Jacob questions him, is unwilling to give his name; though this may be explained by the widespread belief of the ancients that the knowledge of an adversary's name gave one power over him.

Thus Jacob emerges from the conflict victorious, although he is limping, as the result of a dislocated hip joint. In the rest of the narrative there is no mention of such a serious and painful injury. It concludes with the statement that even to this day the children of Israel do not eat the *nervus ischiadus,* "because he" (once more the adversary is only "he") "touched the hollow of Jacob's thigh in the sinew that shrank" (i.e., dislocated the hip joint). The whole character of this verse, and especially the particulars given, show that it represents a late addition. The custom, well-known to the ethnologists, of prohibiting the degustation of certain portions of animal carcasses, makes its first appearance as this tabooing of certain parts of the body. Frazer himself gives many examples of such tabooing in the paper[13] already cited. In the second volume of *The Golden Bough*,[14] and in Robertson Smith,[15] the peculiar sacredness of the sciatic nerve is mentioned, and illustrated by examples. However, it is apparent that the tabooing of different parts of an animal's body has evolved, in these examples, on the basis of totemistic rites, so that its derivation from the animal worship of primitive peoples is obvious, whereas in this case the explanation given for the prohibition is the singular reason that Jacob was struck on the hip joint by "him." However, there is no reference in any other part of the Bible to the exceptional character of the hip joint; thus, the whole narrative leaves us with an unsolved problem.

We have learned that individual and now forgotten commentators—Michaelis, Hensler, Gabler and others[16]—regarded the whole story as the record of a dream or vision. Roscher described it specifically as a nightmare.[17] Are we familiar with dreams of a similar structure? Of course, there are "anxiety dreams" in which the dreamer is attacked, for unknown reasons, by unknown persons. We know that a sense of guilt in respect of sexual irregularities or fantasies, a dread of punishment, or the dread of castration, play an important part in the emotional genesis of these dreams. Perhaps we can deduce, from the dreamlike character of the scene, why God, or whoever the unknown assailant may be, has to disappear at daybreak. It is as though the dreamer were consolingly to tell himself in his sleep: "It is only a dream, and when the morning comes it will all be over." So may Hamlet have reassured himself, if we regard the horrid revelations of the ghost as an endopsychic process; when the first cock crows things will have a different appearance.

---

13 For example, at the ritual feasts of the men of the Aranda and Loritja in Central Australia, youths are forbidden to eat of the flesh of the head or the limbs of the animals devoured (Carl Strehlow, *Das soziale Leben der Aranda und Loritjastämme*, Frankfurt a.M. 1913).

14 Second edition, II, pp. 419–421.

15 *The Religion of the Semites*.

16 Cited by August Dillmann, *Die Genesis*, Leipzig 1842, p. 365.

17 Ephialtes, *Abhandlungen der Kgl. Sächsischen Gesellschaft der Wissenschaften, Phil.-hist. Kl.*, Vol. XX.

As a matter of fact, we do not attribute much value to the dream hypothesis. It explains little. Yet we suspect, on comparing the anxiety dream with the structure of the episode, that similar affects might originally have found their solution here. And now we might listen with greater attention to the author whose work, imbued with abstruse and often fantastic numerical mysticism, gives us many valuable hints as to the real meaning of ancient myths; I am referring to F. Nork, and his *Etymologisch-symbolisch-mythologisches Realwörterbuch.* In Vol. I of this work[18] we find a reference to the tradition that Hercules had to engage in such a wrestling contest on two occasions; once with Hippocroon, when the hero, curiously enough, suffered an injury to the hip, and once in the Palaestra of Olympia, when he encountered his father Zeus, who for some time wrestled with him as an unknown adversary, but finally revealed his identity. Another observation may perhaps appear more significant; the rabbies declare that the vein which the God of Jacob injured is identical with the phallus. The same opinion is maintained in the book of Sohar (Parascha Wajischlach, p. 170). We venture to suggest that psychoanalysis has recognized this and other displacements in the myths in question, and that the symptom of limping has been interpreted as a euphemistic reference to castration.[19] Now we seem to see the whole episode in a new light: The god castrates Jacob, or at least attempts to do so. Of course, by this substitution the difficulties are increased rather than diminished. Who is this god? Why does he attack Jacob? What does the blessing mean? How are the many contradictions to which we have alluded to be explained?

Let us once more consider the whole narrative, omitting— for specific reasons—the beginning and the end, and endeavor to reconcile our present interpretation with the text. It now occurs to us that the whole situation—the attack, the wrestling with a mysterious being, the new name, and finally, what we must call the mutilation of the penis—betray similarities to procedures which are apparently very far removed from it; namely, to the

[18] Stuttgart 1843, under the heading "Jacob."
[19] Cf. "Die Pubertätsriten der Wilden," in my *Probleme der Religionspsychologie,* Wien 1919.

puberty rites of primitive peoples. In these rites the young men are attacked, bitten, and supposedly killed—and the God of Jacob apparently intends to kill his victim—by a mysterious being whom we have recognized as the ancestral spirit—and after their alleged reawakening they are given a new name in token of their new condition.[20] These ceremonies are performed when the young males have reached the age of puberty. So far the details are similar, but we must not overlook the decisive differences, in the light of which our fabric of analogies seems no stronger than a house of cards. Jacob, in the biblical narrative, is a mature man; he even has two wives, as well as a few concubines, and we are told that he has eleven children. For the time being we will ignore this point and, so to speak, annul the whole of Jacob's previous life; we will assume that at the time in question he was still an unmarried youth. We could then say that God attacks Jacob as the Balum monster attacks the young Australian black-fellow, castrates or circumcises him, and gives him a new name. In either instance God may be replaced by the father. What is the meaning of the blessing? We shall find the answer to this question if we recall the content and the essential character of all Old Testament blessings—indeed, we need only adduce, as an example, the blessing which Jahveh conferred upon Jacob in Bethel: "The land whereon thou liest, to thee will I give it, and to thy seed. And thy seed shall be as the dust of the earth; and thou shalt spread abroad to the west, and to the east, and to the north, and to the south, and in thee and thy seed shall all the families of the earth be blessed." If we ignore the later additions and the manifold revisions which the blessing has received, its essential content is the promise of an abundant posterity and the possession of the land—which is the content of all the blessings recorded in the Scriptures.

Now let us turn back to the initiation ceremonies of the primitives. In the book already cited I have endeavored to show that the latent and original meaning of these rites is the repression of the incestuous desires of the youths for their mother. During the initiation celebrations the right to indulge in lawful

[20] Cf. "Die Pubertätsriten der Wilden," in my *Probleme der Religions-psychologie.*

sexual intercourse is purchased by incision of the penis and other tortures. The novices may now marry and beget children. We have noted that in the rites of puberty the desires prohibited by the primitive society are at the same time partially permitted and repudiated. The paternal generation, which after initiation accepts the sons as equally privileged, now consents to their desires. In the course of evolution this consent, conditioned by the emotional trend of the ambivalent attitude, assumes an increasingly prominent position in the foreground, until the original meaning of the initiation ritual is no longer perceptible. With the progressive repression of hostile impulses the paternal affection and care for the young become the central point of the initiation. The incision of the penis originally intended to destroy potency, becomes a means of increasing the power of procreation. We see another example of a highly developed ritual in the blessing which Jahveh bestows upon Jacob; i.e., the blessing of fruitfulness ("Thy seed shall be as the dust of the earth"). The promise of the land, however, replaces the promise that Jacob shall possess the wife who is originally the mother ("Mother Earth"). In subsequent promises to Jacob's posterity the fulfillment of the promise is always conditional upon obedience (i.e., the repression and renunciation of the hostile tendencies toward the father and the incestuous desire for the mother).

If we now survey the incidents of the story of Jacob in terms of its similarity to the rites of puberty—the successive attack of a mysterious god, the wounding of the young man, the change of name, and the blessing—we realize that in this story circumcision represents the expiation and prevention of Jacob's incestuous desires, but the blessing a permission to indulge in sexual congress—of course, with other partners. Now we understand why God asked Jacob for his name—not because He did not know him, but because this question forms a part of the ancient and primitive ceremonies of initiation. In the narrative it is designed to call our attention to the exchange of names, and its significance. And now we are no longer surprised that there is no further mention of Jacob's painful injury; for circumcision was a customary practice, to which all adolescent youths were subjected.

We therefore recognize, in this episode, the considerably

revised deposit of the ancient memories of the Jewish people; memories of the introduction of circumcision, which was accompanied by certain ritual observances, and which may be attributed to the same psychic motives as those which I have endeavored to demonstrate in the case of the primitives. As a matter of fact, Stade, in an ingenious work which is quite unconnected with the legend that we are considering, reminds us, in an article[21] entitled "Der Hügel der Vorhäute" (The Heap of Foreskins), that initiation ceremonies were performed at Gilgal resembling those of certain African and Australian tribes.

A number of details enable us to recognize that the revision of the ancient legend as we now have it was undertaken at a comparatively late period, when the mutilation of the penis, performed by the god or the father, was felt to be repugnant, so that the sciatic nerve was substituted for the penis. This detail of the complicated process of revision to which the ancient legends from the prehistoric life of the people were subjected naturally reveals a tendency which is explained by the date of the revision. A culturally advanced people regards its primitive and not very commendable beginnings from its existing point of view, and seeks to give a new interpretation to the humiliating recollections of its more primitive days. The whole relation of Israel to its God, which originally differed but little from that of the neighboring peoples, can be understood only by referring it to this process, which is characteristic also of the emotional life of individuals. The repression and the tendencious revision of the early stages of tribal history, which may be compared with the individual's recollections of early childhood, will even lead some persons to regard this history as the preliminary to the concept of the "chosen people." This development, indeed, is already implicit in the acceptance of the sons in the community of the adult males among the primitive races.[22]

We may perhaps feel some compunction for dealing so unceremoniously with the venerable text of the Bible. We remind

21 *Zeitschrift für alttestamentliche Wissenschaft*, Vol. VI, pp. 132 ff.

22 For the methods employed in such reinterpretations by neurotic patients see Freud's "Notes Upon a Case of Obsessional Neurosis," *Collected Papers*, III.

ourselves of our solemn undertaking to listen attentively to an objection which threatened to make nonsense of our explanation, and of which we have not yet disposed. We said that this version of the story of Jacob preserved a reminiscence of the original act of circumcision as performed by the father on the sons who had reached the age of virility. Yet Jacob must have been circumcised long before the date of the incident described, since he was married and already had eleven sons. Here the prehistory of the legend gives us a hint. The narrator has localized the whole episode in the place called Penuel, and he has done this for various reasons, etymological and other. Penuel means "the Face of God" or "the Presence of God." There, and only there, thought the old compilers, could Jacob's contest with the Deity have taken place. "Originally," says Gunkel,[23] "the legend is entirely independent, and has no connection with the story of Jacob and Esau. The valiant conqueror of the Deity and the Jacob who trembles before Esau are really quite different characters. Also, in the present version the Penuel episode is only very loosely connected with what precedes and follows it; so that the fact that Jacob has been seriously injured does not emerge in the following passages. Indeed, the Penuel episode really effects a complete separation between the two stories of Esau. The narrative (29 = Jahwist) refers to battles which Jacob has fought in the past; hitherto he has fought with men only, but in this last and sternest battle he overcomes even the Deity. Unless the legend refers to Esau and Laban when it speaks of men, it implies that these are essentially different forms of the story; and in any case a fresh encounter with Esau cannot have taken place immediately afterwards."

To these perspicacious arguments we may add another: that of the contradiction which occurs at the beginning of the whole narrative. We are told that Jacob sent his wives and children and all that he had across the brook, and that he himself "passed over the Jabbok." Therefore the fight could not have occurred on the hither side of the stream. But the second editor says, "and Jacob was left alone," which either contradicts the statement that he has crossed the stream, or implies a second and purposeless crossing. To sum up: the episode has no relation to the story of Esau,

23 *Genesis*, p. 365.

and its whole character is in contradiction to the rest of the narrative. At this point numerous contradictions and improbabilities
occur; in short, the story seems out of place. But if this is the
case—that is, if the episode does not, as the editors have placed it,
fit into the chronological progress of Jacob's career as hitherto
recorded—is it altogether improbable that it may have been trans-
posed from the Jacob who has just attained virility to the Jacob
who is a husband and father? For reasons which we have yet to
divine a fragment of Jacob's history may have been detached from
its original context and inserted elsewhere. But if such a false
position were once established it would be necessary, in order to
make it plausible, to provide at least the semblance of a bridge
to what preceded and followed it—to create some artificial connection. Jacob appears as a married man, eleven times a father—
here we have such artificial connecting links, which conceal the
fact that the fragment originally occurred in another context,
and was subsequently given a different meaning. But can we not
guess the reasons for this detachment and displacement? We can
recall meeting with cases of similar psychic mechanisms in the
symptomatology of the neuroses, whose unconscious purpose was
to prevent the recognition of an actual connection. For example,
obsessional neurotics will build up their symptoms in such a way
as to disguise the real meaning of their obsessional thoughts. The
instinctual demands are generally opposed by moral forces, deriving from the ego, compelling the patient to undertake such transformations. Something of the same sort may have happened in
the history of biblical tradition, as we can understand if we consider the parallel between religious evolution and the mechanisms
of obsessional neurosis. But in every case of such unconscious
distortion and displacement we can show that in the false association, despite all conscious mentation, the choice of the wrong
place and the apparently deliberate ordering is conditioned by
the compulsion of unconscious factors. We shall return to this
point later.

First we must restore the proper context. We have stated
that in the original legend Jacob must have been a youth at the
age of puberty, perhaps immediately before the occurrence of
lawful sexual intercourse, or when intending to indulge in such

intercourse. Also, the attack was made when he was on a journey. Is there, in the story of Jacob, a situation which fulfills these conditions? Yes, there is one;[24] after Jacob's crafty betrayal of Esau the latter determined to kill his brother. But Rebecca advised Jacob to flee, and to absent himself until his brother's wrath had abated. She was actuated, however, by an additional motive: Jacob was to marry one of the daughters of her brother Laban. On his way to Laban, his future father-in-law, Jacob comes to a solitary spot where he passes the night, and there he dreams a dream. The place is called Bethel; and here Jacob has the strange experience which the narrative records.

We have stated that in the puberty rites of primitive peoples the motive of death and resurrection plays the principal part. In all these rites, moreover, recur the features of confinement, initiation in the tribal religion, and the bond with the father's generation. If our interpretation is correct, the traces of such motives must be recognizable in the story of Jacob; though we do not find the period of isolation, the secret initiation in the totemic religion, or the bond with the father. All these motives can easily be detected in the legend of Bethel: Jacob leaves his father's house for a considerable time, and remains in a solitary place. Here for the first time God appears to the young shepherd and makes him a promise; he promises Jacob fruitfulness, and his aid. But in the words, "And behold I am with thee . . . I will not leave thee until I have done that which I have spoken to thee of," God makes a pact with Jacob. And in the morning Jacob makes a vow to God, in which God's promise recurs as a condition; thus he too makes a covenant. After the dream which he has dreamed Jacob awakes; and strangely enough "he was afraid, and said, How dreadful is this place." Here is an emotion by no means consistent with the felicitous promise of the dream, and which the commentators have ingeniously attributed to his consciousness of God's presence. It would indeed be appropriate enough if the contest with God had already taken place here. Without unduly stressing its value, we must seek to divine the meaning of this

[24] Although I regard the following hypothesis as highly probable, I will admit that there are other possible ways of fitting the episode of the conflict into the story of Jacob's life.

dream of Jacob's: "And he dreamed, and behold a ladder set up on the earth, and the top of it reached to heaven; and behold the angels of God ascending and descending on it. And behold, the Lord stood above it"—and there follows the promise. The ladder, as a dream symbol, we know from many analyses, and if we regard God as the representative of the father's generation we must compare the dream with the homosexual rites of initiation. We shall then understand the sequence of a dichronous transaction: first the attack of the god and the mutilation of the penis. Then the dream, the blessing, and the promise: these procedures would correspond with the release of the hostile and affectionate impulses of the fathers in the initiation rites of the primitives.

Here we must expect to encounter the objection, that we have no justification for putting the father in the place of God. But our psychoanalytic researches into the evolution of the idea of God justify this substitution. In respect of this special case, moreover, we recall that the Balum figure of the puberty rites represents the father through the peculiar emotional complexion of the dread of reprisals. But we also recall that the episode of the struggle with God to which Gunkel refers presupposes a character quite unlike that of the Jacob that we know, and that the God of this episode states that Jacob has already prevailed in conflicts with men. At a significant point of the legend of Jacob a blessing is bestowed, and this blessing is obtained only by all sorts of devious procedures. Jacob receives the blessing originally intended for Esau by tricking his father. If we allow ourselves to entertain the hypothesis that this form of the narrative represents a version of the original conflict between father and son mitigated by secular repression, we shall perceive a twofold motivation. One single feature points to this double revision of the story;[25] Jacob goes in to his blind father, saying: "My father! and he said, Here am I, who art thou, my son? And Jacob said unto his father, I am Esau thy first-born." Let us recall God's question while wrestling with Jacob: "And Jacob went near unto Isaac his father and he felt him." Here, perhaps, we catch a glimpse of the original motive of the conflict.

We have stated that in the rites of puberty, as in the story of

[25] Gen. XXVII, 18.

Jacob, atonement is made for the originally incestuous tendencies of the very young men, which are repressed by external power, subsequently replaced by internal authority. If we mistake not, we find traces of such a tendency in the story of Jacob: "And Isaac loved Esau, because he did eat of his venison, but Rebecca loved Jacob." These inclinations may well have been mutual. Is it a mere chance that Rachel, Jacob's bride—who was his cousin on his mother's side—was found by Jacob in the same posture and under precisely the same circumstances as his mother when she was wooed by his father? Is there no significance in the fact that Jacob served seven years for his bride? Is it symptomatic of the unconsciously incestuous significance of Jacob's marriage that Rachel was long barren? She herself blamed Jacob for her unfruitfulness: "When Rachel saw that she bare Jacob no children, Rachel . . . said unto Jacob, Give me children, or else I die. And Jacob's anger was kindled against Rachel, and he said: Am I in God's stead, who hath withheld from thee the fruit of the womb?" In conclusion, it is recorded that Reuben, Jacob's son, committed incest, like his father; "he lay with Bilhah, his father's concubine."

It is true that we hear nothing of any conflict between Jacob and his father Isaac, which in view of Jacob's deception of his father is all the more surprising. But a substitute for the father, a father imago, we might call him—namely, his elder brother Esau —was wrath with Jacob and would have killed him, but was then reconciled with him; a striking parallel with the conflict with God and the subsequent covenant. The jealousy between the two brothers was of long standing; when Esau first came into the world, the Bible relates, Jacob grudged Esau the privilege of the first-born, "and his hand took hold on Esau's heel" when he first saw the light. He was therefore called Jacob (Heel-holder). We see that the Bible, more radical than psychoanalysis, attributes a great antiquity to fraternal jealousy.

As a third instance of double motivation one may cite Jacob's relation to Laban, who withheld his daughter so long from him, and who, when he fled with her, followed him with hostile intentions, and finally concluded a solemn covenant with him, so that again there is a succession of hostile and affectionate impulses. The imagination of the authors of the Book of Genesis endeavors, like that of the neurotic, to represent the same material in the most varied and ever more distorted forms. Like the mysterious god, Laban and Esau both cherish the intention of attacking Jacob. In all these narratives we recognize repetitions of the great primal motive, which was already implicit in the deception of Isaac; namely, the conflict between father and son. It appears to us that the most important reason for this opposition was sexual rivalry, of which we have hints in Rebecca's support of Jacob, in Laban's retention of Rachel, and in the abduction of Laban's daughters. Now, however, we shall have to revise our former opinion. The repetitions of the same event, with very slight variation, allow us to assume that even the scenes in Bethel and Penuel may be referred back to an original event. The mysterious god who falls upon Jacob is a deified father, just as Laban and Esau are originally father imagos.[26] Jacob flees from the father (Isaac-Laban) who pursues him because he has taken possession of the mother (or her substitute). After the conflict with, and the circumcision by, the father, he is set free. A reconciliation follows, and a covenant between father and son is concluded, based on the son's agreement to renounce his childish desires, and the father's promise to aid him. This bond becomes the pattern of the covenant concluded between Jisro-El and Jahveh; all the promises of Jahveh are made on the condition that his people keep his commandments.

There is still one contradiction to cause us misgiving, but we shall soon see that it is of a kind to offer us a final explanation. The most eminent biblical critics take the view that originally Jacob smote the god on the hip. The god expressly admits that he is conquered, and begs for mercy. But then the two versions would stand side by side, the one completely contradicting the other, without any connection beyond the identity of the charac-

26 I will pass over all those interpretations which would have us regard the god at the Jabbok ford as Esau or Laban, since whatever justification there is for this view has been explained in the above interpretation. As in the story of Exodus Jahveh appears to Moses, who is about to embrace his wife, so here he appears to Jacob, who is about to take a wife who is a mother substitute (a cousin). In each instance Jahveh is the deified father imago. After Moses was circumcised the Lord "let him go," just as Laban was reconciled with Jacob, and as Jahveh blessed Jacob in Bethel.

ters. How is this unorganic connection to be explained? Not at all, if we allow the two narratives to run side by side, accepting their superficial meaning. But they occupy different planes; and only a historical and genetic examination can extricate them from their present confusion. We must regard the following narrative as the more primitive, the kernel of the legend: Jacob fell upon the god or the father and overcame him; to be specific, he castrated him. That in the present reading the sense is precisely the reverse cannot surprise us, if we reflect that there were special reasons why tradition should employ this paranoid mechanism.

Among many other obscurities, we are struck by the fact that in the last verse of the narrative there is mention of the fact that the children of Israel are forbidden to eat of the sciatic nerve of animals. It seems very strange that this prohibition should be based upon the blow struck by the deity. Of course, in our present reading of the passage the case is different: The consumption of the sciatic nerve ("the sinew which shrank") is forbidden because Jacob struck the father there. We have then to explain the prohibition as part and parcel of a totemic system; and now, supported by Freud's investigation of the psychic roots of totemism,[27] and the already explained context of the legend, we can assume that the original nucleus of the legend of Jacob preserved the memory of the fact that a son had attacked, killed, and devoured his father, and that it was thenceforth forbidden to slay and devour a man of the same clan. In the prohibition as to eating the sciatic nerve or penis a relic of the original prohibition was preserved, but at the same time the real motive of the ancient parricide revealed itself in a distorted form; namely, sexual envy and jealousy. We shall of course compare the false motivation of the prohibition with the illusory interpretation of the neurotic; the improbability, indeed the senselessness, of the motivation has indicated the true, unconscious reason of the prohibition. We owe it perhaps to the fidelity of the recorder of the tradition, and to the peculiar conservatism of this tradition, that in this—to the best of my belief—unique passage the origin of totemistic practices is derived from a fight.

To sum up: we may say that in the beginning there was a

27 Freud, *Totem and Taboo*, New York 1918.

legend to the effect that at some time or other, before the birth of the tradition, a man overpowered and devoured his father. The legend was the sole recollection of the actual, prehistoric parricide. A second, later legend preserved the recollection that once upon a time the fathers, fearing retaliation, castrated their sons, or at a later period mutilated their penises. This mutilation of the penis, the circumcision, led the way to the reconciliation of the two generations. In consequence of the mutilation sexual intercourse was permitted, since the impulse toward the original incestuous object of the son's libido was inhibited.

As in the excavation of a buried city, deep under the topmost layer of the biblical text a second layer has been discovered, and when we have cleared away the debris of this layer the last becomes visible, affording us a glimpse into the prehistoric ages. What does not this contradictory narrative conceal in its ten verses! Memories of the long-forgotten facts of the turbulent story of the evolution of the human race in its childhood; of prehistoric parricide; of the original significance of the totem; of the origin of puberty rites and circumcision.

The successive emergence of hostile impulses directed against the father, based upon sexual jealousy, and of the dread of castration, may still be studied in our children. Here is a case in point to illustrate this process: A boy of two and a half years cried out, spontaneously, at the sight of his father's naked body: "A knife!" When he was asked what he wanted the knife for he replied: "To cut off papa's gambi!"[28] Some six months later the same child would not try to go to sleep unless his father told him a story. So his father told him a story in which there was much talk of planes, cars, bicycles and sugar cakes. In return the child produced the following story: "Once upon a time there was a little boy. He pulled at his gambi with his hands, and then his papa came and said: Have you been touching your gambi again? And the little boy said, No. Very soon the little boy touched his gambi again, and then again, and his Papa came and said, Jöh!"[29] So the little boy pulled off the gambi and put it in the stove.

28 Gambi = penis.
29 A Viennese expression denoting surprise or alarm.

Schluss-Buss!"[30] Perhaps the kiss is a symptom of the child's affectionate impulse, in contrast to the hostile and jealous impulses already mentioned, which had been repressed. It seems to me worth noting that the child had never heard any threat of castration or similar mutilation in its home, so that one may assume a regression to the primal fantasy.

At this point we must ask how the story of Jacob came to assume its present form. The legends of the Bible, as we know, have a very long history behind them. A tradition changes in accordance with the changing requirements of morality and the secular repression. It is remodeled, the old material being reshaped to serve a new purpose. Distasteful features are thrust into the background, and a new motivation has to confirm the new associations and make them seem more probable, while it conceals the original motivation, which has now become unconscious. The legends thus remodeled were finally separated by the Priestly Code of J. and E.,[31] and at last, by a final editing in the time of Esras, they were given their present form. By this time the original legends were no longer understood in their original sense; the older and more recent fragments of the legends were blended together; characters were condensed, and new motivations—often very insufficient ones—were established. This explains the glaring contradictions which we have been considering; namely, succession was replaced by simultaneousness. The Jahvist and Elohist editors now endeavored, each in his own way, to establish an organic consistency, but they often found it impossible to join up the different portions so that the remnants of prehistoric reality and modern inventions fitted together without perceptible discrepancies. Thus, in the tale of God's attack upon Jacob we have traces of the older version, in which God was attacked and defeated by Jacob. In the end, the Priestly Code[32] and the final editors must have contrived to effect further textual alterations, modifications and additions consistent with

[30] Buss = Bussi: Viennese for kiss.
[31] The usual abbreviations employed in Biblical research and criticism for Jahvists and Elohists.
[32] The Priestly Code or Codex, P, a document which was presumably employed in compiling the Hexateuch.

their religious tendencies. Observe how closely the remodeling of the legendary histories resembles the psychic work of obsessional neurotics; how it welds old and long vanished material and new material into a single symptom, creating new and plausible motivations and rationalizations, perpetrating omissions and ellipses and false associations, in order to obliterate the original and now unconscious meaning of their obsessional ideas. But in both cases it is possible to recognize the apparently intelligent association as artificial, to perceive certain violent distortions as such, despite all the rationalization of the superstructure, and to remove them, and to find our way to the latent and original meaning of the legends and symptoms.

If here we have attempted by means of analysis to study the primary content of the story of Jacob, its development, and its distortions, we do not by any means deny that even in its present form it comprises "spiritual truths," which not only the prophets, but also Herder and such modern biblical scholars as Dillmann have accepted. But we should regard the words "I will not let thee go except thou bless me" as the expression of the eternal truth that no man can enjoy undisturbed happiness in life and love who is still fighting with the shade of his father. The partial conquest of the father is, like the reconciliation with him and his memory, a condition of cultural progress.[33]

We started with the textual criticism of our chosen passages and the motive of the apportionment of sources. It would be tempting enough to attribute, on the basis of our interpretation, the different verses of the chapter to the individual editors; and to establish with exactitude the proper position and the precedence of the various episodes in the framework of the whole legend. Perhaps the attempt already made is a necessary preliminary to such a task. That task, I think, no longer lies within the ambit of psychoanalysis; it constitutes, in the words of one of Fontane's amiable characters, "an extensive field."

[33] *Jadkobs Traum,* by Richard Beer-Hofmann, is an excellent example of a sublimated conception of the material, inasmuch as it interprets Jacob's struggle as a spiritual struggle, a wrestling with God. Curiously enough, the poet makes the events which occurred in Bethel and Penuel occur in a single night.

2. THE DOORKEEPERS

In Jer. XXXV, 4, there is mention of one Maaseiah, the son of Shallum, the keeper of the door. Other doorkeepers are mentioned, three of whom are in the service of the temple. Thus, in the second Book of Kings we are told that priests kept watch upon the threshold of the sanctuary. We learn that the doorkeeper's was a responsible office. But we are not told what was the precise significance of this important functionary. It does not help us much when the modern commentators assure us that it was connected with the sanctity of the temple. No doubt it was, but the precise ritual significance of keeping the door is not explained thereby. But it is certain that such a significance did exist, over and above the task of keeping blasphemers, drunkards, criminals, etc., from profaning the sanctuary.

Perhaps we may find some explanation in another custom of which there is evidence in the Scriptures. In the Book of Zephaniah we read: "And it shall come to pass in the day of the Lord's sacrifice that I will punish the princes and the king's children, and all such as are clothed with strange apparel . . . all those that leap upon the threshold, which fill their masters' houses with violence and deceit" (I, 8, 9). We can understand that the Lord would punish transgressors, but why does he punish also those that leap upon the threshold? The difficulty of interpretation is still further increased if the translation of the text is not reliable.

The first critics who applied themselves to biblical exegesis referred to a passage in the first Book of Samuel (V, 1–5) as affording some explanation. There it is recorded that Israel having suffered a defeat, the Philistines stole the Ark of the Covenant and carried it to Ashdod, where they exposed it in the temple beside the idol of Dagon. "And when they of Ashdod arose early on the morrow, behold, Dagon was fallen upon his face to the earth before the ark of the Lord. And they took Dagon and set him in his place again. And when they arose early on the morrow morning, behold, Dagon was fallen upon his face to the ground before the ark of the Lord; and the head of Dagon and both the palms of his hands were cut off upon the threshold; only the stump of Dagon was left to him." The deductions which the priests drew from such brawls between the two rivals were of a somewhat unusual character, for we read: "Therefore neither the priests of Dagon, nor any that come into Dagon's house, tread upon the threshold of Dagon in Ashdod unto this day."

We have learned that in the temple of Jerusalem there were three doorkeepers, whose office was an important one, though we do not know in what it consisted. We are also told that treading upon the threshold was regarded as a sin. We do not understand this, and we readily listen to Frazer, when he promises an explanation in an exhaustive article on "The Keepers of the Threshold."[1] Captain Conder, writing from Syria, tells us that there the belief obtains that to tread upon a threshold brings bad luck. In all mosques a wooden plank is found in the doorway, so that those who enter are prevented from treading upon the threshold. The same writer has noted the same custom in connection with the shrines and sanctuaries of the country, and the tombs of saints. Similarly, in Fiji all save chieftains of the highest rank are forbidden to tread upon the threshold. All others carefully avoid doing so, for the spot is hallowed, is taboo. Persons of rank step over it; others cross it on all fours. The same precautions are observed in crossing the threshold of a chieftain's house. The chief regards himself as a god, and is often referred to as such by the people, and he claims for himself the privileges of divinity. When Marco Polo visited the palace at Peking in the days of the famous Kublai Khan, he found that two very tall men, two giants, armed with staves, were standing one on either side of the door of the hall—to use the modern expression. It was their business to see that no one set foot on the threshold. If such a thing should happen by mischance they stripped the unlucky offender, and he had to pay a ransom in order to recover his clothes; or instead of depriving him of his clothes they gave him a prescribed number of blows with their staves. If foreigners should arrive who were ignorant of the customs of the country certain noblemen were at their service—whose functions were more or less those of a court usher or master of ceremonies—who instructed them and guarded them—in this case, very literally—

1 In *Anthropological Essays* (pp. 167 ff.), from which the following examples are taken.

against making any *faux pas*. It is a general belief that it is unlucky to touch the threshold. According to Friar Odoric, who traveled in the East at the beginning of the thirteenth century, it would seem that the doorkeepers at Peking gave transgressors no alternative, but administered a beating to anyone who was so unfortunate as to tread upon the threshold. While the monk Rubriquis was living at the court of Mangu Khan as the ambassador of Louis IX, one of his companions accidentally tumbled over the threshold. The doorkeepers immediately seized the offender and led him before the Bulgai, who was the chancellor or secretary of the Court, having powers over life and death. This official was persuaded, with some difficulty, that the offence had been committed in ignorance; but although he pardoned the offender, he never again allowed him to enter the house of Mangu Khan. Piano Carpini, who traveled through the country of the Tartars in the middle of the thirteenth century, some years before Rubriquis' arrival, states that anyone who touched the threshold of a hut or a tent of the Tartar prince's was usually dragged through a hole under the hut, which was contrived for this purpose, and killed without mercy. When Pietro della Valle, an Italian traveler, visited the palace of the Persian king he observed that at Ispahan the greatest reverence was paid to its door of entry, so that it was forbidden to tread upon a wooden step which was situated some distance from the ground. The people eagerly kissed it as though it were a sacred and valuable object. Anyone might enter the palace, claiming protection, because he had kissed the threshold. This threshold was so highly regarded that its name, Astane, was used to designate the Court and the royal palace. We may recall that we ourselves use the words "the Sublime Porte" in a similar connotation. The Caliph of Bagdad required all who entered his palace to throw themselves down upon the threshold, in which a fragment of the black stone from the mosque at Mecca had been inlaid, in order to make the spot more worthy of veneration. The people had to press their foreheads against the threshold, and it was a crime to set foot upon it. In short, we may say that many peoples are familiar with the prohibition against treading on the threshold; and where such action is permitted the crossing of the threshold is accompanied by a ritual which reveals the traces of an ancient prohibition, which was only partly canceled, and under definite conditions.

We now realize that Jahveh's dislike of people who trod on the threshold is not a specifically Jewish eccentricity. It is shared by Fijian chieftains, Chinese emperors, the Shah of Persia, and the Caliph of Bagdad—as we see, one and all great rulers. Frazer adduces a number of further instances which bear evidence to the sanctity of the threshold. The Korva in Northwestern India will not touch the threshold. A Mongolian proverb runs: "Tread not on the threshold, for that is a sin." In ancient India it was the custom that a bride should first step across her husband's threshold with her right foot; but she must not stand on it. In Altmarkt an old custom prevailed according to which a bridegroom bore his bride from the carriage to the domestic hearth. She was forbidden to set foot on the ground. The old Roman custom of carrying the bride over the threshold had doubtless the same origin. It had nothing to do with marriage by capture, which Plutarch believed it to symbolize. Among the Romans there was even a special god of the threshold, the Limentimes, who was afterwards most roughly entreated by the Christian Fathers.

Of the many examples which Frazer gives I will cite only one here. In the Hindu Kush a Kafir seems incapable of quietly stepping over the rather high threshold of a door, as other people are accustomed to do. He has to jump at it, regardless of the height of the lintel, and the necessity of lowering his head. He makes a kind of dash at it, "in a sort of miniature whirlwind," as Frazer says, and leaps over it, his loosely fitting garments fluttering behind him. Although here the forbidden action is perpetrated, it is committed under such peculiar circumstances that the popular belief in the special significance of the threshold is emphasized thereby.

Frazer assumes—and correctly, it seems, as the passage in Zephaniah shows that the doorkeepers in the temple of Jerusalem exercised the important function of ensuring that no one who entered should set foot on the threshold. It was presumably for this reason that the doorkeepers were given staves, so that they could chastise those who transgressed against the enigmatic prescription. As regards the basis of such a superstition, Frazer thinks it would hardly be possible to give a consistent explanation, since in different localities different reasons for it would be forthcoming; the most likely assumption being, perhaps, that the threshold was the habitation of spirits. Certain burial rites of primitive peoples, which Frazer describes here and in his book, *The Belief in Immortality*, suggest the hypothesis that the taboo of the threshold is connected with the belief in the rebirth of the dead. This, in Frazer's opinion, is why the spirits inhabit the threshold. If the spirits are dwellers there they are also the guardians of the house. Respect must therefore be paid to them —since they are really the ancestors of the householder—by refraining from stepping on the threshold. It is certain that this way of regarding the matter, which may be inferred from Frazer's hypothesis, is one of the roots of the threshold taboo. However, psychoanalysis has accustomed us to the belief that all psychic phenomena are overdetermined. Frazer himself offers his attempted explanation with his characteristic modesty: "But it is possible and even probable that other and hitherto unknown causes are responsible for the fact that this portion of the house appears in a mysterious light."

There is, however, another way of explaining one of the most significant reasons for the peculiar attitude toward the threshold. Let us reflect that the door, or the threshold, has a special importance even in the life of quite normal people. To which of us has it not happened that on paying some important call he has lingered, hesitating, at the door, has stumbled on crossing the threshold, and on entering the house has been guilty of all sorts of gaucherie? Freud[2] has called our attention to the peculiar symptomatic behavior of one of his neurotic patients. He was given to leaving doors ajar, and he explained his failure to close them as throwing a light on the caller's relation to the physician. The symptom gave expression to a lack of respect, an unconscious feeling of contemptuousness. We may assume, however, that the caller's behavior gave the discerning observer a glimpse of the feelings which the caller entertained in respect of

2 *Introductory Lectures to Psychoanalysis*, New York 1920.

the person on whom he was calling—feelings of which the caller himself was unconscious.

Even more striking than in such symptomatic actions is the behavior of some neurotic patients in certain symptoms which allow us to divine a special significance attaching to doors. We recall, for example, that many neurotic patients dread to touch a doorknob. I know one young lady who exhibits a symptom not unlike the taboo of the threshold, which is perhaps more general. When she goes out into the street, she is distressed by the compulsion to tread precisely in the center of the flagstone. She will not allow herself to touch the edges or joints of the flagstones, although she is not aware of any reason for this peculiar behavior. This, one must admit, is a very embarrassing symptom, though it occurs more frequently than might be suspected.

If we observe a neurotic patient crossing a threshold in precisely the same manner in which the primitive peoples do so, we may perhaps describe this as a threshold ceremonial. We know that obscure intentions, as well as their simultaneous inhibition, are concealed in the apparently foolish and extremely circumstantial ceremonials of neurotics. These ceremonials diverge widely from their original point of departure, due to the operation of displacement, distortion, omission, etc. It is easy to divine the intentions which are harbored in the case under discussion. We will only point to the fact that in consequence of the violation of the mysterious prohibition the transgressor suffers injury or even death, and that this punishment is inflicted directly by the person visited, or by his agents.

On the basis of the psychology of the neuroses we are compelled to assume that treading on the threshold represents an insult to the person visited. It is as though the tread were rather too forceful; as though it expressed—as in the case cited by Freud —a want of respect and a certain measure of contempt. But if we recall the vigorous nature of the prohibition and the severity of the punishment inflicted upon its contravention, we have to conclude that the visitor to the temple or palace harbors, though unconsciously, much more intensive feelings: strong impulses of complete disrespect, of rebellion and destruction. Their transformation into motor activity is impeded only by the prohibition. That it is the threshold in particular which is placed under taboo becomes intelligible if we reflect that the act of entering is commonly the decisive moment on the occasion of such visits.[3] The psychic process would perhaps correspond to the displacement upon a detail, a mechanism with which the psychology of the neuroses has made us familiar. We may remember that we are accustomed to say, of anyone with whom we are angry: "He shall not cross my threshold again."

To return to our example: We now understand that the threshold ceremonial acquires the greatest prominence in respect of temples, royal palaces, and the houses of chieftains. It is a measure which enhances the effect of the taboo imposed on kings,[4] and like this, is devised to hinder the realization of unconscious aggressive and hostile tendencies. Here we have the explanation of certain details: for example, in Fiji only chieftains of the highest rank are allowed to set foot on the threshold of the temple. They have not such powerful motives for envying God, and for cherishing evil impulses against him.

In the Kafir's eccentric manner of leaping upon the threshold the action originally prohibited is performed, but is preceded by another ceremonial, which through unconscious displacement represents the original ceremonial—the withdrawal before the leaps referring to the inhibition. At the same time, we perceive in

[3] In the discussion following upon this lecture Dr. Hanns Sachs very correctly pointed out that for the unconscious the threshold signifies the vagina—as the house signifies the female body. The connection of this interpretation with the unconscious injury or insult offered to the owner of the house is self-evident. The sexual significance of such customs has been demonstrated by Dr. Ludwig Levy in a valuable article on "Die Schuhsymbolik im jüdischen Ritus," *Monatsschr. für Geschichte und Wissenschaft des Judentums,* Vol. LXII, parts 7–12. If the threshold ceremonial has one of its roots in the taboo of the gods and rulers—a taboo evoked by the fact that the boundary of the ego, in respect of taboo, has been constantly expanded by the unconscious pressure of the aggressive urges—the following derivation suggests itself: The threshold is taboo because the owner of the house is taboo. The transference of the taboo may perhaps be compared with the talmudic "setting hedges about the law." This transference and generalization finds analogies in the symptomatology of the neuroses; and the theory of a guardian spirit of the house can easily find its place in this connection.

[4] Cf. Freud, *Totem and Taboo.*

this manifestation a compromise performance which, as in the shape of obsessional-neurotic symptoms, assists the repressed instinct as well as the repressing instances.

We may now venture to allude to other conceptions which point to the same psychic motives, and to a special treatment of the entrance. There is a threshold ceremony in Goethe's *Faust*. It distresses Mephistopheles that Faust should have to say "Come in!" three times. By the doors of many houses we read such welcoming inscriptions as: "Enter with God, good fortune bring!"— as though it were necessary to suppress the fear that the visitor might bring the very contrary. The holy water of the Catholics and the sacred *mezuza* of the Jews may be regarded as relics of the ancient threshold ceremonial. To this day we may see, before the door of a palace, tall men in fancy dress, bearing gilded staves or maces. We reflect that the ancient predecessors of these doormen performed far more important functions, and that the staff or mace was originally more than a merely decorative accessory. However, what is more essential is the fact that we can now understand the words of Zephaniah, which constituted a *crux interpretum*, and we can explain the nature of the hitherto unknown functions of the doorkeepers in the temple of Jerusalem. But if the Lord, through the mouths of his prophets, utters his condemnation of all who tread upon the threshold, we may reflect, with some satisfaction, that even some centuries before the birth of Christ symptomatic actions, with their unconscious motivation, were not unknown.

3. THE SIN OF THE CENSUS

We read in the First Book of Chronicles, XXI, that "Satan stood up against Israel and provoked David to number Israel. And David said to Joab, and to the rulers of the people, Go, number Israel from Beersheba even to Dan, and bring the number of them to me, that I may know it. And Joab answered: The Lord make his people a hundred times so many more as they be; but, my lord the king, are they not all my lord's servants? why then doth my lord require this thing? why will he be a cause of trespass to Israel?" But David insisted: Joab obeyed, and gave the king the number of those who could draw the sword. God, for some obscure reason, "was displeased with this thing; therefore he smote Israel" with a pestilence that slew seventy thousand. David must already have realized the sinfulness of his behavior, for we read that he now "said unto God I have sinned greatly because I have done this thing; but now, I beseech thee, do away with the iniquity of thy servant; for I have done very foolishly." The punishment of the Lord was administered by the angel which the Lord sent against Jerusalem. But "as he was destroying the Lord beheld, and he repented him of the evil, and said to the angel that destroyed, It is enough, stay now thine hand." There is a variant of this narrative in the Second Book of Samuel, XXIV. The remarkable feature of this version is that here it is the Lord himself who is wrath with Israel, and "moved David against them, to say: Go, number Israel and Judah." These two versions are referable to two editors, who had different opinions as to the source of David's inspiration.

Whosoever it may have been that induced the king to take this step, the result of the numbering was disastrous. What we cannot understand is the Lord's peculiar antipathy to a numbering of the population, and the severity of the punishment inflicted on David and his people. Frazer[1] in his above-mentioned article on "Folklore in the Old Testament," attempts to get over the difficulty by referring to the popular opinion which held David responsible for the outbreak of the pestilence, and to analogous phenomena in connection with other peoples. For example, the Gallas of West Africa regard the numbering of a herd as an evil omen, which will prevent the herd from increasing. And the Lapps were—and probably still are—unwilling that anyone should number them and declare their number, since they fear that such an inquiry might cause a great mortality among the people. Frazer believes that some such belief may have prevailed among the Jews in David's time, and the pestilence which followed immediately upon the numbering would be regarded "as a proof sufficient to confute the doubts of the blindest and most obstinate skeptic." In his concluding sentence Frazer

1 "The Sin of a Census," *Anthropological Essays.*

indicates that he regards the pestilence as a punishment for David's doubt of the ancient promise that the number of the Jews should be as the sands of the sea. The biblical commentators offer another explanation. Wilhelm Nowak, in his *Handkommentar zu den Büchern Samuels*,[2] believes that the numbering of the people may have been connected with questions of fiscal policy, and a more rigid military organization. "We know, from many indications, how difficult the royal power found it to hold its own against the tribes and tribesmen, who jealously insisted upon their rights." Elsewhere[3] it is observed, with reference to this enumeration, that it is only reasonable to assume that it may have been extremely unpopular, since it would certainly have been regarded as yet another step towards consolidating the royal power, and weakening the authority and independence of the tribe.

Perhaps we shall not seem unduly temerarious if with all respect for the perspicuity and scholarship of the commentators, we reject these and similar explanations as unduly rationalistic. Resistance on the grounds of tribal rights cannot explain why Joab should apprehensively ask his overlord: "Why then doth my lord require this thing? Why will he be a cause of trespass to Israel?" Nor can it explain why David afterwards regarded the numbering as his personal transgression and not as a political error. Nor does it explain Jahveh's wrath, and the terrible punishment which the Lord inflicted. If David's procedure had been only a political blunder, the king would not have cried repentantly: "Is it not I that commanded the people to be numbered? even I it is that have sinned and done evil indeed." He would rather have said: "It was more than a crime, it was a stupidity." But such Talleyrandish cynicism was completely alien to the emotional and intellectual world of the kings of Israel, which was still exclusively theocratic.

We are more inclined to believe that Frazer was on the right track when he pointed to similar symptoms of a dread of numbering among other peoples, and presupposed the existence of an

[2] Göttingen 1902, p. 257.
[3] P. 262.

ancient superstition.[4] He had no need to go so far afield as West Africa and Lapland. Ask a Jew in a Galician or Russo-Polish ghetto to tell you his age, and in telling you he will infallibly add, "within a hundred years;" and a mother, asked the age of her children, will inevitably preface her information with an *"unberufen!"* (*Absit omen*—may no evil befall us!) We may surely assume that even among these descendants of the ancient Jews a superstition has survived against the uttering of such numbers— though in this case there is no need to regard it as an inherited burden. It is as if the people wanted to protect themselves against the unconscious envy and hostility of the persons who ask such questions.

In what psychic factors can such a superstition be rooted? The words accompanying the number of years appear to have an apotropaic significance. They are intended to intimidate the demons who threaten to attach a baneful influence to the utterance of the age of the individual or the number of his or her children; in short, to cause his or their death. Freud has explained the psychogenesis of such a belief in demons:[5] Demons are configurations of one's own evil and hostile impulses, projected upon the outer world. We must logically assume that the man who confesses his age, and makes use of some apotropaic locution, is afraid that a voice within him is wishing his own death. This assumption is justified by the existence of unconscious tendencies to self-punishment and an unconscious sense of guilt. In the superstitious mother, in depths which are closed to the conscious mind, side by side with all the love, tenderness, and power of self-sacrifice which are capable of consciousness, there lives an

---

[4] Despite the following attempts at explanation it must be remembered that this fear is rooted in the nature of the number itself. We know that among primitive peoples, and for the ancients, numbers are invested with a sacredness and a magic analogous to the sacredness and magic of names. These qualities may probably be referred to an age when primitive uncertainty was being overcome by the invention of number. The determination of number was once, presumably, regarded as an enchantment; hence the primitives' dread of enumeration. To the savage enumeration seems a magical procedure which confers power over the things or persons numbered. Numbers have a similar significance for our children. Concerning the origin of the sacredness of number cf. Wundt, *Völkerpsychologie*, Vol. VI, 2nd ed., 1915, pp. 357 ff.

[5] *Totem and Taboo.*

impulse that wishes for the death of her children. Here our experience of the ambivalence of the emotional impulses provides an explanation.

Returning to the case of David, let us bear in mind some of its more prominent features—the objections of the faithful Joab, David's consciousness of guilt, and the outbreak of the pestilence after the enumeration. Further, if we remember that David subsequently erected an altar to purge his guilt, we are obliged to conclude that his self-reproach was justified; that he had really committed a transgression in the enumeration. We are accustomed, as psychoanalysts, to observing symptoms in neurotics which show that the emotion which is felt to be painful and immoral, and which ought to be discharged and disposed of by the symptom, actually achieves in the symptom the effect originally intended and repudiated by the conscious ego; and in the effect the result of the repressed emotional trends becomes apparent. The pestilence which followed the census would according to this analogy be a result of those feelings which constituted the most effective unconscious obstacle to the enumeration. Now, what was David's intention in numbering the people? He wanted to know the number of men capable of bearing arms. He would certainly have rejoiced over the great number, but at the same time there was in him an unconscious impulse that wished to diminish this number; that is, there were tendencies toward hostility to and hatred of his beloved people.[6] This people, and the king's own consciousness of guilt, were right in condemning the census, or rather, its obscure motive, as a sin. Here once again we realize that the text, despite all later revisions, confounds, by its construction, conditioned by unconscious motives, the rationalizing exegesis, which is directed by so-called reasonable considerations.

We know that according to Chronicles (I, XXI, 2), it was Satan who induced David to number Israel. The commentators explain that the Books of Chronicles were compiled at a later date than the Books of Samuel, in which the enumeration of the

---

[6] It should be remembered that David had actual reasons for these impulses. This people, which he had saved from the Philistines, had inflicted all sorts of injuries upon him during his flight.

people is likewise recorded. The most important difference consists in the fact that in the earlier version God himself leads David to number the people; but afterwards this passage was felt to be obnoxious, and the responsibility was transferred to Satan. If we recall that the angel of God—that is, his representative on earth—descended upon Jerusalem to destroy the people, and if we refer to the results of our psychoanalytic interpretation, we are compelled to assume that Jahveh also was not inspired solely by feelings of love and devotion to his people, but that he too cherished feelings of hatred, and the will to destruction[7]—an emotional attitude whose effect is plainly enough manifested in the vicissitudes of this people.

But to return to David: We begin to see that beside the taboo of kings there is also a taboo of the people, whose violation cannot be allowed to go unpunished; and this warning to rulers has, I believe, preserved its actuality even in these days of mass murder.[8]

4. THE MEANING OF SILENCE

In Habakkuk (II, 20) we read the admonition: "But the Lord is in his holy temple: let all the earth keep silence before him." Zechariah, the son of Barachiah, describes in his third vision how after all afflictions Jahveh will gather his faithful from the four corners of the earth and will build Jerusalem anew. But first he will pass judgment upon the heathen, and once again we hear the solemn command (II, 13): "Be silent, O all flesh, before the Lord; for He is raised up out of his holy habitation." In a grandiose vision Zephaniah beholds the day of the Lord's judgment, the day of divine wrath. The enemies into whose hands the Lord has delivered his people will execute his judgment (I, 7). "Hold thy peace at the presence of the Lord God; for the day

---

[7] Cf., in addition to many other passages, Exod. XXXIII, 3: the Lord will send an angel before the people, "for I will not go up in the midst of thee, for thou art a stiff-necked people, lest I consume thee in the way."

[8] These studies of biblical exegesis were written, two years before the revolution in the winter of 1917, on the Balkan front. The recent upheaval has shown how fully the above warning was justified.

of the Lord is at hand; for the Lord hath prepared a sacrifice, his hath bid his guests."

Here we are struck by two passages: by the admonition, "Hold thy peace at the presence of the Lord!" and the metaphor by which the judgment is represented as a sacrifice. If we turn to the second passage our surprise is increased, for we find the day of judgment represented as a sacrifice prepared by the Lord in Isaiah[1] and Jeremiah.[2] Isaiah prophesies the fall of Edom; "my sword . . . shall come down upon the people of my curse, to judgment. The sword of the Lord is full of blood; it is made fat with fatness, and with the blood of lambs and goats, with the fat of the kidneys of rams, for the Lord hath a sacrifice in Bozrah and a great slaughter in the land of Edom (Idumea)." Jeremiah describes the destruction of Egypt, and the word of the Lord as reported by his prophet declares that "the sword shall devour, and it shall be satiate and made drunk with their blood, for the Lord God of hosts hath a sacrifice in the north country by the river Euphrates."

We find it difficult to understand that the Lord "brings a sacrifice;" for a sacrifice is generally described as a sacramental rite, something done in the Lord's honor. The passage is comprehensible only if with Robertson Smith we trace the sacrifice back to its origin in the slaying of the totem. This meaning of the ritual of sacrifice, long forgotten by the official votaries of Jahvism, must have suggested itself to the prophets: The anthropomorphic God himself slays the totemic animal. We shall realize at once that this conception is not the only anachronism in these descriptions.

We have learned from Freud to derive the sacrifice from the celebration of the totemic meal which commemorated and atoned for the murder of the father. To all appearances all those engaged in the rite of sacrifice were actuated by motives of love and reverence for the Lord. There is not a vestige of proof that the antithetical components of the ambivalent attitude found ex-

[1] XXXIV, 6: "For the Lord hath a sacrifice in Bozrah, and a great slaughter in the land of Idumea."

[2] XVVI, 10: "For the Lord God hath a sacrifice in the north country by the river Euphrates."

pression in the actual act of sacrifice. As for such a conception of an originally highly sublimated nature as C. J. Jung has suggested,[3] it is quite inconsistent with the pictures drawn by the prophets.

God holds judgment; the sacrifice is his people, and this sacrificial deed is an act of the most frightful vengeance, a discharge of elemental hostility. We shall regard these passages as significant confirmations of Freud's theory of sacrifice, as expounded in *Totem and Taboo,* since they show, as though crystallized in the act of sacrifice, repressed impulses of hatred—significant also because hitherto no one has suspected God of espousing the cause of psychoanalysis.

Here we encounter an objection; we are dealing with the metaphorical expression of prophets in a state of ecstasy. We know that metaphors are only the poetical versions of what were once actual ideas—if the poets speak of "the blood of the grape," this phrase was for the ancients no image, but the reality—and that metaphors, like all the products of the psychic life, are intellectually determined. We have explained that in the time of the prophets the original significance of the sacrifice had long been repressed, and was therefore incapable of reaching the conscious mind. How then is it possible that a vestige, a token of the primary way of regarding the matter, should return, ascending from unattainable depths? And especially in the prophets, whose vital function was to purify the idea of God, and whose ethical glory it was to raise the ancient religion of Jahveh to the level of the most up-to-date morality? The very condition of rapture, of ecstasy, in which they experienced their blissful or terrible visions may have favored such a re-emergence of long-submerged material; reversing its natural tendency, in these circumstances, under the pressure of strong affects, the repressed material returned from the repression.

While we leave it to the experts in biblical research to judge the value of this hint as to the original nature of the sacrifice, we will turn to the motive of the mysterious silence which the three above-mentioned prophets have exacted. Where the context an-

[3] "Wandlungen und Symbole der Libido," *Jahrbuch für psychoanalytische und psychopathologische Forschungen,* Vol. IV, 1912.

nounces the approach of the Lord one might assume that the silence was merely that of reverence. But there are two motives which forbid such an interpretation: the formal wording of the passage in all three prophets, and an argument even more persuasive than the verbal: the consciousness of the approach of Jahveh will spontaneously command such a silence. The admonitory address is needless.

It will not surprise us to learn that the experts have sought and found a reason for this admonition. Thus, F. Nowak explains, in his commentary on the minor prophets:[4] "We know of the ancient Arabs that after the victim was slain they surrounded the altar for some time in silence. This was the moment when one imagined the godhead to be approaching the altar, in order to partake of his share of the sacrifice. It may have been the same among the Israelites." Rudolf Smend,[5] and indeed the majority of biblical critics, are of the same opinion. If we remember that the great judgment which Jahveh is to hold is represented in the form of a sacrifice we shall find the adduction of this sacrificial ritual justified. But it is not this that arouses our interest so much as the nature of the reverence so eloquently expressed in this silence. Reverence is certainly befitting if we imagine those who have offered the sacrifice waiting for God to approach and partake of the offering. But we know that this conception[6] is a comparatively late one, and we have reason to suspect that the silence was a component part of a very ancient ceremonial, that it had a special significance in this ceremonial, and that when the periodical slaying of the totemic animal was transformed into a sacrificial offering it acquired a second and secondary motive.

Let us imagine ourselves for a moment in the situation of the primitive horde, which in the primal form of the totemic meal has perpetuated the dark deed of the united brothers. Let us assume that this feature of silence after the deed is present, as it was among the ancient Arabs after the slaying of the consecrated camel. What can it have signified? Perhaps our psychoanalytic knowledge of psychoneurotic symptoms, which has so

4 *Die Kleinen Propheten*, Göttingen 1897, p. 282.
5 *Lehrbuch der alttestamentlichen Religionsgeschichte*, Freiburg 1893.
6 Cf. W. Robertson Smith, *The Religion of the Semites*, London 1907.

often helped us to elucidate archaic problems, will suggest an explanation. The silence of patients under analysis often seems to us a sign of unconscious resistance. An intelligent lady who was suffering from an obsessional neurosis gave a more special significance for her silence. The greater her resistance, the weaker became her voice, until at last she was quite silent. She once explained, spontaneously, that her silence really meant death. She condemned herself to death as a punishment for ill-wishing her interlocutor. Freud, in his article on the choice of caskets, has given this same interpretation of silence. It seems as though speech were, like thought, a substitute for action, adapted to the state of cultural progress, and subject to the same mechanisms of repression and displacement.

To return to our example: Freud has shown us what mighty reactions in the emotional life of humanity were caused by the cruel and ill-omened deed of the original parricide. Feelings of reactive affection, remorse, and conscious guilt were afterwards awakened in the brothers, having all the violence peculiar to the feelings of natural and primitive men. We ought perhaps to understand this symptom of silence as the first sign of a consciousness of guilt, of remorse and identification with the dead, which overcomes the brothers after the murder. We are all involuntarily silent beside a deathbed. In the silence of the brothers there was disillusion and sobriety after their deed of violence; and at the same time an unconscious identification with the dead; it was as though the silence of the dead had projected itself upon them. At the same time, their silence was a symptom of a somber consciousness of guilt. By this silence they so to speak sentenced themselves to death. So potent and primordial was the operation of the ancient and unwritten law of an eye for an eye, a tooth for a tooth.

Later on, when the periodical totemic feast was being transformed into the sacrifice, the sense of reverence for the godhead may of course have reinforced the original motives of silence, making it profounder, more solemn and significant. At the same time, the pristine emotions, although repressed, were lively enough, and they are still operative in the formal and richly allusive admonition of the prophet who cries: "Be silent, O all flesh, before the Lord!"—perhaps the finest and most pregnant expression of the insufficiency of all human language to describe the great silence.[7]

5. UNCONSCIOUS FACTORS IN BIBLICAL EXEGESIS

It would certainly occur to no one to credit the representatives of biblical scholarship with deliberate and conscious resistance in the exegesis of such passages as are in contradiction to the morality of our own days. Scholars who have been trained in a very strict school, which is characterized by scientific discipline, meticulous conscientiousness, and a sincere striving after truth, are certainly incapable of such petty considerations. The task to which they have devoted their lives shows plainly, for those who have eyes to see, that the path of humanity leads from the obscure depths of animal abjection to the heights of pure morality. Side by side we have evidence of primitive mentalities and proof of an advanced morality. "The radiance of Paradise alternates with deep and dreadful night."

Nevertheless, even here we think some warning of the effect of unconscious factors is not out of place. I should like to show, by an example, how consciousness goes to work in carefully covering up such unconscious intervention, compelling us to follow paths we did not wish to take.

Anyone who has read the narrative that tells us how Abraham sent his servant to bring home a bride for his son, and has followed the story of the wooing and the meeting with Rebecca, will surely be captivated by the charm of this pastoral idyll. The

[7] It goes without saying that the above derivation does not claim to have exhausted all the roots of this ceremonial. We still have to explain why all magical operations must be accompanied by silence. Speech evidently disturbs the compulsive character of all ceremonial. Dr. Hanns Sachs reminds me that in ancient courts of law the injunction held good: Pleasure is prescribed, dissatisfaction is forbidden. (*Lust,* pleasure, is derived from *losen,* to listen in silence.) Possibly further light would be thrown on the subject by the analysis of the ritual howling during the sacrifice, which according to Robertson Smith (*The Religion of the Semites*) was originally an obligatory lamentation over the death of the sacrificed animal, and afterwards became an exultation (*hallel, tahlêl*). Cf. my essay on the Schofar in Part I of *Probleme der Religionspsychologie,* Vienna and Leipzig, 1919.

picture of Rebecca at the well, offering the pitcher to the stranger, and the account of her arrival, when on lifting up her eyes she for the first time saw her future husband, and modestly "took a veil and covered herself," are unforgettable. Many artists, and among them the greatest, have sought to commemorate this scene upon canvas, and Heinrich Heine, when he lay sick in the Rue Amsterdam, reading the Bible again with the eyes of an artist, conjured up the scene for us in words that are touched with the magic of his style. In the concise and laconic but therefore all the more impressive language of the older narrative the episode concludes: "And Isaac brought her into his mother Sarah's tent, and took Rebecca, and she became his wife, and he loved her; and Isaac was comforted after his mother's death" (Gen. XXVI, 67). The sense of the passage is clear as daylight: for Isaac, as for every mortal, the beloved is the substitute for the departed mother. It is therefore understandable, and we feel that it is fitting, that she should dwell in the tent in which the mother had formerly dwelt. In the naive language of the ancient narrative, it is expressly stated that "Isaac was comforted after his mother's death." We, of course, find nothing surprising in this; that Isaac had loved his mother, and that this love had been nourished from earliest childhood, from an unconscious incestuous source, seems to us as natural and unobjectionable as it did to the biblical narrator. We should say: such is life.

We are therefore all the more astonished when we find that the majority of the biblical experts have failed to grasp the real significance of this passage. The text, of course, they have to accept as it stands; owing to the great verbal difference between the Hebrew words for mother and father, there can be no question of a *lapsus calami*. Yet even the Nestor of Old Testament criticism, Julius Wellhausen, assumes that in the original text "father" must have stood where we now read "mother."[1] If this be so, then, of course, as Killmann suggests,[2] the death of Abraham must have been announced, perhaps in verse 62, and afterwards, for some obscure reasons, the announcement was omitted. Ball[3] thought

[1] Wellhausen, *Komposition des Hexateuchs*, 3rd ed., pp. 27 f.
[2] *Genesis*, 6th ed., 1892, p. 307.
[3] *The Book of Genesis in Hebrew*, 1896, p. 79.

the difficulty could be resolved by interpolation. Cheyne[4] assumed that the text was corrupt. Gunkel[5] postulated the existence of two versions, one of which had replaced the original "father" by "mother." Each of these writers produces an absolutely grotesque impression when he translates the passage, "and Isaac was comforted after his mother's death," and quotes the verse at the foot of the page as: "and he was comforted after his father's death." When he speaks of "the graceful conclusion of the charming narrative," one need not be unduly aesthetic to feel that the charm would have been greater had the young wife filled the place of the dead mother. However, such uncertainty as to the sex of the person for whose loss one is consoled by the possession of a wife is, to say the least of it, unusual.

We should like to know the reason for the experts' assumptions in respect of the following details: The commentators remind us that Abraham commissioned his servant to act as deputy suitor or matchmaker for Isaac. But when the servant returned with Rebecca he "Told all things that he had done" not to Abraham, but to Isaac. From this the experts draw the conclusion that Abraham must have died in the meantime. Gunkel, in the passage describing the servant's return, even inserts the statement, in brackets, that the man is now informed of Abraham's death.[6] Is this conclusion necessary? By no means. We are told that "Isaac went out to meditate in the field at eventide, and he lifted up his eyes, and behold, the camels were coming" (Gen. XXIV, 63). They were the camels of the party accompanying the servant, beside whom was riding the lovely young bride. Is it not natural that the servant should immediately tell the young bridegroom Isaac what he had to tell? It can hardly be denied that Isaac was the person most intimately concerned. Yet even if we assume that Abraham had died in the meantime, what right have we to substitute, for the words, "Isaac was comforted after his mother's death," the words "Isaac was comforted after his father's death?" As far as I know, only Cheyne has had the courage to declare (in his above-mentioned book) that he cannot agree with

4 *Tradition and Belief in Ancient Israel,* London 1907, p. 350.
5 Gunkel, *Handkommentar zum Alten Testament: Genesis,* 3rd ed., Göttingen 1910, p. 247.
6 Gunkel, p. 239.

Wellhausen. He questions whether the latter has grasped the problem. Cheyne assumes without more ado that "mother" is incorrect. His own, very far-fetched exposition, which is purely etymological, does not by any means impress us as giving the correct restoration of the text.

The reasons given for altering the passage seem to us both forced and entirely insufficient. We have no adequate motive for distrusting the texts, which are in agreement; especially as we are told that Isaac took his bride into his mother's tent, so that there is a twofold allusion to the natural substitution.[7] We can hardly appreciate the case assumed by the exegetists; it is difficult to imagine that Isaac can have regarded the fresh young maiden as a substitute for the old, wrinkled, venerable patriarch and father. But the mother remains for the son, whose first love was given to her in his early childhood, always unconsciously desirable.

We should describe such an inadequate explanation as that provided by modern biblical exegesis as rationalization. The respect which we feel for such eminent scholars as Wellhausen, Dillmann, Gunkel, etc., warns us against assuming a mere scientific error, or—which would be hardly more comprehensible— one that had persisted for generations without correction. We have already spoken of a kind of rationalization in the acceptance of some of the suggested textual alterations of this passage; but on this very account an important objection presents itself. Could all these serious scholars be subject to such unconscious constraint —men who have accepted without prejudice, and commented upon, much cruder examples of actual incest—such as that between Judas and Tamar, or between Lot and his daughters? Are we to suppose that here, precisely, a resistance built itself up in them, subjecting their keen vision to a kind of intellectual blinkers?

This objection, which seems at first so impressive, is really more easily disposed of than seemed at first sight possible. The peculiar character of the matchmaking scene provides the best

---

[7] It is true that precisely this passage has been described as syntactically impossible (Gunkel, pp. 247 and 260), but the later textual alteration had perhaps another tendency than that which has hitherto been assumed.

argument. Cheyne introduces the chapter in which he deals with this episode—"The Search for a Wife for Isaac"—with the following words: "Who can resist the charm, the gem of purest ray—the story of the wooing and winning of Rebecca? Note above all the Homeric simplicity." Gunkel's appreciation of the narrative is expressed in the passages already quoted. "Naturally: a maiden who treats old people and animals so kindly, and who is so lovely —one could but love her." Similar opinions of the scene could certainly be found in the works of most of the commentators. However they may differ concerning the attribution of individual verses to the various editors, they are all agreed as to the poetical beauty of the idyll. We must not forget that even biblical commentators are subject to human impulses, and liable to surrender to human inclinations. The plastic beauty, the charm and grace of the narrative affect them no less than they affect the unlearned reader. But our pleasure in reading the passage, like that of the experts, depends very largely on an unconscious identification with the hero, with the young and fortunate bridegroom. Which of us would not like to bring home as a bride so lovable, charming, and demure a creature, a maiden in every fiber of her being?

The commentators are unconsciously perturbed by Isaac's relation to his young wife—by the fact that the incestuous source of his love is so expressly stated. It is comprehensible that in this case the unconscious resistance was accompanied by greater sympathy with Isaac's situation than was felt in the case of the actual incest between Judas and Tamar, or Laban and his daughters. There the primitive and archaic was clearly revealed; the instinctive life, in its elementary unrestraint, was too crudely displayed in the foreground; the facts spoke too plain a language and pointed to a cultural period far removed from our own. It is difficult to feel any sympathy with it. But here, in this lovely idyll, every modern reader finds his own youth again, with its hopes and desires; here the identification with the hero becomes a temptation to reinterpret—albeit unconsciously—the natural behavior of the actors. The perturbation caused by the recollection of incest, which is revealed in this alteration of the text, points to a sensitiveness with regard to incest which is comparable only with that of savages.[8] We have been tempted to record this as a case of mental avoidance of the mother.

Perhaps we may conjecture why the editors, with scholarly rationalization, have replaced the mother by the father. It is of course the father who appears to be the greatest obstacle to the incestuous indulgence of our unconscious. That he should be the substitute is understandable; he is the lawgiver of childhood; every thought of him will condemn the incestuous impulses. The first intervener presents himself as substitute for the repressed thoughts of the incestuous relation. But must there not have been other unconscious motives to determine the choice of the version: "And Isaac was comforted after his father's death?" We think it possible to divine at least one. We have already spoken of the biblical scholars' sympathy for the personality of Isaac. We have already suggested that the secret operation of unconscious factors, and the intervention, as censor, of the conscious instances, have resulted in the version in which the mother is replaced by the father. This substitution, however, bears witness to the reactively enhanced affection of the individual for the father, and a partial victory of the homosexual tendencies, in opposition to the unconscious desires. The stressing of his death in the version of the episode proposed by the biblical scholars shows us, however, if we consider the elimination of the incestuous allusion, that an absolute suppression of human impulses is impossible. This "improvised" death serves to repress not only the incestuous tendencies in respect of the mother, but also their realization. If the father is dead—and here the original, unconscious wish breaks through—there is no longer any obstacle to union with the beloved mother. In this indication we still find the trace of the suppression of secret tendencies; it affords us an example of the return of repressed material. If for a moment we were to disregard the barrier between the unconscious activity of the imagination during scientific labors and the actual reality, we might venture to suggest to the exegetists that they must have found Abraham's death very convenient!

We must not neglect to point to the fact that the too energetic reaction against the emergence of unconscious tendencies

8 Cf. Freud, *Totem and Taboo*.

was unable—in spite of the rejection of forbidden thoughts—to prevent a fragment of the unconscious wishes from finding a barely recognizable fulfillment in imagination, in the product of scientific labors. For one consequence of the new version, which records the death of Isaac's father, is that Isaac takes the place of the deceased, whereas the old text suggests that Rebecca replaces the mother. Here the two great primal wishes of childhood emerge —as they emerge in the games of our children, when they play at "mother and father"—in the midst of the most serious and scientific work of the expert, warning all scholars against striving too urgently to suppress the instinctual forces that live in all of us. It looks almost as though the fulfillment of a deeply rooted infantile wish, the desire for union with the mother or her younger representative, had found a complement in the sense of a wish fulfillment of the second infantile fantasy—the elimination of the obstructive father. The secondary elaboration has succeeded in effecting the apparent disappearance of traces of the unconscious and tendencious alteration.

Perhaps it should be counted as an achievement that we were able, by applying the psychoanalytic method, to detect an inherited error. But we must not forget what this error, and its explanation, mean for us: they warn us to be on our guard, in the midst of our scientific work, against the effect of unconscious factors and of the conscious censorship opposing them. Not all are free who make mock of their chains.

This warning of the necessity of self-criticism gives me an opportunity of emphasizing the deficiencies of the foregoing studies—deficiencies of which I become increasingly conscious in retrospect. They may be sought—apart from the tentative character of a psychoanalytic biblical exegesis—in two directions: in the dilettante nature of their preparation, and in the author's defective knowledge, and the fragmentary form of these essays. But perhaps the aim of these studies, which do not seek to be anything more than preparatory hints and examples from a more comprehensive context, is achieved; namely, to call the attention of the representatives of Old Testament scholarship to the application of psychoanalysis, and its fruitful results in biblical exegesis.

MAN THE MYTHMAKER

I

What the religion and the art of antiquity have preserved for us of ancient myths is assuredly not their original content. The myth has been modified, by many psychical processes, through many successive generations. It has adapted itself to contemporary cultures; its primary content has been confused and distorted; and its form has been altered. We cannot hope that in its traditional shape it will surrender the secret of its essential character, and with it that of the mythmakers.

If we turn to the myths of the primitives, of peoples living in a low form of culture—as some Australian tribes, for example —we shall be confronted with hardly less formidable difficulties. Even the primitive peoples are not young peoples. We must not expect to find that they have preserved the original myths, unaffected by evolution and undistorted. Moreover, we are faced with the difficulty of inadequate verbal understanding, the difficulty of entering into the mental and emotional life of primitive peoples, and their extreme reluctance to discuss such sacred matters with strangers.

We have already realized how difficult it is to penetrate to the source of the myth, and to understand the psychic processes of the mythmaker. How did the myth arise? To what emotional needs did it owe its existence, and what are its purposes? These problems were among the first to present themselves to those occupied in mythological research. It was soon felt that the myth, as we have it, requires interpretation, and this becomes possible only if we are able to reconstruct the original nucleus of the myth. In the myth we see, perhaps, how the hero was born; we see that even at his birth he was confronted with obstacles; we learn that he was exposed to dangers, but that he returned to his parents, conquered his enemies, and achieved great triumphs. If we now ask the scientific mythologists for the meaning of such a product of the prehistorical imagination, recurring, as it does, with its typical features, the majority will reply that the myth represents a natural atmospheric phenomenon, or perhaps it symbolizes an astral phenomenon. The youthful hero may be the young sun, emerging from the waters, which has to contend with clouds even as it rises, but finally triumphs over all obstacles. The notion that myths should be interpreted as representations of astral processes, held by such eminent scientists as Stucken, Winckler, and others, would appear to be the predominant view of the modern mythologists. It matters not in the least whether Frobenius favors the solar interpretation, while Siecke supports the theory that all myths were originally lunar myths. The predominant view, which relates the human conceptions of myth to the processes of Nature and the heavenly bodies, is everywhere the same as regards the interpretation of nature myths. Now, there is no doubt whatsoever that this way of interpreting myths is relatively justified; and the part played in myth formation by the impressions produced by natural events is unmistakable.

Considering the problem from our point of view, we have to ask ourselves whether such a mode of approaching the problem will give us any insight into the psychic processes active in the formation of myths. It must be admitted that the gain is slight, since the interpretation of nature myths can do but little to explain the origin of the myths. It enables us to show that this or that mythical motive corresponds with this or that natural process, rather than to understand the psychic processes of myth formation. This kind of descriptive interpretation of myths urgently calls for a dynamic comprehension of the emotional elements. Is it enough for the "nature myth" school to show that a traditional theme can be "referred back" to natural events, when certain elements of the myth can be explained—often in a highly artificial and allegorical manner—as indicative of atmospheric, lunar, solar or astral phenomena? Is it not precisely here that the problem begins? Here we shall not examine the dubiousness of many interpretations, and their incongruity with the content of the myth. As a matter of experiment we will accept the conception of the nature myth on principle; but how are we then to explain, psychologically, the heavenly origin of myths? We may take it for granted that natural phenomena made a profound impression on the man of the prehistoric period in which myths were created, but the way in which he understood them, and his primitive attempts to include them, intellectually and emotionally, in the framework of his philosophy, are of special importance as regards the formation of myths.

The philosophy of the primitives may be described—as W. B. Tylor described it—as *animism*. This most remarkable species of primitive natural philosophy peopled the world with a great number of spiritual beings, which were well or evilly disposed toward humankind, and which were the cause of natural events. Not only plants and animals, but even the inorganic objects seemed animated. When our children, in their games or fantasies, give a chair or a table a soul, and when fairy tales allow not only trees and animals to speak, but even articles of furniture and playthings, and when in poetry (as for instance in Maeterlinck's *Blue Bird*) inanimate objects converse, we recognize in these manifestations traces of the vanished, primeval philosophy from whose soil the mythos sprang. Today we do not rely on a belief in spirits if we wish to understand natural events; we have replaced them by impersonal, physical forces. But the revolutionary changes in the natural sciences show us how imperfectly we have discarded the fetters of the animistic philosophy, and how we still, unconsciously and unintentionally, ascribe human qualities and tendencies to these anonymous powers. It is as though human beings found it difficult to conceive Nature otherwise than anthropomorphically.

We will not here discuss the problems which arise from the primitive philosophy of animism, but we shall maintain that animism is an intellectual system which enables the thinker to grasp the universe as a whole. Wundt[1] observed that the same concepts of animism were held by the most varied peoples, and he came to the conclusion that "they were the necessary psychological product of the myth-building consciousness, and that the primitive animism must be regarded as the intellectual expression of *humanity in a state of Nature*, in so far as this is accessible to observation."

1 Wilhelm Wundt, *Völkerpsychologie*, 2 vols., 1908.

The psychological necessity of the universal animation of Nature, which we have learned to perceive as one of the essential and characteristic features of animism, was already recognized by Hume in his *Natural History of Religion*. There is, he says, a universal tendency among mankind to conceive all beings as like themselves, and to transfer to every object those qualities with which they are familiarly acquainted and of which they are intimately conscious.

We have been told that the interpretation of myths as nature myths explained them as being of heavenly origin, and then—at some later period—allowed them to wander down to earth. As long ago as 1908 Lassmann asked whether the first germ of myth formation "is to be sought in the happenings in the heavens, or whether, conversely, complete narratives of a quite different origin were transferred to the heavenly bodies." Ehrenreich[2] takes the view that the evolution of the myths began on earth, and that the myths were only subsequently projected upon the heavenly universe. Wundt, on the other hand, declares that the astral theory of myth formation is not merely in contradiction to "the history of the myth, which knows nothing of such transmigration, but also to the psychology of myth formation, which must reject any translocation as inherently impossible." The possibility of including the nature-myth explanation in the framework of a far more comprehensive and profounder explanation emerges from the psychological analysis of animism, from whose soil the mythos first arose.

The psychic processes which led to the animistic view of the universe were first successfully investigated by Freud.[3] In comparing the psychic mechanisms which govern the symptomatology of neurotic and psychotic disorders with the forms in which animism finds expression, he was able to show that man's earliest theory of the outer world was a psychological theory. This first conception of the outer world, which was entirely natural to and congruous with the primitive mind, proceeds from the idea that

[2] *Die allgemeine Mythologie und ihre ethnologischen Grundlagen,* Leipzig 1910.

[3] Cf. *Totem and Taboo* and *The Interpretation of Dreams* in *The Basic Writings of Sigmund Freud,* ed. by A. A. Brill, New York 1938.

the various objects in the world are what the primitive human being feels himself to be. Thus, he transfers his own psychic experience, which he perceives by endopsychic observation, to the outer world; and he finds again in the outer world what he experienced in his own person. Thus, we are confronted with the assumption that the essential content of animism has built itself up on the projection of inner perception upon the outer world. The mechanism of projection is, as we know, of great importance in the formation of our view of the outer world, because it determines our sensual perceptions. We shall not here discuss the question as to the origin of the tendency to project internal events upon the outer world; but it is evident that biological as well as psychological necessities may play a decisive part. One thing is certain: that projection represents a primitive mechanism which is of the greatest importance in respect of the total philosophy of primeval humanity.

The processes of projection which are characteristic of animism are possible only on what psychoanalysis describes as a narcissistic basis. In tracing the libidinous development of the individual the psychoanalyst points to a stage of infantile erotism in which the isolated sexual impulses, now reunited, have already found an object, but this erotic object is the ego. The individual behaves as if he were in love with his own ego. The further particularities and vicissitudes of this organization, which we call narcissistic, lie without the scope of this essay; here we will only remark that the overestimation of the power of one's own ideas occurs as a natural consequence of the narcissistic orientation upon the ego. The tendency to project one's own psychic impulses, the conception of the outer world as a mirrored image of the ego, thrives on the narcissistic soil. Thus, the animistic phase of human evolution may be equated with the narcissistic stage of individual development. When the trees whisper consolingly to the sorrowful poet, when he recognizes the uproar of his own emotions in the thunderstorm, he is feeling—and we feel with him—like the primitive man of the animistic era. The narcissistic orientation upon the ego explains, moreover, why primeval man, whose traces we believe we can recognize also in the psychic life of the psychoneurotic, brings the universe into relation with his own human body. The ancients spoke of the navel of the earth. Many cosmological myths of the uncivilized peoples explain the origin of seas and rivers as resulting from the urination of a human being or hero. Indications of this anthropomorphic standpoint, from which the individual perceives the universe as a stupendous enlargement of his ego, are so frequent that any enumeration of them would lead us too far afield. The reader may be referred to the works of Otto Rank,[4] whose psychoanalytic examination of the formation of myths is most important and fruitful. Rank shows how for primitive man the microcosm, the human ego, his physical needs and his psychic conflicts are reflected in the universe, the macrocosm; and what a decisive influence this comprehensive narcissistic ego-projection had on the formation of myths and on his picture of the world.

At this point the interpretation of the nature myth, which has hitherto seemed a vague and quite unpsychological hypothesis, apparently in contradiction to the earthly vesture of the myths, now receives its psychological confirmation. But this confirmation is only relative and restricted. We know that the highly imaginative man of the primeval world projected his own feelings and affects upon the inanimate phenomena of Nature, and thus intimately associated the outer world with his own life. The natural event—as it might be the rising or setting of the sun— does not provide the motive of myth formation, but offers itself as welcome material for the creative imagination to work upon. The animistic philosophy is premythical; the projection of the ego upon the environment originally served the cause of self-preservation as well as that of narcissistic self-representation. It was the readily prepared basis upon which myth creation could begin to operate. The animistic belief in a universally animate Nature, created in his own image, was utilized by myth-creating man in order to set within its framework an image of his own wishes and his strongest emotions. The specific nature of these wishes must explain why in many myths one can detect no relation to natural events, or at most only an obviously secondary

---

[4] Cf. *Psychoanalytische Beiträge zur Mythenforschung*, 2nd ed., 1922; *Das Inzestmotiv in Dichtung und Sage*, Leipzig 1912; Myth of the Birth of the Hero, *J. Nerv. and Ment. Dis.*, XL, 1913.

relation. What is the character of these intense impulses which insist upon expressing themselves in myths, and why do they choose precisely this form of expression, instead of striving for actual fulfillment? These are the questions which the inquirer into the psychology of the myth must ask himself.

II

Here psychoanalytic concepts will be of help to us. One may ask why psychoanalysis, a therapy for neurotic disorders, should feel justified in offering its services in a province so remote from its original field of operation. But psychoanalysis has long ago emerged from its native province; it has proved its merits as a complete system of psychology, until today it embraces in its entirety the evolution of the human psyche, and all its productions; in other words, the whole cultural history of humanity.

It is not my intention here to describe the achievements of psychoanalysis; I will rather assume that the reader is already familiar with them. I shall attempt only to show, as concisely as possible, how psychoanalysis came to extend the application of its method to the investigation of the genesis and evolution of myths. Myths, however greatly they may differ in character, are products of imagination, and are thereby included in the compass of psychoanalytic inquiry. The investigation of the life of the imagination is the main province of analytic activity, whether imagination expresses itself in the genesis of neurotic symptoms, in artistic creation, in childish play, or in philosophical speculation. Psychoanalysis has revealed the unconscious instinctual forces which determine the creation of myths, the psychic mechanisms which were operative in myth formation, and has deciphered the symbolism which, as the language of myths, has so often veiled their meaning.

The specific reason why psychoanalysis applied itself to the investigation of myths was the fact that it had afforded us an insight into the psychic origin and latent meaning of the dream, which reveals so many external and internal similarities to the myth. From Freud's fundamental contributions to the understanding of dreams, the investigator of the myth could anticipate fruitful suggestions and profounder understanding of its prob-

lems. Some of these we owe not only to the creator of psychoanalysis, but also to Otto Rank, Karl Abraham, and Ernest Jones.
It is thanks to them that we can now assert that the psychic life
of myth-forming humanity, and the psychic processes of myth
formation, are no longer a mystery. The interpretation of the
dream, and especially of typical dreams, led to the discovery of
the concealed meaning of the myth. The understanding of the
psychic determinants and aims of the dream, and also of its construction, were of decisive importance for the explanation of the
process of myth formation. The knowledge of the unconscious
forces which determine the creation of the dream is evidently
indispensable for the investigation of the myth. In addition to
the interpretation of myths afforded by psychoanalysis, and in
contrast to the superficial interpretation of earlier investigators,
psychoanalysis has made it possible to consider the myth from a
genetic point of view. In the light of bathypsychology the dream
revealed itself as the distorted representation of an unconscious
wish surviving from the psychic life of childhood. Psychoanalysis
explains the myth as the distorted relics of the wish fantasies of
the peoples; or as Rank expressed it, as "the secular dreams of
youthful humanity." As in the dream creation of the individual,
so in the mythical output of the masses, a fragment of submerged
psychic life rises to the surface in an age subjected to different
cultural conditions and struggling against harsh necessities.

But the wish impulses which the myth, when interpreted,
reveals as its basis, are similar to those which create the dream.
They arise from the conflicts of the childish psyche, and refer
more particularly to the internal life of the family. The special
attitude toward parents and brothers and sisters which psychoanalysis describes as ambivalent, the libidinous impulses and
ambitious tendencies, are always found to be the essential content
of mythical narratives.

As the only essential precondition for the analytic interpretation of the myth, Rank has formulated the principle that the
psychologist must believe in the psychic reality of the narrative.
But what does this really mean? It means that the myth, however
unintelligible it may seem on a first hearing, must have a secret
significance which constitutes its original meaning. The primitive

to whom the myth was related by his forefathers believed in the
factual reality of what he was told; for him gods and heroes,
dragons and sphinxes, goblins and ghosts were nothing extraordinary. We, however, must make up our minds to look behind
the varied images to which the myth introduces us for the figures
which had the greatest significance in the psychic life of primeval
humanity, and to elicit the hidden meaning of the myth by a
complete investigation of its content through the application of
the technique of interpretation which we have learned to apply
to the dream. We must therefore consent to take seriously whatever the myth tells us, and must not content ourselves with
wondering at its unintelligible and often childish or absurd
content.

The primitive sexual and crudely egoistic instinctual impulses which we find, after the retrospective analysis of their
distortions had to be increasingly suppressed before the existence
of a community could be possible. The partial renunciation of
the satisfaction of instinctual impulses is one of the most important preconditions of society. What real life denied the myth-
forming imagination supplied; the wishes whose fulfillment was
prohibited by the necessities of social life and cultural requirements were realized in the myth. Only when man had realized
that he must renounce the satisfaction of impelling desires, only
when repression, in the psychoanalytic sense, had begun, could
the myth be created. It goes without saying that in its primary
form not only the realization of the forbidden wishes and pro-
scribed ambitions will show themselves, but that there will also
be traces of the tendencies which have opposed such instinctual
satisfactions. The conflict between such powerful impulses and
the no less powerful countertendencies constitutes the essential
content of the myth, which thus becomes a direct representation
of the psychic dynamics of our ancestors. The actual renunciation
led to a compensatory instinctual satisfaction in the imagination,
and the myth, in the contrast between that which real life denied,
and that which the instincts were always demanding, reflected an
extremely important fragment of cultural history and human
progress. It gives, as it were, a picture of the secular repression of
the age that gave it birth. What was formerly tolerated, and then

forbidden, is represented in the myth as realized in a distorted form. The wish fulfillment in them points to the operation of those external inhibitions (later on to become internal) which led to the creation of the myth.

The substitution for immediate wish fulfillment of the imagined satisfaction of the forbidden tendencies is therefore the psychological genesis of myth formation. The progressive censorship which the consciousness exerted over the wish fantasies led to increasing distortion of the original content. Condensation, displacement, reaction formation, and the projection of whatever had become obnoxious, upon the transcendent figures of gods and heroes, served to conceal the original realities from the conscious mind. Man renounced his right to the unconditional realization of his wishes, but endowed the gods and the heroes with the faculty of surmounting every barrier.

Here we can only indicate the path subsequently followed by the myth. Based in the beginning on animistic hypotheses, it soon found its way into religion. The religious myth, in its later phases, began to introduce gods and demons where formerly the only actors were the personified powers of Nature. With the emancipation of the myth from its original soil all sorts of profound modifications occurred, some of which we shall examine, since they were of importance in the evolution of culture. The myth-forming man originally imagined the realization of forbidden wishes. Oedipus slew his father and married his beloved mother. The defeat of the father and the breaking down of the incest barrier were actual events. The myth is created by the generation of the sons, which has to submit itself to authority and can attain the goal of its wishes only in the compensatory substitute satisfaction of fantasy. Here an act of the wildest rebellion, a violation of the unwritten laws of primitive society, assumed a definite form in the myth. The modification of the original myth by religion is betrayed by the fact that the wish fulfillment is followed by punishment and atonement for the crime—as in the Oedipus myth, or the story of the Fall of Man. A later reshaping of the myth often endeavors to reinterpret the asocial, destructive deed of the hero as a socially valuable action; Hercules, Oedipus, etc. are social heroes who delivered humanity from destructive wild beasts. The originally crude or barbarous features were mitigated in correspondence with the level of culture subsequently achieved, or were displaced upon indifferent objects, while the amoral tendencies were diminished, and finally transformed into their opposites. Nevertheless, the traces of the ancient impulses are everywhere visible in the myth; think, for example of the narratives in the Books of Genesis: the stories of the Fall, the murder of Abel, the Flood, and the Tower of Babel. Everywhere the essential content consists of references to the revolution against the generation of the fathers (God). But with the religious revision of the myth originally alien tendencies take part in its formation; it gradually becomes ethical, pointing to the terrible consequences and punishments that follow the flouting of authority. Wish fulfillment is now accompanied by a sense of guilt, and the original affects are changed into their contraries; just as a dream which fulfills the profoundest unconscious wishes of the individual often acquires a manifest character of anxiety through the intervention of the repressing forces.

Rank has pointed out the relation between the myth and the fairy tale, and has shown what external and internal processes have forced the myth to survive in so degraded a form. We might say that the fairy tale is the last offshoot of the myth-creating imagination. The weapons of the primeval age, which seemed so formidable to men in their encounters with the enemy, or with savage animals—the bow and arrow—are today found only in the nursery.

But the myth itself proceeded on its way, gradually absorbing all the vital forces of religion and morality. What was once the elementary expression of the wildest instinctual force has become, in the course of countless generations, the vehicle of profound meaning and the ripest morality. Today, when we read a myth, we seem to hear the voice of wisdom speaking, and its external features, often remarkable enough, seem to conceal profound truths, and to give us, in veiled form, the answer to the riddle of our existence. This "anagogic" significance of the myth should not surprise us; after all, the trees whose topmost boughs reach farthest toward the heavens are those that plunge their roots most profoundly into the darkness of the earth.

Where shall we find the myth-creating man today? If we are to believe our explorers, he still survives, after a fashion, among the primitives; but our "backward cousins" are not untouched by modern culture; civilization, gin, and Christianity will soon have made an end of their myth-creating faculties. Yet we shall find examples of myth-creating humanity among our children at play; for them, too, everything is animate, and the profounder meaning which is hidden in childish games is a veiled assertion of the reality of frustrated wishes. The games of our children are as intimately blended with fantasies as the daydreams of later years. Here again we find a denial of the unwelcome reality, and the myth-forming imagination silently and timidly spreads its wings. The youth, in his daydreams, performs valiant deeds, overcomes powerful adversaries, achieves high position, and wins the hand of a king's daughter. We are all, in a sense, creators of myths in our nocturnal dreams, which fulfill our most hidden wishes. The secret impulses which build up our dreams are the same as those which are operative in myths, the secular dreams of youthful humanity.

The poets, so closely akin to the dreamers, are the myth builders of our modern era; where their creations achieve the complete expression of the deepest tides of human feeling they have acquired a kind of mythical significance, and the labors of the artist, despite all adaptation to the requirements of contemporary realism, still involve something of the craft of the myth builder.

It would, of course, be a mistake to assume that the myth represents nothing more than a specimen of the free activity of the imagination. As a piece of amber allows us to see the insect within it, so the myth reveals allusions to a prehistoric, objective reality. Not everything in the myth is mythical. The fighting against wild beasts, the invention of a new weapon, the human struggle against the powers of Nature, the achievements of superior individuals, and other important events, which revealed prehistoric man at the highest points of his existence, and accompanied him on his progress, have formed a kind of precipitate in the myth.

But it seems to us that the myth can tell us a great deal more;

not only does it reveal the most vehement wishes cherished by our forbears, by which we are all unconsciously moved, but it may even contribute to the reconstruction of the early days of the human race.

Freud, in the work which is of greatest importance in respect of the history of human culture—in his *Totem and Taboo*—on the basis of a comparison of ethnological, theological and sociological data with the results of psychoanalysis, has advanced a hypothesis which asks us to conceive the origin of religion, morality and society as the aftereffects of a single great deed of the prehistoric era—the killing and eating of the chieftain of the primeval horde. In the myth there is an echo of this event, though it has left no traces in human memory. Thus the myth leads us downwards into the dark realm of the hidden impulses of the psyche. The present, which admits the psychic reality only in an unwilling and hesitating fashion, takes little interest in the buried treasures of the myth. Yet even for ordinary humanity what Schiller made his hero exclaim holds good:

> "Tell him when he becomes a man
> To pay heed to the dreams of his youth."

OEDIPUS AND THE SPHINX[1]

"... Behold, this is Oedipus
Who unravelled the great riddle ..."
Sophocles

1. INTRODUCTION

The reader of *Imago*[2] will find on the cover of the volume containing this essay a little drawing which, in response to the proposal of Otto Rank, will adorn all the publications of the International Psychoanalytical Press. It represents Oedipus, gazing fixedly and unafraid at his terrible adversary, the Sphinx.

Ferenczi has alluded, in an interesting article,[3] to a passage in Schopenhauer's letters, in which the philosopher praises this hero as the pattern of the serious investigator, who seeks the truth regardless of his own welfare.

Psychoanalysis, which, regardless of the ancient and cherished prejudices of civilized humanity, has indicated the nature of the profoundest psychic impulses, has also revealed the obscure but universal human significance of the Oedipus myth. It has shown us that in the ancient saga the two potent and pristine wishes which are of decisive importance in the development of the individual, as of the peoples, appear to achieve fulfillment.

It seems to us that the picture of Oedipus, the unraveler of riddles, and the Sphinx—a picture so rich in associations—may justly adorn the achievements of psychoanalytic research; especially as a constant warning that we must never be content with what has been attained.

Now, perhaps, is the very time to remind ourselves that the Sphinx itself, that winged monster, is still an enigma to us. But

1 A lecture delivered on November 2, 1919 before the Viennese Psychoanalytical Association.
2 This essay was published in No. 2 of *Imago*, 1920.
3 "Symbolische Darstellung des Lust- und Realitätsprinzipes im Oedipusmythus," *Imago*, Vol. I, No. 3, 1912.

now we shall exchange our roles; we shall ask questions, and the Sphinx, albeit reluctantly, will surrender her secret.

2. THE ORIGIN OF THE SPHINX

The Sphinx of Oedipus, which we see in the little drawing to which I have referred, is a late-born sister of innumerable similar figures which came out of the Near East in prehistoric times. If we wish to learn what she really is we may choose between two methods of inquiry: we may seek to divine her true significance from the context of her setting in the Oedipus legend, or we may look for the solution of the riddle of her existence—and that of her relatives—in the ancient East. The first way is by far the more convenient; it seems to lead directly to the goal, and it has often been followed. Inviting as it may be, we shall avoid it; for the example of so many unsuccessful predecessors warns us that it leads to a very inadequate explanation. The investigators assure us that the story of the Sphinx is a late interpolation in the Oedipus saga—and the Sphinx herself is not autochthonous in Greece—so that we are in danger of taking a frequently reinterpreted and secondary figure of late origin for the original figure. The second way is the more difficult, and it leads us, to begin with, a surprisingly long way from our saga, into the dark regions of primitive religion and mythology, without giving us any assurance that we shall find our way back to the Sphinx of Oedipus. Difficult problems of the evolutionary history of human thought and belief, which would call for more exhaustive treatment, will confront us and threaten to bar the way. Nevertheless, this is the path we shall pursue.

We shall first turn our attention to the early type of the enigmatic being, as revealed by excavation. The Sphinxes of Egypt are lions with human heads, closely akin to the other fantastic hybrid creatures of antiquity—Sirens, Harpies, Gryphons, Cherubim. Wundt speaks of the Sphinx "as indeed the most expressive and therefore the most enduring of the double forms ever produced by art."[1] The Sphinxes represented by the ancient arts of the Near East, of which all these fantastic beings were

[1] *Völkerpsychologie*, Vol. III, 2nd ed., p. 156.

native, include both male and female forms of the monster. In the early period the female form is rare; according to the experts it first acquired its peculiar importance in Greece,[2] though we know of many female Sphinxes from the Middle and Late Kingdoms of Egypt and the adjacent countries. Many Sphinxes, like that of Aegina (about 460), show women's faces of seductive charm, while others reveal masculine features. Their solemn and rigid gaze, and their noble tranquillity, give the observer a peculiar feeling if he gazes at them for long. But even the Sphinxes which possess the face and the shoulders and breasts of a woman seem, as a rule, strangely alien to the modern European. He may perhaps recall Mephisto, who had to confess to his partner in the classic Walpurgisnacht:

> "Above the waist your looks are most inviting,
> But lower down I find the beast affrighting!"

The poses of the Sphinxes are greatly varied; they show them standing, sitting, crouching, reclining. Many have wings, but many are wingless.[3] One can almost follow the development of the Sphinx, which was originally based on realistic animal images, but which, as time went on, departed farther and farther from its prototypes, becoming more and more richly decorated. Even in the late Egyptian examples the lion's tail ended in a serpent, while in still later statues of the Roman period the Sphinxes had become composite creatures whose bodies were admixtures of many different animals.

We find Sphinxes as statues, in the bas-reliefs on the friezes of temples, on household furniture and utensils, on ornaments and gems, their dimensions varying, with the nature and function of such articles, from the colossal—for example, the Sphinx

---

2 Cf. Ilberg in Roscher's *Lexikon der griechischen und römischen Mythologie,* ♯ 1298: "The animals are generally male; female specimens are occasional variants of the male types, but the Greek influence first made them an individual form." In the female Sphinxes a lion's body is surmounted by a woman's head; they rarely have nipples; the woman's breasts were a late addition. In such hybrid forms as the Gryphon and the Criosphinx the female does not occur.

3 In the Egyptian Sphinxes wings are exceptional; in Greece they are the rule. At first the wings were folded; later on they were raised and outspread.

of Gizeh—to the tiny and delicate.[4] We know of many isolated representations of the Sphinx, but Sphinxes often occur in pairs. In the avenues leading to the ancient temples they are often seen lying at intervals of a few yards, their faces turned toward the thoroughfare. In Thebes and elsewhere there may have been hundreds of these colossal images on the processional streets. Many representations show them erect, overthrowing their adversaries with their paws, or tearing at them; but more frequently one sees them on guard before the temples. Later on they adorned, and always guarded, tombs.

3. THEORIES AS TO THE MEANING OF THE SPHINX

In descriptions of the different forms of the Sphinx we often encounter expressions of amazement at the vast number of variants of this monster, which can look back on a history of many thousands of years. Numerous contradictory features, which refuse all attempts to unite them in a whole, threaten to bewilder us and to baffle all explanation. There is no doubt that many Sphinxes are intended to represent the king or the queen; this is proved not only by the facial similarities, but also by the inscriptions and the insignia of the sovereign. On the other hand, it is equally obvious that many Sphinxes represent divinities; of this there is abundant evidence. Moreover, it is not unusual for one of these singular figures to have between its forepaws a statuette which may be identified as the portrait of an individual Egyptian sovereign. Further, as many inscriptions inform us, single Sphinxes were stationed before temples and palaces, where they acted as guardians.

We may think that even the few dates relating to the Sphinx which have hitherto been noted will have told us how many enigmatical features the monster exhibits—features which should prove equally interesting to the psychologist, the archaeologist, the historian, and the student of aesthetics. There has been no

---

[4] The Sphinx of Gizeh is 65 feet in height and 185 feet in length; while many minute Sphinxes appear on decorated vessels, diadems, bracelets and ornaments.

lack of attempts to solve the problems with which the Sphinx confronts us by the mere fact of her existence; but a brief selection of the suggested explanations, which makes no pretension to completeness, will show how little they explain, and how far they are from reconciling all the contradictory facts.

Classical tradition knows the Sphinxes as images of the gods.[1] In Plutarch they appear as symbols of wisdom.[2] Clemens Alexandrinus[3] regarded them as emblems of power, because they possessed a lion's body, and of intelligence, because they had a human face. According to Champollion[4] the Sphinx is an embodiment of the Sun-God. Mariette[5] thinks the king himself keeps guard before the throne which he has erected. Ilberg's[6] view is that the true Sphinx, as distinct from the Gryphon (the lion with a falcon's head), and the Criosphinx (the lion with a ram's head) represents the king. He assumes that only the Sphinxes with animal heads are to be regarded as personifications of the god whose head they bear. He correctly points out that the Egyptians appear to have interpreted one and the same type of relief differently at different periods.

While we find no agreement in the interpretations of the Egyptian Sphinx, and while the explanations provided by historical research entirely fail to unify the many contradictory motives, we are even more surprised at the conceptions of the Sphinx in the Oedipus legend: The old euhemeristic interpretation saw the monster as an audacious robber, while another regarded her as a soothsayer.[7]

Another interesting euhemeristic interpretation makes the Sphinx[8] an Ethiopian species of ape, which many geographers

1 Wilkinson, *Manners and Customs*, 2nd series, London, 1841, p. 302; Wiedemann, *Herodots 2. Buch*, Leipzig 1890, p. 598, cited from the article "Sphinx" in Roscher's *Lexicon*, parts 66/67, ⌗ 1296, Leipzig 1913. From this instructive article of Ilberg's I take most of the footnotes included in this article.

2 Parthey, *De Is*, Berlin 1850, p. 175.

3 Strom. V, 5, ⌗ 31, p. 240, Syll.

4 *Le Panthéon Égyptien*, Paris 1923, no. 24 E.

5 *Voyage dans la Haute-Egypte*, 2, 9.

6 Roscher's *Lexicon*, parts 66/67, ⌗ 1301.

7 Schol. Hesiod. Theog. 326, et al., cited by Ilberg.

8 According to Agatharchides (*Across the Red Sea*), and in other works of the kind. Fully discussed in Ilberg's article, ⌗ 1375.

declare that they have seen! Modern scholars have agreed with the allegorical interpretations of the ancients. K. Bötticher,[9] for example, sees in the Sphinx "a very ancient symbol of the wise, pondering intelligence, concealed within the human head." Interpretations of the Sphinx as a natural force are extremely popular; among other things the Sphinx is supposed to be the all-embracing Helios or Aether, the symbol of the East, the giver of light, the solar zenith, the sunset, the waning moon, and Sirius. Gerhard[10] counts the Sphinx among the powers of the underworld, while Bréal[11] sees her as a symbol of the rain cloud, and Forchhammer[12] as the demon of the winter frost. For Schroeter[13] too she is a wintry demon, conquered by the vernal hero, Oedipus. Keller[14] regards her as the destroying angel of the plague in the region of the Boeotian lakes.

If we now survey this long series of explanations, we have to admit that it passes with suspicious rapidity from heaven, through the earth, to hell. It would be unreasonable to expect that one poor creature should have even further simultaneous meanings.

In conclusion, it should be mentioned that psychoanalysis has turned its attention to the Sphinx. Rank[15] attempts to explain the figure of the Sphinx, in connection with other ancient myths, as indicating the identity of the human and mammalian mother. At the same time he points to the fact that the Sphinx combines the upper part of a woman's body with an animal's hindquarters, which are provided with male genitals. He refers to the infantile conception, which often recurs in dreams, according to which all human beings, including women, possess a penis, and he rightly concludes that there is a concealed homosexual aspect of the meaning of the Sphinx in the Oedipus myth, from which he derives the affect of anxiety. According to this the Sphinx would be a subsequent duplication of the mother; a

9 *Berichte der Kgl. Sächs. Gesellschaft der Wissenschaften*, ♯6, 1854, pp. 53 ff.
10 *Griechische Mythologie*, 1, p. 581.
11 *Mélanges de mythologie et de linguist.*, pp. 163 ff.
12 *Daduchos*, 1875, p. 84.
13 *De Sphinge Graecarum fabularum* (Progr. v. Rogaslu, 1880).
14 *Tiere des Klassischen Altertums*, pp. 182 ff.
15 *Das Inzestmotiv in Dichtung und Sage*, Vienna and Leipzig 1912, pp. 266 ff.

theory repeated by Schmidt,[16] who identifies the Sphinx with Jocasta. It should be mentioned that Laistner, in his well-known work, *Das Rätsel der Sphinx*,[17] agrees with Rank as regards the genesis of the anxiety dream, and equates the Sphinx with the incubus or nightmare. C. G. Jung seeks to interpret the Sphinx by his theory of the theriomorphic representation of the libido:[18] for him the Sphinx is a half-theriomorphic representation of the "mother imago" which may be described as the imago of the "terrible mother," of whom numerous traces may be found in mythology. The libido thus theriomorphically represented would be the repressed "animal sexuality." From this root Jung derives the theriomorphic attributes of deity. Thus, according to this explanation the Sphinx is an "anxiety animal," which clearly reveals the characteristics of a mother derivative, and represents an original incestuously toned charge of libido, due to a cleavage of the relation to the mother. We shall recur later on to these attempted explanations.

4. ONE METHOD OF ANALYTIC INTERPRETATION

Any satisfactory explanation should meet two requirements. In the first place, it ought to make all the prominent and essential features of the Sphinx intelligible, however contradictory they may appear; and in the second place, it should show a natural connection between the Oriental type of Sphinx and the Sphinx of the Greek legend. It obviously will not suffice to give an interpretation which would apply to the one type only, or which would elucidate only one general and essential characteristic of the Sphinx, while ignoring all the mutually contradictory details. On the one hand, then, we maintain that the Sphinx of Gizeh, as a representative of the ancient Sphinxes of the Near East, is closely related to the Sphinx of the Oedipus saga as represented —let us say—on the cinerary urns of the Etruscans. It is probable that the one form developed out of the other, and it will be part

16 *Griechische Märchen und Sagen,* p. 143; cited from Rank, p. 268.
17 Berlin 1889.
18 "Wandlungen und Symbole der Libido," *l.c.*

of our task to follow this development and explain it psychologically; but it is impossible that the two forms are *toto genere* different. The mere similarity of shape tells us that; and in our attempt at interpretation we shall proceed from the external form. We hold the opinion that the Sphinx herself must enable us to form conclusions as to her nature on the strength of her outward appearance. As a creation of the human imagination she is an authentic child of Nature, and we believe with Goethe that Nature has neither kernel nor husk; "She is everything at one and the same time."

But first we must ask ourselves how anyone ever forms the conception of such fantastic animals. It is not an idle question, for we know that the imagination is incapable of creating anything absolutely new; it can only combine, transform and recreate fragments of reality. But this it does in accordance with certain eternal and unchanging rules, which are followed by the artist of the age of cave dwellers no less than by the most recent of Expressionists and Dadaists. The man of antiquity, despite all our knowledge of him, is so remote from our mental and emotional life that our intuition of his feelings will always be imperfect and uncertain. Yet even we, the children of an age which has achieved such wonderful things, know psychic states in which we think and feel approximately as did the men of bygone periods of culture. Psychoanalysis has taught us that our dreams revert to such an archaic mental structure.

One of the principal devices of dream work, through whose operation the understanding of the dream thoughts is made so difficult for us, is *condensation,* in which we must include the production of collective or mixed persons. We believe that this peculiar method of combining a number of features, often mutually contradictory, to form a unity which already exists in the dream material or is newly created, can furnish an adequate explanation of the psychic mechanisms which are operative in the formation of such figures as the Sphinx. The singular composition of the Sphinx's body should disturb us as little in our task of interpretation as the apparently meaningless and unintelligible formation of certain hybrid persons in our dreams. For example, in a dream we often see X, whom we know, sporting a beard like

Z's, together with a woman's hat and a silk blouse such as Mrs. Y might wear, and in the dream this does not trouble us in the least. We may be sure that the ancient Egyptians were as little astonished by the Sphinx. We see psychic creations resembling the dream in structure in the hallucinations of persons suffering from psychosis, in which it is not unusual for imperfect or composite creatures to appear, and we know that psychoanalysis is able to reveal their significance. Those who are familiar with the technique of psychoanalysis have shown that the images which seem so absurd have really a meaning. Owing to the special character of the psychotic disorder—namely, the rupture of all relations with the environment—it may be impossible to make a complete analysis; yet psychoanalysts are agreed that the hallucinatory figures are determined in every feature, and that their production can be explained by the emergence of affectively toned recollections of certain experiences and impressions. It is possible to understand such images only if we realize that they must be granted a definite place in the structure of the psychosis; and if we place ourselves on the same footing as the patient, refusing to take exception to the absurdity of the hallucinatory images. A woman patient of Dr. Bertschinger's, who drew the hallucinatory pictures that passed before her, furnished explanations of the images which gave one an excellent notion of the way in which they were produced.[1] Twofold creatures appeared with especial frequency; she might see a stag with the upper part of a human body, or even with two human torsos; a horse's body with a human head; a spotted hyena with the head and shoulders and bosom of a woman; a crocodile, which in addition to its own head displayed the head of a man, etc. The individual components of these compositions proved to be determined by the patient's reminiscences. For example, she saw a spotted hyena, and on the following day she offered this explanation; she had compared a wardress who had annoyed her to a spotted hyena because she had such wicked green eyes, and wore a spotted blouse. At the same time the hyena was a young woman who resembled the wardress; the patient had recollected this young woman, and remembered that when she

[1] Bertschinger, "Illustrierte Halluzinationen," *Jahrbuch für psychoanalytische und psychopathologische Forschungen*, Vol. III, 1912, pp. 69 ff.

was eleven she had a particularly painful experience in connection with her. The image of a billygoat with a human head was intelligible when one learned that as a little child she had been the unwilling witness of an act of coition, when she compared the man to a billygoat. But this picture too was overdetermined, for during a holiday in the country she had seen for the first time the erected penis of a goat. In the same way analytic investigation traced every individual hallucination back to certain memories. Stimulated by recent impressions which suggested comparisons, the imagination kept on returning to certain affectively toned events of the past. The hallucinations which often occurred at such times presented persons or thoughts in a peculiarly compressed form, unintelligible to the normal mind. If the patient had at some time compared someone to an animal he now actually appeared as the animal. Another person, associated with the first through some real or imagined connection, was blended with the first in the hallucinated image, or was represented by a human head set upon an animal body, while a specific quality was symbolized by a physical attribute, etc. In every case it could be seen that the hidden meaning of the hallucination could be made intelligible only by the adoption of a historical perception, which went back from recent events to the events of early childhood. At the same time, as in solving a picture puzzle, one had to consider the components of the vision singly, and only to survey their combination when each isolated portion had been understood.

If now we return to our consideration of the Sphinx, profiting by the analytic experience of interpreting the mixed beings in dreams and the hallucination of the psychotic, we shall have to confess that every portion of the portrayals of the Sphinx, and every attribute of the Sphinx has been separately explained, and that an interpretation *en bloc* must necessarily miscarry. Further, the high degree of condensation of the image makes it necessary carefully to remove stratum after stratum; for the recollections of the individual, in superimposed layers, which are drawn upon in creating the dream, correspond with the sedimentary deposits of the experiences of successive generations in the formation of the mass psyche. Thus the historical or rather the genetic standpoint must supplement the psychological in a survey which proceeds from the consideration of the individual components of the figure of the Sphinx. As in the analysis of a dream, we shall for the time being disregard contradictions between the individual elements; in this case, as in that, we shall finally recognize, if our interpretation is correct, a latent connection, which will show even the apparently absurd to be necessary and significant.

5. THE SPHINX AS THE BELATED REPRESENTATION OF A TOTEMIC ANIMAL

The most conspicuous motive in the personification of the Sphinx is the blending of a human and an animal body. The individual analogy of this phenomenon in the dream and the hallucination tells us how we are to understand it; there a man was represented as an animal because the patient had likened him to an animal. The similarity or identity was expressed by replacing one object by the other, to which it had been compared. In this way the dream also represents similarity and correspondence. Here one may recall the grimacing animals of Rodin, and the works of Ibsen's sculptor Rubek, whose genesis he himself explains.

The ethnopsychological analogy leads us back to an age when man did not yet arrogantly point to the distance that divided him from the animals; indeed, he was peculiarly impressed by the animals, and felt the comparison with an animal to be not an insult, but an honor. Many evidences of prehistoric culture tell us that there was once a time when in primitive conceptions the bridge between animal and man was not so completely broken down as it is today. Even our children hurry swiftly across it, without any special effort; they find no difficulty in assuming that the person whom they know as an uncle is also a lion. Just recently I saw a little boy, who had been crawling on all fours and baying at his playfellows, run to his mother and inform her, with every indication of terror: "Max is a wolf and wants to eat me!" Protected by his mother, he shouted to his little playfellow, of whose identity he was absolutely positive: "Max, are you a boy again yet?"

The totemic system is based on such a primeval outlook. We

have heard that in the opinion of many scholars the Sphinxes were originally personifications of the king, and later on were interpreted as symbols of divinity. We, however, shall be more inclined, proceeding from the animal body of the Sphinx, to assume a development in the reverse direction, which in broad outline we should describe as follows:

The first comprehensive religion of mankind, totemism, regarded the animal as divine. Many thousands of years later the totem god was transformed into an anthropomorphic god; or, remembering the original prototype of deity, the father of the primal horde, we might say that it was changed back into an anthropomorphic god. Nature, who does not take sudden leaps, makes no exception in respect of the evolutionary processes of human thought; the progress of culture is infinitely slow; for thousands of years the image of the animal god must have held its own beside that of the new god in human form, and when at last, after many vicissitudes, the anthropomorphic god advanced into the foreground, there remained, simultaneously with feelings of aversion, the memory, associated with powerful affects, of the important part which the animal had once played in religious worship. The figure of the Sphinx must be regarded as a *very late* reminiscence of the primary totemism, for the god of the dim primeval era reappears in the animal body, while the anthropomorphic deity of a later age is reflected in the Sphinx's countenance. We are therefore inclined to say that the archetype of the Sphinx is not the king, but a powerful animal, probably the lion, which had once been the god of human beings. Let us recollect the lion-headed gods of the Egyptians—Hathor, Neith and Bast—apparent relics of totemism in Egypt, in which the lion figures as a totemic animal. In our opinion the images of animals —of lions, for example—which were cherished and regarded as sacred in the Egyptian city of Leantopolis, were the immediate prototypes of the Sphinx. There may well be a single, long line of development from the crude animal drawings in the caves of the Aurignacian era to the Sphinx of Gizeh and her contemporaries. The human head which the Egyptian Sphinx so often displays would thus be of late appearance, determined by the anthropomorphization of the gods, and replacing an original animal head. The combination of man and animal is a token of identity; but it tells us that a historical process has preceded it, whose traces we see before us. The psychic process which led to this mode of representation is entirely analogous to the process of condensation in the dream; here too we see, combined in a single image, elements which are to be conceived as a unity, although to our consciousness they are separate; the idol of a primitive age which one knows is superseded, and that of the present day, which cannot deny its relationship to the former.

The difference between the psychic activities of the individual and the collectivity is clearly indicated by the fact that in the dream persons in actual existence are condensed and combined with persons taken from our childish memories, whereas prehistoric art combines in a single structure creatures from bygone stages of evolution with those which are now attracting its attention.[1] The representation of the two historical aspects of the deity, the animal and the human, compressed into a single form, seems absurd to us, and if we are to credit the psychology of

[1] A few references supplementing the above definition may be welcome here. In some of the Sphinxes of the twelfth Dynasty the face is still surrounded by a huge lion's mane. M. Hoernes (*Urgeschichte der bildenden Kunst,* Vienna 1915, p. 58) gives a similar explanation of the origin of hybrid forms: "Plastic art is a firm anchor of religious ideas. Absolute conceptions also are fixed by art, yet even though obsolete and belonging to the past they continue to be current. They enrich the present with the memory of the bygone, and still find a fitting place for the latter in the artistic expression of ideas. This explains the origin of the oldest hybrid figures, the oldest group formations." The interpretation of the Sphinx as a deity is entirely in harmony with the oldest traditions, which assert, with curious persistence, that the Sphinx of Gizeh represents the Sun-god; but they also insist on the analogy to the meaning of the Gryphon and the Criosphinx; for the Falcon is sacred to Horus as the Ram to Ammon. This explains, also, the many representations of the Sphinx with the statuette of a king between her paws; she is the king's guardian. When she appears before the temples as a guardian it must be remembered that in this late form she figures as a kind of degraded divinity, having become a servant of the godhead. Only in this sense is it understood that the god himself is guarding his temple. It is evident that the Sphinx, in her function as doorkeeper, is closely related to the hybrid creatures of the Assyrio-Babylonian culture, the lions in the palaces of Sargon, Sanheribs, etc. Such guardian lions and bulls are seen not only by the doors of ancient palaces; for the cathedrals of Ferrara and Spalato, and the palaces and *piazze* of Venice and many other Italian cities show similar animals. Even the monsters that stretch their necks from the gables of our churches are reminiscent of these ancient and originally totemistic animals.

dreams, we must assume that such representations conceal a trace of unconscious derision. But it would be quite erroneous to associate such a feeling with the conquest of "animal" sexuality—nothing could be more alien to ancient Egypt—or with any sort of contempt of the animal. The originally high estimation of the animal may, in the course of the gradual evolution of culture, under the influence of many motives, have been followed, at last, by a diminished estimation, which in historical times could lead to a symbolical representation in the manner of C. G. Jung. But as regards the early period which we are considering such an anagogic conception, which might be called the repetition of a fragment of evolution rather than its explanation, is quite out of the question.

From the manner in which the images of the Sphinx originated in totemism[2] one might regard the further development of the type as an ever more and more fantastic production of derivative forms. Factors of a different kind may have co-operated in the final product; among them tendencies making it unintelligible, and lastly the erroneous comprehension of obsolete configurations of the Sphinx by later generations. At the same time, a fragment of the political and national history of the Egyptian people may be reflected in the evolutionary history of the Sphinx. The Egyptians of the earliest period, according to the Egyptologists and other experts, were by no means a homogeneous unity, but a mixture of various peoples.[3] Further, we know how many hetero-

---

[2] The well-known American expert, Morris Jastrow, has expressed the opinion that "this same factor of resemblance between men and animals in conjunction with the ignorance as to the processes of nature led to the belief in all kinds of hybrid creatures, composed of human and animal organs" (*Babylonian-Assyrian Birth-Omens and Their Cultural Significance*, Giessen 1914, p. 79). He is inclined to derive from this belief, in connection with the Babylonian doctrine of birth-omens, the fabled creatures of the ancient religions of the Near East and also those of the Greek, Egyptian and Indian mythologies, in so far as they represent such hybrid creatures. Similar views are expounded by Professor Friedrich Schatz (*Die griechischen Götter und die menschlichen Missgeburten*, Wiesbaden 1901) and Dr. Bab ("Geschlechtsleben, Geburt und Missgeburten" in *Zeitschrift für Ethnologie*, Vol. 38, pp. 209–311). These theories alone do not provide an adequate explanation, although they elucidate many individual features.

[3] Cf. F. Hommel, *Grundriss der Geographie und Geschichte des alten Orients*, pp. 108–129; A. Wiedemann, "Ägyptische Religion," *Archiv für Religionswissenschaft*, Vol. IX, 1906, p. 482. That the Egyptian people consists of

geneous elements were absorbed and assimilated by the primitive population of Egypt. The tribal organization and the local distribution had for the peoples of the ancient East, who were comparatively late in forming States,[4] a special significance in respect of religion. We see, for example, in the history of Babylon, that it repeatedly happened that with the prolongation of the political and cultural supremacy of a particular tribe all sorts of religious transformations occurred; one god would be assimilated by another, various features of the prevailing religion would be condensed, and a divine attribute would be replaced by quite a different attribute. Such happenings, in the phase of totemism, led to mixed formations of different kinds; combinations of the totemic animal of one tribal group with that of another might have been formed as the result of the prolonged juxtaposition of several totems. As such evidences of conflict and compromise between old and new, between the conquered and the conqueror, between different tribes, we may note such creatures as the Criosphinx, the Gryphon, etc., which preceded the creation of the Sphinx with a human head. This form was the last of a long series, whose progress we cannot exactly follow.[5]

---

an admixture of many different peoples and racial remnants is indicated not only by skeletal remains (Cf. J. Kollmann, "Die Gräber von Abydos," *Korrespondenzbl. für Anthropol.*, Vol. XXXIII, 1902, pp. 119–126), and the illustrations of types from the earliest period (cf. J. de Morgan, *Recherches sur l'origine de l'Egypte*, Paris 1896–7), but also by the examination of the ancient Egyptian language. This proves to be a mixed language, comprising various African and Asiatic components. According to the researches of A. Ermann ("*Die Flexion des ägyptischen Verbums*," *Sitzungber. d. Berl. Akad.*, 1900, pp. 317–353) and Graf Schack-Schackenburg (*Ägyptiologische Studien*, Vol. V, Leipzig 1902, pp. 209 ff.) and the anthropological discoveries of von Luschan, one may assume that the primitive population of Egypt consisted of African peoples which at a very early period were subjugated by Semitic Bedouins.

4 The wars of the different city kings of Babylon were concluded in the third century B.C. by the formation of the kingdoms of Sumu and Akkad; not until the latter part of the predynastic period of Egyptian history were the northern and southern provinces of the country combined to form two larger kingdoms, although the provincial organization was not abandoned (about 3400).

5 The above schematic and simplified account can give the reader no idea of the multifarious events which led to the developments that occurred within totemism, but can do no more than hint at a few possibilities out of many. However, it may be noted that many obscure passages of the Bible can be explained by the connection of the tribes with their totems inside the larger

The historical mode of consideration, if we combine it with the psychoanalytic method, is to understand why in the image of the Sphinx one sees not only the god, but the king; for to the ancients the difference between god and ruler was conceived as vaguely as it is among the modern primitives.[6] The kings of antiquity were accustomed to being honored as gods, and their statues were accorded divine honors. Thus, the Babylonian sovereigns, from Sargon I to the Fourth Dynasty of Ur, laid claim to the statue of gods: Indeed, the monarchs of this dynasty had temples built in their honor, and commanded the people to bring offerings to their images. The Egyptian kings were deified during their lifetime and were reverenced as gods in special temples, by a special priesthood. By the people the king was regarded as "the

---

political union. A grasp of the subject is even more important in respect of the much-debated question, whether monotheism or polytheism lies at the origin of religious evolution. Andrew Lang (*Myth, Ritual and Belief,* and *The Making of Religion,* London 1904, 3rd ed., *Magic and Religion,* London 1901) and the Viennese Father, Wilhelm Schmidt (*Der Ursprung der Gottesidee,* 1912) are of the opinion that a monotheistic form of belief preceded all other and cruder forms of religion; they are definitely opposed to the majority of investigators in this field, who regard polytheism as the more primitive form. If with Freud we regard totemism as the first comprehensive religion, we come to the conclusion, after a conscientious survey of the ethnological and historical material, that there is a great deal of truth in the opinion of both the above investigators. It is not correct in so far as it holds that monotheism (the exclusive belief in *one* god) is the primary religion, but henotheism may claim such precedence over other forms of religion. The tribe which traces its descent from a totemic animal, which it worships, is first and foremost an exclusive whole. Its connection with other tribes, which takes the form of a peaceful union, or the subjugation of one or several tribes by an alien tribe, first introduces the possibility of a change of totem, and the more important possibility that new totems shall be valued and worshipped together with the old. In conjunction with other motives, this may be regarded as decisive for the development of polytheism from a primitive henotheism, but for the later development of a primitive monotheism, which has to contend with the older multiplicity of gods, the factor of the racial or tribal organization must be regarded as especially effective and explanatory. Thus, the suppression of the Elohim by Jahve on Sinai seems to be codetermined by the prolongation of the hegemony of the tribe to which Moses belonged. An exhaustive treatment of the relevant problems will have to be reserved for a separate volume.

6 J. S. Frazer, in "The Magic Art" (*The Golden Bough,* Vol. I, Part 1, pp. 373 ff.) gives numerous examples of such "incarnate human gods" from all parts of the world; and also of the divine states of the ruler in ancient Babylon, Egypt, Peru, Mexico and China, and he explains this by the evolution of kingship.

great god," "the golden Horus," and especially as "the Son of the Sun-God Ra." He was addressed as "the Sun, Lord of Heaven and Earth," as "Creator and Shaper of mankind, Life of the great world," etc. The history of Egyptian culture explains how the Sphinx came to signify not only the god, but also his human incarnation. As tokens of their divine nature the prehistoric kings wrapped themselves, just as the chieftains of savage peoples do today, in the pelt of the totemic animal. The rulers of prehistoric Egypt wore the skin of the lion long after the totemistic religion had been replaced by a religion of a higher order.

6. THE SPHINX AS SUN-GOD

The interpretation of the Sphinx as the Sun-God takes its appropriate place in the development we have sketched; she has indeed some claim to be regarded as a secondary divinity.

We cannot here discuss the psychic hypotheses on which the astral conception of the gods was based, or how this conception came to be entertained, or to what actual and psychic necessities it owed its continued significance. The researches of Otto Rank have corrected and modified the theories of the astral mythologists in essential details, and have demonstrated their value within certain limits; but in these pages—at the risk of exceeding the limits of our subject—we shall do no more than briefly indicate the evolution of the astral mythology. I think we may be certain that the astral religion evolved from the totemistic philosophy, and that the gods were relegated to the heavens under the combined impression of natural events, psychic revolutions, and changes in the conditions of human life. It may be assumed that the Zodiac, in its very composition, bears witness to the totemistic origin of astral mythology and astral religion. The promotion of the gods to the heavens reveals itself by many indications as a more highly developed and loftier phase of religious evolution. It exiles the gods from their home, the Earth, where they originated, and where in the beginning they peopled forest and brake. Primeval humanity, like the child in its first years, took no interest in the heavens and the heavenly bodies; the appointment of the upper regions as the dwelling place of the gods is a sign of the advanced spiritualization of religion.[1] This becomes possible only where man has lifted his gaze from the earth to the heavens.

The projection of the totem upon the heavens was the typical method of disposing of them; it happened at a time when the evolution of religion had already advanced beyond the totemistic idea of the god to higher conceptions; so that now the totem, being of no further service, could be relegated to the celestial lumber room. In this connection it should perhaps be noted that this kind of disposal finally became a euphemistic representation of death, and that it recurs in dreams, in poetry, in folklore, and in the formation of myths. One is reminded of a dream cited by Freud, in which a child of four saw her playmates put on wings and fly away.[2]

This ascension of the god signifies, in this sense, not only a promotion, but also, unconsciously, a banishment, a sort of latent dispossession. In this new religious conception the old psychic mechanisms which were at work in the formation of religion are still conspicuous; respect and esteem for the god have increased to the maximum, but in the same degree the unconscious revolutionary wishes that aspire to his removal to a distance assert themselves. This expression of an intensified ambivalence—for as such we must regard the relegation of the gods to the heavens— was repeated when the status of the anthropomorphized deities was imperiled. The ancients could still allow the gods to wander about the world and die a physical death; but later on they were made immortal and had to swell in heaven. The effects of unconscious hostile tendencies and reactively reinforced love and reverence are clearly perceptible in this religious conception.[3]

1 There are still skeptics who profess their lack of interest in the heavens and their divine inhabitants:

"The heavens we resign
To angels and the sparrows."

Heine

2 *The Interpretation of Dreams.*

3 The reference in the text of the astral cult to the projection of gods, first animal and then human in shape, upon the heavens, calls for a more exhaustive consideration. In so far as this projection was part of a more comprehensive and primitive process, that made use of psychic paths which were already conditioned, it is a subject of extraordinary interest, which should be examined from other aspects. In this connection I will add only a few supple-

The Sphinx must have participated in the long evolution of the deity from the animal on earth to the animal in the heavens, to which in the last resort we owe the nomenclature of the Zodiac,

---

mentary remarks, whose fragmentary character is obvious. In connection with the above exposition they may perhaps help to exhibit the astral mythology and religion of the Near East as of secondary importance. The Babylonian cult of the seven planetary gods, Sin (Moon), Sumas (Sun), Nabû (Mercury) Ishtar (Venus), Nergal (Mars, or Saturn), Marduk (Jupiter), Kaimanû (Saturn, or Mars), shows, by the very names of the planets, that these were identified with the gods. We know that the names given to the stars and planets by the Babylonians were retained by the Greek astronomers. As to how the gods became stars, we can only make assumptions on the basis of certain indications in the religions of antiquity and in those of modern savages. The Egyptian deities were mortal, but when their bodies lay swathed and bandaged in their earthly tomb, their souls shone as brilliant stars in the firmament. The soul of Isis shone in Sirius, that of Horus in Orion, that of Typhon in the Great Bear (Frazer, *The Dying God*, p. 5). The primitive peoples of today see in the stars either demons or the souls of the departed. It seems to me that this is an advanced phase, in which the gods of old appear as demons. (Example in Frazer, *The Dying God*, pp. 61 ff.) A star makes its original appearance when a great man dies; the heroes of Greece and Rome were set in the skies as stars by the gods, in reward for their achievements. Compare the words of Caesar's wife in Shakespeare:

> "When beggars die there are not comets seen,
> The heavens themselves blaze forth the death of princes."

The same motive appears, otherwise expressed, in the numerous sagas of primitive peoples in which God, discontented with conditions on earth, takes refuge in the heavens. The existence of the twelve signs of the Zodiac can be traced to the middle of the second millennium B.C. in Babylon (Schrader-Winckler-Zimmern, *Keilinschriften und das Alte Testament*, 3rd ed., Berlin 1903, p. 627). It has been noted that the boundary stones or "landmarks" mentioned in the text, which display emblems of the Zodiac, the better-known Babylonian-Assyrian deities are indicated; "in the planets of the Zodiac they have, so to speak, their abiding manifestations." The nature of this relation remains obscure; it becomes clearer if we recollect that even the planetary gods were originally totems. This conception of the Zodiacal circle as a gradually emerging pantheon of the totems of different tribes, which finally assumed a permanent form, would be consistent with Peiser's bold interpretation of a passage in Psalm XII (*Orientalische Literaturzeitung*, 1910, ♯ 5). According to Peiser Psalm XVI, 4, should read:

> "Other Baals are many
> wandering on the wall of the Zodiac;
> Their blood-offerings I will not bring to them
> nor take their names upon my lips."

The significance of this interpretation becomes apparent if we compare it with the opinion of Winckler, Stucken, Jeremias and others, that the astral character of the Babylonian religion was primary. How far it differs from the

in a definite form. As Horus, from being a totemistic deity, became a solar god, so his plastic representation, the Sphinx, may have become a solar symbol. Other attributes of the solar deity were allotted to her in a secondary degree, and subsequently many functions were ascribed to her which were not consistent with her original character as the image of a totem.

But we are constantly astonished by the fact that what we perceive as the consecutiveness of a very long and gradual evolution of culture appears to be a simultaneousness in the figure of the Sphinx; the past does not wholly disappear, although new and important conceptions assert themselves. It is as though the unconscious mind of the peoples were incapable of completely discarding its outworn and obsolete ideas and feelings. The unconscious mind of the mass is equally indestructible and immortal, and withdrawn from the influences of victorious innovations.

7. THE WINGS OF THE SPHINX

The evolutionary history of the celestial deity may have covered a thousand years, and it may have been extremely complicated; but all the indications seem to show that the removal

---

estimation of totemism by the astral-mythological school may be judged from a passage in a recent book, *Sternglaube und Sterndeutung* (Leipzig and Berlin 1919, 2nd ed.) by Prof. F. Boll: "The discoveries of the last few years have shown that zodiacal research is dealing with one of the most important fossil indications of the ancient cultural stream which has proceeded from the great central point of the spiritual life of the ancient world. In correspondence with the notion that the earth and earthly life are a copy of the greater life of the heavens the human world has been divided from the astral standpoint. Thus, the Peruvian capital of Cuzco was built as a zodiacal monument. Further, the tribe was everywhere divided into groups which were subordinated to the animals of the Zodiac. It was thus that totemism arose, which from this time onwards was no longer regarded as a universal and independent phase of human evolution, but as a derivation from the cultural circle which derived from the Zodiacal circle." In opposition to this view, we believe that the form thus described represents an end product which the history of totemism explains; it corresponds to a retroactive projection of the zodiacal emblems upon the earth. We cannot here explain what consequences for the development of astrology and astronomy have resulted from this derivation; but it should be emphasized that in antiquity, and throughout a great part of the Middle Ages, the dominating position of astrology, and the kind of relation which it establishes between the constellations and human destiny is explained by the religious significance which was originally attributed to the stars.

of the god to the heavens was gradual, and that it took place, according to the views of the prehistoric East, as in those of the primitive peoples of today, in a perfectly natural and obvious manner. Tree totemism and the cult of mountain peaks represented definite evolutionary stages in this important cultural, historical and religious process, in which the bird plays a part of special significance.

Here we come to a conspicuous attribute of the Sphinx—its possession of wings—which seems inconsistent with its lion's body. The interpretation of this quality as a sign of speed is, of course, reasonable enough, but it needs supplementing in many important respects. It is evident that the wings, with which the religion and mythology of antiquity endowed not only the mixed animal deities, but also such deities as were human in form, as Mercury, and such messengers of God as cherubim, seraphim and angels, were taken from man's natural environment.

The task we have set ourselves in these pages allows us only to touch upon the significance of the bird in respect of religious conceptions; but we may be sure that a more special treatment of the problem would lead to interesting and valuable conclusions. Here we can do no more than give a few indications. In the final development of the totemistic system the vulture, eagle or other such bird must have been adopted as a totem at certain definite points, which would be different in the case of the individual peoples. The swiftness of the bird may have impressed the primitive mind, just as the overcoming of gravity, and the ability to disappear and reappear in the ether, might perhaps at a later period serve as the criteria of the omnipresence and omniscience of the gods. There is no possible doubt that at one time the bird was regarded by men as a god; the later conception of the bird-soul must, I think, have developed from the fact that birds alighted upon the corpses of the beloved dead, ate of them, and flew away again. It is probable that the totemistic significance of the bird appertains to a later religious development; the bird then becomes the being that flies to the astral deity, the Father-Sun, representing the soul, and its flight becomes the symbol of the translation and resurrection of numerous heroes, from Moses and Elijah to Jesus.

For the time being we cannot precisely determine the point when the bird was introduced into the totemistic form of religion, but it seems as though it had been totemistically adapted at a time when totemism was already disappearing—that is, that its function and its task were described in totemistic language. It may be for this reason that it afterwards became one of the totemistic incarnations of the Saviour, and an emblem of the hero. The sparrow-headed and vulture-headed gods of the Egyptians, the doves of Aphrodite, and the raven of Wotan, the vulture that devoured Prometheus's liver, and the cranes of the Ibykus, the birds whose flight all the peoples of antiquity regarded as an oracle, the vulture which appeared when Abraham offered up a sacrifice, the doves sent forth by Noah, and the dove which plays its part in the Annunciation to Mary—all these birds were originally gods, who subsequently became the auxiliaries and the messengers of anthropomorphic deities. Thus the Sphinx also, from being a deity, became a winged guardian in the service of God, like other familiar figures. She too had at first a place in the pantheon, before she became a mediator between Jahveh and mankind; I mean the angels who bore wings, and whose originally totemistic character we still perceive in the Old Testament descriptions of their predecessors, the Cherubim.[1]

Here again it should be noted that the oldest Sphinxes known to us have no wings, and that the Sphinx was first generally represented as winged by the Greeks.

8. MALE AND FEMALE SPHINXES

We had perforce to trace the far-flung and hardly recognizable paths which were followed by the primitive society before it reached the religious stage at which we find it in early antiquity. We were able to detect traces of this evolutionary progress in the form of the Sphinx; for like the annual rings of a tree, the bygone phases of her development have impressed themselves upon her shape. Owing to the remarkable conservatism of primitive cultures, the ancient characteristics did not disappear when the new

---

[1] Among such forms we include the colossal winged and human-headed bulls of the late Assyrio-Babylonian period.

arrived, but, mingled with the new, they survived to serve modified purposes, long divorced from their original significance. All
progress, in the religion of antiquity—and not only there—occurs, in a similar fashion, through the transformation and the
reinterpretation and assimilation of inherited forms. This fact
may throw some light on that peculiar form of the Sphinx which
we can only describe as hermaphrodite. We know that in Egypt,
in very ancient times, the male Sphinxes were in the great majority; later on female Sphinxes appeared with increasing frequency beside the male Sphinxes, until in Greece they completely superseded the male forms. How far is the female form
consistent with our explanation of the totemistic derivation of
the Sphinx? If we remember that in the early period the female
Sphinx was rare, and that later on both male and female forms
appeared, it seems obvious that we may accept a historical development which replaced the original male by a female form.
The penis which the female Sphinx bears would thus be a relic
of her original masculine form. It seems that we have now to enhance the probability of this hypothetically accepted development by facts relating to the prehistory of humanity. We know
that the present form of the family was preceded by the matriarchate, in which the members of the horde were grouped about
their natural center, the mother. The relics of the matriarchal
organization, as we find them in certain very primitive tribes, as
well as traces in the organization of the ancient peoples of the
East,[1] give us, even when we consider the numerous alterations
which have occurred in thousands of years, an approximate picture of that first, primitive group organization. It is difficult to
establish the influence of the matriarchal system on religion, if
only because we have no direct access to the prehistoric stage of
human development. Freud assumed that the great mother divinities may in general have preceded the father-god in the course of
evolution. There are two facts in particular which support this
opinion: the relatively late character of totemism, which, by reason of its source, presupposes that a more complicated form of

[1] Cf. especially Frazer on Attis, Adonis, Osiris (*The Golden Bough,* 3rd ed.,
Vol. IV, London 1907, pp. 382 ff.) and also the older works of Bachofen,
Dargun, etc.

family preceded the fraternal class, and the improbability that the libido-cathected figure of the Mother, which was for so long the center and head of the family, had not been previously raised to the divine status in the primitive philosophy. Nevertheless, one must observe a certain caution in assuming the existence of an original mother religion; we know that the cults dedicated to the mother deities of the Orient—Isis, Ishtar, Cybele and other embodiments of the Mater Magna—were originally of a very different character from the father religion; they were characterized especially by their emphasis on the sexual factors, their celebration of fertility in man and in Nature, in contrast to the father religion, which kept the social motives in the foreground and created a sort of social anxiety in the consciousness of guilt. Even if we regard these ancient cults as late developments we must nevertheless agree that their characteristic features were already contained in their prehistoric and preliminary stages; indeed, we shall rather be inclined to assume that they appeared there in cruder and less inhibited forms, unaffected by external cultural progress.[2]

It is, of course, only a question of nomenclature if we regard religion as existing in this or that stage of human evolution, or if we date it from another stage, but it seems to me that two of the essential and indispensable motives of the formation of a religion are precisely the social nexus, and with it the powerful agency of the consciousness of guilt. Consequently, though the veneration of the mother in the age of the primitive matriarchate may seem religious in its sincerity, we cannot really speak of religion in this case, since the essential characteristics are lacking.[3] The Mother of the matriarchal era was worshipped with all the signs of the overestimation of sex, as she brought to a head the object choice of the anaclitic type; for a long while she was un-

[2] One cannot agree with the theory that the difference of the cults of male and female deities rests on externalities, that are the indelible and indestructible signs of a profound difference rooted in the instinctual life.

[3] In order to avoid misunderstanding it should be expressly stated that the above roughly indicated scheme refers to a period prior to any historical experience; the mother cults of the early East, compared with this, belong to one of these phases, divided by thousands of years. In them a genuine mother religion, capable of development, already makes its appearance. It is naturally impossible to say anything definite regarding their development.

doubtedly the object to which the libido of primitive man was chiefly dedicated; she became his idol, mainly in consequence of the urgent power of the heterosexual instinctual components. Here, through the factor of the first, elementary erotic choice and the overestimation of sex, the difference between the original veneration of the mother and the primitive father religion is clearly demonstrated. If the mother of the first organization of the matriarchal epoch became an idol, as many discoveries relating to the late quarternary seem to indicate was the case in an earlier phase, so the father of the primitive horde subsequently became the father ideal of the members of the fraternal clan. But in the contrast between the *mother idol* and the *father ideal* we find, in addition to an essential trait of the attitude of primitive man to the archetypes of his religion, an indication of the kind of object choice which provides the basis for later and highly significant developments. It has already been noted that the object choice of the primeval era, of which we find indications in the matriarchal period, is mainly of the anaclitic type, whereas later on the object choice of the narcissistic type moves into the foreground. The libidinous veneration of the mother, which was connected with the glorification of the crudely sexual, could of course become, subsequently, in a more or less sublimated form, a religious cult, but first of all the god must exist as such, and the father religion, in the form of totemism, must make its entry into human history.

In accordance with the pattern of the father religion the Mother was subsequently deified. She now appeared as a rival beside the father-god, but the right to function as a religious creator was reserved to the father as the prototype of every god, and was bound up, not with the elementary and unbroken power of the first libidinal cathexis, but with the reactively enhanced and perpetuated power of paternal yearning.[4]

4 The features of the mother and the beloved, united in the first libido object, are still united in the form of the original female deity. Later on the maternal character is more and more strongly emphasized, while the sexual motive recedes into the background or appears only in the more spiritual form of mercifulness and love of humanity or womanly kindness. But even the most advanced development cannot quite exclude it; the female divinities are always the guardians of love and wedlock. The Gretchen of the Faust tragedy

The matriarchate undoubtedly gave an impetus to many significant developments in human society, but it did not give birth to religion as such. In the contrast between the mother idol and the father ideal, which we construed as the preliminary to the divorce between mother divinity and father-god, those motives are already latent which were afterwards, with their progressive intensification, to become so important. The cult of the mother divinity led to the excessive glorification of sexuality, and only very much later did it achieve a partial sublimation, such as we perceive in the cult of the Madonna; but it was always responsible for encroachment upon the prescribed though unwritten laws of the father religion, because it was constantly receiving reinforcements from the depths of the eternal powers of the instincts. The strength of Antaeus was renewed when he touched the Mother.

But the father ideal, which had become a god, now became the secret lawgiver of mankind, its personified conscience and its protector against the instinctual assaults that threatened to disintegrate the social order. Within the compass of this work, which has other aims in view, we cannot attempt to gauge the importance of these mutually conflicting principles, which continue to play a significant part in the evolution of religion. We can do no more than observe that one of the most important points of the irruption of sexuality into the social institution of religion may be found here, and that the conflict between mother religion and father religion corresponds with the lifelong hesitation between masculine and feminine object choice in the individual. Further, it must be emphasized that the exhaustive psychoanalytic, re-

---

who turns to Mary in her sorrow is only a modern embodiment of innumerable sisters in the ancient world, who in similar situations sought the help of the local goddesses. The witty Anatole France tells in *La pierre blanche* of a lovely maiden who addresses the Mother of God in the following delightful prayer: "Holy Mother of God, you who conceived without sin, grant me this favor that I may sin without conceiving!" This contrast reminds us of the time when even the mothers of gods conceived in the earthly fashion—for as yet it was not sinful to do so. Another anecdote of the French skeptic's recalls the same epoch of mundane divinities: An Italian, whose wish Jesus had not granted, despite his fervent prayers, returned to the chapel where the image of the Madonna and her child was displayed, and cried: "I am not speaking to you, son of a harlot, but to your sainted mother!"

ligious and historical evaluation of this important theme is still in arrears. It would constitute one of the most important and informative additions to and continuations of Freud's introduction to the birth of religion.

The excursion, which, by the hypothesis of the subsequent deification of the Mother, maintained that the totemistic father religion was the first and most primitive religious creation, was only apparently superfluous, for without considering the course of evolution, as we have sketched it in broad outline, it is impossible to understand how the Sphinx should be represented as female as well as male. As we have said, the mother divinities were created after the pattern of the father: and only so can we understand how the god—for the Sphinx was originally a god— should now appear as a woman. The attempt has been made to associate the female form with the victory of the anthropomorphic embodiment of divinity, on the assumption that it was the female form which first and most powerfully impressed the primitive believer when the totemic god came to be replaced by a human god. The process by which god became man, one of the most tremendous events in world history, is still unknown to us as regards its most important psychic conditions; and it is not impossible that it was precisely here that the image of the mother goddess first made its appearance. However, the female form of the Sphinx is secondary, for totemism—and it is to a very late recollection of totemism that we owe the figure of the Sphinx—was purely a father religion and a creation of societies of men. The first prototype of God, the father of the primitive horde, was a strict, powerful, terrifying chieftain; the totemic animal which the primitive regarded as a god must have had a similar character. To no being of milder nature would the primitive savage have bowed; and even the Jahveh of the Bible is a terrible and revengeful god. The transference of such traits to a mother divinity was possible only when profound changes in the relation of prehistoric man to woman, and in the mutual relations of the sexes, had made themselves felt. The image of the "terrible Mother" constructed by C. G. Jung—even if we ignore his anagogic interpretation—is by no means primary, and it presupposes definite changes in the psychic relation to the mother. Tremendous revolutions must have occurred, attributable perhaps to a decisive modification of living conditions and their repercussions on the primitive human family, resulting in a radical transformation of domestic emotions, before the image of the loved and cherished mother could change into the terrifying figure evoked by Jung. In the psychical productions of neurotics we have valuable indications as to the processes which led to this result: I mean those unconscious processes which led to the transformation of the positive into the antithetical oedipus complex. To those whose attitude toward the mother may be so characterized she appears as a terrible and hateful female; often indeed as a persecutrix and a tyrant. It can be demonstrated by analysis that this particular psychic attitude is a late transformation of the original positive relation, which occurred under the compulsion of certain psychic necessities. But among the motives which condition a disturbance of the original relation to the mother we must include the paternal policy of sexual intimidation and the fear of castration as especially effective. Sexual intercourse with the mother, so ardently though unconsciously desired, resulted for the child in the loss of the cherished member, so that the beloved mother became the dreadful mother, an object of terror.[5]

If we now turn back to the products of the mass psyche we shall surmise that the stern prohibitions of the father generation, in respect of incest, representing or taking the place of actual castration, which were first impressed upon the young generation from the outside, and later on became part of their psychic property, afford a good analogy to every individual evolution. The creation of the mother divinities was in itself an attempted irruption on the part of those impulses which were urgent toward the practice of incest. It was only partially successful, for simultaneously with the deification of the first libido object that seemed to encourage the actual realization of those infantile wishes there emerged unconsciously the prohibition of incest received by many generations, which changed the beloved object

5 It goes without saying that the events which had the effect of altering the conditions of life would also have changed the relation of the mother to her sons, and must have led to the development of the feminine character in a definite direction.

into an object of anxiety, all contact with which threatened disaster. To the primitive mind, the result of this complicated process of transformation could be imagined only by giving the mother image the features of the father; the prohibition came from the father, and its effectiveness depended mainly upon the unconscious homosexual tendency toward the fathers. But when the father god in animal form was blended with the image of the mother goddess, this was likewise a sign that the homosexual tendencies which played so decisive a part in the evolution of religion had frustrated the irruption of the incestuous impulses; that the attempt to replace the terrible image of the totemic god by the more kindly image of the mother and wife had failed, for the taboo of the incestuous object was inextricably bound up with the mother imago, even though this became a goddess. The victory of the homosexual impulses, which was so plastically manifested in the animal hinder parts of the Sphinx and so disturbingly in the addition of the penis, could not, of course, be enduring; from the very first it was not undisputed, and later on the penis often disappeared from the representations of the Sphinx, whose femininity became ever more pronounced; so that the Greek Sphinxes have gracious and comely faces, far removed from the gloom and the grave virility of the Egyptian Sphinxes.[6] Nevertheless, they retained the animal body as the permanent sign of their descent and a warning of their perilous nature.

What have we gained from this genetic survey? I think we have obtained several interesting results. It has explained the contradiction between the female sex of the upper portion and the male sex of the lower portion of the Sphinx's body. At the same time it must be emphasized that the formation of the lower portion of the body, like that of the most attractive portion of the mother image, has masculine characteristics, so that here also the process of repression of the heterosexual object by an object of the same sex in a later stage of development is most vividly manifested. We have come to understand why the representations of the Sphinx should be now male and now female, and we know

[6] Siegfried Bernfeld, in discussing this lecture, pointed to the fact that the emphatically feminine form of the Greek type of Sphinx corresponded with the temperament of the Greek people.

that this fact is related to the religious development. In this connection, I believe, we have reason to correct the opinions hitherto held concerning the Sphinx, and not only those which are beyond the scope of psychoanalysis. In the ingenious interpretation of the Oedipus legend given by Rank in his work on the incest complex he refers to the infantile sexual theory mentioned by Freud, according to which women as well as men possess a penis. Rank explains the theory by the homosexual anxiety dream. Without prejudice to the correctness of this explanation, our historical interpretation of it may claim to have contributed to the understanding of the psychic processes in the formation of the figure of the Sphinx.

Our interpretation, however, requires a more radical modification of Jung's conception of the Sphinx. A critical examination of Jung's arguments will reveal the inadequacy of the superficially symbolical interpretation of the Swiss author; as in the analysis of individuals, so in the theological field, Jung makes no attempt to go back to the earliest developmental stages of psychic formations. It is highly probable that at some time the Sphinx, in a very late and culturally advanced period, became a theriomorphic representation of libido, and that she must be regarded as the half-animal representation of that mother imago which was described as the terrible mother. But we do not see that this symbolical representation explains anything. It does not enable us to understand how such a figure as the Sphinx was ever conceived; and the interpretation of the Sphinx as an incestuous libidinal charge derived from the relation to the mother will satisfy neither the psychoanalyst nor the inquirer into the evolution of religion and culture. While this kind of interpretation—in the sense of our modern sublimated symbolism—contributes nothing to the explanation of the figure of the Sphinx as represented in early antiquity, it rightly and instinctively refrains from entering into the many mutually contradictory motives of such representations or considering them in detail.

We will conclude by a summary of all the various features of the Sphinx of the Near East—features which are often so mutually contradictory; the ancient conception of the Sphinx as god, as king, as guardian of the sanctuary;[7] her half-animal, half-human form, now male, now female.

9. THE SPHINX OF OEDIPUS

Unless we are greatly mistaken, we should now, in the light of our recent discoveries, be justified in returning to the consideration of the legend of Oedipus and the Sphinx, and in anticipating, from their application to the ancient myth, fresh explanations as to the still hidden meaning of this episode. In our opinion the unity of the Sphinx may be accepted, and we do not think that even the legendary monster which oppressed Thebes can have been so remote from its original stock that the results obtained there can be without bearing upon the interpretation of the mysterious part which it played in the destiny of Oedipus.

But before we attempt to wrest from the Sphinx of Oedipus the secret of its nature, we must first of all clearly understand which features of our legend are accepted by the mythologists and philologists as primordial, and which they have regarded as subsequent expansions, embellishments, variants, or what not. No complete reconstruction of the original version is practicable; but the scholars tell us that the legend must once have existed in a much cruder form, and that originally the slaying of the father must have been followed immediately by the violation of the mother, who was present at his murder. The notion of a marriage, which continued for several years, was first introduced by the tragic poets. According to Gruppe, the episode of the Sphinx was first included in the myth where a fresh justification for the marriage was adduced: "Inasmuch as the old romantic motive was exploited, according to which the hand of a king's daughter was won by the conquest of a monster, this terrible creature, which

---

[7] The Sphinx's function as guardian signifies that the god guards his own sanctuary. As a matter of fact the situation is even more complicated; for if we consider that the temple of a god is originally part of the god himself, an enlargement of the divine personality, then the Sphinx is really guarding herself. This peculiar situation is intelligible only if we associate the twofold presence of the god—as in the analysis of the ritual of sacrifice—with the course of religious evolution.

the legend has localized in Bocotia, presented herself as a matter of course." Further, according to Bethe the original form of the Sphinx legend is that in which the Sphinx was put to death by Oedipus without any previous solving of a riddle. Hesiod knew nothing of any riddle.[1] A red-figured Attic lecythos in the Boston Museum[2] shows the Sphinx (without wings) with forepaws up-lifted, like a cat preparing to strike, on the point of attacking Oedipus, who is named in an inscription. The hero's right hand holds the club with which he is about to strike a deadly blow. Robert has justly observed that there can have been no question here of solving a riddle either before or after the encounter, but rather of a fight like that of Hercules with the Nemean lion. Robert also argues, with much ingenuity, that the Sphinx began to ask riddles only in her later history, and that the intellectual contest cannot have been the original form of the monster's en-counter with the hero. One should have realized that a creature represented as having a lion's body and a lion's talons must originally have been conquered, not by the ingenuity of a solver of riddles, but by the physical strength of a hero.[3] "It seems to me that the notion of turning a man-killing monster into an in-genious riddler of riddles, who could be overcome only if con-fronted by her intellectual equal, can hardly be of earlier date than the period when the poetical enigma was the fashion in Greece."[4] A gem illustrated in Furtwängler's monograph on gems[5] shows, like one of the Boston vases, that the version in which the Sphinx, when her riddle is solved, flings herself from her rock, can have nothing to do with the original content of the legend: Oedipus, standing behind the Sphinx, plunges the sword into her breast. Perhaps the story of the Sphinx's suicide origi-nated in a late assimilation of the fate of the Sphinx with that of the traditional Lucasta. Many pictures show the hero killing his adversary with his sword. It is our belief that the version of the legend in which nothing is said of any riddle, but in which a

[1] H. von Hofmannsthal omits the riddle in his tragedy *Oedipus und die Sphinx.*

[2] Carl Robert, *Oidipus,* Vol. I, Berlin 1915, p. 49.

[3] *Ibid.,* p. 49.

[4] *Ibid.,* p. 57.

[5] Plate XXIV, 21, 22.

terrible monster, which is laying the country waste, is killed by the hero Oedipus, must be regarded as the oldest accessible form of the Oedipus legend. But now the question arises as to the relation of this part of the legend to the myth as a whole. Is it really an episode, a late addition, without any close relation to the essential content, as it may seem at the first glance, and as the majority of the philologists believe? Robert gives an excellent summary of the difficulties of incorporating the episode of the Sphinx in the legend of Oedipus. He suggests that the Sphinx is not unconnected with the fate of Laios—and the legend itself seems to hint at some such relation, but its exact nature is very obscure.[6] "If one sought to introduce her as avenging the murder of Laios, as his Erinys, in a manner of speaking, it would be absurd that his murderer should also kill the avenger of the murder, without suffering any harm himself. If one imagines her as a punishment for a crime committed by Laios himself, it would be absurd that she should not appear until after his death, so that Laios himself did not suffer at her hands, but only his innocent subjects. Thus, nothing remains but to conceive her as an instrument of the decree of Fate, and to ascribe her despatch to the god who emitted this decree, or else to seek a motive for her appearance unconnected with the Oedipus myth." Robert, things being as they were, thinks it unnecessary to look for a motive; the monster was there, and to ascribe her appearance to human guilt was a later and secondary notion.

We think, however, that the author has resigned himself too soon. The ancient legend speaks of a mysterious relation between Laios and the Sphinx, and psychoanalysis tells us that such relations have a psychic—that is, a real—motivation. If we do not perceive its nature we must wait patiently until we find it; at all events we must not simply deny its existence. Even the parallelism between the slaying of Laios and the slaying of the Sphinx seems to indicate that the two figures are somehow related.

Perhaps we shall find an explanation of the relationship if we consider the result of one analysis of the Sphinx; the Sphinx, a late development of the divine totemic animal, confronts the young Oedipus. He fights and kills her, and the city is his reward.

[6] Robert, *Oidipus,* Vol. I, p. 63.

If we accept the results obtained by the analysis of the origin of totemism we must assume that in the last resort the Sphinx is equivalent to Laios, the father of the young hero, so that her slaying repeats the murder of the king. But through the symbolism of dreams and myths and poetry and wit we have learned that the significance of the city, and of the country, is, in the unconscious, woman. Moreover, we recognize in this disguise a repetition of the great event which constitutes the kernel of the human, all-too-human story of Oedipus: the slaying of the father and the seizure of the mother.

If we accept this interpretation we are again confronted by difficult questions which have to be answered. Which form of the legend is the original one, and why is its content repeated in a different form? How did it come about that the earlier, male figure of the Sphinx was translated into a female figure? What psychic motives determined the change, and through what psychic mechanism was the transformation effected?

The Oedipus myth hands down to us in its antique forthrightness and simplicity a theme whose emotional content is so universally human that as psychoanalysts we are accustomed to cite it as typical of the strongest unconscious wishes of childhood. But the very naïveté of the Greek tradition, which develops this theme in historical time, in all its crudity, before the eyes and ears of the auditor, should give us cause for reflection. One should always be distrustful when a myth openly relates crudely sexual themes; almost invariably the myth conceals other significant motives, and the emphasis laid on the one sexual subject often serves to conceal other fragments of sexual or innocuous themes.[7]

If we omit the oracle, the episode of the Sphinx, and other specific mythological features of the Oedipus myth, what is left? The life and the actions of a criminal, a patricide and an incestuous son, for whom we cannot even feel compassion, a man whose destiny strikes no profounder note of tragedy. We should not understand why this particular criminal was chosen by so many of the Greeks to be immortalized as a tragic hero, and why for him especially the tribunal should become the stage.

[7] This may best be illustrated by the analysis of the biblical legend of the Fall.

Reflection, as well as the particularly crude form of the tradition, the obscure connection between the role of the Sphinx and the fate of Laios, and its mythological significance—all these motives justify our assumption that the Sphinx legend is not a later interpolation, as the majority of mythologists believe, but is one of the most essential components of the original myth. But if this be so, the question of the relation of one part of the legend to another, which repeats the same story on another plane, now becomes urgent. We will answer it briefly thus: The Sphinx plays much the same part in the life of Oedipus as the Ghost in the tragedy of Hamlet.[8] The episode of the Sphinx is older than what we may call the human legend of Oedipus in its present form. There, in the description of the death of the Sphinx, the typical event of the Oedipus legend occurs in its first, elementary, terrible force; in later versions the superhuman crime has become a deed that rids the country of a monster. But the motive—the fact that the action was that of a young hero, and the victim a late representative of the ancient totemic animal, of the inviolable god—reveals it in all its tragic momentousness, and its true significance, which far exceeds the fate of the individual. Here, in the murder of Laios, all happens, so to speak, within the setting of private life, and the ambit of a legal code; but as regards the slaying of the Sphinx, from which the action subsequently received the strongest subterranean repercussion, it is obvious that the exploit of the young saviour Oedipus was a crime against deity, since the god was its victim. The human actions and mundane events of the legend now appear in the light of higher powers. The tragic note is greatly enhanced by the fact that Oedipus has not only offended against the transitory morals and questionable customs of mankind, but that he has violated the sacred and eternal laws decreed by the gods. Oedipus has not only slain his father, but in his father he has struck at the supreme authority, the God himself.[9]

8 This comparison is not merely superficial. The following inquiry will show us what close relations exist between the theme of Oedipus and that of Hamlet—themes whose unconscious significance Freud justly compares.

9 In this connection it should be noted that Robert, in the work already cited, holds that the oldest form of the legend is that in which the hero goes from Eteonos to the Phix mountain, where he slew a monster which had its

One may indeed say that it was just because the terrible gravity of Oedipus's crime was concealed by the story of the Sphinx that it was possible to represent his action as that of an ordinary human being, and to describe it without disguise. We should then assume that the Oedipus of an earlier form of the legend killed the divine totemic animal and had to pay dearly for his crime. Subsequently the original slaying of the totem was no longer recognized in its momentous real significance by the Greeks, who had progressed to the creation of anthropomorphic deities. The totemic animal, degraded by progress to the status of monster, was retained in the very late transformation of the legend as the Sphinx; and the killing of the totem was likewise retained; but now, by a conversion of affect, it acquired a meritorious character.[10]

The whole event was thus misunderstood owing to the influence of the tendencies of a more highly cultured period. We

---

lair there, and was devastating the countryside; thus becoming the saviour of the country (p. 58). Proceeding from other points of view, the writer comes to the conclusion already reached by E. Meyer (*Geschichte des Altertums*, pp. 2, 101, 103, 167), that the Oedipus myth had originally a religious significance. Meyer rightly sees in Oedipus a figure like that of Herakles: one of the great gods in whose life the cycle of Nature finds expression. Oedipus, who weds his mother, the Earth, but is then blinded, and dies, may have derogated to the rank of hero, of whose remarkable vicissitudes the poets had much to tell. Robert regards Oedipus as a chthonic hero from the Demeter cycle—the Earth-Goddess is originally his mother; "Where the Earth, the divine, primal being, is the universal Mother—as she certainly is among all the Greek tribes—her sons are naturally at the same time her husbands" (p. 44). Here our interpretation is consistent with the symbolical role of the country (Thebes). How far Robert, despite his discernment, has diverged from the original meaning of the myth may be judged from the following passage: "The child of Mother Earth originally needed no father. If he had a father, that father, according to the Nature religion, could only be a being like himself—the ancient god of the year, whom he had to slay in order that he himself might become the king of the year, even as Zeus dethroned Kronos. . . . So every year he was given the prophet-god Laios for his father. Every year he slew Laios, and every year he married his mother. *There can hardly have been a causal connection between the parricide and the slaying of the Sphinx.*" (The italics are mine.) The author adds that here we have the most difficult problem in the poetical form of the Oedipus myth, and that all attempts to establish such a connection have failed.

[10] The new interpretation resembles that which was effected in the tradition of the shattering of the Golden Calf by Moses. Cf. my *Probleme der Religionspsychologie*, Part 1, Vienna and Leipzig, 1919.

must not forget that the gods had already assumed human form, that religious feeling had become more sensitive and refined, and had suppressed, even though unconsciously, any impulse of sympathy with the monstrous act of deicide. But then another crime offered itself as a substitute for this unique act: a crime grievous enough, and resembling the other, but without the character of a violent insurrection against the deity. This crime was parricide.

However, we do not believe that the choice of this substitute was directed by chance. Let us consider what the substitution of the father for the totem meant: The totemic animal itself had been a primeval substitute for the Father, and the slaying of the totem revived memories of the murder of the chieftain of the primeval horde. If the legend now made Oedipus kill his father, what it recorded was a form of the primitive legend not uninfluenced by the anthropomorphization of the gods, and adapted to the later cultural standards of the period. If we consider this process of evolution, which started from a primitive era that had no conscious memory of the actual event, that found a late echo in the Oedipus myth, and which in the slaying of the totemic animal revealed the act in its religious significance, and later on, compelled by the impatience of the repressing forces, allowed it to be replaced by the parricide, we then have the following aspect of the matter: *The myth as we know it does not reflect the primary content of the legend, but already represents a late recurrence of the repressed matter.* An episode broadly resembling the present events of the Oedipus legend may have formed the content of the original nucleus of the legend.

We may understand why this myth, as one of the few of which we have any knowledge, has told us what it has to say in such a crude and naked form. We must not ascribe this peculiarity to its primitive character; we must rather regard it as due to an irruption of repressed material after thousands of years of repression. Disregarding all such considerations as might on principle apply to this example of myth formation, we will confine ourselves to establishing the fact that here, as in other myths, the first form of this imaginative production to reach us already bears traces of religious elaboration and interpretation. Nowhere can we find the prereligious myth in its pure form; but where the divinities, the demons, and the rest of the *personae* of the ancient religions do not occur we can at least envisage a newer form of the myth, which has grown out of the religious phase, and which must not be confused with the primary form, with its animistic associations. Noting that here we are faced with the difficult problem of the relation between myth and religion, we return to the story of the Sphinx.

We have realized that in the Oedipus legend, side by side with the more recent form, the older version of the story of the Sphinx persists, erroneously conceived and interpreted; and further, that the chief emphasis, which formerly rested on the story of the Sphinx, is now transferred to the fate of Oedipus, struggling against a human father. Such a displacement of accent is not unknown to us in the psychic field; in dreams also what was once the kernel makes its appearance as the shell.

Hitherto we have disregarded, with intention, the motives that seem to assign the maternal character to the Sphinx. Rank's view of the meaning of the episode is that the Sphinx and the mother originally coincided; that is, the introduction of the Sphinx should be regarded as the isolation of certain obnoxious features of the mother. But after the introduction of the Sphinx her proper maternal character was effaced by subsequent waves of repression. The original violation of the mother was replaced by a conflict with the Sphinx, and only in later versions was this transformed into an intellectual contest. The Sphinx mother— formerly the violated mother—asks the youth who is struggling to understand the sexual problem a sexual riddle regarding the nature of man, and only when the hero has solved the riddle— that is, "only after the violation of the mother in the original version"—can he consummate the marriage. According to Rank the Sphinx episode represents a "doubling" of the rape of Jocasta, introduced in the course of repression and mythic stratification. But Rank, sagaciously realizing that this interpretation is inadequate, has adduced the story of Chrysippos, associated with the figure of Laios, whereupon the homosexual significance of the figure of the Sphinx becomes apparent.

It now appears possible to reconcile Rank's interpretation with our own. The one supplements the other; Rank's hypothesis, in our opinion, suggesting a later version. The Sphinx, as a duplication of the mother, has interposed herself before the more primitive image of the totemistic father substitute, concealing it, even as the simply human form of the Oedipus myth has interposed itself before the heroic-religious form. The slaying of the Sphinx is originally the killing of the totem; but it is equally certain, as Rank has explained that it afterwards became the rape of the mother. Then, were duplications of the father imago and the mother image combined in the figure of the Sphinx? As a matter of fact, they were, as another consideration tells us: The human Oedipus legend, which as a recurrence of the primitive legend reflects all the essential details of the latter in a more civilized form, has evolved from the Sphinx legend by a process of humanization and cleavage, so that the essential and significant elements of the later stratum must already have existed in the tale of the Sphinx. We thus arrive at the assumption that in the Sphinx legend as we have it now a wholesale condensation is concealed, the work of many generations, which has compressed the slaying of the father and the violation of the mother into the single act of which the Sphinx is the victim. Homosexual and heterosexual, sadistic and masochistic emotional trends overlap, inextricably blended. The psychic processes which psychoanalysis has detected in the individual provide us with an explanation of the situation. The child who observes the sexual intercourse of adults identifies himself not only with the father, but also with the mother; he not only wishes to have sexual intercourse with the mother, as does the father, but he also wishes to be treated by the father as the mother is treated in coitus. This sadistic-masochistic fantasy corresponds with the first heterosexual and homosexual associations of the child. The infantile-sadistic notion of coitus makes it seem a conflict in the eyes of the child; so it is possible that the child, following the misunderstood example of the father, may wish to overthrow and wound the mother. The transference of this experience to folk psychology draws our attention to the alternate rise and fall of homosexual and heterosexual waves in the life of the peoples. Love for the father may coincide with unconscious hatred for the mother, and vice versa. We may now perceive the Sphinx as an embodiment of these two primeval, powerful and antithetical trends; since Oedipus accompanied parricide with the violation of the mother, and yet in violating the mother made the father the object of his love.

If we now try to elucidate the historical sequence of the predominance of these libidinal trends, we shall realize that the slaying of the father, of the totemic animal, *seems* to have preceded the violation of the mother, who appears in the more nearly human form of the Sphinx. But the components of the hybrid form, in which the male, animal hinder quarters are apparently the older elements, and the human, female features the more recent, gives us reason to suspect that here, as in the whole legend, we have a recurrence of an ancient, repressed theme. The condensation of the slaying of the father and the sexual relation with the mother, which is divided in the Oedipus legend into two separate actions, is in our opinion a throw-back to a primeval state of humanity when the erotic choice of youth did not declare itself so decisively for the woman as it does today, but also when erotic play and erotic conflict were not so sharply separated as they are today; to a phase which would be analogous to the sadistic-anal period in the libidinal evolution of the individual. If the possibility of return to this atavistic evolutionary phase of instinctual development is the precondition of the existence of condensation, we shall have to assume that the first impetus toward the creation of the Oedipus myth was the fantasy of (sadistically colored) sexual intercourse with the mother, an obstacle to which was the sexual intercourse of the father. Like the primal form of every myth, this is no more than the objectified hallucination of fulfilled wishes. We know from individual analysis that this formula corresponds with the biogenetic law that the child originally fulfills, by way of hallucination, the wishes whose fulfillment is denied to him by reality. If we have thus traced the Oedipus myth back to its first germ, the fantasied, violent sexual union with the mother, it will not surprise us if we find, in one of its latest forms, and in a significant position, a sign of this derivation; I mean the dream chosen by Freud as the starting point of his analysis, the dream of which Jocasta speaks in Sophocles' tragedy:

". . . Many a man ere now has seen himself in a dream
Mated with his mother . . ."

So that Freud is justified in his assertion that the legend of Oedipus is derived from dream stuff of great antiquity; as we think we have proved by the historical and psychological reconstruction of the later form of the legend. The universal incest fantasy of the mass of humanity is threatened by an obstacle to its formation and hallucinatory fulfillment in the anticipated intrusion of the father. The tremendous event of the father's murder casts its shadow before it, in the form of the picture which emerges in the dream of the forcible removal of the intruder. The possession of the mother is so closely associated with the condition of parricide, the fulfillment of the instinctually rooted wish is so impossible without the removal of this chiefest hindrance, that the one event can be regarded as representative of the other. This psychic constellation later on, in combination with the motives already mentioned, provides the possibility of the condensation to which we have pointed in the legend of the Sphinx.

This possibility could first be realized when the psychic reactions to the actual deed of the father's murder had long been established and when a primal myth had already taken shape. The rape of the mother, as manifested in the subduing of the Sphinx and the slaying of the totemistic father, would be equated with the recurrence of the wish which provided the impetus for the creation of the myth. The possibility of condensation was increased by the reactively enhanced affection for the father and the hostility towards the woman, which after each act increased the originally sadistic component of the incest fantasy. In the duplication of the Oedipus legend, by which the figure of the Sphinx is again divided into the figures of Laios and Jocasta, the hostile and affectionate tendencies in the young hero's relations to his father and mother re-emerge separately as before. As in the legend of the Sphinx, sexual intercourse and murder synchronize in one act, affecting one object, so they coincide in our version of the pre-Sophoclean tragedy of Oedipus, when Oedipus, having slain his father, takes his girdle and his sword.[11] The ungirt body is a familiar erotic symbol in Greek antiquity, and the taking of the sword is a symbolical substitute for castration, so that here also, in dichronous action, we have the successive expression of affectionate and hostile emotions in respect of the same object.

We can understand how, under cover of this homosexual motivation, the hybrid figure came into existence. The Sphinx is both man and woman, because both were desired as sexual objects; she is killed, and sexually enjoyed, because for the child both actions coincide in the sadistic-masochistic, infantile notion of sexual intercourse, as they possibly did in reality, in the earliest period of the differentiation of the sexes in the evolution of the human organism.

We have already stated that the absurd hybrid forms, like that of the Sphinx, which occur in dreams suggest that the dreamer feels derision or contempt for the object represented. If we transfer this rule to the creations of the mass psyche we may assume that in the curious mixed creations of primitive art certain tendencies express themselves whose direction is analogous to that of these emotions. One might perhaps maintain that the hybrid form of man plus animal in the Sphinx corresponds with the unconscious resistance to the superseded totemistic divinities in a culturally advanced period which was already familiar with human divinities. The synthesis of the Sphinx, with her male and female components, would thus reflect an unconscious hostility to the father-god, an impulse of repudiation which directs the heterosexual libidinal tendencies against the religion based on homosexual associations. We should compare this aggressive trend with a repression which set in during the period of late antiquity, and a modified judgment of homosexual practices, whose last remnants we see in the derision of homosexuality by

11 Another association, of later date, leads once more to the condensation which we have noted in the legend of the Sphinx; the Sphinx, according to Peisandros's account, was sent by Hera as a punishment, because Laios, the father of Oedipus, had kidnapped the handsome Chrysippos. According to the legend Oedipus, homosexually inclined, killed his unknown father on account of Chrysippos, whom he also loved. We shall not be unduly venturesome if we see in Chrysippos himself a duplication of Oedipus. Thus, legend records the murder of the father out of homosexual jealousy, as well as from motives of heterosexual desire.

the Greek and Roman satyrists.[12] Yet this remains only an assumption, no more probable than another in respect of a period so alien to us in feeling as the prehistoric Orient.

10. THE RELIGIOUS SIGNIFICANCE OF THE OEDIPUS MYTH

I do not know how far I have succeeded in giving the reader of the foregoing pages a notion of the great importance of the Oedipus myth in the religious life of the Greeks, and of the close and cryptic relation of the performance of the *Oedipus* to the religious ritual of Hellas. The profound and lasting influence of the Oedipus legend in antiquity must, I believe, be ascribed to the religious motive which revealed the instinctual life of men in conflict with the laws of the gods. For here, as in the Dionysian games, and the ritual of Attis, Adonis and Osiris, a young revolutionary saviour was represented, rebelling against the old and powerful father-god and suffering a terrible punishment for his offense. I believe the influence of these performances may be compared with that of the ecclesiastical Passion play on the faithful in the Middle Ages, for it depended on the same psychic precedents. The prehistory of Christ is not unlike that of Oedipus. It should be emphasized that in the Oedipus myth, as we now have it, the profoundest psychic motives, which led to the formation of religion, though unrecognized by the auditors, were nonetheless plastically represented, and that here an unconscious sense of guilt was evoked.

Elsewhere I shall try to show that the hidden kernel of this myth is the same as that which underlies the story of original sin in the biblical narrative, on which the sense of guilt of the masses was fixated for hundreds of years. Here we will only note that in Assyrian and Babylonian paintings and reliefs, on cylindrical seals and the like, Sphinxes, Gryphons and similar winged animal forms are seen to be guarding the Tree of Life. Everyone knows that in the story of the Fall of Man a cherub, whose original animal form we find in the visions of Ezekiel, stands beside

[12] I think the story of Chrysippos and the punishment of Laios by the Sphinx is not unconnected with this change.

the Tree of Life as the Sphinx lies before the Egyptian temples, and as the leonine or tauriform guardians keep watch before the palaces of Assurbanasirpal and Sanherib. All these guardian animals are late descendants of totemistic deities. Further, it can be shown that in the tradition of the Tree of Life precisely the same condensation has occurred as in the Sphinx episode of the Oedipus myth, and that in the biblical narrative the Tree plays the same apparently subsidiary role as the Sphinx in the Greek legend. Recent research has convinced me that the Oedipus myth might be called the Hellenic version of the legend of the Fall.[1]

However, we must not forget that what was struggling for expression in the religiously emphatic form of the *Oedipus,* and what thrilled and moved the Greek auditors, and moves us even today, was just those decisive psychic impulses whose operation first provided the impetus toward the formation of religion. In this sense also the Oedipus legend is a creation which reveals the recurrence of repressed material.

We have intentionally excluded from this interpretation, as a secondary feature, the riddle propounded by the Sphinx. On this occasion we are more concerned to solve the riddle of the Sphinx herself. Or rather, one of her riddles. For these are many, and they still challenge our endeavors to solve them.[2]

This sends us back to the little drawing of which I spoke in the Introduction: a sketch which the analyst may regard as a token of what has been achieved, but also as a constant encouragement to further research.

[1] By this I do not intend any reference to the still unsolved and complicated problem of the relations between the Semites and the Greeks.

[2] The position of the riddle in the Oedipus myth corresponds with the place which the knowledge of good and evil occupies in the legend of the Fall of Man. Cf. "Die Erbsünde," in Part II of my *Probleme der Religionspsychologie.*